IT CAME FROM THE 80s!

# IT CAME FROM THE 80S!

*Interviews with 124 Cult Filmmakers*

Francesco Borseti

McFarland & Company, Inc., Publishers
*Jefferson, North Carolina*

LIBRARY OF CONGRESS CATALOGUING-IN-PUBLICATION DATA

Names: Borseti, Francesco, 1981–
Title: It came from the 80s! : interviews with 124 cult filmmakers / Francesco Borseti.
Description: Jefferson, Norht Carolina : McFarland & Company, Inc., Publishers, 2016 | Includes index.
Identifiers: LCCN 2016031756 | ISBN 9781476666044 (softcover : acid free paper) ∞
Subjects: LCSH: Cult films—United States—History and criticism. | Motion picture producers and directors—United States—Interviews.
Classification: LCC PN1995.9.C84 I83 2017 | DDC 791.43/6535—dc23
LC record available at https://lccn.loc.gov/2016031756

BRITISH LIBRARY CATALOGUING DATA ARE AVAILABLE

ISBN (print) 978-1-4766-6604-4
ISBN (ebook) 978-1-4766-2563-8

© 2016 Francesco Borseti. All rights reserved

*No part of this book may be reproduced or transmitted in any form or by any means, electronic or mechanical, including photocopying or recording, or by any information storage and retrieval system, without permission in writing from the publisher.*

Front cover: The cast of the 1982 film *Parasite*; (from left) Joannelle Nadine Romero, Freddie Moore, Al Fann, Robert Glaudini, Demi Moore and Natalie May (Embassy Pictures/Photofest)

Printed in the United States of America

*McFarland & Company, Inc., Publishers*
*Box 611, Jefferson, North Carolina 28640*
*www.mcfarlandpub.com*

# Table of Contents

| | |
|---|---|
| Preface | 1 |
| *Blood Frenzy* (1987, U.S.A.) | 3 |
| *Blue Monkey* (1987, U.S.A./Canada) | 20 |
| *The Carpenter* (1987, Canada) | 40 |
| *Cavegirl* (1984, U.S.A.) | 51 |
| *The Chilling* (1989, U.S.A.) | 58 |
| *Creepozoids* (1987, U.S.A.) | 72 |
| *Deadly Intruder* (1984, U.S.A.) | 81 |
| *Death House* (1987, U.S.A.) | 89 |
| *Edge of Sanity* (1988, U.K.) | 96 |
| *The Evil Below* (1988, U.S.A./South Africa) | 107 |
| *Ghost Town* (1987, U.S.A.) | 110 |
| *Ghost Warrior* (1983, U.S.A.) | 122 |
| *Hunk* (1987, U.S.A.) | 128 |
| *The Lamp,* a.k.a. *The Outing* (1986, U.S.A.) | 134 |
| *The Masque of the Red Death* (1989, U.S.A./South Africa) | 146 |
| *Munchies* (1986, U.S.A.) | 159 |
| *Never Cry Devil,* a.k.a. *Night Visitor* (1988, U.S.A.) | 168 |
| *The Oracle* (1984, U.S.A.) | 173 |
| *Parasite* (1981, U.S.A.) | 175 |
| *The Pink Chiquitas* (1985, Canada) | 189 |
| *The Rejuvenator* (1987, U.S.A.) | 195 |
| *School Spirit* (1984, U.S.A.) | 204 |
| *Shadowzone* (1989, U.S.A.) | 210 |
| *Slave Girls from Beyond Infinity* (1987, U.S.A.) | 217 |
| *Sorority Babes in the Slimeball Bowl-O-Rama* (1987, U.S.A.) | 239 |
| *Terror Night* (1987, U.S.A.) | 251 |
| *Time Walker* (1982, U.S.A.) | 264 |
| *Transformations* (1987, U.S.A.) | 272 |
| *Index* | 285 |

# Preface

I started gathering the material for this book about four years before publication, with the aim of offering all B-movies aficionados like myself an entertaining overview of horror, sci-fi and fantasy movies made in the 80s. I plunged into this project moved by curiosity and by a generous supply of enthusiasm and recklessness.

All the interviews in the book are original. Although the interviews in each chapter appear to be a one-sided conversation, they were gathered through the classic Q&A format. The questions were left out because they are really not needed to get the flavor or meaning of each person's statements. An occasional clarification is added in brackets. Each interview was edited only for grammar, style, length or to correct obvious mistakes (a punctuation error, a misspelling or a misstatement of a person's name, for instance). Anything added to the interviews are indicated by square brackets. Most of the interviews were done by e-mail, a few by telephone. Screenwriters, directors and producers (the most important, job-wise, of the filmmakers included in this book) were the most interviewed, although statements by actors, cinematographers, special effect artists, and others were also included.

Other than being part of my personal collection, all the movies appearing here have a second and more important feature they share: very little has been written or said about them since they were released. For most of these movies, this book represents the first time much appears in print about them.

All the movies included in the book were produced in English speaking countries. Most of them—and it couldn't have been otherwise—were made in the United States. Although I love movies made in my home country, I specifically decided from the start to avoid including Italian B-movies for the simple reason that a lot has been written and is still being written about them. My interviews would have, thus, added nothing new to the field.

The movies included in the book were not chosen on the basis of their objective artistic value and this book was never conceived as a work of film criticism. So, you will not find any critics' quotes or reviews done by myself regarding the movies. Any aesthetic critique would have been completely out of tune and out of place in a documentary work like this.

Prepare yourself to meet directors on the brink of a nervous breakdown, wretched producers always fleeing creditors, scriptwriters under pressure due to impossible deadlines, older actors—once riding high—now compelled to accept any role to pay the bills, porn filmmakers who go mainstream, to cite but a few examples.

Bon Voyage.

*Postcriptum:* To properly enjoy the interviews, it is advisable to watch the movies described first. Maybe several of them are already in your private collection. If this is not the case, there is a remedy: Today most of the movies are available on DVD. For the rest, a search on eBay can produce results for the old and dear VHS.

# *Blood Frenzy*

## (1987, U.S.A.)

*Genre:* Horror; *Director:* Hal Freeman; *Writers:* Ray Dennis Steckler (story, uncredited) and Ted Newsom (screenplay); *Cinematographer:* Rick Pepin; *Editor:* Ruben A. Mazzini; *Special Makeup Effects:* John Goodwin & Ron Wilson; *Producer:* Hal Freeman; *Co-Producer:* Claire Cassano; *Production Company:* Hollywood Family Entertainment; *Cast:* Wendy MacDonald (Dr. Barbara Shelley), Tony Montero (Rick Carlson), Lisa Loring (Dory), Monica Silvera Nadon (Jean), Lisa Savage (Cassie), Hank Garrett (Dave Ash), John Clark (Crawford), Chuck Rhae (Lonnie), Eddie Laufer (Little Lonnie), J'Aime Cohen (Little Dory) and Carl Tignino (Dory's Father)

A psychiatrist leads a group of mentally ill patients into the desert convinced that the isolation and the mutual confrontation may help them. A mysterious murderer starts to reap victims. Hal Freeman (1936–1989) made a brief foray into mainstream cinema with the slasher movie *Blood Frenzy*, but he was best known for working in the West Coast porn industry since the late 70s, with his production company, Hollywood Video. The biggest success of Hollywood Video was the franchise *Caught from Behind*, which started in 1982. In October of 1983, while he was shooting the sequel *Caught from Behind 2*, Freeman was arrested on the set, becoming the first director of adult movies to be arrested in California due to the controversial "Anti-Pimp Law." This law was approved in 1982 to free Hollywood of rampaging prostitution. According to the district attorney, the actresses paid by Freeman to have sex in the movie *Caught from Behind 2* were considered prostitutes and so the director was guilty of pandering. In July of 1985, the Van Nuys Superior Court considered the sentence of 3 to 6 years of imprisonment set by the anti-pandering law as too harsh and sentenced Freeman to 90 days and a small fine. The judge of the Superior Court commented that even if he found the adult film business deplorable, the objective of the law, when it was approved, was certainly not to incarcerate people like Hal Freeman. The district attorney's office appealed to the California Supreme Court to impose a full and exemplary sentencing on Freeman. In August 1988 the California Supreme Court acquitted Freeman of the pandering accusation, establishing that the explicit sex acts seen in the movie were protected by free speech rights, and that paying actors to perform in them did not constitute a crime. The sentence legalized de facto pornography in California. Hal Freeman died in October 1989, a few months after his definitive acquittal by the U.S Supreme Court, while he was trying to shoot his second horror movie, "Judgment Night." Due to my intense passion for movies that haven't been produced, movies that will never be seen (maybe), I asked Ted Newsom to shed some light on "Judgment Night."

# Ted Newsom
## (Writer)

The porn industry was a thorn in the side of upstanding citizens of Los Angeles, and elsewhere. It always had been. Anything sexual was automatically no damned good, in the eyes of a lot of people. It was a multi-million dollar business and brought huge amounts of capital into the area, employed hundreds of people, and generally speaking, those who owned the companies were as honest as any other movie makers or distributors. (Stop snickering. Laugh out loud. It was meant to be funny.) But "getting tough on crime" is always a publicity goal for District Attorneys. The D.A. in Los Angeles at the time was Ira Reiner.

He'd had quite a little bit of success in cleaning up street hookers in Hollywood, who'd be just all over the place, on Hollywood Boulevard, Santa Monica Boulevard, Sunset Boulevard. The legal system was just a revolving door. A girl would get arrested, give a fake name, her pimp would bail her out, and she'd change her name or leave town ... and the hooker population didn't drop at all. Reiner came up with a legal theory to target the pimps rather than the girls, and they made it a crime to profit from having someone doing sex work for you. This actually did work, because pimps learned quickly it wasn't going to be their whores in jail, it was going to be them.

Reiner theorized that he could clean out the entire San Fernando Valley of porn companies using the same legal theory: that producing a sex movie is the legal equivalent of being a pimp, because you're supervising someone whose job it is to have sex for pay. All they needed, so they thought, was one chump who they'd nail to the cross. When they did their worst to him, everybody else would leave town. And he'd get re-elected as "The Tough D.A. Who Cleaned Up the Porn Scourge." So went the theory.

Some actress scheduled to be in a film of Hal Freeman's got herself in trouble with the law: hooking, or a drug bust, an expired license—doesn't matter. They leaned on her, and she told them she was scheduled to do a film called *Caught from Behind Part 2* [1983] for Hal Freeman, and that they were going to shoot at a house within Los Angeles County. That's just what they needed. So they arrested Hal on the shoot (by the way, my partner and my names are on that movie, although we didn't write it). Anyway, the arrest led to several years of court battles, which drained Hal's finances and his health. Eventually, the California State Supreme Court overruled the conviction, establishing the obvious: making a movie with sex in it is obviously not the same as pimping a hooker.

I never set out to work on either adult movies or in men's magazines. I'd always wanted to make a living writing and making films. Some of the opportunities which presented themselves led me to writing for *Oui Magazine* regularly, during its days as the "classy European" spin-off of *Playboy*, and in 1982, an editorial job at Larry Flynt Publications [LFP]. I had no particular publishing background, but it was fine, it paid well, and I was there for a year or so.

Through another editor, Lonn Friend, I got to know Hal Freeman. I was looking to write movies, and Hal needed a script to link some footage he'd shot of some porn actress walking around Chicago. That had been some convention trip, and he brought his cameraman and one actress along to take advantage of the "production value" of a rarely-seen city. My job was to come up with a story to go around the footage—but without the actress, who was no longer available. She'd had a fight with Hal, or was off on a coke toot, or whatever. Misty-Something was her stage name. So I looked at this generic footage of her walking around Chicago, riding an elevator, looking at sites, and so on. There was only one sex scene, her solo in a bathtub. Hal's idea of imagination was explaining why this Misty woman wasn't in the rest of the movie. He said, "Have one of the other characters ask where Misty is, and somebody else says, 'She's taking a fucking bath.'" That was his idea of clever. I came up with a script, got a minimal amount of pay, and began writing semi-regularly for him. I don't think he ever actually shot that movie, but immediately after that I wrote a movie called *X-Factor* [1984] for him. That was the biggest-budget movie he'd ever done, and probably the best.

Big budget for Hal is relative. *X-Factor* probably cost $40,000. They shot it soft-core (hardcore insert scenes were shot later), all on location and in studios in San Francisco, and actually did a fair job of it. The softcore version actually played on the Playboy channel later on. It was a love story with a metaphysical angle, which I liked doing. The one-page outline from which I worked, written by someone else, used the name Ted as the lead character. Naturally I kept that. I named the lead female character Susan after an old girlfriend. I seem to recall the original story idea was written by a guy named Ray Wells, with (I recall this distinctly), a description where "lazer beams" (sic) come out of the eyes of the couple when they're making love. He certainly should have received story credit on that movie, but there's no fairness in writing adult movies. The Writers Guild does not cover them.

After I was fired from LFP (a badge of honor, which everybody receives sooner or later), I avoided writing scripts for any porn companies other than Hal's Hollywood Video. They would have paid more since their budgets were usually higher than Hal's three-day "Charming Cheapies," but I did not want to create a reputation as someone who wrote only sex movies. After I left LFP and magazines, my then-partner John Brancato and I wrote together for several years. Notably we adapted "Spider-Man" [1985] for Cannon, which ultimately led to the Columbia movie ten years down the line. We also adapted "Sgt. Fury, The Sub-Mariner," and did a script from a Stan Lee story called "Decathlon," which really was Hunger Games a couple decades too early. The first thing I was ever paid to write, 'way back in about 1979, was a Disney-esque kid's adventure called "Helga & the Little People," about a little girl who flees from East Berlin with her St. Bernard and joins up with a circus act of seven little people.

I always had a fondness and respect for horror films, but that didn't make me want to only write for those, either. As it turned out the first mainstream movie on which I had writing credit was *Blood Frenzy*. I can surmise that Hal Freeman wanted to do something more than just two- or three-day sex junk. It is not as if he was a "good" director. He did not have any particular talent for camera placement or cinema art. Anything that worked visually in his movies was thanks to Rick Pepin, who shot all his films.

I'll point out this, which I think is funny. Hal wanted to establish a legitimate, non-sex spin-off company for his non-porn films. He also didn't want to lose whatever cache his established company name might have had in the non-porn world (which, truthfully, was minimal). So he called his new production/distribution company Hollywood Family Video, using a logo identical to his old one. Well, that backfired big-time when he took this movie to the MPAA to be rated. They were outraged. "Hollywood FAMILY Video?!?! On a movie called 'BLOOD FRENZY'?!?! What kind of FAMILY watches something like THIS?!?!" I think they wanted to slap an X-rating on it for the blood and gore, just because the company name made them so irate. Hal eventually released it without a rating. The gore in *Blood Frenzy* is not excessive for this kind of movie.

Like *X-Factor*, the original story was actually written by someone else. I have a feeling it might actually have been Ray Dennis Steckler [1938–2009], who was infamous for *Incredibly Strange Creatures Who Stopped Living and Became Mixed-Up Zombies*, and a number of other semi-amateur features. I know that I ran into him editing or something at Hal's place years later, so I'm sure they knew each other, anyway. The original title of that script was "Warning—No Trespassing," and in general it followed the same lines: a group of people in the desert, "Who is the killer?" and a cave. When Hal asked me to rewrite the thing, I used the basic outline, making it into a cross between "Ten Little Indians" and a *Friday the 13th* gore fest. Early on, I renamed it "Blood Frenzy" because I figured that quality-wise, it would fall somewhere between the extremes of Hitchcock's *Frenzy* and Herschel Gordon Lewis' *Blood Feast*, which covers a LOT of ground. Thus, *Blood Frenzy*.

I think the budget was plus or minus about $100,000, and Hal spent an equal amount on publicity, package design, and so on. He hired a really brilliant woman [Claire Cassano] to help him mount the movie and, later on, work on sales and publicity. She was drafted into appearing in the movie, as the waitress in one of the first scenes. As far as I know, Hal financed the entire movie out of his own pocket. The porn business was thriving at that time, his own company in particular was making a lot of dough, and he wanted to do something different. It was that simple. What was interesting was his enthusiasm for this project, and the other couple of non-porn projects I wrote for him later. He was very gruff, very crude, but not 100% unlikable. I never had any ill feelings toward him. He did, however, consider the performers "the animals"—that's performers in his sex stuff. I never heard anything like that during prep or production of *Blood Frenzy*. I think he got a big kick out of being around real actors with legitimate credits.

I was excited, because one way or the other, it was going to be a real movie. When I wrote it, I kept about half of the script as interiors, so that the company would not have to spend all the time out on location. They'd do the exteriors for week, then come back and do the interiors of the Winnebago, the interiors of the various tents, the interior of the cave, the night-time exteriors, which would be easy to fake on a stage. At least that was my plan. Instead, Hal, possibly with Rick agreeing, decided the whole thing had to be shot on location in the desert.

What probably did hurt the film a little was the total absence of sex. There's a suggested scene or two, but there's not one bit of nudity. He was really trying to make a "real movie." I would've enjoyed seeing Lisa Loring naked. Or the girl who played the blonde, Lisa Savage. I thought she was a lot better actress than her role would allow. I felt sorry for Lisa because I'd written such a "brainless bimbo" role, figuring it would be played by some bubble-head Hal knew from porn. The actress who played the doctor [Wendy MacDonald] did some topless dancer stuff in a movie later on, and … eh. Monica Silvera, the petite actress who played the character who didn't want to be touched, was a hoot. She became part of an improv comedy group run by my friend Ron Wilson, who was make-up assistant on the film. Monica was incredibly sexy in the way Mary Ann was sexy on *Gilligan's Island*. Very funny, too.

Speaking of make-up. I knew what we needed, since I wrote the thing, so I suggested Hal talk to my pal John Goodwin. John and Ron Wilson had worked together for me in a spoof called *The Naked Monster*, originally titled "Attack of the B-Movie Monster" [1985, Ted Newsom] and they were wonderful actors, very inventive. John made a living doing make-up and prosthetic effects. He knew what he was doing, and now has two or three Emmy awards to prove it, from his work on *CSI*, with all the corpses and torsos and such. But Hal was convinced he had his make-up guy. He showed me a portfolio some guy had left there, and raved about him, "He's the guy who did the mermaid in *Splash*!" Well, I KNEW the guy [Robert Short] who did the mermaid in *Splash*, and it sure as hell wasn't this guy. Maybe he was part of the crew at one point, maybe he even slapped latex or plaster on Daryl Hannah's ass once, but he sure as hell didn't design the suit. I knew the guy was going to be trouble. But would Hal listen? Nah. Hal had his man. The guy—who I'll call Tex because I mercifully have forgotten his name—was this burly, hairy guy with fat tattooed arms, a beer gut, scraggly beard, and a way of talking a lot without saying a thing. I'm not a make-up man, but I know something about it and about prosthetics. And when I know more than the make-up guy, that's a bad sign. He was affable enough, in a redneck way. He was as full of shit as a Christmas goose, but nice about it.

I know that the cast was on a most-favored-nations status: everybody got the same pay rate. I think that was probably at John Clark's insistence. He was a very canny businessman, and fair. Hal wanted to avoid porn names in the cast, lest they make someone think this is a naughty movie. Ron Jeremy plumped for a role but Hal said no. I think it was through Ron Jeremy, however, that Hal got two of the performers, Lisa Loring and John Clark. Lisa, of course, had been a child actress [*The Addams Family*] and had an incredibly rough adulthood. She'd married the porn actor Jerry Butler, and that was not working out so well. He'd promised to get out of it, then secretly went back, that sort of thing. I had originally suggested Brinke Stevens for the role of the smart-ass, bisexual fashion model. I think Lisa came off a bit too earthy for my take on the role; I was thinking high fashion model, not someone who'd appear in *Swank* [the adult magazine]. But she was a really wonderful actress and did fine. John Clark was another friend of Jeremy's. John had acted since he was a boy in England, and was then about 45. He was married to Lynn Redgrave. I think he met Ron Jeremy when John rented out his home for a porn shoot. Quite a few people do that (not necessarily movie star families), and how are you going to turn down a thousand dollars a day? (Actually, it's easy when you realize what a mess any place is after ANY sort of movie is shot in your home. And a sex movie? Eeeuuuw.)

Hal took the project seriously. Perhaps too seriously, as it turned out. He didn't give the entire script to the actors, he left off the last ten or fifteen pages. He wanted them to be surprised at who the killer turns out to be. Looking back on it, I think it's obvious. Or maybe not. Anyway, most of the actors (the ones who still were around by page 75) didn't know how the movie would end. As an actor myself, I think that's silly. It's all pretending, and you can certainly pretend to be surprised on film. That's where it counts.

There was no particular reason for the writer to be on the location, but Hal asked me to come out, so I did. The base was Barstow, a little town out in the desert in California, on the way to Palm Springs. He put everyone up at a place called the Super-8 Motel, which I found funny ... it seemed appropriate. And actually, he was shooting 35mm film, which I think was the first time he'd ever done that. All his previous movies were on 16mm. Videotape started replacing that soon afterward, as shown in *Boogie Nights*.

I watched the shoot, got to know some of the cast ... and saw the make-up effects guy. He had some equally-scraggy friend with him, with a prison-style Fu Manchu mustache, long dark hair, and, of course, tattoos. I got the feeling these guys were both quite familiar with the joint. And joints, for that matter. They looked like two thirds of the Furry Freak Brothers. Or Laurel and Hardy crossed with Cheech and Chong. They showed me, rather proudly, their secret effects stash for the movie: a couple dozen arms and legs from department store mannequins, painted red to be "bloody." God, they were so proud of that shit! It looked exactly like what it was: a pile of dummy legs and arms with red paint smeared on them. "We're gonna scatter those all over the cave for decoration. Cool, huh?" Oh, yeah. Cool. Very cool.

The primary location was a canyon about ten miles from Barstow, and once the story was situated, they were planted there permanently. It offered some nice rocky mountains, some distant vistas, and had a real abandoned mining cave right there. It couldn't have been better for that if we'd planned it from the script stage. I remember there were actually bats out there at night. They'd fly out of the cave at twilight. I'd never seen real live bats. Not exactly right for a slasher movie, but atmospheric.

Lisa Loring got upset when she finally got a copy of the entire script, with the final pages. She said, "I'm an actress! I can't work this way! I've studied what you gave me, I created a character and a way to play it, and now it's all different. I can't do this. I can play a Lesbian photo model, or I can play a murderer, but I can't play a Lesbian photo model murderer!" (I wondered why not. And in the end, she did exactly that.)

I stayed out there a couple of days, everything looked like it would be fine, and I drove home. When I got back, I had this emergency call from Claire: "Call back immediately, we need to replace the make-up guy!" I found out what had happened: Tex and his pal got roaring drunk in some Barstow bar and got themselves thrown in the jug. Hal would not bail them out—but the police had also confiscated their vehicle, which had all the make-up and effects stuff in it. Perfect. I called John Goodwin, and he came in at the last minute—halfway through the shoot. That is not the best way to do things.

With Ron Wilson to help, John went out and worked nights in a cramped room of the Super-8 Motel to come up with effects which were at least serviceable. The air in the place filled with the stink of chemicals, solvents and latex and both Ron and John got goofy from the fumes. But he did a respectable job under trying circumstances, and got a couple funny stories out of the experience.

One story that Ron tells is about shooting the final confrontation in the cave, with Lisa going crazy, her halfwit brother [Chuck Rhae] drooling, the blonde strapped to the table being carved up, and the doctor looking on in horror. Ron and John both swear Lisa's first take went like this: "You thought it was my brother all along, didn't you, doctor? You're so smart with your diagnosis. Genitally insane, you said!" Genitally insane. I guess that means, he was nuts. The halfwit, by the way, was the husband of Danica Rhae, who acted in adult films. I think *Blood Frenzy* is Chuck's only acting role. I named the character Lonnie (I think I did, anyway ...) after Lon Chaney, crossed with Lennie. And I named the doctor character after the English actress Barbara Shelley.

After the movie was wrapped (it was a two-week shoot, six days times two), Hal asked me to come up with a teaser scene, so I wrote the opening, with the little kid (Little boy? Little girl? Aha, we can't see!) with the musical Jack-in-the-Box, and the abusive father (who gets his throat slashed). Another insane story Ron and John told me. Since the cops had impounded old Tex's vehicle, they no longer had the prop Jack-in-the-Box. Well, that was essential. Hal asked John to create one with make-up. Ask yourself how the hell you create a metal Jack-in-the-box toy with nose putty and latex—and have it match the one you've already shown in close-up? Somehow they managed to get the thing back. They left the sawed-off dummy legs, though.

I know John was unhappy with the way the special effects were used. He thought they were shot just fine, but that they were on screen too long. He's right. The longer an effect is on, the less shocking it is, and the easier it is to see how it was faked. On the teaser effects gag, for instance, it was written as one swipe of the tool across the dad's throat, a burst of blood, and out. Well, I guess Hal considered these effects the visual equivalent of the "money shot" in porn, because he just loved those things. He had the actress (daughter of friends of mine) poke and gouge, wiggle the metal around in this gushing wound, oh, it just went on and on. The one murder which I think comes off well is when the unseen crazy is stalking John Clark in the cave. Rick shot it exactly the way I wrote it, shot for shot. That was the only scene in the whole movie I broke down like that, otherwise there was a general description of the action. For what it's worth, I think it works.

I know Hal had rather grand plans to push the film theatrically, and had talked to the people in Barstow about having a grand premiere there. I don't think it was ever shown in

**Filming the opening sequence of *Blood Frenzy* in Hal Freeman's garage. This is the front of his house in Woodland Hills, California. Claire Cassano (Co-Producer/"Waitress") is the woman with folded arms in the middle of the photograph. The woman sitting behind Claire Cassano is J'Aime Cohen's mother (J'Aime Cohen played Dory, the Lisa Loring character, as a little girl) (courtesy of Claire Cassano).**

theaters, however. The video box was pretty grand: oversize, with a folding lid, glossy four-color art, photos of all the principal suspects. I came up with the idea of the Jack-in-the-Box getting stabbed. Either Claire, who was in charge of publicity, or, I suspect, Hal, had a line on the front of the box, "Shot in 35mm!" Well, gee whiz. That was so charmingly silly. Yes, in the porn world, that would be unusual, but in the real world, that was absolutely standard. You might as well have put "NOW with SOUND! See People Really TALK ON SCREEN!" It was charming in its naiveté. I'm sure Hal wanted the "35mm" line on the box to show the world he was now a real professional. I'm also sure any professional who saw the line on the box thought, "God, what an amateur."

After *Blood Frenzy* was wrapped, Hal wanted to do another horror movie. Since the officials out in Barstow were so cooperative and had said they'd let him use their courthouse as a location, I wrote a horror script called "Judgment Night" [1988/1989], basically, entirely set in and around that one location.

A convicted murderer has escaped prison, and seeks revenge on the people who supposedly "betrayed" him: the prosecutor, the judge, his defense attorney, and their assistants. One night, he manages to lock the courtroom building up—with all of them inside. One by one they are targeted for "execution" for their crimes against him. Having done the old "slash 'em up" routine with *Blood Frenzy* I wanted to have some fun. Since the story was set in a courtroom and involved the law, I decided the killer would use methods of legal execution, albeit in a grotesque way: shooting, beheading, death by fatal injection, strangulation. I had hoped John Goodwin would do the make-up effects again, since this would have given him some interesting challenges. So I was essentially following the standard pattern of a limited budget film: limited cast, limited locations, limited time frame. It all took place over one night. I think there were only two sequences set outside, a driving sequence where the defense attorney comes into Barstow, and the final shot of the two survivors exiting the court in the morning.

I remember one special prop that would've had to be made or procured: a small-ish statue of "Blind Justice," the blindfolded woman with a sword in one hand and a scales in the other. And after one particular murder, I think the scales would've had either a pair of eyeballs or a decapitated head on it. Ya-hoo!

Hal and Rick Pepin, and me, saw fifty or sixty actors read for the various roles. One young guy was particularly intense when he read a monologue where the killer gives his crazy philosophy. Oh, Hal fell in love with that guy. After he was gone, Hal said, "That kid's good. Real good. But I gotta tell him to bug his eyes out more." That's Hal the Director. I had envisioned Brinke Stevens as the prosecutor, Linnea Quigley as a legal assistant. I forget how she died, but I do remember a scene with her in the women's rest room. It may have been a wonderfully gratuitous sex scene. That may sound silly, but when you're limited to rooms in a court, you don't have a whole lot of variation. There's the hallways, the court rooms themselves, offices—and the bathroom.

I started to get other, rather more socially-acceptable, work elsewhere, and I drifted away from Hal. Last time I saw him at work, he was ill, had lost about 40 pounds, and his doctors could not figure out why his system couldn't keep anything in. I visited him once a short time later, when he was up in the UCLA Medical Clinic, and we talked about "Judgment Night." He was still ready to go. Some more time went by—a couple months, I think, and I was busy with other things. I got a weird call on my message machine, someone who apparently knew me, but I couldn't recognize the man's voice. It drove me crazy. Finally, somehow, I figured it out. It was Hal, calling from home. He had lost so much weight and was so sick, he did not even sound like his blustery old self anymore. We talked for a time—I could tell he was deathly ill, though he still talked about wanting to do one more horror film. I told him he was the nicest director I'd ever worked for, and it had always been fun. He was apparently very surprised anyone would say that. He started to bust up. He died about two weeks later.

## Claire Cassano
### (Co-Producer/"Waitress")

I graduated from the American Academy of Dramatic Arts in New York in 1981, and was awarded the Max Fisher award for the most accomplished actress. Like most classically trained actors, I took my acting career seriously by beginning in the theatre. I became anxious to move west to California, to experience the film business, warm weather, and to begin my own life away from home. I found film to be less serious, but that is where I could make money and perhaps achieve notoriety.

Hal Freeman and his eldest daughter, Cindy, were impressed with my salesmanship, and public speaking ability. They were very personable and asked if I would come and help Hal begin his new company, Hollywood Family Entertainment [HFE]. I believe they liked that I was a young professional with strength of character. The fact that I was a legitimate

**Hal Freeman (Director/Producer) and Claire Cassano (Co-Producer/"Waitress") posing for publicity photos for *Blood Frenzy* (courtesy of Claire Cassano).**

actress from New York, gave them creditability. I had street smarts, and was a good people person, so was destined to represent their company in a solid, credible and positive light.

Hal and I also had a lot in common, we both came from humble beginnings. He was Jewish from Chicago, and I am Italian from New York. We both spoke a similar street language and wanted to continue to better ourselves and reach higher ground.

Hal wanted desperately to crossover from adult entertainment and make mainstream independent pictures. He liked the horror genre and so decided to enlist Ted Newsom to write the script for *Blood Frenzy*. Ted had already worked for Hal in the past. The story was by Ray Steckler, another person who had worked for Hal. I wasn't a fan of the script or the genre, but I wanted to make my first movie.

Hal and I produced *Blood Frenzy* together. I was always by his side. We were very close friends. We always believed that we could make it a success. We were not happy about a lot of it, but it was our first attempt, and we had to stick to the budget and the timetable. There was little time or money to correct mistakes.

Rick Pepin was the director of photography for many Hollywood Video presentations. He worked for Hal for a long time. He had a family and was also anxious to crossover to mainstream films. Rick left HFE to form his own company, City Lights, with Joe Merhi. He hired Wendy MacDonald for his first City Lights production [*Mayhem*, 1987, Joseph Merhi], after he met her on *Blood Frenzy*.

I posted all of the casting notices in the Los Angeles trade papers, and conducted the auditioning/casting with Hal. Lisa Loring was a good find for marketing purposes. She answered our audition ad just like everybody else did, including Lynn Redgrave's husband, John Clark, who played Crawford.

I wanted to play Cassie. I played her in a couple of rehearsals and did a fine job, but Hal didn't want the sales professionals to see me as an actress. He said that it would lessen my effectiveness as his vice president of sales and marketing. He was right. I sold the hell out of *Blood Frenzy*.

We shot the entire movie in two weeks in the Mojave desert, near Barstow, CA. One stunning on-location memory.... Cassie was to take her top off in one scene, giving the gratuitous T&A shot for the film. Hal and I made it clear at auditions that Cassie's part required nudity in one scene. Everyone who auditioned agreed to it. Lisa Savage who got the part because of her look, agreed. On location in the Mojave Desert in 120-degree heat, right before we were to shoot the scene, she decided not to do it. She remained locked up in her hotel room and would not come out unless we promised her that she didn't have to do it! After conferring with Hal, I told her that she had to do it because she agreed to it in writing, and that we weren't changing the script just for her. She protested and then challenged us that her fiancé, a lawyer in Los Angeles, was coming to the set and would pull her out if we didn't agree. Sure enough, the boyfriend showed up in the middle of the desert and threatened to sue us and drive her away if we didn't change the script for her. Of course, the movie would have cost much more if we didn't agree. We had already filmed many scenes. We would have to get another Cassie and begin again. I told Hal that I should have been Cassie! He reluctantly agreed that Cassie would not have to take her top off! The scene was filmed with so much tension that worked well for the scene, but was a result of a primadonna who went back on her word, and her lawyer boyfriend who was protecting her breasts. I did not like either of them for behaving like that. We were honest from the start and they were not.

Picture taken on location for *Earthquake Survival* (1988). Hal Freeman, Shelley Duvall, and Derek Scott, assistant cameraman on *Blood Frenzy*, cameraman on *Earthquake Survival*. *Earthquake Survival* ("Learn How You Can Survive the Critical First Seven Days After a Major Earthquake") was a documentary directed by Hal Freeman. The screenplay was by Brinke Stevens. Shelley Duvall was the host of the documentary (courtesy of Claire Cassano).

All of the actors did their best and were generally a pleasure to work with. Some who were more professional of course didn't understand or like Hal's background. But, as an actress I know that there are always primadonnas, downright bad actors, and professionals. When you are staging any kind of show, you simply need to get along with all of them, just as in life.

We could not secure theatrical release in the U.S. Independent films were not welcome to theatrical release as they are now. There was a Hollywood star only system back then. Thank goodness that has changed. I was in Milan for MIFED as VP of sales and marketing. We sold the film to many countries. I remember we did well in Japan, Benelux, Germany and Italy.

After the success of *Blood Frenzy*, we believed that we could conquer anything. So, next we made *Earthquake Survival* [1987, Hal Freeman] with Shelley Duvall and Matt Murray. Our next independent success. The first video to be sold by two grocery store chains at the point-of-sale, as a "sell-through" product. "Judgment Night" was scheduled next, and it would never be made.

I was to produce "Judgment Night" with Hal. Ted wrote that one, too. It was a far better script, more like a Hitchcock murder-mystery. Hal became ill. He was undergoing all kinds of tests. We never knew what was really going on. He and his family kept his illness and his care secretive. It made us all fear the worse. He and the family said that his health was compromised because of a stomach reduction surgery, but the rumor was that he had contracted AIDS. I don't know what the truth is. The family was always very secretive, so I don't know. But, I do know that Hal confided in me often, and never said that he had anything except complications from his stomach having been stapled, and that he was very angry with the doctor. Something had gone wrong.

Hal was a profound mentor, dreamer, pragmatist, and a very generous man. He changed my life and how I look at it. He loved hard workers and working hard himself. He was tireless. He was hopeful. He was a father, a grandfather, and a best friend to me. I miss him very much. I am forever thankful for meeting and working with him. I will love and remember him, always.

## John Goodwin
### (Special Makeup Effects)

I was visiting Ted Newsom when he was writing the script for *Blood Frenzy* and I suggested a plot device that was borrowed from Agatha Christie's "Ten Little Indians," so you could get an unknown murderer killing all these people on a campout in the desert. The trick would be one of them was blown up beyond recognition but that would be red herring and he would turn out to be the surprise murderer at the end. I made a few suggestions for gory deaths and Ted was going to pitch me to Hal Freeman, a former porn movie producer, to do the make-up effects. I never heard anything more.

Then many weeks later I get an emergency call from Ted saying that Freeman & Co. are out on the desert outside of Barstow, California, and the police have arrested his make-up effects expert for having automatic weapons in his van. Well, at that point I felt like saying good riddance, for not hiring me in the first place. I had just finished the last year of the TV show *Moonlighting*—I didn't hold much regard for these low budget slasher films, and had no idea what Hal Freeman—although a nice enough guy—was doing.

I called Ron Wilson, an enormously talented fellow and jack of all "Cinema trades" and we drove out to Barstow. We negotiated a daily rate and promised to come up with what we could on location if they could postpone most of the bloody effects as long as possible while Ron and I set up a humble lab in our room at the Holiday Inn and bribed the maid to keep away. I told them from the start I had no way to blow up a fake body I didn't have so I know that part of the film was changed.

I vividly remember this cave in Barstow that looked so fake it couldn't play in a Three Stooges short. The floor was flat and they wouldn't let you water down the walls or anything. I think Hal Freeman learned an important lesson: just because it's on location and real doesn't mean it's going to look that way on film.

One night they had to match something from the first few days of the show—where an actor has to march out of the dark carrying this musical jack-in-the-box. Well, the prop was in possession of the police so Freeman tells me, "You genius make something that will match." Well, I try and be a nice guy which is not easy in this industry sometimes, but at times you've got to dig your heels in. I told Freeman that it was just a waste of time to try and cobble something together that he'd better shoot around it or send someone to the police station to see if he could get it. I don't think he knew what I meant by "shooting around it," but he certainly understood my tone of voice, so they went and got it from the police station!!!

We shot the opening in Hal Freeman's garage weeks after the rest of the movie was complete. I remember this kid is supposed to kill his father with a garden weeder which is ridiculous, but Hal was afraid to change anything Ted wrote. So Ron Wilson and I talked them into the kid tripping the other actor so at least he was down on the ground. But it's not another day "for love" as W.C. Fields would say. We had all these complicated blood lines—and they kept changing the position of the actor—and I knew we could only do it once. They wasted so much time there was not going to be time to put another neck piece on. I think we got it on the first take and of course Hal Freeman kept yelling for more blood like he was living it. Actually with a little more controlled environment that shot could have been twice as effective…

## Tony Montero
## ("Rick Carlson")

I was in the Army for three years during [the] Vietnam war. Then I lived in Hawaii for a couple years going to college. I came back to the mainland, got married and started acting in commercials in San Francisco. I did a major campaign for Toyota then moved to Los Angeles for the big time, ha ha! Los Angeles was great, I did a lot of episodic TV and got another big commercial campaign (I was the first "Mr. Goodwrench"). I did many Stephen Cannell shows (*A-Team, Hardcastle, Riptide, Scarecrow and Mrs. King*), soaps (*General Hospital, The Young and the Restless*), and then occasional films. I got started late in life (I was 30 when I got my first acting gig).

I got the *Blood Frenzy* gig through Hank Garrett. Hank was a good friend of mine and a good friend of Hal Freeman's. Hal had been doing only porn prior to this project and he wanted his legacy to be something more than just porn. I never minded that Hal and the crew were porn makers: there was no direction. Poor Hal passed away shortly after the film's release. I believe it was AIDS that got him—in those day it was rampant in his industry.

Hank Garrett is a real solid guy, with a great film history. We worked very well together. Wendy Macdonald was the director's sweetheart. Lisa Loring was a pro. She was the only actress who would show her tits after we got on set—all the others flaked out. Lisa Savage was a model and didn't want to do any nude scenes. This after she told Hal, "No problem"—prior to this she had done a billboard of her lying on an air mattress, ha ha!

It was hot working in the desert! Imagine it's 110 degrees F and Hal Freeman is cooking chili in the motorhome for lunch for everybody, eating out side with scorpions running around and a PA who is sympathetic to rattlesnakes not killing them but pushing them out of the camp just out of sight…

Ted, the writer, wrote a great script and it could have been so much more but … well, that's history, the people with the money rarely have the artistic instinct to go with it.

The film needed a better soundtrack. You can take a shitty film and put a great soundtrack with it and people will say, "Hmmm that wasn't so bad"—but take a great film and put a shitty soundtrack and people will go away and say, "It sucked." In the scene where I am in a tent talking about my experience in Vietnam, if Hal would have added a soundtrack of combat it would have made that scene pop. Also, there was a time when we were leaving a restaurant and I dropped my keys. I asked him to take a shot of that showing my dog tag on the keys then overlay some combat sounds as I picked them up that would have really helped develop the PTSD [Post-Traumatic Stress Disorder] that my character was suffering from.

I am now playing jazz at various upscale restaurants and clubs in Mexico. I sing and play sax and clarinet. I can honestly say my worst moment as a musician is better than my best moment as an actor. (Un-sophisti-cat.com. I'm on Facebook too: Tony Montero.)

## Monica Silvera Nadon
### ("Jean")

I grew up in California, the middle child of nine children. I went on camping vacations with my family and the Girl Scouts. I started gymnastics at the age of 12 after seeing Olga Korbut in the Olympics. I competed in gymnastics in high school and college. I taught gymnastics while in college, then moved back home near San Francisco and taught gymnastics while trying to pursue my acting career in the San Francisco Bay Area. When I moved to Los Angeles, I also taught gymnastics. And in my current hometown, I taught gymnastics for five and a half years.

As a young girl I performed in plays for the recreational department in summers, then acted in plays in high school and went on to receive my Bachelor of Arts Degree in Theatre Arts from California State University of Fresno. Both gymnastics and theatre have played a large role in my life.

After graduating from college I worked in the box office of Roger Rocka's Good Company Players by day and performed in musicals at night. Later I moved to Los Angeles to pursue an acting career. I studied film acting at Film Industry Workshops (FIW) in Studio City. Some of the FIW classes were held at the CBS Studios lot. For a budding actress it was always exciting to see the "stars" of the television shows as they were leaving for the day.

While studying acting at Film Industry Workshops, I auditioned and got cast in *Blood Frenzy*. I met John Goodwin and Ron Wilson, make-up artist and his assistant who specialized in make-up for horror films. Both John and Ron were also improvisational actors. Not long after the movie was filmed, I took an improv acting class from Ron Wilson. Ron trained us to the point that we started performing improv at local venues.

It was after our first performance that I met my husband in 1990. We got married twice, in 1994 and then again in 1995. Our 1994 wedding took place on a game show called *Here Comes the Bride*. Three couples were interviewed about how they met, their romance/dating period and the proposal. Then the studio audience voted for the couple's story they liked best. My husband and I won and got married on the show, legally! Television star, Lyle Waggoner, was the host of the show and also walked me down the aisle. That was a fun way to get married but it was not the wedding of my dreams so my husband and I got our marriage con-validated by the Catholic Church in 1995 and had all our family and friends in attendance. My husband later joined the improv troupe and performed with us for a few years. We have two teenage boys who were born in 1998 and 2000. I took time off from acting when my boys were young. We moved to a mountain community and I got involved in the local community theatre. I have been the board secretary for eight years and am in my fourth year as President. I act, direct plays, teach acting to young children and run our improv troupe. I acted in and worked on another low budget film in 2007. I work as a substitute teacher during the school year, am involved in my church community and stay very busy without community theatre.

While studying film acting at Film Industry Workshops, Hal Freeman, the director, called the workshop and asked them to send actors over to audition for the film. I don't remember much about the audition but I do remember talking about the auditions with my roommate and our friend, both of who were studying at FIW and had auditioned for the same part I did. We all shared our audition experiences. The more we talked, the more I was convinced that one of my two friends would get the part. Each talked about how well their audition had gone and the positive response they'd gotten from the casting people in the room. They were both very good actresses. Needless to say, I was quite surprised when I got the call that I had gotten the part in the movie. A horror film was not in my acting career dreams. I never liked horror films. I didn't like being scared and I had told myself that I would never act in a horror film. Well, when the first part you're offered is in a horror film, you don't say no. As it turned out, filming a horror film was not scary at all.

The location for the film was just outside of the city of Barstow, California, over the mountain from Calico Ghost Town. Barstow is in the desert. Every day was hot, hot, hot. The temperature was in the high 90's or even over 100 degrees Fahrenheit. I remember filling up my car with gas and washing the windows. By the time I got the window wet and made my first swipe with the squeegy to clear the window of the water, the water had dried on the rest of the window leaving dirty streaks all over the it.

I remember we had a read through of the script in Hal Freeman's hotel suite. The crew members sat and listened while the actors read the script out loud. The make-up lady, who did the regular make-up, told me she thought I was a good actress. I was very flattered to hear that she thought I was as good as the other actors.

Being the most inexperienced actor in the film, I wasn't sure what to expect. I was pleasantly surprised to find the other actors to be friendly and accepted me into their group. I gave Lisa Loring a ride in my car to the location. She told stories from her soap opera days. Hank Garrett was very nice and friendly. He had the biggest smile. He offered to help me with my acting scenes. I remember Hank, who had acted in the television show *Car 54 Where Are You?*, told the story of when he had acted with Sir Laurence Olivier. Sir Laurence told Hank that he liked his work, meaning that Olivier had actually seen some of Hank's previous acting. Hank had been very impressed that Olivier had bothered to see his work and compliment him on it. Wendy MacDonald was very friendly and asked if she could stay in touch with me after filming. She said it wasn't always easy to find good actresses to work with. I was very flattered by her compliment. Lisa Savage and I shared a hotel room during the filming. She was also very nice and friendly. We would run our lines with each other in our room at night before going to sleep. I think my favorite scene with another actor in the film was the one I filmed with Tony Montero. It was an intense scene and I thought it turned out well and that Tony and I worked well together. John Clark was just a big teddy bear. He was easy to talk to and he gave me some acting tips. His then wife, Lynn Redgrave, came to visit him on location twice. I enjoyed talking with her in the hotel swimming pool. One evening, the whole cast went to dinner with John and Lynn. I could have been very intimidated to be around someone of her talent and stature, but she talked to me like I was on her level and put me at ease.

I don't have a lot of memories of director, Hal Freeman. I picture him in my mind sitting in a director's chair the most. He didn't schmooze much with the actors. He directed the scenes with minimal direction to the actors. I do remember one of the crew members saying that, in a meeting with just Hal and the crew, Hal told the crew that actors were "a dime a dozen" and he could replace any of the actors easily but that the crew were the important people in the filming process.

[Here are some stories from the filming…]

"Dead Fall" … In one scene in the movie, my "dead" body is pulled off a crude table and dropped on the floor of the cave. Before the filming of the scene took place, Ron Wilson, make-up assistant, approached me and told me that I should request they put some padding on the floor to cushion my fall. There were small rocks all over the ground. He told me it was totally within my rights to ask for padding to protect my landing on the rocky ground. This, being my first movie, it hadn't even occurred to me that I would need to ask, or even that I could. A crew member managed to provide a blanket to soften my landing. It might have been a painful landing otherwise.

"Cry No More" … Another scene in the movie had the characters doing "intensive" group therapy. My character, Jean, was supposed to cry. I had yet to master the technique of crying on cue and was unable to summon the tears that director, Hal Freeman, wanted. Lisa Savage and Wendy McDonald were able to cry tears of sympathy for my character during the scene. Nothing I did was able to bring forth tears so Hal Freeman shouted for someone to bring onions, leftover from lunch. Unfortunately, the onions no longer had the potency to bring tears to my eyes. Finally, we used eye-drops to produce the desired effect. Later I learned that Lisa and Wendy had been using eye-drops all along to make it look like they were crying.

"Tent Up, Anyone?" … At the beginning of the movie, when the characters had just arrived at the campsite, we filmed a scene in which we were supposed to pitch the tent. No one gave us instructions on how the scene was supposed to be played. They just left a tent on the ground with the actors, walked away and called "action." We unfolded the tent and laid it out on the ground. Hank Garrett looked up and said, "I don't know how to put up a tent." None of the other actors knew how either. Except me. I had been a Girl Scout and had gone camping many times with the scouts and with my own family as well. I knew how to pitch a tent! So I did my best to instruct the other actors how to pull the corners tight and find the tent stakes and poles. As it turned out, we didn't have to pitch the tent at all. Hal Freeman just wanted a shot of us starting to pitch the tent. The crew pitched it later in a different location from where the shot originated.

"Cracked Egg" … In another scene I had to crack an egg with a knife in order to fry eggs for breakfast on the camp stove. The knife was supposed to lend suspicion that my character might be the murderer. In the first take, I cracked the egg perfectly. Hal Freeman asked for another take just in case something went wrong with the film in the first one. For some reason, my right hand would bring the knife just shy of cracking the egg open. We tried numerous takes, but I still couldn't get my hand to make the final strike. A crew member even showed me that the knife was dull and wouldn't cut me. He rubbed the knife on his hand to demonstrate. I was frustrated. I didn't consider myself a chicken, someone who was scared to crack an egg with a knife. I mean, I had done it the first time. But for the life of me, I could not crack another egg with that knife. Finally, Hal Freeman decided that the first take would have to do.

"Die Screaming" … My favorite story to tell about filming the movie *Blood Frenzy*, is when I got my throat slit. In the scene, I'm checking out the cave and the murderer comes up from behind me and cuts my throat. We did two different versions of having my throat slit. In the first version, the make-up guys, John and Ron, put an "A" solution on my neck and a "B" solution on the knife. When the knife slid across my neck the "A" solution made contact with the "B" solution and a streak of red appeared. That version was easy. In the second version, John and Ron fashioned a prosthetic piece of skin to go on my neck that covered plastic tubing that wound from my neck down my back and into a bottle with a pump mechanism. Chuck Rhae, playing the murderer, would slide the knife across my neck and Ron, off-camera, would push the mechanism up and down to pump the blood from the bottle, through the tube and out through the prosthetic piece of make-up. I screamed and blood, lots of it, came rushing from my neck and down my chest. With each take we did, I was directed to keep screaming. Don't stop screaming. And like a good little actress, I did as directed. In watching the movie later, many of my acting friends laughed hilariously during that scene, because once your vocal chords are cut, you wouldn't be able to scream anymore. My friends got a big kick out of this and hooted with laughter. Dummy me! I just did as I was directed and didn't think to question it. But of course, what is a horror film without a lot of screaming. The other funny part of this story is that during all the takes with Ron pumping blood through the tube to my neck, the blood mixture didn't know what the assistant director meant when he called cut. The blood just kept dripping, lower and lower down my chest and further. When the mixture made its way down my bosom it was a bit of a shock. They had used cold water to make the mixture and my body was hot from the heat of the desert. My eyes got big at the feeling of this cold "goo" going down my chest. Okay, I managed to get through that chilling effect and did a few more takes, all the while, Ron kept pumping more blood through the tube to come gushing out of my neck. Again, the blood mixture didn't know it was supposed to stop when they called cut. By now the blood was oozing its way down my pants. My eyes got even bigger when I felt the cold sticky blood mixture in my underpants. You know when you first walk into a swimming pool and you get your feet wet? It's cold but you can handle it. Then you walk further into the pool and your knees get wet. Okay, that's cold, but you can still handle it. Your thighs get wet, you can still handle it. But when the water hits your skin under your bathing suit, it's a heck of a lot chillier and you gasp to take a breath because it is so much colder. That's the best way I can describe the feeling when the blood mixture reached my underwear and kept oozing its way down my legs. Cool swimming pool shock! One of the female crew members said she laughed at my facial expression when that moment happened. We all had a good laugh at my expense.

I would have to say that the whole filming process was a good experience for me. I learned a lot and found that I could hold my own with the more experienced actors. The whole filming was done in less than fourteen days. I remained friends with Ron Wilson and John Goodwin after the filming was over.

# *Blue Monkey*
## (1987, U.S.A./Canada)

*Genre:* Horror; *Director:* William Fruet; *Writers:* George Goldsmith and Chris Koseluk (uncredited); *Cinematographer:* Brenton Spencer; *Editor:* Michael Fruet; *Special Makeup and Creature Effects:* Sirius Effects; *Producer:* Martin Walters; *Associate Producer:* Risa Gertner; *Executive Produces:* Sandy Howard, Michael Masciarelli and Tom Fox; *Production Company:* Howard International Films; *Cast:* Gwynyth Walsh (Dr. Rachel Carson), Steve Railsback (Detective Jim Bishop), Susan Anspach (Dr. Judith Glass), Ivan E. Roth (The Creature), Don Lake (Elliott Jacobs), John Vernon (Roger Levering), Helen Hughes (Marwella Harbison), Sandy Webster (Fred Adams) and Philip Akin (Anthony Rivers)

An elderly man is accidentally stung by an insect while observing an exotic plant in a greenhouse. He dies in hospital, and a strange parasite crawls out of his mouth. While the larva is dissected and analyzed in the laboratory, a strange insect emerges from it without being noticed by scientists. When several other patients, who are presenting the same symptoms of the elderly man, die (the parasite lurks within the human body and feeds on the bones), the hospital is quarantined. Due to exposure to an accidental genetic growth promoter the insect quickly reaches abnormal size, spreading death and terror inside the building. A female doctor, an entomologist and a detective face the monstrous creature, which has since started to breed: an egg-laying female has originated and hundreds of eggs are ready to hatch.

## Michael Masciarelli
## (Executive Producer)

I went to Film School at Loyola Marymount University in Los Angeles. Some of my fellow class and roommates included: Jim Wong and Glen Morgan (*X-Files/Final Destination*), Patricia Whitcher (*Thor/The Avengers*) and David Witz (*Star Trek/Moneyball*). We all helped each other and worked on our student films together. I worked on my first feature film while still in college: *Deadly Sunday* [1981, Donald M. Jones], a very low budget horror film shot in about two weeks during the summer. After I graduated college my first job was as a video editor on a television show for the Disney Channel called *You n' Me Kid*—before getting a job with Sandy Howard [1927–2008].

I and Jim Wong started working for Sandy Howard editing movie trailers as part of the films' foreign delivery requirements. It was a lot of fun and allowed us great creative freedom. Sandy would give us some of his notes but we learned very quickly if we just told Sandy we made the changes he wanted and showed him the trailers when he was tired at the end of a long day, he would just thank us for a great job. And we didn't change anything ... we just got to use our choices. Jim Wong and Glen Morgan later wrote their first feature film which got produced for Sandy Howard called *The Boys Next Door* [1984, Penelope Spheeris].

I then started to work on different Sandy Howard films in different roles. As either a production assistant or 2nd assistant director on films such as *The Boys Next Door* with Charlie Sheen and Maxwell Caulfield. I eventually started to do all the production budgets and schedules for the company and eventually became VP of International Productions. "Green Monkey" [which was the original title of *Blue Monkey*] was part of a number of scripts that were sent out for financing and was chosen as part of a multi picture deal.

Sandy Howard always had a lot of projects in development at one time. 95% of the time the original idea or concept was his. He would hire a writer to develop/write the script for him. Such was the case with George Goldsmith on "Green Monkey." The writer would turn in a first act or draft and Sandy usually had script notes that were twice as long as the draft. Part of the reason for developing the project was the success of *Aliens* [1985, James Cameron]. But Sandy had [a] wide range of subject matters to his film. The writer normally got paid very little up front maybe $2,500–5000 for the script against a back end deal if the film got made of perhaps $50,000.

The film's budget was around a modest $3 million (Canadian). Sandy had theory on a $2–3 million budget: unless you were totally drunk and didn't know what you were doing ... it was hard to lose any money. But if you made a low budget film for 5–10 million dollars and it was a piece of crap ... you could lose millions. *Blue Monkey* never did well or made any money in the U.S.A. but I think it made a modest profit in the international markets.

"Green Monkey" was part of a (3) picture deal Sandy made with RCA/Columbia Pictures Home Video. There were a number of scripts that were submitted to them and the three that were chosen were: "Green Monkey," *Dark Tower* [1986, Ken Wiederhorn & Freddie Francis] and *Nightstick* [1987, Joseph L. Scanlan]. Some of these films were produced in Canada as part of "Canadian Content" films. At the time the U.S. dollar was worth almost 30% more and by having the film a "Canadian Content Film" you got tax rebates and supplemental funding. There was a point system that you had to have to be Canadian Content. Of the writer, the producer and the director, two of the three needed to be Canadian. Also the 2nd highest paid actor needed to be Canadian. Gwynyth Walsh, one of the stars in *Blue Monkey*, was Canadian. Steve Railsback, the main lead, was from the U.S.A. William Fruet was brought on board to direct as he was Canadian and had made some successful horror movies [*Cries in the Night/Trapped/Spasms/Killer Party*]. Martin Walters was a very experienced 1st assistant director whom I had worked with on a Sandy Howard film called *KGB: The Secret War* [1984, Dwight H. Little]. He was from Canada and someone we could trust as being in a sense our "Front man Producer" in Canada. But he actually worked as the day-to-day producer during production.

Sandy Howard, Tom Fox [1935–2004] and I not being Canadian ended up as Executive Producers on the film. Tom Fox had made some films on his own [*The Return of the Living Dead*] and had some involvement but he was basically an investor and put in I believe $200,000 towards productions costs. Risa Gertner was a smart young woman we met there with a lot of knowledge of the film industry so Sandy made her an Associate Producer on "Green Monkey" and another project [*Street Justice*].

Sandy Howard and I did most of the pre-production work (finding special effects person, and key department heads, and scouting locations). We first were looking into Vancouver, Canada. There were a lot of films being made there and it was only a 3-hour flight from Los Angeles. We ended up in Toronto because they seem to be deeper in crews there. We had more experienced people to choose from.

As I said earlier, the main reasons for going to Canada were first because of the value of the American dollar at almost 30% the Canadian Content tax benefits and Toronto had a bigger film community to choose from. We ended up making a number of films up there. *Prettykill* [1986, George Kaczender] was one of the films in which I was the Associate Producer on and *Street Justice* [1987, Richard Sarafian] in which I was the Producer. These were both made in Toronto, non-content films. The story line in each of those films took place in New York. So it was a short flight over with the cast to film some establishing shots or scenes in New York City, but most of the film was really shot in Toronto. We would also have a few pickup days of filming back in Los Angeles—most of the time without main cast members for insert shots. Toronto is a beautiful city and looks like a clean New York.

We were filming both "Green Monkey" and *Street Justice* at pretty much the same time. I was mainly on the set of *Street Justice* but would check in on "Green Monkey." It was VERY COLD during filming. We shot right in the middle of one of the coldest winters ever in Toronto. I remember we lucked out as we needed a hospital to film in and found one there we could use. I remember there were a lot of one-way streets in Toronto and I would get lost trying to drive around. I got a ticket for driving down a one-way street. I told the police officer I was from the United States. He said, "They don't have sign in English there?" and gave me the ticket.

I remember more of pre-production. We first met with Carlo Rambaldi who designed *E.T. The Extra-Terrestrial*. He worked up his budget for doing the Alien special effects for the firm. It was like $2 million also; as much as our whole budget. We also met with Tom Savini (*Dawn of the Dead/Creepshow*). We finally lucked out when we found an up and coming special effects artist, Steve Neill [Sirius Effects]. He was talented and could work with our limited budget.

[Why did the title change from "Green Monkey" to *Blue Monkey*?] During the 80s AIDS/HIV was still a very taboo subject and not a lot was known. Actor Rock Hudson had just died of AIDS and there was a great fear of getting it. A theory came up from scientists that AIDS had been started by infected African green monkeys and at the time and for a number of years people still believed that's how AIDS started. So

The main creature in *Blue Monkey* (courtesy of T. Dow Albon).

of course the title "Green Monkey" had to be changed as not to be associated in any way with AIDS. Calling it "Blue Monkey" never really made any more sense since the alien was never really blue, but that's why the title was changed so as not to be associated with the African green monkeys.

Before the film was released Sandy had an idea to hire someone to spray paint on the White House or the Statue of Liberty "The Blue Monkey is coming…" That never happened. But I remember one night on Hollywood Blvd. while we were filming another movie, I saw a blimp (Zeppelin) airship flying overhead saying "The Blue Monkey is coming…"!

Sandy Howard was a unique personality. One could write a whole book on him. He was quite the character in Hollywood and looked the part of a big time Hollywood producer. There was a joke that he owed money to nine out of ten people in town. As he was always borrowing money in between projects to keep thing going. He was bigger than life. He loved the process of making films and traveling the world making them.

I remember the first day of shooting on *Street Justice* I was just this young kid producer. Sandy told me to go fire someone on the crew—that I needed to show them I was the boss and they would respect me. Lucky I refused…. I told him I wasn't going to fire someone for no reason. He could fire me. I think he respected that I stood up to him. Later on that same film, there was someone I wanted to fire and Sandy told me not to, that it would be too disruptive to the show…. Ha ha! So go figure.

The last feature film I produced was a film called *Ricochet River* [2001] with Kate Hudson. The past few years I have been producing/directing live multimedia shows. They are mostly either awards shows or celebrity fundraising events. I have also got involved in Thoroughbred Horse racing and own some race horses—more of a hobby with the horses … and I have made a couple award-winning documentary short films on the subject.

## George Goldsmith
### (Writer)

*Force: Five* [1981, Robert Clouse] was my first feature film credit. I was already a published newspaper and magazine writer before I went out to California in 1975. Once there I started writing for films and TV. My attitude was that I didn't know if I was any good, but I knew I could write at least as badly as the stuff that was getting made, so I gave it a shot. I quickly optioned several movie ideas to studios and producers, including MGM TV, Columbia and Universal Studios, and then wrote all 28 episodes of a direct to video series called *Masters of the Martial Arts* starring John Saxon, of *Enter the Dragon* fame.

Steve Ecclesine, the producer and creator of that series, and later many TV shows and films, found me teaching in a karate studio next to Doug Weston's famed music club the Troubador on Santa Monica Boulevard. This was 1979. I was living in the karate school, paying for my keep by teaching in the evenings. I was also a bouncer and a bodyguard, primarily for music acts, including the Runaways, and would teach in the evenings and then bodyguard until 3 in the morning, then come back to the karate school and sleep until about 9 in the morning, then get up and write until it was time to teach again. I was living on a couple of dollars a day. It was a wonderful life. Vicki Hearst, Patti Hearst's sister, was a student at the karate school. We were dating around the time Patti got kidnapped by the

SLA [Symbionese Liberation Army] and the FBI used to follow Vicki and I when we went out. Really hard to spot; guys in suits with black shoes and white socks and sunglasses which they wore at night! I taught Berry Gordy, Jr. (dad founded Motown Records)—a great kid—and Bob Dylan's sons and a lot of famous Hollywood personalities. Dylan's kids were great too, really nice and fun to work with. I used to really torture the students and one night Ecclesine walked in, was really amused at how I abused the students and asked me after class if I knew any writers who were also knowledgeable about the martial arts. The rest, as they say, is history. I did *Masters of the Martial Arts* for him, then he got me *Force: Five*, which was produced by Fred Weintraub and Bob Clouse, the producer director team from *Enter the Dragon*. A year or so later I got the call to do *Children of the Corn* [1983, Fritz Kiersch]. [Author's note—I couldn't resist asking George Goldsmith something about *Children of the Corn*.]

"Children of the Corn" was originally optioned by Hal Roach Studios, a small independent. Stephen King had written a script based on his own short story by the same name [1977]. They could not work with the script and a friend of mine, a story editor in town, recommended me for the rewrite, so I went over to meet with the Hal Roach executive after I read the script.

The first 35 pages had Burt [Peter Horton] and Vicky [Linda Hamilton], the protagonists, driving in a car arguing as they drove through these endless cornfields and back country roads. In my view it was not cinematic at all; interesting dialogue, but sort of claustrophobic and intense and angry. Burt and Vicky's marriage was not a happy one, but of course that was King setting the stage with tension, claustrophobia, a remote setting, all good elements for a horror story, but to an audience, 35 minutes of this was not going to fly, nor was the very narrative style King had employed throughout. So I came up with an idea to tell the story visually through the eyes and ears of these two little pack rats, Job [Robby Kiger] and Sarah [Anne Marie McEvoy]. They were a completely new invention but to me it worked and gave me an opportunity to visually and cinematically tell King's story.

Stephen felt otherwise, and the story editor at Hal Roach was on the fence. He liked my ideas but Stephen King was Stephen King, and so we had a conference call, the three of us, which Stephen opened up by informing me I did not understand horror and I countered that he did not understand cinema: horror and fiction are internalized, just like his script. Cinema is external: visual, auditory, a more sensory experience. In the end I prevailed. Hal Roach went with my script and sold it to New World Pictures, which kept my version and kept me on the project all the way through editing.

Then they tried to hose me on the credits ... Gotta love Hollywood! That was about money; they admitted it openly to me, "No offense, George, but King's name on the script means more than yours." It had nothing to do with fairness, just money. *Children of the Corn* was, needless to say, a hit, and after it came out I saw Stephen on a TV talk show. He was asked what he thought of it. He hesitated for a moment and then very thoughtfully and deliberately said, "I think it's the work of people who are going to do better." I really chuckled at that. I'd like to think he learned from me just as I learned from him. We both "did better" as our careers progressed, just he did a heck of a lot better than me! But his movies got better, that's what I mean; they got more visual and cinematic. I felt his comments on that talk show were gracious and I always appreciated him for that. He has always been a phenomenal storyteller.

I should add that working with Fritz Kiersch was a really pleasure. He and the actors were surprised when I accepted Fritz's invitation to attend some early read-throughs of the script with Linda Hamilton and Peter Horton. They were even more surprised when I had zero problem changing lines to suit the characters and the actors playing those characters, which I think is an important role a writer can play. I didn't want them stumbling over any of my lines, and I wanted to make it easy for them to convey the ideas I wanted to get across, so why wouldn't I change words to suit them, or listen to their take on it? My only disappointment was later on, during shooting, when Linda started winging some of the scenes and doing extemporaneous dialogue that I thought diminished those scenes. But all in all, it worked out pretty well, especially for her. Fritz did a great job managing egos, unpredictable Iowa weather and non-actor actor stand-ins—no small feat for a relatively inexperienced (at the time) director working on a shoe-string budget.

By the way, did anyone get that *Children of the Corn* is the story of the revolution in Iran, and the consequences to America? That Burt and Vicky were symbolic of the American public, and the Blue Man was the CIA, Malachi was the Ayatollah and He Who Walks Behind the Rows was the monster of unbridled religious zealotry, i.e., ISIS?

It was fun working with Sandy Howard and he was one of those larger-than-life characters, a real B-Movie "macher," which is a Yiddish term that loosely means "important person" but it combines humor, sarcasm, maybe a bit of jealousy and a pinch of respect into the definition. Sandy, Roger Corman, the wonderful Sam Arkoff [1918–2001], Charles Band (I liked Charlie. I did some script doctor work for him)—they were the "B-Movie Machers" who gave us so many wonderfully corny, terrible, fun, entertaining films. These individuals were human "genres" in and of themselves. Burt Reynolds did a great takeoff on that type of character in *Boogie Nights*, except the Reynolds character had zero taste, whereas Sandy, Roger, Sam and Charlie at least had quite a lot of taste—most of it corny, much of it bad, but at least it was taste!

The process that went into making films such as these was about marketing first and story second. It was about the poster that could be used to raise funds. The poster would be created before the film, even before the script. An "hauteur" or "filmpresario," as we used to call them (like Sandy), would get the Big Idea. It wouldn't really matter how corny it was, or if it could be made into a good or great movie. That was the writer's problem, and/or the director's. Once the poster got a distributor or investor excited, then Sandy would sit down with the writer (in this case me) and give him or her the Big Idea and the Big Set Pieces or Big Moments that they truly believed would wow the audience. In these meetings there would often be a lot of bad acting by Sandy as he described how he envisioned the Big Moments that would captivate and enthrall the audience, literally have them on the edge of their seats … at least in his mind. Then I would be sent off to try to make it all make sense, to build a story around the Big Idea and the Big Moments (Big Scenes) that he wanted. The story was really somewhat secondary—it was simply the glue that held the Big Things together. The story had to justify the poster, not vice versa. It was really fun, and very challenging, and a certain "genre" of film audience lived for it. This is what in my view led to the "Rotten Tomatoes Culture" within the film community. In some cases the worse a film was, the better it was. I mean, who could resist going to see *Attack of the 50 Foot Woman*? That picture made more than five times its budget!

I was known as a writer who could write really quickly, and had a lot of ideas I could articulate on the spot. Many writers would agonize for weeks over a few pages; not me. For me writing was actually "reporting." My process was that I would "see" the film in my head and then just write down what I saw and what I heard the characters say. Once I got into what I called "the zone," I might just black out for an hour or ten hours, and I would produce anywhere from three to thirty pages. That's the most I ever wrote; thirty pages in a day. That was for *Nowhere to Hide* [1987, Mario Azzopardi] which I completely rewrote into a shootable script in six days—but that's another story. I was known as a script doctor and an idea man so a lot of producers, especially the B film guys who often needed things done quickly, came to me. And I liked all genres; I hated the way the major studios pigeonholed everyone into these stupid categories like this one is an action writer, that one a comedy writer, that one a dramatist ... as if all us creative people were mono-maniacal and could only do one thing. So I knew Roger and Sandy and Sam and all those guys and they liked me. I would often tell them I thought their ideas were terrible and they should go a different way, but I also said if they insisted, I'd do my best to give them what they wanted, and I did. They trusted me.

I met Sandy after *Children of the Corn*, which was a big hit, and all those guys wanted me to work for them but I was trying to break out of the lower end films. On the other hand, I hated the monumental egos at the studios and just wanted to create. I didn't want to direct or act or produce, just write, and there was a lot of competition, so I paid more attention to the "B movie" world than a lot of other writers who had had some success. I doctored a couple of Sandy's really bad scripts—fortunately I declined to be named on them (one was *Dark Tower*)—and we became friends. Finally he came to me with the "Green Monkey" idea which eventually became "Blue Monkey." Why it changed colors, I will never know.

I honestly do not remember whether I approached Sandy with this concept or whether he approached me. I was working a lot in the horror genre, before and after *Children of the Corn*, because I had always loved science fiction and horror. "Green Monkey" was certainly an original story and script, but not a title I would have chosen. As for concept, Sandy wanted to do a "big" horror story about a creature in a contained space. Could be anything: an aircraft, a hotel, a submarine, a spacecraft ... didn't matter. That was pretty much what he knew at the time we discussed doing the film. Like all B movie makers Sandy was focused on genre, not originality, and horror was always a profitable genre if done right. For some reason "Green Monkey" was the title he wanted to use—I don't recall why. Titles were considered important, and I think that remains true today. One of my all-time favorite films, *The Yakuza*, suffered for having that title. So did another fine film, *Who'll Stop the Rain*, even though that's the title of a great Credence Clearwater Revival song. But Sandy didn't even care if there was a monkey in it. It was never about the damn monkey—and I am laughing as I write that! I was given a title and a very broad concept and told to "make it work," and since I was already doing stories with similar concepts, I was pleased to do it. I got a check for what I suspect was more than Sandy had ever given any writer, at least to start a script.

[Was *Blue Monkey* somehow influenced by *Alien*?] I don't recall any influence from *Alien*. It could have influenced me but would only have done so in the sense that the "terror" was locked in with the victims, but this was not terribly new. Dracula films had been doing that since day one in the castle, and haunted house films had been locking victims in forever—so Ridley Scott was not original with that. But what he was original with was that you couldn't really get out. I mean, it was outer space, right? Where are you going to? But *Alien* came out in 1979, and *Blue Monkey* in 1987, so there was a lot of time between the two films.

In my first draft I used the outer space element of a space rock that turns out to be an egg coming back on the space shuttle because my father-in-law at the time, Dr. Nicholas Renzetti, was heavily involved in the space program. He was head of Ground Space Telecommunications for Jet Propulsion Laboratories (JPL) in Pasadena, where my wife and I lived. Dad Renzetti is the one individual singly most responsible for the Deep Space Network, and the definitive 800-page book on that subject, "Uplink/Downlink," published by NASA, is dedicated to him. He and I used to talk for hours about space travel, science, etc. He was also the Director of SETI for five years, around that time, so those were big influences on me.

Another influence was my friend Harlan Ellison, whose science fiction I devoured. Harlan is a legend. So Harlan calls me up one day out of the blue. I don't know how he got my number, and he says, "This is Harlan Ellison. I'm writing an article on why Stephen King's stories don't translate to the screen well." And I thought, "What a punk!" So I say, "*Carrie* was a huge hit, and now *Children of the Corn* was a huge hit, so you'd better rethink your article, bub." He hears the tone in my voice, which was not friendly, and we argue for awhile, and then he suggests we meet at Barney's Beanery on Santa Monica Boulevard that night. Barney's was a kind of low rent Joe Allen's, but it had a pool table which was infinitely cooler than standing around with a bunch of poseurs talking about themselves for five hours and then saying, "Well, enough about me, what did you think of my last film…"

So I go up to Barney's and Harlan has already secured the pool table, and he's working it nonchalantly. Harlan is not a big man. He is in fact very small and slight. But what he lacked in size he made up for in ego—and talent. We start talking and we're not getting along great. Something comes up about my previous work in martial arts films and he says he studied martial arts with Bruce Lee. That was the red flag to the bull, so I tell him that I would be so honored to fight anyone who studied with Bruce. He declines, saying he only studied the really nasty stuff and he would be afraid of hurting me. I tell him I have no problem getting hurt, I had fought some of the best, and in fact I would consider every bruise, every broken bone, a badge of honor and would even write up a waiver that under no circumstances would I sue him or press charges if he hurt me, and as soon as I wrote it up we should go out in the alley behind Barney's and get busy. Well, he didn't want to do that.

So we talked some more instead of fighting, and he invites me up to his place off of Coldwater Canyon, which is a truly amazing house with weird angles and architectural oddities so you're walking down this hallway and you look like you're ten feet tall, and the person at the other end of it looks like they're two feet tall. It has gargoyles looking out from the roofline. Inside, we come into this truly grand room, the central living room, which is about twenty feet high, and all the walls are floor-to-ceiling book shelves completely filled. It was fantastic. I started to like the guy just a little bit more, but we were still a bit testy with each other. So we're hanging out and then the phone rings and he goes into the kitchen and I hear him start talking to what is obviously a woman writer who had just been rejected in some way, or criticized, and it was clear she was distressed. Harlan was so unbelievably kind to her, so supportive, so warm, that in that moment, just listening to the way he was talking to her and building her confidence right back up, I suddenly "got" him, what he was all about. I had always been a huge fan of his work, which is probably why I took exception to his criticism of my work, but I got over that and for awhile I considered him a good friend. I've never stopped admiring his work, nor his true personal character, although he was really good at making enemies in Hollywood. [Famous is] the story about him taking a billboard across the street from Paramount to let the general public know they had ripped him off … or the time he took out his .45 during a story meeting and started cleaning it.… Gotta love a man who does that!

Anyway, it was easy to come up with the "Green Monkey" script. I tried to make the creature that evolved out of the egg, which was initially thought to be a space rock that had hit and damaged a satellite, into a sort of monkey-like monster, but that was as far as I could go. Mine had wings and big teeth and was pretty gooey, as I recall. But again, as I have written earlier, what the writer sees in his head and what comes out on the screen are often very different things. So I had this astronaut who comes back from doing a repair job on a damaged shuttle or satellite, and he brings back this "rock" that did the damage, and it turns out to be an egg. The astronaut falls ill and is hospitalized. He brings the rock with him. Of course since he's just been in space, he and the hospital are quarantined. Total lock down to prevent any space borne, unknown virus from getting out. The doors are chained shut and there is panic in the hospital and in the city. The "rock" starts to crack because, of course, it's an egg, not a rock and this creature squirms out. Now here is where my memory gets a bit hazy (after all this was thirty years ago and I have not found my original draft), but I think a tiny worm or weird kind of alien insect crawls onto the unconscious astronaut and either slithers into his mouth or nose or eyes. A day or two later it emerges from his mouth as a kind of larva, much bigger, and holes up in the closet, where it begins to grow into … the Green Monkey! From there it was pretty easy to block out the rest of the story, somewhat predictable given the circumstances, but I do think that having the chase scene in the air ducts was pretty novel. Talk about enclosed places…! Imagine being chased by a monster through an air duct where you can only crawl, not walk or run.

Back then we did not have canned CGI or special effects that could be created with a couple of right clicks on a computer, so Sandy probably killed the whole space angle to save money. I don't specifically recall but that would be likely—for the "B movie machers" it was always about squeezing the most production value out of the least dollars. When I brought him my original draft, I was really excited about it. I thought it had the makings of a very successful film. *Children of the Corn*, to my surprise, was a huge hit and on its way to becoming a cult classic, and I felt this could be too if it was cast and directed the way I was seeing it in my head, and I still think that is the case. The film could have been a classic because sooner or later everyone gets ill, or visits a hospital, so they can relate to being there, and they know it's kind of an institutional horror set just as it is—from there it is easy to imagine being locked in, and then having a monster chasing you. That was one of my goals, to make the setting as universally identifiable as possible.

Having an internal logic to a story was, and is, very important to me and it always bothered me that so-called story editors would use "lack of logic" as an excuse to turn down scripts when films like *E.T.* have such gaping logic holes in them, like right from the very beginning when *E.T.* can't escape from his captors, or is in danger from them, yet with the wave of his finger he can make this kid's bicycle he's on fly over them. He has all these powers but he needs the kid and the family to hide out with? That always galled me—there are such double standards in Hollywood. Tom Hanks can walk in with the phone book and it gets made; some unknown genius walks in with a brilliant script and some overpaid kid with family connections playing "story editor" for a studio tells him or her "the third act needs work…" Right.

So for whatever reason—but probably cost—Sandy asked me to lose the origins in space. I'm not sure if I came up with the bug from the South Pacific island, but I do recall that I had been working separately on a similar type story (it never got made) that took place on a hospital ship that had gone out to the South Pacific to pick up survivors of a deadly storm, and an insect-like monster grew out of a parasite—I was trying to execute on the concept first done so well by *Alien* where you had a number of potential victims in an inescapably enclosed environment against an otherworldly foe (I still think that concept, the hospital ship afloat out on stormy seas, is a wonderful setting for humans versus aliens). I may have shared the idea, or even some pages, with Sandy, and then taken the script in that direction. I wrote more than one draft, but I don 't recall which draft was turned over to Chris Koseluk by Sandy Howard (they never told me they were rewriting me). Whatever Chris did (with or without Bill Fruet's input) was almost certainly heavily influenced by Sandy's "input." I don't know exactly what changes they made. What I do remember is: no monkey I ever created was blue—so at a certain point the script went in a different direction from my original. Bill Fruet was not part of any of my work. I think I talked to him a couple of times on the phone. I may have met him at Sandy's once but I don't think so. I think he was hired after I started my work. So the evolution from a "monkey" of any color to an insect was due to whomever rewrote the script—some combination of Chris, Bill and Sandy. But they would have gotten the idea for an insect from my "larva" that crawled out of the astronaut's mouth—that scene was definitely in my original draft. I always made it a practice to try to disgust my wife as much as possible with graphically visual scenes. That one really got to her.

Susan Anspach and Steve Railsback wound up in the film. Susan, of *Five Easy Pieces* fame, as the doctor and Steve, having fallen somewhat from the lofty perch of *The Stunt Man* with Peter O'Toole—one of my favorite films ever about the film business—as a detective who happens to be in the hospital at the time it gets locked down.

Janet Maslin, the longtime film critic for *The New York Times* even called *Blue Monkey* "an angry larva story." I got a great laugh out of that one. She actually liked the film, or at least didn't dislike it. I especially liked the comment by one Canadian critic who accused me of "career slumming" with *Blue Monkey*.

Sandy Howard was a big guy, kind of a big, rough-around-the-edges tough guy. More street smart than smart. I have never read a biography on him, just knew him from personal experience. He was a guest in my home a few times, and I in his. He was dating a friend of mine for awhile, but that ended. Sandy oozed a manufactured kind of charm. He was always well-dressed, well-groomed. It was kind of a caricature, but it was great. He was playing a part and he knew it, you knew it, but you bought into it. So everything was understood. He was the minor mogul, and everyone around him was generally a sycophant to some degree. I think he liked me because I'd just as soon throw someone out the window before I kiss their ass, but I was respectful. I genuinely respected Sandy and his accomplishments even though they didn't measure up to any standard of art. But why should everything be art? I think Sandy understood my fondness for him and respect for him was genuine, and not based on what I thought he could do for my career.

## Chris Koseluk
### (Story Editor)

I began working as a story editor for Howard International Films in 1986. It was a small operation led by Sandy Howard. Sandy was a veteran film producer who had made his mark many years before with *A Man Called Horse* [1969, Elliot Silverstein]. Following that, he had managed to put together a string of films—often by the skin of his teeth.

Sandy was established enough and savvy enough to cash in on the VHS craze that was sweeping through the film industry at that time. Companies wanted titles to put out on tape and were willing to bankroll low budget films to secure these rights. He had gotten lucky the previous year with a couple of films—*Vice Squad* [1985, Penelope Spheeris] and *Angel* [1984, Robert Vincent O'Neil] (The latter featured the infamous tagline "High School Student by Day, Hooker by Night"). Based on this, Sandy strung together enough money to put five films into production.

His strategy was usually the same. He'd come up with an idea and find a hungry writer to turn it into a screenplay. Next step was to hire a journeyman director he knew wouldn't mess things up by trying to be too "artistic." He cast a line-up of familiar names. This ensured that the films would sell well in foreign territories while making the investors happy because, by all appearances, this would be a "classy" production. Then he'd pray that there'd be enough money left after all was said and done to get the film through post production.

*Blue Monkey* was pretty much done this way. The film was budgeted at 1.2 million. Whether Sandy ended up spending that amount, I couldn't tell. He was "cross-pollinating" funds between this and four other films and I'm not sure anyone would have the accounting expertise to sort it out. When I first became involved with the project, George Goldsmith had already completed the first draft. At that time, it was called "Green Monkey." I believe George was playing off the idea that the green monkey was rumored to be spreading the AIDS virus. And since our "monkey" was spreading an unknown virus through the hospital, it seemed to make sense at the time. But by the time the film had evolved, AIDS had also evolved into a full blown epidemic. Sandy was afraid of the association, and insisted on changing the name. At various times I believe it went by the name of "Infected," "Infested," "Virus" and "Insect." None stuck and Sandy finally decided to call it "Blue Monkey." It made no sense, but seems fitting as the movie doesn't make much sense.

Sandy's strategy was to cash in on the popularity of *Aliens*. George's script wasn't bad, it involved an alien invasion of a hospital. The main problem with it was the timing. *Aliens* had just hit theaters when he turned in the draft. Enough of what George had written was a little too close for comfort to the sequel—purely unintentional—but problematic just the same. Sandy decided to go back to the drawing board. He came up with the idea of turning the alien into an insect. It would come to life in some remote locale (Bora Bora I remember joking). Sandy figured that would be enough to throw off suspicion as to where the idea had originated. George went about revising the script. The script came in and George had devised an insect that appeared to be unlike any species this world had ever seen. It was a hybrid that exhibited traits of everything from an ant, to a beetle, to a grasshopper to … well, you name it … when the script called for it. If memory serves me correctly, at one point, the insect impregnated itself and gave birth to another creature. It made little sense, but when has that ever slowed down a good B picture?

Sandy wanted to tinker with the script, but by this point, George was ready to move on. He had just landed a gig doing an episode of *Hill Street Blues* and felt he had grown beyond "Green Monkey." That's when Sandy turned the script over to me. That's also about the time William Fruet came aboard as director. Fruet was enthusiastic and encouraged me to have fun with the script. I decided to put my tongue-in-my-cheek and see what happened. Fruet knew the insect was so absurd—we had to put it back into outer space to gain any iota of credibility. If the creature were alien, we could have it do everything George had devised and still have an audience believe it.

I came up with what I thought was a great opening. The audience would see a giant meteor plummeting towards Earth. We'd intercut that with a greenhouse in a nondescript rural town. Suspense would build as we cut back and forth between the hurtling, flaming rock and the greenhouse. Each time, the second shot would be closer and closer to the greenhouse—eventually focusing on a pane of glass in the roof. Finally, the object hits the greenhouse. But it turns out it was only about the size of a pebble. It goes through a glass pane in the greenhouse with a resounding "plunk." The camera angles into the little hole in the glass to a plant in the middle of the greenhouse. Suddenly, an eerie burst of green (blue?) light bursts from the plant. Roll opening credits. I thought the scene set up the movie perfectly. We're playing by our own set of convoluted rules. Nothing is going to seem quite right. We're pulling your leg, but don't be surprised if we scare you, too. Fruet really liked it. Sandy, unfortunately, hated it. Seems a few years before this he had produced the film *Meteor* [1978, Ronald Neame] and ended up losing his shirt on it.

I remember the morning after I had written that scene. Sandy was in Toronto filming something else and I had sent him the pages. He called early in the morning LA time, actually waking me up (I had worked late the night before). He told me it wouldn't work. "I'm not making a science fiction film," he yelled. "Sandy," I replied. "You're making a film about an insect that grows to be nine feet tall! Whether you like it or not, you're making a science fiction film." After making my case as to why this would make the film work, he agreed to think about it. If you saw the final film, you know who got his way. Ironically, about ten years after that, I was watching a commercial promoting U.S. beef and it was essentially my opening. A guy thinks he's going to die because a meteor is hurdling towards Earth. So he puts a steak on the barbecue to enjoy one last good meal. The steak tastes even better when the meteor hits the ground and it is only the size of a pebble. It gave me some small satisfaction in the knowing that—in the end—it was an idea worth doing after all.

Another funny idea came to me as we were researching the film. Sandy wanted an expert to give us some bug tips. Seems the go-to guy in Hollywood for this was Steven Kutcher, a.k.a. "The Bug Man." We made an appointment and one afternoon, Sandy and I travelled to a remote part of the San Gabriel Valley to Steven's house. Not surprisingly, there were insects everywhere: on the floor, in tanks, on the counters, even in the refrigerator. Steve invited us to sit. Without thinking, Sandy plopped down on the couch. Looking around, I wasn't going to take any chances. I saw a wooden kitchen chair, and could see that it was bug free. I grabbed it, put it in the middle of the room, and stayed there through the whole session. I also declined Steve's offer of a drink. He was very helpful and I learned quite a bit about bugs that day. As Sandy and I were riding back from our appointment, I joked about his sitting on the couch. I told him there was no way I would have gotten near it, thinking about what could have been crawling around in it. Sandy laughed and said, "That's a great idea. You should write a scene based on that." I can't remember specifically in what ways Steve influenced our insect, except to say that he gave us the idea for the scene when the heroes (Steve Railsback and Phil Akin) first encounter the film's entomologist (Don Lake).

Another fun day was our visit to the effects house in Glendale to see how the bug was coming along. Steve Neill and Mark Williams [1959–1998] of Sirius Effects put it together [Mark Williams did a lot of the sculpting and design work] and I remember it looked great! In my opinion, they had gone far beyond the call of duty for the amount of money they were getting. Somewhere buried deep in my closet I still have the model they created.

Slowly but surely Sandy started assembling a cast. It was filmed in Toronto to take advantage of Canadian tax credits and the very favorable exchange rate on U.S. dollars. This is another reason Canadian native William Fruet was brought in to direct.

With Fruet's constant input, I put the script through quite a few rewrites during this period. The basic structure and plotline didn't change much. I estimate that about 90% of the dialogue was written by me. It was George's idea to make alcohol the cure for the virus. We didn't see any reason to change that.

A major character change I did make concerned the expectant couple "George and Sandra Baker." I completely rewrote them, trying to beef up the comedic aspects. One of the Toronto producers, Risa Gertner, had a connection to the Second City group and, based on my changes, was able to talk Joe Flaherty and Robin Duke into playing the Bakers. That was probably the biggest kick of the film for me. Flaherty, in particular, was a favorite and I was thrilled at the idea that he would be playing a character I had created.

I also enjoyed the idea that John Vernon was brought in to play the head of the hospital. I used to joke that he was going to stop the bug by putting it on "double secret probation." Another funny casting note is that one of the young kids in the film is Sarah Polley. Sarah grew up to be not only a very well-known indie film actress, but also a respected director. And it all started with *Blue Monkey*.

Because *Blue Monkey* was filmed in Toronto, I wasn't on set for any of it. Most of it was filmed at an abandoned asylum in the area. Fruet loved it for its endless stone corridors. At that point, I was getting a little itchy. Another colleague enticed me to leave and join him in our own filmmaking enterprise. Plus, Sandy was hemming and hawing about giving me a writing credit. Because of these two factors, I decided to move on. I get first end credit on the film as "story editor" rather than co-writer. In hindsight, had I stayed, I probably would have ended up with an opening credit. What can I say? I was young and dumb.

I saw the movie when it finally hit theaters later that year. I was disappointed that the opening was gone. Another scene I devised, which I called the "goopy" body scene, was also a big disappointment. When the paramedics bring the first victim into the hospital, they try to revive him using a defibrillator. Because the bug has invaded his system, it had eaten all the bones in his body. The defibrillator pads were supposed to go all the way through the body, causing a "goopy" wave of flesh to pour all over those trying to save him. It played much better on paper then it does on screen. "Sigh." The other thing that struck me is how dimly lit the last third of the film is. You can thank Sandy for that. From what I heard from a friend who stayed through post production, Sandy deliberately had the film darkened to cheat the scenes with the bug and try to hide the fact that it was basically an actor (Ivan E. Roth) in a suit.

Side note: I was at a charity event about a year and a half after the film. "Celebrities" volunteered to be waiters to raise money for the cause. It turned out Ivan Roth was one of the volunteers. He came to our table, introduced himself and said, "I'm your waiter." I hadn't met Ivan prior to this but recognized his name. I said to him, "You're my bug!" After explaining, we had a nice talk and he told me how much fun he had playing the blue monkey.

What else do I remember about *Blue Monkey*? The reviews were horrible. But *Variety* did say something along the lines of, "It has its own sense of whimsy and convoluted logic." I'd like to take credit for that. The Los Angeles *Herald Examiner* included it on its list of the top ten worst films of the year. How can you not appreciate a distinction such as that?

## Michael F. Hoover
### (Special Makeup and Creature Effects—Sirius Effects)

I believe (the late) Mark Williams designed it [the bug]—at least he was the man I went to with questions, and so forth. I remember he designed and built the eyes, a remarkable bit of business. He applied rhinestones to the surface of the eye (quite an expanse of eye, too) then covered the rhinestone surface with a vacuum-formed clear shell. This he painted with transparent paint to give it a rainbow-esque surface. When the rhinestone bit moved under the shell just a little, in person, the effect was wonderful.

The design of the bug I recall was a matter of debate. The trick is, of course, to disguise the human in the suit to the point where you don't even think of a guy in there. With that thought in mind, there was some talk about the actor running backward, with the bug facing forward—if you get me. The director—or the director of photography [Brenton Spencer]—obviously knew the old adage "Less is more," in that you rarely saw much of the bug—just like *Alien*, oddly. He shot it perfectly.

I remember that there were two big arm-things on the back [of the bug]. The mechanisms for those were salvaged from some sort of desk lamps, and activated by cables, as were the eyes. The entire heavy rig was attached to the actor with a motorcycle vest-thing. Really heavy-duty plastic body armor for crazy people who go off-roading on their bikes. I believe Todd Masters was the point-man on-set. I recall Todd telling me that when they got into the main part of the hospital with the Bug, it was too tall to run down the corridors, so the upper arms (the desk-lamp ones mentioned), had to be broken, and dangled from the body, only to be repaired later for other shots.

## Todd Masters
## (Special Makeup and Creature Effects—Sirius Effects)

I was a kid when I did *Blue Monkey*, around 18 or 19. I had just recently moved to Southern California from Seattle. I had arrived in late 1985 and had already done a few projects—as monster making assistant—before *Blue Monkey*. I had worked at Boss Film on *Big Trouble in Little China*, *Poltergeist II* and *Predator*; elsewhere on *The Twilight Zone* and *Night of the Creeps* (my first on-screen credit). Sirius Effects was Steve and Gilly Neill's home-brewed effects company (which was really Steve and Gilly's garage, and their backyard).

Mark Williams was a mainstay at Sirius Effects and he was quite the character. Over 6 feet tall, clad in tight leather—including tattoos, gauntlets and bleached blonde hair. It was like working with a member of Slayer or Twisted Sister, but it was the 80s and monster makers were known as rebels, a bit rough around the edges—and in some cases, a small step from "rock star." Mark played that to the nines, daring to be different, even extreme. He even walked with swagger: you'd hear him clang with metal, as he walked towards you ... before you saw him. But, he was cool and funny, a sweet person behind that rough, dangerous exterior. He was head artist on many of Sirius Effects builds at that time and led the charge on main bug monster suit. Narrow and tall actor Ivan Roth was hired to portray the monster and they had already started when I joined the group. Steve Patino [1960-1994] had helped supply the Ivan Roth mannequin, and most of the sculpture was well along when I arrived. I jumped in as needed and sculpted one arm of the creature. I mainly spent my time on the big egg sacks and few of the other gags. Steve Neill did the "Mama Bug" puppet [the creature with a large egg abdomen that at one point of the film lays eggs in the basement of the hospital].

*Blue Monkey* was filmed in Toronto—it felt like an above average Roger Corman film of the time. I took over leading the charge on the show when it went to set, probably for no other reason than Steve or Gilly were not going to go to location. And I was more a diplomat, more patient than Mark Williams—and dealing with the AD's and Production came easy for me. Mark, clad in leather and studs, could be a bit intimidating—nicest guy in the world, but sort of out of place anywhere but Sunset Blvd. Ivan came with us—or maybe better, we, with him. We were his monster-making posse, so to speak and had gotten to know each other during the prep, prior to flying to Toronto. Then we joined our new local assistant—and our driver—sometimes punk rocker—Jill Compton, in Toronto. So, we all were an unusual foursome: Mark, Ivan, me and Jill. We looked even scarier than our monsters! All of us spent a lot of time together on location, trying to make the suit work. It was an interesting experience—all working in an old, haunted and dilapidated insane asylum just outside the city. The entire film was produced there, and our "monster department" took over a wing of the building, to get the effects work prepared.

Prior to shipping all of the effects work and the suits to Canada, from Steve and Gilly's backyard, I had expressed concern that the light and narrow Ivan was going to be challenged by the weight of the "hero" suit's upper mechanical parts (his head and some his shoulders seemed to be taking the entire stress of a very large part of the costume). Essentially, the

The entire shop crew of Sirius Effects, not all of whom worked on *Blue Monkey*. From left to right: Ricky Schwartz (a make-up artist working on creature effects between jobs, holding the cocoon mold); in the back, the guy who nobody seems to remember; Makio Kida (probably he went back to work in Japan, after he built up enough U.S. film credits); Beth Hathaway, seated (she went on to become a well-known creature effects artist in her own right); Mark Siegel, behind Beth Hathaway (recently, he worked for DreamWorks); Todd Masters, behind Mark Siegel, upside down, and wearing Blue Monkey forearms; T. Dow Albon, in his IBM lab coat, holding a tongue depressor; Gilly Neill, seated; Mark Williams, holding some kind of alien entrails; Tony Defont, pointing at C-clamp; Steve Neill, the boss, kneeling in cap; J. Paul Moore, an actor and magician, working between gigs; Mike Hoover, standing off to the right. The big friendly dog is "Puck." The Cat is "Momma Cat." Gilly Neill, who started out as Steve Neill's girlfriend, and then became the office manager, and finally became Steve's wife, loved animals. So besides "Momma Cat" and "Puck," the shop had several other cats and dogs. At some point Steve Neill had an iguana (courtesy of T. Dow Albon).

original concept had all of this resting on his narrow neck. I requested that the Sirius Effects team add a harness to help support the weight (it was a reinforced motocross harness) but still, it was too much for poor Ivan. By the time we all arrived on location, he confirmed that the hero head was too much for him. So I began looking at the other, lighter-weight "non-moving stunt head," and designed ways to turn this into the suit's hero head. This required me sourcing whatever I could onset from craft service, local hardware stores (Canadian Tire!) and anything else I could steal from the nut-house. I was really young—so had endless energy—and spent many weekends and nights in that haunted place, trying to retrofit the suit and the effects. As example, I stole all the mayonnaise lids that I could find in catering and craft service, to make pulleys. I cabled these up and worked pretty well. Then, I "borrowed" some great invisible wires from the special effects supervisor and wound them around the arms of the creature in order to pull the creature's strings like a marionette. It was surprising how much more life I was able to get, on the lighter-weight version—big lessons for me, about design and physics ... and onset reality. The original hero head had great mandible movements, but that was about it. The build hadn't really considered the challenges of the shoot, and that "hero head" ended up being turned into a puppet that worked without Ivan. We'd often strap it to a stolen wheelchair, and would push it around set for lower bandy movement for many of the bug's close ups.

The director, William Fruet, was stoic, general-like—and I just-off-the-turnip-truck, following directions ... as best I could with what we had. I was still a youngin', so regarded Mr. Fruet as really ... "Mr. Fruet." At least, that's how I felt of my status to him. As the time went on, I grew to know him only a little bit, on off/hours, and he was really a cool guy. He handled the pressures of being leader of this crazy train very well—and still knew when to take a step back and laugh (it was a big bug movie, after all).

The rest of the cast was amazing. The banter was snappy and silly, since we were hanging with a 10-foot bug—everyday, comedy gold. Don Lake was so funny, and enjoyed being around our weird team ... in an insane asylum. I was also a big fan of Steve Railsback, as I loved *The Stunt Man* growing up, and here he was sort of playing the same part, in a way: the confused protagonist, struggling through a ridiculous action plot.

Mark Williams sadly passed away in 1998. He had opened his own shop a few years before, and had worked with Alice Cooper and had created effects for many other films. He was way too young to go, filled with life—and seemed strong enough to handle anything that came at him. He's well missed by many of us effects dudes. Gilly Neill died only a couple years ago. She is terribly missed. Many of the "Blue Monkey" artists reunited at a backyard wake for Gilly not long ago. It was at her talented daughter Beth Hathaway's house. Beth carries on the family tradition of monster making art (she has worked on *Jurassic Park*, *Narnia*, etc.). She also carries on Gilly's great sense of humor and smile.

I haven't seen *Blue Monkey* in a long time—and last time, I was really enjoyed it. I love B movies and this was definitely rated B. I love looking at some of our crude effects and think often of all the madness it took to create some sequences. Of course, this was 10–15 years before believable visual effects, so we certainly didn't have this to rely on. Everything was in camera, and it's fun to watch, on that level. It's a bit cheesy, but it's a lot of fun. I need to watch it again....

Not long after *Blue Monkey*, I went on to start my own company, and—with credits on *Look Who's Talking*, *Horse Whisperer*, *True Blood*, *Elysium*, *Stargate*, and many hundreds more—we're still going strong ... 28 years in biz (www.mastersfx.com).

## T. Dow Albon
### (Special Makeup and Creature Effects—Sirius Effects)

I joined Sirius Effects in the last week or two of 1986. Work had begun on *Blue Monkey* before I arrived at the shop. Todd Masters championed the idea of putting the guy in the suit "backwards," so that he could bend his knees "forward" (for him in the suit) but it would look like an animal/insect with the joint projecting backwards. I think that the idea was abandoned because the creature needed to run/chase the hero at some point. The set crew wasn't determined until the very last moment, I knew it wouldn't be me, but when Todd and Mark Williams got the gig everyone, including Todd and Mark, laughed about how they were the losers in the "Blue Monkey Lottery."

Back in the old days "Creature Features" would require more than one suit. There would be the "Hero" suit, for tight close ups. Then there would be the "Running/Chasing" suit. Then maybe there would be the "Specialty" suit, say if the monster had to sit in a car or something. Frequently the production would dispense with a "Sitting/Car" suit if they could get away with just putting the actor into the top half of the suit. And then maybe you'd need a "Death/Explosion" suit, because if you shot the (empty) suit with a flamethrower, you'd want to see bones, etc., on the inside, and not a bunch of mechanical junk. Depending upon how shots were scheduled, you could use the "Hero" suit for the death scene, but then you had to shoot all the close ups first, and the death scene last. I mention this, because the director [Fred Olen Ray] on *Deep Space* [1987], shot the monster's death scene, with chain saws, on the day BEFORE he needed the monster for the close up.

*Blue Monkey* was from a time before CG, and at the very beginning of servo-motors in creature effects. So the idea was that "The Guy in the Suit" would work the lower arms. Then there would be two more sets of arms above the lower/human level arms, that would work through cables. The upper/cable arms would have far more limited function than the lower/human arms. So the idea was that the upper arms would "act" and "menace" whilst most of the action would have to be done by the lower arms. But the director intended to shoot around these limitations. There might also have been some talk about shooting anything where the monster grabbed hold of a victim as a "Reverse." (Monster starts out holding the victim, then lets go. The footage is edited into the film backwards, and it looks like the monster is grabbing the victim … if it's done right. If it's done wrong … then it looks like something from Benny Hill.)

If I remember correctly, Steve Neill cut some sort of a deal with the production company, so then he built ONLY a hero suit. Then he instructed them to disconnect the Bernoulli-Boxes [the cable controllers] from the cables, make sure that the lighting was "dark" and have the monster run around with cables hanging out the back.

This brings us to Todd's story about having to break the upper arms, so the monster could run down the hospital corridor, because the ceiling was too low. This problem was actually discussed early on in creature development, but the production company didn't seem to do anything about it. Very early in my time at the shop, everyone went to a meeting with someone from the production company—I don't remember if it was the director, or just the effects coordinator. Anyway, we were all pretty quiet, and he explained his vision for the film, and then waxed eloquent about this great location that he'd found. Apparently they were going to shoot in some sort of hospital, before it was demolished—or something. And after he explained his plan, the new guy (me) asked what he was going to do about the fact that hospitals were government buildings, and had standard ceiling heights? Because standard ceiling height was around 8 feet, and we were building a monster that stood 7½ feet tall, with arms that projected up to around 10 feet. And there was silence, and I suggested that he should have a plan about the ceiling height, or they'd have to pick another location to which the monster would lure its victims—where it could stand up straight—say like the nearest football stadium. And there was an uncomfortable silence. And the client left.

And Todd laughed. And then Steve, the boss, said, "Dow, you're not allowed to come to the client meetings anymore."

It's my understanding that somebody, somewhere, wanted to make allusions to the 1954 film *Them!* [directed by Gordon Douglas], which had lots of rubber monster giant ants. At some point a little girl would try to explain the horror she had seen, and only be able to describe the creature as a "big, green monkey." So, almost to the very end of the job, the title was "Green Monkey." We all referred to the job as "Green Monkey" and the creature as the "Green Monkey," or sometimes as the "Rubber Monkey." Now during the 1980s a mysterious and deadly disease arrived on the U.S. West Coast. The disease was named AIDS, and no one knew where it came from. Round about half way through 1987 scientists began considering that AIDS might be a recent cross over to humans from other primates. Probably in West Africa. The candidate that they finally settled on was a species commonly known as … "the green monkey." Everyone from the client now agreed that the film could not be titled "Green Monkey," but no one seemed to know what to re-title the thing. It was looking like there would still be a "Monkey" in the title, but maybe they'd use some other color. In the shop we worried that they might decide "red" or "purple" and they had us painting the thing "green." Eventually, they just shot the film with the creature in its original, green, paint job. Then, in post-production I think, they decided on "Blue Monkey," changed the titles/credits, and released the film.

## Gwynyth Walsh
### ("Dr. Rachel Carson")

*Blue Monkey* was my first lead in a feature. I have very fond memories of the entire shoot. I was so excited to have the opportunity. The cast was lovely. Steven Railsback was a dream to work with. Don Lake was—is—a great guy and a lot of fun to work with. Susan Anspach shot her scenes in a couple of days so wasn't around that much. But she gave me a great piece of advice which I still use: always make sure that the cinematographer gets to light you at the end of the camera rehearsal process. Don't let your stand-in do it all. That way you get better lighting. Many actors let their stand-in do all the preliminary work and only step in at the very end. I've also found that you get to understand the shot and what you as the actor need to be doing in it better that way. Plus you end up with more rehearsal which is sometimes in short supply on a set.

When we were shooting the chase scenes in the tunnels, Ivan couldn't run quickly enough in his creature costume to make some of the shots work. So they put him in a wheelchair and had a grip push him as fast as he could through the frame. So that's what we were supposed to be frightened of: a bug in a wheelchair! We all broke out laughing at the end of the shot.

## Ivan E. Roth
### ("The Creature")

I became involved with *Blue Monkey* because I had played an alien in some TV commercial for a children's toy. The special effects person, Todd Masters, liked working with me and he recommended me for the part of the creature. I auditioned and got the part. At that time, I was 135 lbs. and 6 feet tall! We worked together on a few other projects before and after *Blue Monkey*. Anyway, we went off to freezing cold Toronto, where we shot the film in an abandoned mental hospital. I spent most of the time having a lot of fun chatting with cast member Don Lake, one of the funniest men in show business, and of course, my friend Todd. We had a lot of fun, despite the cold. Then the heat in the hotel went out for a few days! It was two degrees! I believe I was there for about three weeks, but it seemed like much longer!

# *The Carpenter*
## (1987, Canada)

Genre: Horror; Director: David Wellington; Writer: Doug Taylor; Cinematographer: David Franco; Editor: Roland Pollack; Special Makeup Effects: Michel Bougie; Special Effects: Andrew Campbell; Producers: Jack Bravman and Pierre Grisè; Production Company: Gold Gems; Cast: Wings Hauser (Ed, the Carpenter), Lynne Adams (Alice Jarett), Pierre Lenoir (Martin Jarett), Barbara Jones (Rachel), Louise Marie Mennier (Laura Bell), Jon Cuthbert (Roland), Robert Austern (Barns), Anthony Ulc (Landis), Bob Pot (Farnsworth), Richard Jutras (Mr. Mort) and Ron Lea (Sheriff J.J. Johnston)

A young woman and her husband move to an unfinished house in the countryside and hire a team of contractors to finish it. The most hard-working and energetic worker is a carpenter, who not only was the previous owner and builder of the house, but has also been dead for several years, having been executed on the electric chair after killing some repo men. The young woman, neglected and betrayed by her husband, is not indifferent to the charm of the ghost, who has returned to finish his work eliminating whoever gets in his way.

In the mid 70s and early 80s Jack Bravman worked in New York for Bunny Atlas's Bunco Films, a company active in the porn industry. Between 1985 and 1990 he produced a few genre films in Canada. The first was *Zombie Nightmare* (1986), co-directed with John Fasano (1961–2014). The second was *The Carpenter*, that preceded *Invasion of the Mind Benders* (1987), *Voodoo Dolls* (1988), *Madonna: A Case of Blood Ambition* (1989) and *Night of the Dribbler* (1990).

## David Wellington
## (Director)

I became involved with the film because I'd been an editor first. I was the editor on *Zombie Nightmare* [1986, John Fasano and Jack Bravman] and Doug Taylor and I pitched Jack Bravman on the idea of making a film. He said sure so we sat down to hash it out. Doug wrote the film very quickly, in less than two weeks I think. In any case, Jack and Pierre Grisè were keen to do it. We were young and fresh out of art school and very idealistic. They just wanted to make as many movies as possible because of the Quebec tax credits at the time.

I think the budget was about $350,000 but I can't remember exactly—not much. We shot it in about 15 days. We shot most of the film in an old house outside Montreal. The owners were about to gut the place and do a major renovation so they let us do whatever we wanted. Perfect situation for a young, inexperienced crew. (That said, a lot of those inexperienced people went on to big things. Steve Campanelli, the camera operator, now works with Clint Eastwood and David Franco; the DP shoots the TV series *Boardwalk Empire*.)

Jack and Pierre were vaguely charming, happy-go-lucky vulgarians who were making money with the tax credits. We didn't give a shit, we just wanted to make a movie. We were 24 years old. Pierre used to have tons of porn videos in his trunk; Jack was getting money from some mysterious guy in New York. All a little shady but it was like that in Montreal in those days. Wings Hauser was a great guy. He didn't know what to make of us and I'm sure thought the whole thing was pretty low rent. And in all this here's me and Doug trying to make this genre busting horror movie. God, we were young. And here we are 25 years later and I'm talking about it.

## Doug Taylor
### (Writer)

David Wellington and I had been co-students and close friends together at Montreal's Concordia University in their Specialization in Film Production program. We'd both been quite successful as students in this very challenging program and both wrote and directed our own short films with full crews of fellow students, shot on 16mm film. I don't think it's being boastful to say we were among the top of our class.

Coming out of school, David was by far the most ambitious and self-confident of my contemporaries. While I was scratching my head wondering how a young man can find his way into a rather limited Canadian feature film industry, David was masterful at making the right connections and inspiring those contacts to give him the breaks he needed to get started. And … he had the talent to capitalize on those breaks.

Among those acquired connections was Jack Bravman, and David managed to get involved with *Zombie Nightmare*, a film that I don't think holds up very well, but it was a foot in the door with which David could convince Jack that he should direct Jack's next low budget horror film. Jack asked for a story idea or two. David turned to me and we agreed to each come up with one. I don't remember what David came up with, but I came up with "The Carpenter," more than a little tongue-in-cheek at the time. Possibly enticed by all the opportunities for power tool mayhem, this was the story idea Jack wanted to go with. And so I was hired to write my first feature film screenplay. I believe I was about 23 years old at the time I started writing. 24 when it was completed. And I imagine that David was of similar age. We were delighted at the opportunity to cut our teeth on a "real movie."

I think it began as a bit of a joke. The idea suggested so many horrifying murder possibilities. At that time, many horror films were functioning almost as comedies, or at least with a sly sense of humor. I'm thinking of the sequels to *A Nightmare on Elm Street* with Freddie's one-liners. Or *The Texas Chainsaw Massacre II*. Also at that time there was some pretty serious film criticism digging into horror films. I'm thinking in particular of a Canadian magazine called *CineAction* that dealt very seriously with issues of sexual politics and subversive themes in the works of directors like David Cronenberg, Brian De Palma, John Carpenter, or Tobe Hooper. So … somehow this strange combination of tongue-in-cheek slasher horror movies and serious film criticism influenced the direction of *The Carpenter*. I believe Cinema Canada referred to it once as a kind of feminist slasher film. I think the strides it made on that level are pretty slight. But in retrospect I am a tiny bit proud that my first exploitation horror film ends on a triumphant note for a strong female protagonist. Given our limited resources and youth, and the low standards of the producers, we could have ended up with a movie that would be quite an embarrassment. I still feel a great fondness for *The Carpenter*.

There was an extreme heat wave in Montreal the summer I was writing *The Carpenter*. It was so hot, I was writing on an ironing board, so that I could stand up, and feel less hot with my legs straight. When I had completed the draft that would go into serious pre-production, we were on a very tight deadline. This, of course, was before the internet was commonly available. I printed out the hard copy from my very early model word processor, and handed it to David Wellington, who then jumped into his car to make copies and deliver the script to the production offices. Almost immediately after he left my place, the skies opened up and the most memorable flood in Montreal's history fell from the sky. Tons and tons of rain. Manhole covers flew up into the air. People had to swim out of their cars from our sunken freeway. It was crazy. And the timing seemed so funny, as though finishing the script for *The Carpenter* had somehow angered the Gods.

*The Carpenter* happened very quickly and was quite a rushed production. But we wanted it to be as good as we could possibly get it. So rewrites continued to be done on various scenes just a few days ahead of the shooting schedule. I have a memory of deciding that the carpenter (Wings Hauser) should catch on fire. A week or two later, I was watching a stunt man being set on fire and I distinctly remember thinking, "This is amazing!" This is a perfect creative outlet … where you can just make up crazy stuff and weeks, or even days later, a group of busy, talented people make it come true. I would later learn that this kind of immediacy is extremely rare in the feature film business. But at age 24 … I was seeing it happen.

I believe the budget was about ¾ of a million dollars—perhaps a little more or less—not much—definitely less than a million. I believe that most of the financing for *Zombie Nightmare*, *The Carpenter* and *Invasion of the Mind Benders* [1987, Genie Joseph] came from investors in New York, through Jack Bravman. Pierre Grisè ran an equipment house for lighting and camera equipment, etc., in Montreal. To my knowledge, Pierre's contribution had a lot to do with providing technical resources and crew, while Jack brought cash to the table. As my memory serves me, the New York investor's last name was either Gold, or Goldman, or something like that. So the company name "Gold Gems" came from Jack and the New York side of things, though Pierre might have shared in the company. *The Carpenter* was shot in Montreal (where I still live) and in surrounding areas.

*The Carpenter* premiered at the Montreal International Film Festival (of all places), then had a short theatrical run in several major cities across Canada, which I believe is more than can be said about any other of Jack's projects. There was also a French dubbed version playing in Quebec cinemas (Canada's French speaking province).

I quite liked Jack Bravman. He came off as the nice guy among the producers and financiers. His wife Nancy appears briefly in *The Carpenter* as a real estate broker showing Martin [Pierre Lenoir] the house in a silent shot. Jack and Nancy were New Yorkers, with evident New York accents. I had heard that he came from some kind of porn background, and I seem to recall him mentioning it without any embarrassment, but when I knew him, he considered that very much behind him and was focused on the horror genre. His wife was a school teacher, which might be why he had given up porn. My experience with Jack was that he was honest and fair. So while he worked in the "exploitation" film business ... I certainly didn't feel exploited by him. He was giving us young guys a chance to do something and paying us (not a lot, but at the time, it felt unbelievable to be paid to make a movie).

Soon after *The Carpenter*, I wrote the first (uncredited) draft of *Invasion of the Mind Benders* which I eventually walked away from due to creative differences with the director, Genie Joseph. She was nice enough, but I felt like the movie was going to be a disaster and I decided to leave them to it. At the time, I was too young and naïve to think to protect my writing credit, and since there was no money to be made in doing so, I think I was happy not to be associated with it. I've never seen "Mind Benders" but I didn't have a good feeling about what they were going to do to my script. Perhaps I'll see it one day.

Recently, I received a cheque from the Writer's Guild of America. It was a royalty cheque for about $17 for *The Carpenter*. This was the first time I had received money since writing it 24 years ago. I imagine this has something to do with the new DVD release. Though, it is listed as "foreign sales" so I don't really know. I was certainly not a guild member or member of any writer's guild at that time. It was great to buy lunch with money earned from *The Carpenter*.

## Lynne Adams
### ("Alice Jarett")

*The Carpenter* was my first lead role in a feature film. I was thrilled to get the job, to be on set and see the movie put together scene by scene.

This was before fancy special effects and computer anything. The ingenuity of the crew to pull shots together never ceased to amaze me. Yes, I admit, the effects look hokey and amateurish; it's part of their charm. Everyone rose to the creative challenge of making things work with no budget, limited resources, and lots of ingenuity.

And I got to deliver one of the most memorable lines ever. When my husband [Martin Jarett, played by Pierre Lenoir], who has been cheating on me with one of his students [Laura Bell, played by Louise-Marie Mennier], comes home to find me calmly sipping a cup of tea with said young girl slumped in the chair next to me, very dead and bloody from being shot with a nail gun (the carpenter's work, that ghost-man who cares for me with homicidal efficiency), he freaks out and yells, "What happened?!? What's this?!?" To which I calmly reply, "It's your girlfriend. Kind of hard to fuck her now," and resume drinking my tea. Perhaps not award-winning dialogue, but oh-so much fun to do.

Another moment I won't soon forget is when, at the end of the movie, my sister (played by Barbara Jones) holds me in her arms to comfort me as my house, and the carpenter, burn to the ground. The stuntman doing the full body burn, one of the most dangerous stunts to do, was Barbara's then husband, and as he ran towards us, arms flailing and fully on fire, we were both praying he'd be okay. I was holding her to make sure she wouldn't rush to him for most of that shot. As it turns out he was fine and the sequence looked great.

Most of the cast and crew on that movie established solid careers for themselves in film. Little did we realize then how entrenched our paths would be in this crazy business. David Wellington is a well-respected director whom actors love to work with. David Franco is a much sought-after DOP. Arden Ryshpan, our line producer, has been an instrumental force in establishing and protecting performer's rights across Canada. Most of the crew members are still working on film sets around the world. Barbara Jones, Richard Jutras, myself and many other actors in the film have flourishing careers as working artists.

Summertime, an outlandish story, a crazy creative team, and power tools. What more could a girl ask for?

## Pierre Lenoir
### ("Martin Jarett")

I've been a professional actor and singer for almost 40 years. I am a graduate of the Conservatoire d'Arts Dramatiques de Montréal (The Montreal Conservatory of Dramatic Arts). *The Carpenter* was not my first movie, but it was the one in which I'd had the biggest part. I was third billed and worked 15 days on it. As a matter of fact, this has turned out to be my biggest part so far, followed by 10 days on the Leslie Nielsen vehicle, *2001: A Space Travesty*, and five days on another horror picture, *Discopath* [2013], which fans of *The Carpenter* would do well to seek out. I am not a star but I am a working actor, also known as a "day player" which means I've mainly had one or two days' work on nearly 100 movies and TV shows.

I've also appeared in over 125 plays and musicals. I've been in over 180 TV commercials and I've been doing cartoon voices for nearly 30 years. I am also a musician, having composed the music for 7 musicals, which have been produced in Quebec and Canada, with one of them being mounted in a small theater in Switzerland.

I auditioned for *The Carpenter* the way one does these things: my agent at the time sent me the sides and set up an appointment. I went in, but I don't remember who I auditioned for. Two days later, I got a callback—they had liked what they had seen. That's where I met David Wellington for the first time. He looked young and intensely serious. He was cordial, but no more than that, after all, he hadn't decided we were going to work together yet. I read through the scenes once or twice. During this, the phone rang and someone answered loudly, and someone else entered the room noisily. I didn't flinch and read the scenes to the end. David thanked me and I went home. A few days later, my agent told me I got the part. When I met David on the set on my first day, he smiled and told me I had gotten the part mainly because of my look, but also because I didn't let the noises in the audition studio distract me.

David didn't give me much direction when we filmed. As a matter of fact, I found him a bit aloof. But I knew he had more pressing problems on his mind, and so, as many movie directors say, once you've cast the part the best you can, most of your problems are over. Actually there was only one instance where I had to redo a scene not for some technical reasons, but because he felt I could have done better. It was interesting to see the camera operator nodding as David said this. We did take two, and it came off fine.

Some actors will not do anything on a set until they've been told what to do by the director. And that's fine if it works for them. I'm the kind of actor who has suggestions for every line, every movement, every gesture, every intention. Yeah, one of those. I read the script I'm given several times and sometimes I will find that an action or a line might need to be set up properly several scenes before, and because they are not shot in the order in the script, an actor has to do his homework. David would very cordially listen to what I had to say, and sometimes he'd say yes, and other times, no. Sometimes, he'd come up with a suggestion of his own. Other times, someone like the director of photography would have a suggestion, and again, sometimes David would say yes, other times, no. And that's basically how the whole shoot went. As far as I could tell, there were no screaming fits, nobody stalking off the set.

I put in very few ad libs. They were discussed with David, and I think he let me keep two. One I'll talk about later. The second one was during the lecture scene where I talk about Paul Bunyan. Two close friends of mine were extras in the back row. When the bell rings I say, "All right, we'll pick it up next time. Do the readings. Don't forget, Michaelson, chapters 4 and 5." That was my homage to Indiana Jones. That's what Professor Jones says when the bell goes off in his classroom in *Raiders of the Lost Ark…*

I didn't meet Wings Hauser until we shot the scene where I enter the room after following a blood trail from the driveway. I see Laura [Martin's mistress] dead and covered in blood on the sofa, and Alice says, "Pretty hard to fuck her now…" and that's when I slap her. A pretty rational response if you ask me: Dead mistress + Sarcastic wife = Physical response. Then the carpenter appears out of nowhere and knocks me to the floor. The rest of the scene where he pins my hands to the floor with screwdrivers and pops open my head with a carpenter's vise would be shot much later that night. Wings had his own room at the house, and I was told he didn't come out of it until he was needed for a scene, which is why I had not met him before.

He wasn't hired for the movie until late in production, and he only worked for a few days. As a matter of fact, during the shoot, there were rumors about who the producers were talking to for the title role. One day we heard they had approached Peter (*Easy Rider*) Fonda. We all went, "Cool…" Then we heard it might be Keir Dullea. Most of the crew said, "Who?" I said, gently, "Does the movie *2001: A Space Odyssey* ring a bell?" When we found out that Wings Hauser had been hired, I'm the one who said, "Who?" And they told me, gently, that he was a very popular low-budget horror movie star, with a bit of a cult following. Lots of horror film buffs would come and see this movie. More than for Keir Dullea…

Anyway, we were introduced but he didn't talk much. We went over the scene, and then it was time to do it. They set up the camera and lay a couple of sound blankets for me to fall on. We rehearsed it once and after he knocked me to the floor he said, "You okay?" I said I was fine as I got up and it was time to do it. "Action!" He knocked me to the floor. "Cut!" And by the time I had gotten up, he had left the room, done with the scene.

My death scene was my own final shot, and it was going to be filmed at the end of this long day's shoot, hopefully before the sun came up. I think this was the last chance they had to shoot in that big house, so it was the part of the production where you try and shoot all the leftover stuff. When we finally got around to it, it was very bright, little birds were chirping, everybody was mainlining coffee…

They were using two cameras because it would take too long and be too expensive to shoot this scene more than once. So I lay down on the floor, the screwdrivers were glued to my palms, and the special effects vise was attached to my head so that the tubes carrying the blood would remain out of sight. They had prepared a rag attached to a small plastic bottle containing stage blood, which I would hold in my mouth and bite down on as the carpenter tightened the vise, making blood come out of my mouth as well as from my head. I don't think this part worked very well.

So now we were really ready. Wings came in saying nothing. There was a tiny bit of urgency in the air: we had to wrap things up. He sat on my thighs and reached for the vise handles over my head. I got a whiff of the alcohol on his breath and I was suddenly concerned about how much control he would have during the scene. Well, I needn't have worried, the whole thing went off without a hitch. They placed the rag in my mouth, David told everybody to concentrate, we were only doing this once, and then "Action!"

Wings started doing his monologue and turning the handles of the vise. I started screaming, as much as I could with the rag and the bottle stuffed in my mouth and I felt the blood come out through the tubes and start pouring down around my head. It was cold! After a bit, I let the screams die away and started doing little whimpering sounds, like a small animal that knows it's about to die. At one point David yelled, "Cut! Nobody move!" Some sort of technical adjustment was made and he yelled "Wings, back up a few lines! Action!" And he did it again, more blood poured out.... And we were done!

Wings got off of me and they asked me to stay there while they took pictures. After a few minutes, someone helped me up and handed me a towel to wipe away some of the sticky blood. Someone yelled, "And it's a wrap for Pierre!" Which is what you say when an actor's final scene is done. There was applause, the guys shook my hand, the girls gave me a kiss. I turned to shake Wings' hand, but he had already left the set. Done with the scene.

Actually, the special effects in this movie were pretty elaborate. All the killing had to be spectacular, and yet totally safe for the actors. I had seen some of the props used to kill the victims, all those tools, and I was impressed how cleverly they had been built. Especially the sander that tore away that young man's face.

In my case, they had wanted to build a fake full-sized reproduction of my head so they could actually crush it in the vise. So before filming began, I had gone to the special effects' technician's studio in Longueuil, near Montreal. It was actually a nice suburban house on a quiet street. The perfect horror film cliché. When I arrived, I was met at the door by the creator of the special effects. I entered and I looked around: there were bodies dumped here and there all over the hallway. Severely burnt bodies. He said it was something else he was working on.... They started by getting a mold of my teeth, exactly like they do it at the dentist's. That took about half an hour. Then, after a trip to the bathroom, they covered my hair with a skull cap and smeared my whole head down to my shoulders with a special latex mix. Small straws had been inserted in my nostrils so I could breathe during the process, which would take some two hours before it dried. And I had to keep my face in position like I was screaming. For two hours.

It got pretty quiet and peaceful in there, and once in a while, he or his assistant would ask if I was okay. Apparently, some actors develop severe cases of claustrophobia, which some of them don't even know they have. I had lost all sense of time, but after two hours, they pulled off the mold and it felt wonderful just being able to breathe clearly again. My face felt fresh, because when they removed the latex, it also cleaned out my pores. When

I saw the results on the set, it sort of looked like me, and they did shoot some inserts with it with plenty of blood, but I don't think any of those shots made it into the movie.

While I was shooting this movie, I was also performing in a play at night. This had been understood by the producers and the director and everybody was fine with it. When my day was done, I would be driven to the theatre in time for the show. It worked very well and only once was there a snag during the shoot and I arrived at the theatre with ten minutes to spare. So I didn't get to do any socializing with the crew or my fellow cast members. If, let's say, people went out for a beer at the end of the shooting day, I wouldn't be able to come along. The play I was in ran for two years, a huge success by English Montreal standards and I stayed with it for a year, or 277 performances. Luckily, the producer of the play was very understanding, so for the few times we went to night shoots, he found a replacement for me.

Which is why I only met the producer, Jack Bravman, once, during a lunch break. We didn't talk much, he seemed more interested in the newspaper he was reading. He said something I found interesting: he was leafing through the movie advertisements and he said, "I don't think I'm gonna do any more horror movies.... Look, it's all teen sex comedies.... That's where the money is now..." Well, that was back in 1987.... Nancy, his wife was an absolute sweetheart, I got along with her quite well. As a matter of fact, in the scene in the movie where I buy the house, she's the agent quoting me a price. Which, of course, I find ridiculously high.

I first met Louise-Marie Mennier, who played Laura, my mistress, something like ten minutes before we were to shoot our first intimate scene. I was sitting on a bench outside the bedroom where we were going to shoot it when David brought her over and introduced me to her. She was very pretty, sweet and young. This may have been her first movie. David said, "Here, you can get acquainted.... We'll be starting in about ten minutes." We looked at each other and chuckled.... What can you say in ten minutes that will prepare you for your first semi-nude scene? "So, where are you from.... Oh, you sing as well? ... Is this..." David interrupted and said they were almost ready. I reached into my bag and pulled out my toothbrush. When I looked back at Louise, she had done the same.

We went and changed in the room set aside for costumes, which means I stripped down to my shorts and she stripped down to her panties. They gave us big thick robes and we made our way to the set. It was mostly dark, just enough to highlight the bed. We slipped under the covers and gave our robes to the dresser. That's when I noticed the room was very crowded. So did Louise. She called David over and asked him to clear the set like he had promised he would do. He said of course and apologized and asked all non-essential personnel to leave the room. Well, out of maybe twenty, two or three left. She said, "I guess they're all essential..." So we did the scene. It went fine. But this one didn't make it into the movie.

One of the other scenes that did make it is the one after the lecture scene where we're having wild sex, each one of us trying to get on top of the other. At one point, I got on top of her and made like I was thrusting. Suddenly, I felt something hit my ass. It was the camera operator's foot! The camera was on a crane that made it swoop over the bed, and this time it got too low. Or my ass was too high.

There's the scene in the motel honeymoon suite, where she pretends to be tied to the bedstead, and when I come in she says, "You're on time..." And I say, "I've got an alarm clock between my legs..." We had to do that one more than once: the giggling...

Lynne Adams was a sweetheart. I had known her for several years before *The Carpenter*, working together in commercials and corporate films. *The Carpenter* would not be the only time we acted as husband and wife. After that shoot, we continued doing more videos and commercials.

I was slightly nervous about the love/sex scenes I would be doing. These were my first and I wasn't sure how to approach them. Lynne had appeared in a feature film the year before where she had had a fairly explicit love scene. So I asked her for some advice. She kindly listened. I said, "What if I get … excited during the filming…? You know… What if something comes up? … What would the actress think? That I was trying to take advantage of the situation? …" She told me to relax and have a good time, that the whole thing is going to be so technical, getting excited is the last thing I'm going to think about. And, if, by chance, something does come up, she'll take it as a compliment, and will mean she's probably excited too.

The day I showed up for the first scene with Louise, Lynne had left me a note, saying she had seen rushes the night before and we were great. And then she told me to relax again and have a good time, Darling.

There's a scene in the movie where Alice dances with the carpenter and he pulls away, smiles, undoes his fly and we cut to a close-up of her horrified face as we hear the sound of an electric drill. Alice wakes up from her nightmare and tries to get comfort from Martin. But he's taken his sleeping pills and doesn't wake up as she hits him, and hits him, and punches him again and again and again. She was hitting me for real, with all her strength. I was under the duvet, covered with several of those thick sound blankets so she could go at it as hard as she wanted. We did several takes and it didn't hurt at all, but for the next few weeks, my back and side were covered with bruises. The kind that start out black and blue, and then turn a sickly, yellowish green.

There's a scene towards the end where I find my mistress dead on the sofa and Alice says, "Pretty hard to fuck her now…" and I slap her. I'm not sure but I think I slapped her for real. Lynne and I had both been on stage several times, and we were both familiar with this technical way to give the slap and to receive the slap so that it sounds great without anybody getting hurt. A few years later I was in a play with another actress who had to slap me. She was so nervous and afraid she would hurt me, she forgot how to do it technically and ended up slapping me for real. For 32 performances.

During a lunch break, I was sitting with David and Lynne and I suggested to him a new scene. I started by saying it was a Horror movie cliché, and then I said no, it was a Horror film archetype. I thought that would impress anybody listening. My idea was that after I was killed, Alice would take a shower to wash off all the blood and the red paint and this was in the script. But while she's in there, naked, she turns around and (Music sting!) there I am! All bloody, skull cracked, eye hanging out, and so on. Then she blinks, and I'm not there. David smiled, and before he could say anything, Lynne said, laughing, "Oh come on, Pierre. I know why you want to be in that shower!"

About ten days after the shoot, I was invited to the wrap party in a bar in Old Montreal. Most of the crew was there. Wings wasn't, of course, because as soon as he had wrapped, he went back home to Los Angeles. I don't think I saw David there, and I can't remember if Lynne was there or not. But Louise was, and we ended up talking to each other for most of the evening. Someone had brought a videocassette with a preliminary rough cut of the movie, but the VCR in the bar didn't work. So someone said he would go get his own VCR and be right back. Well, it seemed like he was gone for hours. Finally he returned, they plugged the VCR into the monitor, inserted the cassette, and this one didn't work either. So we all went back to our drinking. As I said, I got to talk with Louise, and it's amazing how doing a handful of love scenes with a person can really break the ice. I found out she was studying to be an opera singer, but I have no idea if this was brought to fruition.

I didn't hear anything about the film for a year. Then, I was told it would be presented at the Montreal International Film Festival at the end of August 1988 for two showings, one on Thursday night, and the other on Saturday afternoon. I had met this young woman, Carol, and had gone out with her once. I asked her if she wanted to come and see me in the movie and she said yes. We arrived at the theatre Thursday evening and I went to the box office to get the tickets under my name. No, there was no big opening night premiere with searchlights, limousines, a red carpet, paparazzi and screaming fans. No. Just me going to ask for my tickets and being told by the teller that the showing of *The Carpenter* had been cancelled. He wasn't sure why, something about the reels being in the wrong order or the sound being out of sync. It would probably be shown on Saturday. I returned to Carol and told her this, and she said, "You sure you're an actor? …" We went for a drink, and I don't know if this has to do with anything, but I never saw her again.

That Saturday, I was in a bad mood for some reason and I decided I was going to skip the showing. It was going to be presented at 3:30. Well, finally, at 3:10 I said, "Fuck it!" ran out of the apartment, grabbed the bus and arrived at the theatre just as the opening credits came up. It was too dark to find a seat so I just stood there in the entrance as the names appeared. And there was mine. Twenty feet high and eighty feet across. Or so it felt. I had seen my name on the credit roll at the end of TV shows, or in small type at the end of other movies, but this was the first time I saw it like this. And the last. So far…. I was slightly disappointed at the fact that my name appeared below Lynne's. My contract had stipulated that my name was to have appeared on its own. Oh well (my contract also stipulated I was supposed to get a copy of the movie but that never materialized).

But never mind that. I found a seat and stared at the screen. And there was Lynne, cutting up one of my suits. And me, entering, and saying, "Rough day, huh?" And it got a laugh. Good. This was that other ad lib of mine that David had let me keep.

An hour and a half later, it was over. How did I feel? That I had shared something very personal with a roomful of strangers. I wasn't embarrassed, as a matter of fact, I was very satisfied with the great majority of my scenes. The other stuff? Well, if they ever remake it with the same cast, I would approach some of it differently. I don't know if anybody else from the production was there, I suspect they were because of the way some of the names got applause during the closing credits. But for some reason, I didn't feel like seeing anybody, maybe a leftover from that bad mood. I left the theatre just before the lights came on and made my way home. When I got there, I felt pretty good about what I had seen. Pretty damn good.

As I said, I never got a copy of the movie, but a few years later, I was in Toronto shooting a commercial, and I went to Sam's the Record Man, many years gone now, and went to their large Laser Disc section. And right there, under the C's, the garish image of Wings Hauser grinning maniacally and coming at me with a chainsaw! I bought it on the spot, and it was only when I got back to the hotel room that I noticed they had misspelled my name on the jacket. I was "Pierce Lenior!" But then I thought that if I ever needed a stage name for an American film career, this wasn't so bad.... And this was the way my name was spelled for many years afterwards, when the movie was mentioned in video catalogues and reference books. But luckily, it has now been spelled correctly in the recent DVD release.

One last note about my career: as I've said, I've been in dozens of movies and TV shows, and it's always a pleasure to catch them or to be recognized from them. But there's this one time.... I had a day's shoot on Roland Emmerich's *The Day after Tomorrow*. Many people saw it and I received a ton of emails and Facebook notifications. But a few years ago, Katharine, my partner, and I were in downtown Istanbul, Turkey, crossing a public park. We met a class of young teenage girls who were greeting tourists to their city. They offered us Turkish coffee and sweets. They were very happy to learn that Katharine was a teacher and they introduced their own teachers to us. Then they asked me what I did. When I said actor, they got very excited and asked what they had seen me in. When I told them about *The Day after Tomorrow*, they said they had seen it! When I described the scenes I was in, they all jumped and down: they remembered the scenes! Yes, Istanbul.

# *Cavegirl*
## (1984, U.S.A.)

Genre: Fantasy/Comedy; Director: David Oliver Pfeil as "David Oliver"; Writers: David Oliver Pfeil as "David Oliver" (Screenplay) and Phil Groves (Screenplay "Primal Urge"); Cinematographer: David Oliver Pfeil as "David Oliver"; Editor: Robert Field; Special Effects: Gregory Landerer; Producer: David Oliver Pfeil as "David Oliver"; Associate Producer: Reed Fenton; Executive Producer: Mark Tenser; Production Company: Crown International Pictures; Cast: Daniel Roebuck (Rex), Cynthia Thompson (Eba), Darren Young (Dar), Saba Moor (Saba), Jeff Chayette (Argh), Charles Mitchell (Char), Cynthia Rullo (Aka), Tom Hamil (Casey), Bill Adams (Bill), Chris Noble (Hank), Bill Sehres (Ralph), Sydni King (Karen), Stacey Swain (Brenda) and David Castro (Catso)

Thanks to a strange crystal, a shy student finds himself in the Stone Age, where he falls in love with a beautiful cave woman and saves her clan from a tribe of cannibals.

## David Oliver Pfeil
### (Writer/Director/Producer/Cinematographer)

I came to California in 1969, having won an international photography competition to study at Art Center College of Design in Los Angeles, graduating with distinction. I'd been working for 14 years in Hollywood when the *Cavegirl* project came along. I'd worked on countless motion pictures and television series as a second unit director, director of photography, and film title cinematographer/designer. After *Cavegirl*, I won two Emmys for television series titles (co-designed with Wayne Fitzgerald) including *The Bold and the Beautiful* (CBS). I also shot the iconic opening title sequence to the classic '80s *Knight Rider* TV series and the movie *Footloose*.

In 1997, I moved to the SF Bay area to become Director of the School of Motion Pictures and Television, then VP of On-Air Advertising, for Academy of Art University in San Francisco. Currently, my wife Valentina and I own a high-end video production company based in Marin County, CA. I'm an active member of the Directors Guild of America (Director's category), the Academy of Motion Picture Arts & Sciences (Oscars), and the Academy of Television Arts & Sciences (Emmys).

Mark Tenser of Crown International Pictures came up with the basic idea for *Cavegirl* and hired Phil Groves to write it. That script was called "Primal Urge." David Baughn, the VP and General Manager of Crown (his half-sister was my girlfriend, now wife), recommended me to Mark as a potential director. I got the script to read. At the first meeting with Mark, he said he wasn't totally happy with the script, and it was not a script I wanted to direct. So, I was given the opportunity to do a rewrite. Phil did get story credit, and my final version went on to be produced. I wanted to make a movie that played to Crown's "youth market," but was also silly fun. Nudity was always required in a Crown movie. While writing the script, I took some inspiration from the Monty Python movies, and (spoofing) the movie *Quest for Fire* [1981, Jean-Jacques Annaud]. "Primal Urge" was the title all the way through preproduction and shooting. During post-production, Mark showed me the poster art he'd commissioned with the new name, "Cavegirl." I liked it … I thought it would market the film better.

Mark and I almost parted company over my proposed budget. Mark expected me to shoot the location scenes in Griffith Park (in the middle of Los Angeles). I had only worked on "A" studio productions, where a complex 3-minute title sequence alone could cost $100K. I had too much emotional investment to let the story go, so we agreed to co-finance the production and I became its producer as well. I think the total original budget was about $300/350K. Theoretically, we each were putting up half. I did what a lot of first-time feature film directors have done, and still do … I mortgaged my house to get the money! Then, to complete the movie, I went over budget. Remember the production value of the giant bear, mountain lion, the helicopter shots, etc.?

All principal shooting took place between September and December of 1984, although there may have been some pick-up or insert shots in early 1985. The "prehistoric" exterior sequences were shot in Twin Oaks, California, which was barely a town at the time, surrounded by two large cattle ranches. Twin Oaks is in the Sierra Foothills, halfway between

Dan Roebuck ("Rex") and David Oliver Pfeil (Writer/Director/Producer/Cinematographer) discuss a shot in early morning light (courtesy of David Oliver Pfeil).

Tehachapi (at the edge of the Mojave Desert) and Bakersfield. I knew the area because I owned 40 acres of land there and had befriended a few of the local residents. We shot the school scenes at a high school in Arvin, the closest real town. We also used a couple of locations in North Hollywood, and shot on my stage off Sunset Boulevard in Hollywood.

About the cast, Mark Tenser wanted Cindy Thompson [1959–2009] to play Eba—she'd been in another Crown picture [*Tomboy*, 1984, Herb Freed]. We had a casting call for the lead (won by Danny Roebuck) and a few other roles. For the cave people, I cast people I knew who I thought would make great cavemen and cavewomen. Darren Young was a photographer who also worked as my camera assistant. Charlie Mitchell (another photographer) had assisted me on other projects. David (Davide) Castro owned a Mexican restaurant, El Compadre, on Sunset Boulevard near my studio.

There are many things I'd do differently if I were making this movie today. Still, a lot of positive things came of it. Three new hires who worked on my team, Jack Isgro (1st AD), Reed Fenton (Associate Producer/UPM), and Craig Leary (PA), are friends with whom I've stayed in regular touch. Jack became my associate director for the film school at Academy of Art University. I'm pleased to know that I gave Danny Roebuck his first film job, and he's gone on to have a career in film and TV. I was so sorry to learn that Cindy Thompson died in 2009.

All in all, everyone on our side of production pulled together and gave 110%. If they gave out awards for good intentions, hard work, and camaraderie, we would all have come out big winners on this movie.

## Valentina Laurence Pfeil
### (Assistant to the Producer)

I met David Oliver Pfeil on my first day of work, at my very first job (with Wayne Fitzgerald FilmDesign) following my graduation from Art Center as a Graphic Design major. Ironically, I met both Darren Young and Charlie Mitchell that same day. Later, I was freelancing and had been in a relationship with David for about four years when *Cavegirl* happened.

It became a "family" enterprise. David hired people he'd worked with before on other projects, and a few actors he'd known for years: his ex-girlfriend, Cher Slater, did hair and makeup; our neighbor, Earl Klasky, helped us with casting; and so on.

The interior cave set was built inside David's studio in Hollywood. It was an impressive, studio-caliber piece of construction, as were the skulls and crystal props. I hated that we had to tear it down afterwards, but there was no way and no place to save it. Today, David could've probably resold it on Craigslist!

When the cast & crew went on location in Twin Oaks, I'd drive up most weekends. My main job was to run things or people back and forth and basically, try to prop up the Director. David could always work ten people under the table, but even he showed strain from the demands of *Cavegirl*. My preferred (more scenic) route to get there was via Hwy 14 through the Mojave Desert, west on the Barstow-Bakersfield Hwy past Tehachapi, then a short stretch of mountain road with a couple steep hairpin turns before following Caliente Creek Road up the valley to our location.

Twin Oaks was a whole other world, coming from Los Angeles. The location accommodations (a rented house and trailers) were as comfortable as we could possibly make them. It got pretty cold up there in November. We even saw some snow. I didn't envy the "cave people" in their skimpy little costumes, but then that kind of commitment comes with the territory of making movies. Apparently, being experienced behind the camera makes a person unselfconscious in front of the camera as well; it amazed me, how good Darren and Charlie were performing as actors.

## Reed Fenton
### (Associate Producer/UPM)

After graduating from film school I became an advertising photographer, shooting many national campaigns. I started getting requests from my clients to direct and shoot commercials of the projects I had been shooting stills on, an opportunity I jumped at. This continued and expanded to corporate films, music and fashion videos, and more commercials.

I had met Darren Young in the early stages of my career, as he was a photographer as well. He was close friends and worked with David Oliver Pfeil, so that was my introduction to David and *Cavegirl*. As I had a strong production background, it seemed like an excellent fit.

David, Jack and I were getting by on about four hours of sleep a night after going to post. We would shoot from dawn till dusk, then review dailies on location from the prior day's shoot. As I recall, I tried to keep my seventh day of work in a week to 12 hours.

It was my job to go around and make sure that the rest of the cast and crew got up by banging on their trailer/bedroom doors. Food service was provided by a local Twin Oaks woman named Bonnie, who would arrive around 3 a.m. to start cooking breakfast. She and her assistants delivered lunch on set, and provided dinner.

We shot the locker scene with topless coeds at the high school in Arvin. We got the girls from this agency I knew of on Santa Monica Blvd. We did not tell the school we were shooting topless, and I recall having to watch out for the security guard to have them cover up if and when he came around. We needed a shot in the mountains with flowers, and by this time it had gotten cold and even snowed. We made a trip to a desert location and gathered a bunch of flowers and transported them to the mountain location and strategically placed them for the shot.

It was a terrific experience working with David from pre-production through post, and we remain in touch today. *Cavegirl* was a great launching pad for my future work in film and television, which I am still involved with currently.

## David Baughn
### (Former VP and General Manager of Crown International Pictures)

My entry into motion picture distribution was with MGM in Denver, CO, as a booker, then San Francisco as a salesman and assistant branch manager. I moved to independent distribution when I was hired to be Russ Meyer's National Sales Manager, in charge of sales, advertising, and marketing such hits as *Vixen*, and *Cherry, Harry, & Raquel!*, etc. I joined Crown International Pictures in 1984, and spent six years as the VP and General Manager overseeing their U.S. and Canadian sales and marketing. I was also their Director of Acquisitions.

*Cavegirl*'s sales were light theatrically because it had major studio competition when it was released. However, the movie did well in ancillary sales (foreign markets, TV/cable, VHS & DVD). In those days, we had to play a minimum of 25 theaters (advertised) to get those ancillary sales.

## Darren Young
### ("Dar")

My background is as an advertising photographer; a graduate of the Art Center College of Design (1972), I had my own photo studio for several years. Through that business, I formed an association and a friendship with David Oliver Pfeil; we worked together on various projects for years, including main title shoots for television and motion pictures. In the process of doing these, I got cast as minor characters: drug dealer, photographer, construction worker, etc. I even played Jesus in a scene at the end of *Omen III!* So, acting roles were a sideline fueled by opportunities via the projects we worked on. Because of our history, when David asked if I'd be interested in a featured role in this movie he was putting together, I accepted. I mean, what a fun thing to do and to tell your grandkids about when you're old! I didn't have to audition, since David knew me well enough to know I was zany enough to fit the character of Dar perfectly!

On the personal side, my other interests besides photography are music (I've played guitar since I was 10), skiing, kayaking, and I also spent several years racing sports cars (in fact, I currently make my living teaching high-performance driving at racing schools and safe-driving clinics, and do manufacturer programs). I sold my photo studio in 1995, about ten years after doing *Cavegirl*. The business had changed to the point that I was no longer enjoying it, and I've made it a point in my life to only do things I enjoy. "If you find a job you love, you'll never work a day in your life," good words to live by!

While *Cavegirl* didn't win any awards, for me it was one of the more memorable times of my life. We all worked our asses off and had some tough times ... and we didn't make much in the way of salary. It was a "low-budget production," remember? Being a low-bucks movie, most of us had one or two extra jobs—I was the stills photographer, acted as a camera assistant for David, also did a lot of rigging, and some of the special effects; I even got to blow up a porta-potty (GREAT fun!) and drove one of the motorhomes to the location. That was the great thing about this whole bunch of people: we all did whatever was needed to make it happen. David was very appreciative of that, too (he bloody well had to be).

I have to say, everyone on the cast was fun to work with and be around. I learned quite a bit from them, and even though I wasn't an actor by profession, there wasn't any "attitude" put out by anyone. Danny Roebuck (who's gone on to become a well-known character player) was probably the guy I learned the most from. I was amazed at how he'd put small details into what he was doing that would really expand the scene. For instance, when he and I were playing a bit where I steal his shoe and won't give it back, Danny's comic turns of expression made it hard not to burst out laughing and ruin the shot. I'm really glad that he became a successful working actor—he deserved it.

Jeff Chayette almost took himself too seriously, but was a funny guy to be around. He really got into his role; like, in the hunting scene where I "chickened out" and ran away from the animals, he had to slap me to force me back to hunting. He actually whacked me, and hard. As a result, the very shocked and hurt look on my face was 100% real! But I got my revenge ... I would regularly beat him in our chess games back at the ranch where we were staying.

Cindy Thompson was a lovely lady. I was very saddened when I heard she'd passed away. While she may have come off as the quintessential "dumb blonde," as I got to know her better, I found Cindy to be a sweet and surprisingly introspective girl. We had some good late evening conversations after the day's work was in the can. I don't know where she went or what she did after *Cavegirl*, but I hope she found her place in her shortened life.

Saba Moore has to be one of the funniest people I've ever known. She could put an expression on her face that would make you absolutely die laughing. She probably had the most energy of all the cast. I'd known Saba for years prior to *Cavegirl*; she and I had posed as a couple of bikers for an ad that a mutual photographer friend, Jim Wood, shot when I was working as a photo assistant in the late '70s. I wish I knew where she was now...

Charlie Mitchell was another real character. Charlie was about 6'5", 280 lbs. and looked very scary indeed, due to a scar on his face from an old accident. But Charlie was/is truly a "gentle giant" and great human being—a nice Texas boy who didn't say that much, but when he did you paid attention. Charlie also did not suffer fools lightly! He was the perfect caveman, really just playing himself while dressed in a rabbit skin!

One other player who stands out in my memory is Bill Adams, who played the caretaker of the mine. Bill was a film editor by trade, but he had such a great character-actor look, he got more than one role in various productions. He and I had a great rapport, and in the final scenes where it's revealed that his character and mine "knew" each other, he was the one that made that scene work with his mimic of my funny caveman wave—a great surprise "reveal" that carried the movie's ending. I'm sure he's no longer with us, but what a cool guy he was.

There are plenty of stories ... like that hunting scene.... We were shooting in the mountains in November, and it was about 26°F that morning. Even with leather soles glued to our feet, standing out there on the frozen ground wreaked havoc on us. After doing one part of the scene, I went to sit in one of the trucks to keep warm for a few minutes. Reed, the UPM, called me back for another scene, so I jumped down from the truck onto the ground—and almost passed out from the pain! It seems my feet had gotten a little frostbitten, and when I landed hard on the frozen dirt, my nerve endings went ballistic. Took a few minutes to recover, but I was able to get it together and go work.

Then there were the helicopter shots. We had two of the best picture-chopper pilots in the industry, Harry Hauss and Jim Deeth. On one of the takes, the picture bird was supposed to make a low pass over the camera—one of those great fly-by shots. I was on the ground at the camera with David, and Harry was next to us, relaying David's directions to the pilot. After one take, David said he wanted the bird to come in lower and faster. Well,

Deeth decided, "OK, you want low? I'll give you low..." and came tearing up this ravine at us with the skids ripping bushes out of the ground! Needless to say, I hit the deck, the rotor wash blew over us like a tornado and David looked up from the camera with a big grin on his face—"Great!!!"

David is an amazing guy. He is immensely talented and a perfectionist. His perfectionism caused some friction for the production—he was trying to do a vintage champagne movie on a beer budget. But without that drive, I think *Cavegirl* would never have made it to the screen. Even though I'm a bit of a perfectionist in my own right, I wish I had 20% of David's energy. When David and I worked on projects before *Cavegirl*, I was his right-hand man for many of them, doing everything from handling the cameras to putting together the logistics for the shoots. I learned an astounding amount of skills in the time I spent working with him. We've now been good friends for close to forty years (yikes!), and keep in touch regularly, even though our paths have gone in different directions with David continuing in the film business and me going into the automotive realm. We still share a kinship born of our common background in the visual arts, and probably will until one of us checks out of this spinning dirtball we're all on. If there is anything I would have wished for David, it's that *Cavegirl* had been more of a commercial success. Had *Cavegirl* been given better support by Crown, I think David would be a well-known director in the industry. But sometimes the industry can be pretty cruel.

As I said earlier, even though making the movie *Cavegirl* put us through a grinder, it was one hella ride. I myself wouldn't trade that experience for an easier way. As the saying goes, adversity builds character.... At day's end, I imagine many involved in the making of this film look back on it as the unique collaboration of a diverse group of people, and a great growing and learning experience. I still look back upon it with (a perhaps warped) fondness. I can't say I regret anything about doing *Cavegirl*.

# *The Chilling*
## (1989, U.S.A.)

Genre: Horror; Directors: Jack A. Sunseri and Deland Nuse; Writers: Jack A. Sunseri (Story) and Guy Messenger (Screenplay, uncredited); Cinematographer: Deland Nuse; Editor: Beth Conwell; Special Makeup Effects: Peter Konig and Lionel Orozco; Special Effects: Matthew Riley; Producer: Jack A. Sunseri; Associate Producer: Arthur Aravena; Production Company: Trans-Bay Pictures; Cast: Linda Blair (Mary Hampton), Dan Haggerty (Sergeant Vince Marlow), Troy Donahue (Dr. Miller), Jack De Rieux (Joseph Davenport, Sr.), Ron Vincent (Joe Davenport, Jr.), John Flanagan (Steve Carson), Michael Jacobs (Mark Evans), Steve Gluck (Jerry Kardell), Neil O'Neill (Dr. Nevin), Peggy Duncan (Lisa Burton) and Rick Blanchard (Tony Rizzo)

A cryogenic center hibernates people who have died of an incurable illness, waiting for science to resuscitate and cure them. What the clients of the center don't know is that the evil director of the institute is selling their family members' organs on the black market. During a storm a lightning strike damages the machinery, causing the corpses to defrost and transform into zombies. The brave security guard of the center and one of the director's assistants face the monstrous and famished reanimated cadavers.

## Guy Messenger
### (Writer)

I played one of the "Delta House Pledges" in *Animal House*, but didn't get screen credit.

I had worked as a volunteer or low paid production assistant on a couple of films shot in San Francisco. I was on set for every day of *The Dead Pit* [1988, Brett Leonard]—I worked as production assistant, actor (I played the first mental patient seen through a window, at the opening credits), and as editing assistant at Brett Leonard's house in Santa Cruz, and, later, an editing suite at Skywalker Ranch.

I got to know Jack Sunseri [Jack Sunseri was one of the producers on *The Dead Pit*] and in conversation he learned I had a Literature degree. He could not write or spell well. He hired me to write the whole script for a "treatment" he had thought of. He had written the first one page "treatment" idea. It was originally to be called "The Frozen Dead." Sunseri asked me to be the ghostwriter, but he did not ever ask for secrecy in that matter. Years later, I posted my credit on the IMDB website and they kept it in. I don't think he cares any more. I had not intended to be a writer, really: I am an actor and musician, and have not tried to ghostwrite since. It was born simply out of the need for a job. After I quickly wrote the script, Jack Sunseri changed certain things in it. The entire plot (except the ending) stayed the same; the characters and their names stayed the same—but he changed something that made a poor script even worse.

Jack Sunseri was a construction person. He wanted to direct and star in the film and do everything. But he did not know how to write, direct, or produce.

## Deland Nuse
### (Director/Cinematographer)

After completing undergraduate studies in psychology, I continued on in a PhD program at the University of New Mexico. After realizing that I preferred working in the visual arts, I entered into and completed the Master's degree program at San Francisco State University. While living in San Francisco, I worked on several music videos, including Santana's "Say It Again," documentaries, and short films. In 1986, I made the move to Los Angeles to have more opportunities. Fortunately, I knew quite a few people in Los Angeles and immediately got a job as a 1st camera assistant to DP Gary Graver (one of Orson Welles Cinematographers). After that experience, I worked regularly in different capacities on many features, documentaries, music videos, and corporate films. For most of this period, I worked as a gaffer, best boy, and electrician. *Heaven and Earth* [1987, Ulli Lommel] was my first feature as a DP.

For *The Chilling*, the job came to me through Arthur Aravena [associate producer on the film], whom I met at San Francisco State University. He gave me a call about the film during the summer of 1988, if I recall correctly. He mentioned that Jack Sunseri was to produce and direct *The Chilling* and they wanted me to be the DP. In the fall, I returned to the SF Bay Area where their production offices were set up in Berkeley, California. The locations for the film were to be in the San Francisco East Bay Area including the communities of Berkeley, Concord, and Walnut Creek, with a studio facility set up in an old Gerber baby food factory in San Leandro, California.

I met with Arthur and Jack and discussed the lighting and camera requirements and began to consult with the special effects department for preproduction. I don't recall what the preproduction time period was, but it was at least a week, perhaps even two weeks. Only a few days after I arrived, Arthur came to me to request that I co-direct the film with Jack since he had only been a producer on his previous films [*Deadlock/The Dead Pit*]. I agreed to do this and while I didn't think much about the implications of this position at first—I usually end up giving a great deal of help to directors anyway—it became something else entirely.

On the first day of production, we were set up to shoot the scene where Linda Blair meets the father in the hospital for the first time. I lit the scene and we waited for Jack Sunseri to show up. After about 30 minutes, he did not show up and apparently didn't answer his phone. Arthur looked at me and said something to the effect of, "I guess you're directing too," which I proceeded to do for the remainder of the film in addition to serving as DP. My guess is that Jack panicked and realized that he didn't have the skill set to direct. For the remainder of the film, the pattern of Jack's involvement became showing up and observing during filming for brief periods of time—then suddenly leaving to manage the details of producing. At one point during filming, he showed up asking to say action and cut for one shot—then left suddenly for the office or the periphery of the set. In other words, he did not contribute to the direction of the film.

Jack wrote a first draft of the screenplay and then brought in Guy Messenger to flesh out a very thin screenplay in terms of plot and characterization. Guy continued to contribute to the screenplay during production since many of the structural and characterization problems in the story were addressed each day during production. On several occasions, I needed to change plot elements that could not work each day. Often, Linda Blair, myself, and the assistant director (whose name I don't recall) [Jon Sullberg] would discuss script problems on set, change them and improve them. I think it can best be said that the script evolved to take maximum advantage of locations, my own stylistic preferences, and Linda's suggestions concerning the best way to make her character work for the story.

I'm not privy to the exact budget. The budget I hear was in the area of $250,000.00, not including the many contributions of free locations, hotels, and other promotional advantages. The budget question is also complicated by the fact that while the first part of the film's production took place during the fall, we returned in March of 1989 to do some additional production for at least a week or more—a very necessary and helpful decision for the film. My estimate would be that in terms of real costs, the budget would probably be in the $750,00.00 range.

The filming locations were: San Leandro, CA (for the Cryogenic Lab); Berkeley, CA (for Troy Donahue's office and the helicopter); Concord, CA (for the hospital); Walnut Creek, CA (for the motel and the bank robbery); Oakland, CA (for the protest scene).

For me, the most beneficial experience of directing *The Chilling* came from what I learned about working with the three "star" actors: Linda Blair, Dan Haggerty and Troy Donahue [1936–2001]. To begin with, I had no part in selecting these actors. Jack mentioned to me that he had always wanted to work with them and that was the primary reason they were chosen. That reason aside, they did fit the parts very well visually. As it turned out, this was the most challenging part of directing and it became apparent immediately. There were three problems created by the selection of these actors.

First, Jack hired them to be present at the same time for most of the production. This turned out to be very inefficient since in most cases I only needed to work with one and occasionally two stars at the same time. Apparently no thought was given to the question of how best to utilize the actors' time and consequently the actors not on call ended up spending a lot of time waiting. Second, there was no time scheduled for me to meet and work with the actors before actual production begin (I have found it best to have a table reading with the cast for a few days before shooting in order to get to know each other and problem solve dramatic challenges in the script). Literally the first hour of the first day was when I met Linda Blair. There was no chance to establish a working relationship with her before calling action. This turned out to be true of Troy Donahue and Dan Haggerty also. Third, I soon realized just how important casting is. I had worked on many films by that time but I had never observed the details of casting from a director's point of view. While Linda, Troy, and Dan look perfectly fine in their roles on screen, I quickly discovered that they each had a completely different approach to acting.

The most immediate challenge for me was that each actor was at his or her best in different numbers of takes. That is to say, Linda Blair always gave her best performance on her third or fourth take. Troy was also a third or fourth take actor. That worked out OK with Linda and Troy but unfortunately they were not in many scenes together. With Dan Haggerty on the other hand, I ran into a major problem, namely, he would always be at his best the more takes you could shoot of him—in his case, that might mean 20–25 takes. This fact turned out to have a major impact on my decisions of which of these actors I could use in the same shot. For example, if I blocked a scene with Linda and Dan in the same shot and also involving camera movement, I would end up having to shoot many takes to get them at their best at the same time. Since our time schedule did not allow the luxury of time for actors to do 10–20 takes, I ended up using more single and separate shots of these actors than I had planned for.

The other related issue to performance was the fact that Dan Haggerty was an alcoholic. When I first met Dan as the Director, he asked me if he could keep a bottle of vodka on the set and my immediate reaction was to deny his request in no uncertain terms. This ended up working against me very dramatically. In the first scene I shot with Dan, I called action in a scene that ran about three minutes and Dan missed his lines; I called cut, I pointed out the problem to Dan and said that we would do it again. Immediately Dan began cursing at me and his tirade lasted at least three minutes. At first I was shocked over his outburst, but I keep my cool and said we would do it again. Dan complied and we shot another take. During the second take, Dan flubbed his line again and the same result, another tirade of profanity. I soon realized that this was just the way Dan behaved and he was just frustrated, probably with himself more than me. So we would do another take until he got it right followed by another outburst. Interestingly, he never walked off the set. Apparently it was just the way he operated. So now I had to make the decision of how many takes did I want to live through in order to get Dan to the level of performance I wanted? To complicate matters, there was also the fact that paradoxically Dan got better and better with each take. If I had the time and tolerance for his childlike tantrums and do 20 to 25 takes, Dan's performance would be fantastic.

We have to remember that Dan came up learning his craft in Hollywood along with actors like Jack Nicholson, and I think we see flashes of this gift in *The Chilling*. Dan absolutely had every bit as much talent as Jack, but his growth as an actor had clearly been limited by his alcoholism. It was very sad and painful to watch and to consider what might have been for him. I ended up dealing with this problem by adopting the attitude of a stern, unflappable, but tolerant parent to Dan's child. Very strange since he was twice my age, but it worked.

About two-thirds the way through production, Dan even disappeared for several days, probably on a drinking binge. His hotel room was checked and they found his wallet and other items on his bed. His agent was called and he had no idea where he was. When he did return, he only said that he had some things to deal with.

Also, on a more humorous note, we soon realized that once we gave Dan the shotgun for the scenes when he battles the zombies, we had no problems with him. He really took well to action scenes where he could shoot. In fact, we started out giving him small loads for the shotgun blanks, but when I realized that he was really getting into it, I had the property master give him full loads that were much louder. It really helped center his performance although I'm sure the sound mixer was not happy with my decision.

I worked most closely with Linda Blair since she was in most of the scenes. Linda was at a difficult point in her career at the time of *The Chilling*, attempting to make that transition from the juvenile roles that made her famous, to the more age appropriate roles she desired. I suspect that one of the reasons for accepting her part in *The Chilling* was just that, she could play the role of a woman in her thirties. In fact, at one point Linda discussed this with Jack, and myself namely that she wanted to work toward getting on top again with good roles. Personally I enjoyed working with Linda. She had a very good sense about what her character needed to do and this became part of our daily discussions and script changes. About half way through the first phase of production, I caught a flu-like illness for two days and ran a temperature of 102 degrees Fahrenheit. Linda was instrumental in keeping me together and made some useful directorial suggestions that I adopted. For the zombie scenes, we filmed in a very cold building that necessitated the crew to wear heavy winter clothing. My favorite memory of Linda is when she wanted to discuss something really important to her, she would stand in front of me, grab the lapels of my jacket, look me in the eye, and make her request. Great memories.

Troy Donahue was the most interesting actor on *The Chilling*. I really enjoyed working with him and he brought a great sense of humor to the set. Troy was also an alcoholic, but a recovering one who had successfully emerged from a dark period in his life into a career of low budget genre films. He did this without resentment and complaint and had a great work ethic. While I very much enjoyed his sense of humor, his stories of various life experiences, and his uplifting presence on set, he was also very reliable. He showed up on time, knew his lines and was able to offer me several choices on his delivery of his lines. I had a good laugh while we were editing when I noticed that during some takes Troy appeared to be taking on the personality of William F. Buckley, a well know public intellectual in the U.S.A. at the time, as a model for his role. I also had the pleasure of having lunch with Troy back in Los Angeles after filming had ended.

I have fond memories of the film despite some very challenging working conditions. If I haven't made it clear so far, the challenging experiences came from trying to overcome script weaknesses and poor production management. I had some very dedicated and creative crew personnel, and supporting actors. Of the supporting cast, Ron Vincent, Jim Thrasher, Jack De Rieux, Peggy Duncan, John Flanagan, and Neil O'Neill really stand out. For the crew, I have to mention the heroic efforts of Arthur Aravena and my gaffer, Alan Steinheimer, who always had my back. For the second part of the production in 1989, Arthur Aravena served as my gaffer.

There were two theatrical screenings of the film in 1989. The first was a sneak preview at a drive-in theater in the Walnut Creek-Concord area (Jack De Rieux, mentioned to me that he had seen it there). The second screening was at the Grand Lake Theater in Oakland. The Grand Lake screening coincided with an informal wrap party that occurred directly after the screening—informal since it was more of an ad hoc decision for everyone in attendance to walk across the street to a restaurant and have food and drinks. I recall the "party" as a very enjoyable event. Everyone was very happy to get together again since it had been a few months since the production had wrapped. After that, I don't recall hearing anything about distribution possibilities. I know that Jack attempted to sell it to various film markets but I don't know why it never got distributed theatrically.

Eventually, I got a VHS version of the film and I was very disappointed to find it in 1.33:1 TV aspect ratio. It was only last fall that I was able to acquire a DVD version of the film, and dismayed even more to find that the TV aspect ratio remained. I shot the film in a 1.85:1 ratio and this format was a very specific choice. I feel that much of the impact of the film is lost in the 1.33:1 ratio. My hope for the film now, is that it can be seen in the intended 1.85:1 aspect ratio.

Currently, I'm a Professor teaching at UCLA in the Film, TV & Digital department. I teach Cinematography classes and Film Aesthetics classes. In 2010 I taught a workshop in Cinematography at the Accademia Nazionale del Cinema in Bologna, Italy. During the last two years, I have been shooting a documentary and preparing to shoot a new feature film, *The Curse* for director Fulvio Sestito.

## Ron Vincent
## ("Joe Davenport Jr.")

In the 1980s and 1990s San Francisco was a prime location for filming television commercials. Both American and international film production companies shot there; occasionally a movie or television show also shot there; also a lot of print advertising was shot in San Francisco and San Jose—so there was quite a bit of work for San Francisco actors.

My first paid acting job was in 1986; it was for a local television station in Concord, California. The instructor of the television commercial acting class I was taking worked there and hired me. *The Chilling* was filmed in January through the first week of February 1989 (in April there were 3 days of reshoots). In 1991 I became a member of AFTRA. In 1992 I had principal roles in two episodes of NBC's *Unsolved Mysteries*—that got me membership in SAG. In 1994 I played six different characters in the play *The Heidi Chronicles* by Wendy Wasserman at the California Conservatory Theatre in San Leandro, California. In July 1995 I left acting to get married and have a family. I intend to return to acting in a couple years.

In late November 1988 I received a telephone call from my former TV commercial acting instructor. He said one of his students saw a help-wanted advertisement in the *Contra Costa Times* (a local newspaper) looking for actors to appear in a feature film shooting locally. He gave me the address and dates and times for the auditions. The auditions were an open cattle call at Jack Sunseri's business office in Lafayette, California. He had multiple businesses. For *The Chilling* he had set up a business called Trans Bay Pictures. At the audition I was handed a brief synopsis of the film's storyline and the featured actors who would be in the movie (Linda Blair, Dan Haggerty and Troy Donahue). So I knew it was going to be a B-movie. I arrived at the audition late Sunday afternoon around 4 p.m. There were about three people ahead of me waiting to audition. In talking to them I realized most of them had not acted before, they were just there to see if they could get into a movie. A young woman, about 19 years old, came in after me and told me she was not an actress; she was just there to see if she could get into a movie. The auditioning was taking much longer than any other I had ever been to. It was just about my turn to audition when the casting director came out into the waiting room. He asked how many of us were serious actors and how many of us just came there to see if we could get into a movie. The young woman raised her hand as being one who was not a serious actress. He said ok you come in and audition now. I didn't think that was very professional so I got up, gave my photo and resume to the receptionist and I left without ever auditioning.

In the first week of January 1989 I got a telephone call from Jack Sunseri. It was about 10pm and I was getting ready for bed (I worked a part-time shift loading trucks from 3:30am to 7:30am so I would sleep about 5 hours before the shift and 3 hours after the shift). My answering machine took the call. I heard him say he was Jack Sunseri and he was filming a movie in the morning and they had a last minute cast change and he wondered if I could come in and read for a lead part. I picked up the phone and spoke with him. He told me that he saw my photo I had left at the audition and that I had the look for the character of Joe Davenport, Jr. He said filming would start at 8am the next morning and it paid $100 a day. I agreed to read for the role and then got dressed and drove to his office about 30 minutes from my home (I figured I had the part because it was so late at night and he didn't mention anybody else reading for the part). When I got there it was close to 11pm. The office building was dark except for a light in his office. I found my way to his office and met him and one of his assistants. I read from the script and got the role. I signed the contract and went home and read the entire script. I then went to work loading trucks and afterwards drove to the filming location in Walnut Creek, California, to shoot the bank robbery scene. I didn't get any sleep that night.

I found out later that Troy Donahue was originally cast as Joe Davenport, Sr.; Jack De Rieux was originally cast as Dr. Miller; and Rick Blanchard was originally cast as Joe Davenport, Jr. Troy had a last minute scheduling conflict so Jack De Rieux was recast as Joe Davenport, Sr., and Troy was recast as Dr. Miller. Rick Blanchard was only 9 years younger than Jack De Rieux and he looked too old to be his son, so they had to recast the role of Joe Davenport, Jr. (and that's how I got the part the night before filming started). However Rick did appear in the movie as the guy who got his throat slit in the hotel room by Joe Davenport, Jr.

These are the locations that I remember being at, and the sequence that they were filmed in…

—The bank robbery. [This is the scene in which Joe Davenport, Jr., is fatally injured. After his death his father Joe Davenport, Sr., submits his son to the cryogenic treatment.] This was the first scene filmed. The location was Walnut Creek. It was filmed in the former building of a San Francisco Savings and Loan branch (they had either moved or gone out of business just before filming started, so it was a very good location for a bank robbery scene).

—The hospital/Cryogenic lab dissecting room. The hospital scenes were shot at Mount Diablo Hospital in Concord. Linda Blair did some scenes here. It also served as the dissecting room of the cryogenic lab. The scene where a dead Joe Davenport, Jr., is getting his guts taken out was shot in the basement morgue of the hospital. That's also the same place where, at the beginning of the film, a dead Mrs. Davenport was given cryogenic fluid.

—The cryogenic lab. The bulk of the cryogenic lab scenes were filmed at a vacant warehouse in Oakland, California. This is where Linda Blair had most of her scenes. Troy Donahue and Dan Haggerty had all of their scenes filmed here. During the day a truck drivers training school used the facilities, so all the filming was done at night.

—The motel room. This was where Joe Davenport, Jr., and his gang stayed before the bank robbery. It was the last scene to be filmed. The location was The Hillside Motel in Lafayette.

Jack Sunseri was a very entrepreneurial person. At the time *The Chilling* was made, I believe he was in his early 40s and had a number of successful business ventures. *The Chilling* was another business venture. As producer he had to keep tabs on all different aspects of the filmmaking process. I respected that and kept my dealings with him to a minimum. I mainly dealt with the assistant director and the director.

Deland Nuse was a film aficionado. He was really into films and filmmaking. I met him the first day of filming, and he gave me his ideas on how he saw my character (I had got the role about 9 hours before filming began, so I had no time to develop the character). At first I thought he was just the camera operator, but after a few days I realized he was actually directing the film. He was very patient and pleasant to work with. I kept in touch with him after the filming of *The Chilling* until 1995 when I left the business.

Of the three "name" actors in the movie, I only worked with Troy Donahue. I met Linda Blair and spoke with her briefly, but I did not meet Dan Haggerty. Troy had made a number of movies, particularly B movies, and he was very adept at film acting. I remember him explaining something to me about the camera lens and how wide a shot that would fit in the scene. He was very accessible to the cast and crew members of *The Chilling*.

I had met Troy the first night of filming in Oakland. I had one scene with him. It's the scene in the film where he had retrieved his files and was trying to leave the cryogenic lab. I was in the silver cryogenic costume running up a staircase after him (I was the zombie with hair). It was a very brief scene in the movie. I had a prosthetic mask glued to my face so you really can't tell that it's me. I was supposed to be Joe Davenport, Jr., as a zombie. However, when filming ended that night, I peeled the mask off my face and my face was all red; I had an allergic reaction to the glue that they used to glue the mask to my face— I couldn't wear the prosthetic mask anymore. Because of that, all the scenes that I was to appear in as a zombie were rewritten without me in them. In the original script the zombie Joe Davenport, Jr., was supposed to be a very menacing presence in the film, appearing in most of the zombie scenes as the leader of the cryonoids. For the next 10 days I did not work on the film, and therefore didn't work with Linda Blair and Dan Haggerty. When I came back, the "name" actors were gone. I shot a few scenes as zombie Joe Davenport, Jr. Instead of a prosthetic mask, the makeup people put greenish make-up on me and frosted my hair and eyebrows. I was the only zombie that was recognizable, but I did not have very many scenes as a zombie. When I met Linda Blair, I was wearing the prosthetic mask (it was on the first night of filming in Oakland). She asked me how could I see under the mask. I told her there were hidden eye holes to see out of.

I met Jack De Rieux the first day of filming at the bank. He did not appear in that scene, but he showed up to check out the production. He had a beard that he grew for the part of Dr. Miller that he was originally cast to play. Jack was a local high school drama teacher and community theatre actor. In talking to him I found out we had some things in common. He also had taken a TV commercial acting class at the same talent agency as I did, and was represented by them. He also acted in a TV commercial that the class instructor directed. The day before the film's premiere screening in Oakland, Jack and I did an in-studio interview on a local radio station. We also got represented by the same large San Francisco talent agency about a year later. Last year in 2014, Jack retired from teaching; the local newspaper did a big story on Jack's retirement (*The Chilling* was not mentioned in the article).

John Flanagan was an actor I met during the first night of filming in Oakland. That night he was also in a play in San Francisco. He had a conflict and was hoping Jack Sunseri would let him off to go be in the play (as I recall, he missed the play).

Steve Gluck and I had a scene in the hospital morgue. He took out Joe Davenport, Jr.'s internal organs. I had met him also on the first day of filming at the bank. He too had come by to check out the production.

I met Michael Jacobs the first day of filming at the bank. He also came by to check out the production (as did Jack De Rieux and Steve Gluck). All his scenes were shot in Oakland while I was off so I did not work with him. I saw him again at the premiere in November 1989.

Jim Thrasher played the role of Jerky. He was one of Joe Davenport, Jr.'s gang. His character spoke with a stutter and twitched his head. He was a method actor that meditated to get into character. He worked a regular job as a projector operator at a movie theatre. He was a good actor. He appeared in the bank robbery scene and motel scene. Unfortunately most of his dialogue was cut from the script.

Tavia Cathcart played the bank teller that Joe Davenport, Jr., grabbed and threatened. She had a small role but was a very good actress. She went on to work quite a bit in industrial films, TV commercials and theatre in the San Francisco Bay Area. A few years after *The Chilling* I saw Tavia on the set of *Mrs. Doubtfire* (the film starring Robin Williams shot entirely in the Bay Area). She was the stand-in for Sally Field. I had been sent there for the director, Chris Columbus, to look at me for a featured extra part of a maître d' named Hector. Tavia saw me on set and came over and we hugged. I didn't get the role but they gave Tavia a small one-line part as a hostess in the restaurant scene.

[Here are some stories from the filming...]

At the bank:

—On the first day of shooting at the bank, I noticed there was a snack food table loaded with sugary frosted pastries and Jolt Cola (Jolt Cola advertised itself as having "twice the caffeine and all the sugar" of regular cola). I guess it was meant to keep the cast and crew wide awake for the long hours of the shoot. It made me on edge though.

—When I first arrived on the set I was introduced to Deland Nuse. He told me he saw my character, Joe Davenport, Jr., as being like "Charles Manson with a sense of humor."

—The first scene took quite a while to set up technically. I was talking to Tavia Cathcart, the actress who played the bank teller that my character threatens. Since we had a lot of time to kill I thought that it would be good to improvise the scene. We went upstairs to an empty room and improvised. We were both in character and as the improv progressed I started yelling at her and she let out a scream. Immediately I heard footsteps running up the stairs. The yelling and screaming alarmed the crew downstairs that they came up to see what was going on.

—The first scene filmed was Joe Davenport, Jr., and his gang entering the bank. As we entered the bank I grabbed hold of an older woman and announced that the bank is being held up. That older woman was Jack Sunseri's stepmother. On the first take she tripped and we both fell flat on our faces. She didn't get hurt thankfully.

—They only had 2 days to shoot all the bank robbery scenes. It was taking longer than anticipated, so some scenes and dialogue between Joe Davenport, Jr., and his gang got eliminated.

—I was developing the character of Joe Davenport, Jr., as we were shooting. To help get in character I carried around a boom box and listened to hard rock music (Guns N' Roses and Aerosmith were particular favorites).

—The entire dialogue of the bank robbery was unscripted; we improvised it; my first scene after getting the role the night before is improvised. I didn't even know much about my character, I basically winged it.

—When Joe Davenport, Jr., got shot, his head drops down and then slowly lifts up until his gunshots at the ceiling and he falls backward. As I was lifting my head I was directed to look at the middle of the lighting pole stand in the distance and follow it up with my eyes to the top, then shoot the gun. I wasn't aware that by focusing on the pole my eyes were crossed-eyed. In seeing the film I was embarrassed because it looked like I was over-acting.

—The film's editor showed up the first day of filming to see how they were filming and get an idea of what he would be working with. I was surprised to see him as I knew him from a previous independent film I had acted in that he edited. He later helped me obtain a copy of an early trailer for the film that I made copies of and sent out to casting directors.

—I had brought an acoustic guitar to the set. I would play it when I had a lot of time to kill waiting. A number of cast were sitting around waiting upstairs at the bank. I was playing guitar. Valerie de Ropp (an actress who played a bank teller), and I were trying to sing the REM song "The One I Love." We couldn't figure out all the lyrics though.

—I wore my own clothes as Joe Davenport, Jr. The torn pants were my work pants I had on when I came to the set after I got off my "regular" job.

At the hospital:

—At Mount Diablo Hospital they shot the scene where Joe Davenport, Sr., and Mary are discussing the arrangements for putting Joe Davenport, Jr.'s body in cryogenic freeze. That scene was filmed in the hospital cafeteria. It was scheduled to shoot in the morning and be done before the cafeteria's lunch hours. However the filming took a lot longer than expected. The hospital staff, doctors, and other employees had to wait outside the cafeteria's locked doors. The line of people got quite long and very angry at the production assistants who were stationed outside the doors keeping people from entering (many of the people missed lunch that day).

At the warehouse (Cryogenic lab):

—The zombie scenes were filmed at a vacant warehouse in Oakland. This location was where the bulk of filming took place, about 3 weeks' worth. The warehouse was on the property that a truck drivers training school used during the day. It was in a bad part of Oakland. Two weeks before filming began there, an instructor at the school was robbed and murdered as he was closing up at night.

—There was a lot of excitement amongst cast and crew when filming moved to this location. The three "name" actors would all be here, and the zombie horror elements would be filmed here. However by the end of the 3 weeks the mood had changed. A number of crew members had either quit or got fired (I heard even Linda Blair got fired).

—Upstairs at the warehouse there were offices. One was fairly large. It had chairs and tables, and it was where the cast and crew had their meals. There were smaller offices along the side of the larger one. One of these smaller offices was shared by Troy Donahue, Dan Haggerty, Jack De Rieux and myself as somewhere to hangout when we weren't filming a scene. During the first night, I was hanging out in the smaller office with one of the special effects crew. I think his name was Peter [Peter Konig]. I had my guitar and we wrote a song about *The Chilling*. The lyrics were quite clever. I can remember some but not all. One of the verses was about Linda Blair. It went like this: "Now we got that young lady whose head spun/In that movie with Ellen Burstyn/She hovered above her bed/And now she's running from the frozen dead." We finished writing the song before the dinner break. During the meal that night I had the make-up assistant, Colleen ("Cool" was her nickname) announce that Joe Davenport, Jr., would be singing for the dinnertime entertainment. I came out in my zombie mask with my guitar and sang the song in front of the entire cast and crew (Linda Blair laughed when I sang the verse about her). When I finished I got a big applause. I think Peter videotaped it. It would make a great YouTube video if it ever got found.

—When I came back to the set after 10 days off, I was disappointed to learn that the "name" actors had finished their scenes and were gone. I was hoping to work with them. I never met Dan Haggerty. A number of crew members were gone, some were replaced with new people. The offices upstairs were dark and no longer being used. They only shot a few scenes of zombie Joe Davenport, Jr. (as I said before, I didn't wear the prosthetic mask). I think I worked the last night of the shoot in Oakland. There weren't any zombie actors there so a couple production assistants put on the masks and costumes. I did a scene where Dan Haggerty's character shoots me and I fall back against some pallets. Since Dan Haggerty was no longer there, Jack Sunseri put on Haggerty's security guard uniform and was filmed from behind, making it appear Dan Haggerty shot me. It was a real let down for me. I was there at the beginning of the Oakland shoot when everyone was excited—now at the end of the shoot they couldn't wait to end it and get out of there.

At the motel:

—These scenes were filmed on the last week of the production, but they appear early in the film (this is where Joe Davenport, Jr., and his gang stayed before the bank robbery). The production rented two rooms at the motel. One for filming (downstairs) and one for the cast, crew, and make-up to occupy when not on set (upstairs). After having survived the Oakland shoot, the mood was relaxed in anticipation of finishing the movie. It was a relatively easy shoot. Most of the action took place in the motel room.

—In the scene where Joe Davenport, Jr., slits the throat of one of his gang (Rick Blanchard), the special effects crew had made a neck prosthetic for him. It was attached in front of his neck, with two tubes inside that ran down underneath his shirt and down each pant leg. During the scene when I grabbed his hair and pretended to slit his throat, there were two guys on the floor next to Rick's legs (one at each leg) each pushing a pump that shot fake blood out of the tubes in his prosthetic neck piece. We only did two takes of this scene because of its complexity (and the mess it made on his clothes).

*The Chilling* finished filming in the first week of February 1989. Two months later, in April, they had to do some additional filming at the warehouse in Oakland. They needed to see more of Joe Davenport, Jr., as a cryonoid. I worked three days on the reshoot as a zombie. I got paid $300 for it. But my contract stated that I would not be paid if they had to do any reshoots with my character. A few days later Jack's production accountant called me on the telephone. He told me I wasn't supposed to be paid for the three days of reshoots, according to my contract. He told me Jack had put a stop payment on my check. Unfortunately I had already spent the money.

After the last week of filming, there was a "wrap party" at Jack Sunseri's office in Lafayette. It was a fun and relaxed party for cast and crew. There was a film projector set up and we got to see some of the rough footage of the film, without sound. Deland had his camera and was taking pictures. We all said our good-byes and vowed to keep in touch. I got many phone numbers and did keep in touch with some people for years after that, even working with some on other projects.

When the filming ended, I decided to send out press releases to local newspapers and other local publications. The press release was about me, a local actor, having just finished acting in a feature film with Linda Blair, Dan Haggerty and Troy Donahue. I included my acting headshot with the press release. I had mentioned where I went to high school and the local acting instructors who I studied with. Every publication printed the press release with the photo. Two of them called me and interviewed me over the phone for special articles. One newspaper, the *Contra Costa Times*, sent over a photographer for a featured article in their weekly "Time Out" section (the article appeared in April 1989). In addition they did an article a few days before the premiere in November 1989 telling about the movie and giving the day and time of the premiere.

In early November 1989, *The Chilling* had its premiere at the Grand Lakes Theatre in Oakland. (However, two weeks prior to that, in the last week of October, it played outdoors at the Bridgehead Drive-In in Antioch, California, over the Halloween weekend.) At the premiere in Oakland, there were spotlights and an early poster of the film outside of the theatre. The general public could buy tickets to see the film that night too. The entire cast and crew were invited to the premiere. In addition we could invite as many guests as we wanted. (I invited all my family in the Bay Area. Parents, siblings, cousins, aunts, uncles; not to mention my fellow actor and actress friends. I probably had close to 30 people there.) Jack Sunseri presented each cast and crew member with an "Oscar" trophy. He called each person out of the audience by name. Each person gave their thoughts on working on the film. It was quite long and dragged on. However before Jack began, a young woman who nobody knew, interrupted Jack and came up to the microphone. She said Linda Blair sent her, and then she proceeded with a 10-minute monologue about nothing. After she finished, she left the theatre. Jack just said, "Weird," and proceeded with the presentation.

After the showing of the movie, I was in the lobby talking to some co-workers from my "regular" job who had come to see the movie. A couple of women came over to me and asked me for my autograph. I wasn't sure why they wanted my autograph because I was just a local actor. Anyway, my co-workers were impressed.

About a month after the premiere, I was exiting a BART (Bay Area Rapid Transit) train in San Francisco. As I was leaving the station I heard someone saying, "Ron. Ron Vincent." I turned around and a man introduced himself to me as Guy Messenger, the writer of *The Chilling*. I didn't say anything. I just looked at him. I always thought Jack Sunseri wrote *The Chilling* (I also didn't understand how he knew who I was). He explained that he was the "ghostwriter" hired by Jack Sunseri. He had seen the movie at the premiere and that's how he had recognized me. I had to confirm this, so I called Jack Sunseri's office. I spoke with Jack's assistant (who was the production accountant) and he confirmed it, but said that he (Guy Messenger) should not have told me about being the ghostwriter.

The Chilling did not get theatrical distribution in the United States—nor did it appear on television here. In 1992 it was released on video tape by Hemdale Home Video through their Coyote Films division. In 2008 it was released on DVD by Code Red. When I signed the contract to act in The Chilling, my compensation was $100 a day (it was a non-union film and I was a non-union actor at the time so the pay was not very good). However I was also to receive 3 points of net profit (3%) for the first year after filming ended; I was to receive 2 points of net profit (2%) for the second year after filming ended; I was to receive 1 point of net profit (1%) for the third year after filming ended. The movie didn't get released until 1992 on video: since that was over 3 years after filming ended I never received any additional compensation from my participation in The Chilling.

## John Flanagan
### ("Steve Carson")

I've been an actor in San Francisco my entire adult life. I do the occasional film, commercial, or television shoot, but mainly it's theatre. I'm a member of SAG/AFTRA, and Actor's Equity, the theatre union; although, I was not a member of SAG at the time of The Chilling.

I found out about the film audition from an actor friend of mine, Neil O'Neill. He plays a doctor near the beginning of the movie. Neil told me they were looking to cast a number of people as zombies. It didn't seem very interesting to me, but Neil talked me into going to the audition. At the audition, there was a big line of young people that were going to be looked at to play zombies. Others were waiting to be looked at to read for particular roles. I let them know that I wasn't interested in playing a zombie for no money. They told me to go ahead and read for the role of Steve, the boyfriend of Linda Blair's character. I read for the role, and they must've been fairly impressed because they offered me the part on the spot. I was, obviously, excited to be offered the role because it was an opportunity to work with some fairly famous/infamous actors, and I thought it would be a very good payday.

When I inquired about contract and pay, they let me know that there was no pay for the role. They tried to sell me on the fact that it would be a great opportunity and experience to get to work with Linda Blair and the others. I was fairly shocked, and told them that I could not do it for free. Later that night, they offered me the role again, and if my memory is correct, I was offered 50 or $100 a day for the shoot. I think I worked three or four days on it. I would have liked to have made more money, but I was a young actor and it did seem like an interesting project.

Like with most films, everything took forever. In this case, it took even longer. I don't think they got all the shots they would've liked, which is not uncommon, but even more so with this film. My understanding was that they only had the three stars for a certain amount of days, and then they were leaving. So, there was a certain amount of pressure to get their scenes shot, especially those with Linda. I think there were one or two scenes where they put a wig on another woman, and shot her from behind because Linda had already gone back to Los Angeles.

Linda would show up on set fully made up. She was nice to me—but, I got the feeling that she was irked by the way some of the things were being run … annoyed by some of the disorganization.

At the time, I was learning lines for a production of the Greek tragedy, "Orestes." The world of theater was very foreign to her. Obviously, she came from the world of film. Troy Donahue was a nice man, kind of quiet. He was a fan of the Raiders football team, so we talked sports. Dan Haggerty was really great … fun and boisterous. He had had so much experience in television on the *Grizzly Adams* show that he knew an awful lot about cameras, lighting, and how scenes should be shot. I think he even directed two or three scenes himself on a second unit, but am not 100% sure about that. I guess he had been good friends with Andy Gibb, the singer and brother of the guys in the Bee Gees. Dan thought that I looked a lot like him, that I reminded him of him.

Deland Nuse was a very nice man, as well. Not really sure if Deland knew what he was getting himself into when he took the job because of the fact he ended up being the de facto director. I enjoyed working with him. He seemed to have a fair amount of experience.

The film is a pretty basic B movie—no better nor worse than many others of its kind. The fact that it stars Linda Blair, Troy Donahue, and Dan Haggerty is what gives it its cachet. For a young actor like myself it was an interesting and, at times, a fun and exciting experience to be a part of it all. I rarely even think about *The Chilling* today, but for a while there it was sort of my claim to infamy. It was just cool to have a part in a movie. What actor wouldn't want that? Obviously, there's a part of me that would have liked for the film to have had a wide release, and gotten a lot of positive recognition, but that never really happened.

# *Creepozoids*
## (1987, U.S.A.)

*Genre:* Horror; *Director:* David DeCoteau; *Writers:* David DeCoteau and David Eisenstark as "Burford Hauser"; *Cinematographer:* Thomas Callaway; *Editor:* Miriam L. Preissel;*Special Makeup and Creature Effects:* Next Generation Effects; *Special Mechanical Effects:* John Criswell; *Special Makeup Effects:* Thomas Wayne Schwartz; *Special Effects:* Thomas Callaway; *Producers:* John Schouweiler and David DeCoteau; *Associate Producers:* Jackie Snider, Rozanne Taucher, Linnea Quigley, Steve Lustgarten and Gary P. Ryan; *Executiver Producer:* Charles Band; *Production Company:* Cinema H.V. Productions; *Cast:* Linnea Quigley (Bianca), Ken Abraham (Butch), Michael Aranda (Jesse), Richard Hawkins (Jake), Kim McKamy (Kate) and Joi Wilson (Woman)

Five survivors of a nuclear catastrophe find refuge from the acid rain in an old abandoned research laboratory. They face a horrible mutant creature as a result of genetic experiments, its monstrous offspring, and a pack of giant rats.

*Creepozoids* was originally called "Mutant Spawn 2000." I asked Will Schmitz to shed some light on his unproduced screenplay for *Creepozoids* and, on the same occasion, I asked him to give more details concerning (no, it wasn't a porn film!) "Space Sluts in the Slammer," which never became a film.

## Will Schmitz
### (Writer, "Mutant Spawn 2000")

After earning my Master of Fine Arts from the University of Iowa Writers Workshop, where I won accolades from Donald Justice, I was invited to join the PhD program by the head of the English Department based on my academic work. I declined. My wife, in the meanwhile, began to earn a master's degree in film production. She introduced me to a fellow student, Jerry O'Brien, for whom I wrote a script that was later made as *Rites of Passage* [1997]. Before moving to Los Angeles, I had written six feature scripts. I met David DeCoteau through Jackie Napoli who I met in response to an ad for a writer in a magazine. I met Robert Strauss [director/producer of *Blood Nasty*] in the same way.

I wrote the 1st draft of "Mutant Spawn 2000" (made as *Creepozoids*), an alien ambulance chaser, and a treatment for "Space Sluts in the Slammer" [1987] for David DeCoteau. Dave butchered my script "One Woman Death Machine" for what he shot as *Lady Avenger* [1987]. He seemed to have no ambition to ever get out of ultra-low budget, we never spoke again and he turned over my version of *Creepozoids* to someone else to rewrite. I pretty much stopped writing low budget scripts since the Roger Corman/John Sayles days of fun low-budget movie-making seemed to be over.

Dave paid me $500 per script. His was the idea for "Space Sluts in the Slammer," which he said was a line muttered by the character of Nick Cage in *Valley Girl*. I wrote a treatment. The company raised money for it based on the treatment and a sexy poster. It got written up in *Time* magazine, but the money was never invested in "Sluts" and put into other projects instead. "Space Sluts" was a women-in-prison movie with the usual exploitative lesbian tones like in the old Susan Hayward *I Want to Live* [1958] but way cheesier. It never got past the treatment. Dave wanted to shoot it in a warehouse using locks bought at a hardware store. Not much sci-fi about it. For the lowest budget possible was Dave's over-riding concern—he used to boast he could shoot them faster than I could write them (I usually wrote them in a week).

["One Woman Death Machine" was rewritten.] When I complained about the result, Dave threatened to take my name off the credit, which was acceptable to me, but not to him because it would have cost money to do—it was already set. The script for "Mutant Spawn 2000" was already done, Dave and I were splits, so that went the way it did. At the wrap party for *Lady Avenger*, Dave said I could sell the original if I wanted to since his was nothing like it.

In "Mutant Spawn 2000," the alien injects its victims with a venom that excites the human body's pleasure centers and the victims die in ecstasy even as they are consumed by the creature. I tried to stay as far away from an Alien imitation as possible. Since that was Dave's purpose, he did not go with that. My script was actually fun and good before Dave performed his usual butchery.

I started teaching English in high schools and wrote at night. My sci-fi stories "Bots, Come!" is coming out next year. My association with these low budget people was brief and, mostly, humorous. They were a nice opposite to the serious "creative" and academic types I had been around for the previous years.

## David Eisenstark
### (Writer)

During the 1980s I had a dozen low-budget horror/exploitation scripts optioned, hired-to-write, or sold, which is why I went with the name "Burford Hauser," not wanting to get stuck in that ghetto forever. Of course, the market was soon saturated, and the signs went up, "will look at any script except horror."

I met David DeCoteau, who read one of my scripts and liked it enough to hire me to write *Creepozoids*. That was a great experience and pretty straight-forward: I went to his office and he told me the story and I wrote it down. It took about a half-hour, I think. It's a blatant steal from Alien, of course, which was big at the time. David had a warehouse full of refrigerator boxes which could be made to look like air-ducts, so the whole thing was to put a big chunk of the action in the ducts and save money on production. I think he gave me a week to write the script, during which time he called a few times to ask why I hadn't finished it yet! When I did finish, he thought the way I'd done the last act would cost too much to shoot, so I rewrote that. Maybe the credits should read "Story by David DeCoteau, Screenplay by Dave Eisenstark" but nobody cares, and certainly not me. I went to the film in downtown LA when it opened and was surprised to see the third act was nothing like the two versions I'd written, so I give him credit for that.

I've heard *Creepozoids* was a hit in England theatrically. The possibility of a sequel was definitely on David's mind. Also, I think he liked the "The End…?" 50s B-movie style of it. He mentioned a sequel a year or so later, but as far as I know, nothing was ever done about it.

David called me about writing another film for him, but in the end that never materialized. The film was *Sorority Babes in the Slimeball Bowl-O-Rama* [1987], if I remember correctly. Not much to it as far as my involvement: got the job, then he called a few days later to say he had somebody else, don't know why. The pay on these things was so low, it really didn't make much difference to me one way or the other. Even the producers, I think, would say it was too much work for too little money, and sadly, most never went on to bigger things (self included—great life, lousy career).

I've continued to write since *Creepozoids*, mostly writing screenplays on assignment, six of which have been made. My horror/black comedy novel, "The Video Killer" [2014], was just published by Spanking Pulp Press and my Western novel, "Bleeding Kansas" [2014], will be published soon by World Castle Press (http://DaveEisenstark.com).

## Thomas Callaway
### (Cinematographer/Special Effects)

*Creepozoids* was my first feature shot on 35mm film. The film was very low budget, I think around 60k. I was hired to do some pyro effects on the film. The original DP had some scheduling conflict and Dave DeCoteau asked me to shoot it. It was a great opportunity for me and it really started my career.

I remember having to pick up the camera gear for the shoot at an apartment in Hollywood. I rang the doorbell and Ron Jeremy, the porn star, opened the door. He was talking on a cordless phone and only wearing pink bikini briefs. I didn't know who he was at the time but I prepped the camera in record time and couldn't get out of there fast enough. Unfortunately he was there two weeks later (early March 1987) when I returned the gear. I left the gear next to the dried up Christmas tree he still had in his living room. I guess he was part owner of the camera package. I insisted on using Panavision after that.

*Creepozoids* was a 12-day shoot with 1 day of pickups a couple weeks later. We shot most of the film in an old warehouse on Washington Blvd. in LA and a half day at a storage unit somewhere downtown. The title sequence was also shot downtown LA—without permits. It was just me, a 1st AC and the actors. Dave was great to work with and we had a lot of fun making that film. At first he didn't trust my operating skills so for the first day or so he operated. He eventually let me operate and it all worked out.

## Thomas Floutz
### (Special Makeup and Creature Effects—Next Generation Effects)

I had worked on other Charlie Band movies (at John Buechler's MMI) for about a year before *Creepozoids*, but only in the capacity of making things for them. My first on-set experience was *Ghoulies 2* (we shot in Italy, outside Rome) where I also played the giant Ghoulie. But *Creepozoids* was Peter Carsillo and [my] first film together.

I had been doing some side jobs with Peter, some commercials, some wax figure work, some mold work. At the time, I did almost all tech work—molding, casting, seaming, while Peter did the artistic work—all the sculpting and painting. The same was the case on *Creepozoids*—Peter did all the designing, sculpting, and painting. He was a great artist then, and is still amazing.

Peter lived in an apartment complex with a DP/camera man [Thomas Callaway] that he was friendly with. He talked with Peter about doing the effects for a new feature that he was going to work on. One thing led to another, and eventually we were talking to the director, Dave DeCoteau. He told us everything in the script, there was a huge amount of stuff—make-ups, transformations, full-body mechanized creature suit, giant mechanical rats—and that he had a total of $6000 for the whole make-up effects budget. We were really excited. It was our big break! We barely slept during the build, and called in favors from all of our effects friends. I think we broke even, we made no $ at all on the film.

I played the Zelda creature. It was a backwards suit, inspired by a much cooler suit in the film *Xtro* [1982, Harry Bromley Davenport]. I was walking backwards on these short crutches on my arms. It was all triceps to support myself and "walk." I trained at the gym to try to beef up my arms, but there was no way to really prepare for the physics of it. It was exhausting to walk a short distance in the suit. Between takes, we would take the head

The "Zelda" creature in *Creepozoids* and Peter Carsillo (Special Makeup and Creature Effects). Thomas Floutz (Special Makeup and Creature Effects) is in the suit (courtesy of Thomas Floutz).

off, so I could cool down and get some air. I have pictures of me in the suit with the head off. There is a band-aid on my nose to help protect it from the weight of the mechanics in the fiberglass under skull. And I am asleep. Pete and I were exhausted from trying to build everything in time, and would pass out whenever we weren't moving.

I mentioned that there were giant mechanical rats in the show? I was puppeteering one of them on set, and I remember trying to motivate one of the actors, telling him, "'Rats' backwards is 'star'!" I think it's easy to see that he used this in his inspired performance!

Apparently after they shot and edited everything, they found that they were short time-wise, so we were asked to give as many credits as possible, in order to stretch out the running time. We submitted a list of everyone, and I think they were all included. It was funny, I'd run into our crew people after the movie was released, and they would say, "Man, I only worked a day on that show and I got a screen credit! Amazing!"

When the film was over and done, it didn't really lead to other projects, like we'd hoped. We had a friend that wrote an article about us and the work on *Creepozoids* in *American Cinematographer* magazine [December 1987 issue], emphasizing how cheaply we could do things, and still have a decent product. We got a couple of meetings from that, but no other projects really came of it. Pete continued to do wax figure work, and now is a designer for Disney. I kept working in film and TV. I got into the make-up union on *Hellboy 2* (I got nominated for an Academy Award for the work on that show), and I currently do the on-set prosthetic work on *Grey's Anatomy*.

I look back on *Creepozoids*, and I have warm memories of working on it. We were young, and really passionate, and we were our own bosses for the first time! And we had something to prove, to other people and to ourselves, that we had it going on, that we could do something cool and different...

## Ken Abraham
### ("Butch")

*Creepozoids* was my first film. The only other thing I had done professionally up until that point was playing a car thief on a bad TV show called *Superior Court*. The audition for *Creepozoids* wasn't even mine. It was my friend Billy Frank's, who later appeared with me in *Vampire Knights*, *Hobgoblins*, *Deadly Reactor* and *Dead End City* [they were all shot in 1988/1989]. Back then we were trying to bill ourselves as the "Hope & Crosby of the horror world." Since I was there to support my buddy at the audition, Dave DeCoteau asked me to read for the part of Butch Minnelli. Whaddya know, I landed the part.

*Creepozoids* was an ultra-low budget film shot in a warehouse in Culver City, with some exteriors downtown LA. There's one scene during the opening montage of the movie that was shot downtown on the bridge over the LA River. For anyone not familiar with LA, the LA River is nothing more than a bed of concrete that carries rainwater away—and it barely rains in LA—meaning this thing was dry as a bone. The cast members were asked to walk on the OUTER ledge of the bridge—no railing, no safety net, just 40–50 ft. straight down to solid concrete. And to make matters worse there was a huge pillar jutting out that the cast had to cling their backs to in order to get around the column. Not me. No fucking way.

I'm afraid of heights and there was no way I was stepping out on that ledge. For a low-budget, 50-dollar a day B-movie? You kiddin' me? Fuck that. I freaked out. Literally. I started panicking and cursing and losing it completely. The DP Thom Callaway had to talk me down. "Ken, you don't have to do it. Chill. You don't have to do it!" I didn't do it. That's why in the scene it's shot as if I've already crossed the bridge and I'm giving a "C'mon, let's go!" to everybody else, as if they're holding me up. Truth be told, I was terrified. That scene's only about a second long and as mentioned is in the opening montage. It's a shame you can't appreciate how dangerously high up everyone was because of the poor angle it was filmed. I would have died had I attempted it.

Dave DeCouteau directed the film but credited himself as "Ellen Cabot." After our first read-through as a cast, Dave asked me to stay behind when everyone had left. It was my first movie role and I was nervous. Wanting to please, I asked Dave how he felt the reading went. To my chagrin Dave said he felt zero chemistry between me and Linnea Quigley—which is hard to believe considering I was in love with her…—and he was actually kind of harsh about it. In hindsight, it seems to me that he was the kind of guy that wanted to keep you on your toes by shaking you up a little—likes to fuck with your head…. So, after he tells me he doesn't feel the chemistry he blows my mind by asking if I had jerked off to Linnea yet. I had auditioned a bunch by this point but had never had anyone ask me about masturbation before. I was more stunned than I was creeped out—and I was creeped out. "Um … no." I answered, which was the truth. I mean, I had only just met her at this point. I had no idea she was a scream queen. I just knew she was this really amazing, beautiful girl. Petite, sexy, you name it. I was in awe of her. But had I beat off to her? No. I hadn't.

Making me feel even more insecure by my answer Dave prodded me further (no pun intended). He asked, "Well what do you jerk off to? You can tell me: I jerk off 4–5 times a day myself." It was awkward, especially for a newbie just starting out. I never did answer those questions. But it did the trick; he intimidated me from the get-go.

As for his directing style, it was fast and to the point. Film was expensive back then and there was no time for take after take after take. In fact, that's why so many of those B-movies from the 80s were so bad … they just didn't have the budget for multiple takes. I mean once in a while, yeah, but for the most part we raced through scenes. I think only having one take is a legitimate or at least believable excuse for bad acting or bad filmmaking. For instance if you took Robert De Niro and made a movie in which he only had one take of everything—it'd probably be his worst movie. OK, bad example, he'd probably still be brilliant—but my point is in these days of digital filmmaking when you can afford the luxury of take after take after take then there's really no excuse to deliver a poor scene or bad performance. Just do it until you get it right. Not back then. One take, Jack.

Let me elaborate with the most embarrassing scene of my career: the *Creepozoids* shower scene. This nude kissing scene was shot in one take and it's arguably the worst screen kiss ever. On action Linnea started making out with me, I mean she went for it tongue and all—god bless her!—but I wasn't ready for it and started countering the maneuver by making out right back at her. It was horrific, our faces were fighting each other like two dogs slobbering over a bone. Gross.

If I could go back in time I'd yell, "CUT! Hang on a second here. Linnea, I'll lean in and start to kiss you, and we'll start real slow and ease into it. OK?" Note to aspiring filmmakers, actors, or whoever gives a damn: screen kisses should not involve tongue. It's vile. You've been warned. But no, instead we heard. "Moving on!" Ugh. Other than that horrible, abomination of a kiss the shower scene was pretty intense. As Linnea can probably attest I did many, many, many pushups gearing up for that scene. Linnea loved pranking me and would say, "They need us on the set!" and I'd hit the floor and pound out pushups, only to hear her say, "Just kidding!"

Instead of soap we used shaving cream because it looks more sudsy on camera. The shower, located in a dank warehouse, was nothing more than piping and a shower head standing in the middle of a kiddie pool. Right beside it off camera was a guy on a ladder pouring water down the pipe so it would spray out of the shower head. Not very romantic. As we were setting camera I had to drop my robe and stand facing Linnea (and a crew of people) completely naked. It was nerve wracking. The direction Dave gave me was to run my hand down the small of her back through the sudsy shaving cream, cup Linnea's absolutely amazing bottom and continue to run my hand along her outer thigh to her knee. That was ridiculously hot. I had to start counting ceiling lights to take my mind off things. Talk about getting a swelled head in Hollywood…

Linnea was the kindest, most genuine actor I'd have ever met. For someone who was so smart, sexy and funny, she was extremely down to earth. I was such a goober, like a stupid wide-eyed puppy around her. As mentioned *Creepozoids* was my first film and I was super nervous. She made me feel so at ease, and she teased me a lot. I remember one scene in which we were eating yams and I hate them heartily. I ate them during my scenes, during other people's scenes, during other people's close-ups, I just pounded these yams. Linnea let me eat them until I was nearly sick before finally cluing me in. Don't eat unless the camera is on you, period. She laughed. In fact, as a parting gift when the movie was over Linnea gave me a can of yams autographed by the cast. She was awesome.

I remember working with Richard Hawkins. He was funny and we goofed around a lot, but it seemed that David hated him. I don't know why, I just know he did.

One scene in *Creepozoids* stands out in my memory because of the circumstances with the mechanical rat. Basically, it didn't work. We had effects guys on that movie that created this mechanical rat that had like 22 different moving parts to it. It could snarl, sneer, wiggle it's ears, all kinds of stuff. Then of course they had a cheesy foam rubber one that served as a stand-in to set up camera. Well just like in the movie *Ed Wood* when they couldn't get the mechanical octopus to work and Martin Landau is reduced to having to flail around with a lifeless dummy octopus, they couldn't get the mechanical rat to work on *Creepozoids*, and I was told by a frustrated David DeCoteau to just pick up the dummy rat, hold it against my arm and scream. That's exactly what I did. Try it sometime. Pick up a stuffed animal, hold it to your arm and scream. That was me in *Creepozoids*.

## Michael Aranda
### ("Jesse")

In 1985, I had finished a play in San Francisco (my home town) and left for Los Angeles to study with Stella Adler who opened a conservatory on Hollywood Blvd. I had worked in Los Angeles before working in a variety of musical theater productions in Southern California as well as films (small background parts in some of the teen films of the 80s: *Back to the Future, Teen Wolf, Secret Admirer, Soul Man, Fright Night, St. Elmo's Fire*, etc.).

I replied to a casting breakdown for *Creepozoids* and about a week later got called in for a read. As it turned out the casting office was walking distance from my acting studio—just off Hollywood Blvd. I met with Dave DeCoteau. I remember thinking how young he was, not more than a few years older than me. The audition was unique in that it was very informal. We talked about subjects not correlated to the film or acting; then he told me a little bit about the film; then had me read briefly from a script of another film. To this day I think this was and is the best way for an actor to audition for film—very spontaneous. I do not like auditioning or cold reading. I find that process very stiff and non organic.

I remember getting together with Richard Hawkins to rehearse the script a few days before the shoot. As it turned out the three of us—myself, Kim [McKamy] and Richard—lived about a quarter of a mile from each other in Pasadena.... Funny we never saw or bumped into each other after the film despite our close proximity to each other. I was impressed with Kim. I thought she was a good actress. I felt working with her would be working at a high acting level. Richard was very focused and intense. Linnea Quigley was full of life, very nice and energetic and so pretty. I was aware of her work and knew she was a B-movie queen on the rise. And Ken Abraham "was" Butch, nice man. I remember him giving me business advice (on becoming a lawyer instead of an actor). He was no-nonsense and realistic about the biz and he would talk to me about it at breaks in the shoot.

Funny note: the shower scene with Ken and Linnea, is my voice overdubbing Butch. I am the moaning coming out of Butch. Ken was not available so Dave called me one day. A month after the shoot to moan for Butch. I had a difficult time doing the overdub. I found it kind of silly standing in a room alone with headphones moaning into a microphone while watching the nude shower scene.

The whole film shoot took about two weeks. The process was very quick, most of the scenes were one take—no rehearsing. I recall the scene where I die at the breakfast table took more than one take. I had a mouth full of corn syrup and black food coloring that I had to hold in then exploded it out as I writhed in pain. For some reason Dave shot it more than once—and I believe I went through more than one t-shirt that day. All in all it was a great experience shooting *Creepozoids*. I got a big kick when it opened theatrically in Los Angeles and surrounding suburbs.

Since *Creepozoids* I have worked in TV and film. I left acting for a bit to complete a BA in psychology. I returned a few years later to acting (stage, TV and film work). My last project was playing Norman Reedus' (*The Walking Dead* fame) brother in an independent feature, *Leave Bad Enough Alone* [2008]. I am an abstract artist in Los Angeles and Long Beach and have done many shows for charity alone and with other artists. I enjoy painting very much and find it much more relaxing and satisfying than acting. I have a great passion for travel and have seen much of the world…

## Richard Hawkins
### ("Jake")

*Creepozoids* was my first time in front of a camera in a principal role. I had attended drama school—the American Academy of Dramatic Arts—and was working with a writers developmental group in Los Angeles called First Stage where I performed staged readings (on our feet, fully blocked and with the book in hand), of newly, unpublished plays. My background was in theatre.

I had answered a casting notice—sent my picture and resume—from an industry paper called *Dramalogue*. I was called in to audition. I think the director called me back two or three times and on the last time told me he had cast me in the role.

Other than it was a very fast shoot and that it was great fun working with everyone, one moment stands out in memory. In one scene I was directed to shoot the monster with a powerful rifle, special effects of the rifle fire to be added in post-production. We rehearsed the blocking a couple of times and the blocking and action of shooting the monster felt a lot like when I was a little kid playing "army soldier" shooting at an invisible enemy. When the director said, "Action," I launched into my blocking, pointing my weapon at the monster while making the "brrrrrrrrrrrrrp" sound of the rifle firing just as I had done as a kid playing "army soldier." The director yelled, "CUT," turned to me and very calmly said, "That was good, but this time, don't make the 'brrrrrrrrrrrrrrrrrp' sound with your mouth—we can see you doing it on film." Everyone laughed including me. Such is life.

# *Deadly Intruder*
## (1984, U.S.A.)

*Genre:* Horror; *Director:* John McCauley; *Writer:* Tony Crupi; *Cinematographer:* Thomas Jewett; *Editor:* Bruce R. Cook; *Special Makeup Effects:* Roger Kelton; *Producer:* Bruce R. Cook; *Co-Producer:* Tony Crupi; *Executive Producer:* John McCauley as "John Walton"; *Production Company:* Channel One Productions; *Cast:* Stuart Whitman (Capt. Pritchett), Chris Holder (Bob), Molly Cheek (Jessie), Tony Crupi (Drifter), Danny Bonaduce (John) and Laura Melton (Amy)

A girl makes the acquaintance of a new guy at a dinner party and starts going out with him. At the same time the young girl starts being troubled by a drifter just arrived in the small city. The sheriff and the police investigate a series of brutal murders that started after the escape of a psychopath from a mental institution. The girl is frightened as that drifter could well be the mad murderer responsible for the crimes, or maybe not: thinking about it, also her boyfriend is a complete stranger.

## John McCauley
### (Director/Executive Producer)

[Author's note: Do you remember *Rattlers*? After the effort it took to find John McCauley, it would have been a crime to interview him only on *Deadly Intruder*, neglecting his first film as director. I also asked him why he left the movie business altogether.]

The story of how I became involved with *Rattlers* [1976] and *Deadly Intruder* is interesting, and while I never became successful like others I worked around during that cult era like James Cameron, I did make some money, learned a lot, worked many 20-hour days and enjoyed the ride.

Like anything in life, being at the right place at the right time and knowing the right people is critical. I was painting and remodeling houses when someone noticed that I had a good ability with a camera and asked if I could load film in a motion picture camera that weekend. They were shooting what was called "nudie" films where there was no plot, but lots of young girls running around bare breasted. I loaded a lot of film and watched a lot of jiggling young breasts. I quickly learned how to operate the camera and one day when the operator went off on another job suddenly that became mine. It was certainly better than painting houses, where there were never bare breasts to be seen. In the next few years the nudie films began evolving into porn as the laws changed. Suddenly I was turning into one of the guys of the crew shown in the film *Boogie Nights* (I actually had to walk out of the film in the theater because it took me back to those creepy days with sleazy producers).

I forget what year the famous American Woodstock Festival was held, but I turned down a job offer to work on that because I was making more money shooting porn.

I also shot commercials, short films or whatever else legitimate work showed up, and a reel of these got me a fellowship to the American Film Institute. It started in the Doheny Mansion above Sunset Boulevard in Los Angeles, an old oil money estate part of which is shown in the film *The Big Lebowski*. Of course in its early days there was really no organization, but people like Gregory Peck or John Cassavetes could be seen wandering down its marbled halls. This was about 1971, before I even did *Rattlers*. Looking back, this was a great opportunity for me but not having a hustling personality I didn't take advantage of it. John Cassavetes was making quality low-budget dramatic films and editing there at the time. Of course, looking back I should have asked Cassavetes if he needed someone to sweep the floors or some way to enter Hollywood properly. I would hang around there in my spare time trying to hook into some project, but there seemed to be mostly talk of movies and people like Franz Kafka who I had never heard of since I never went to film school like most of the people there. After five or six months I stopped hanging out there and continued shooting whatever paid the bills which usually involved naked people with dirty feet. Since porn actors (can I really call them actors?) don't wear clothes or shoes, their feet are always dirty but the only ones who see it are the crew members. I had an Eclair 16mm camera and tried to keep it working—commercials, student films, etc.

At the time another way to make more legitimate films was what was called "B" movies, which were low-budget films that played second bill to studio features or in drive-in theaters that were popular at the time with young people. Mostly these were horror genre where a young girl would always for some stupid reason wander into the darkened basement where a killer lurked. I wrote a script following the genre more along the lines of a monster film like *The Blob*. I took the idea from a true story where a scientist in South America had discovered honeybees crossed with an aggressive African strain that turned them into a deadly variety. The script was called "Killer Bees." I dropped it off to the porn and low-budget producers I knew of, but didn't really get any bites, probably because the dialogue was so bad. Later, when I wrote *Rattlers*, also with pretty awful dialogue, someone at the distributor gave the writer's credit to the script supervisor [Gerry Golding], which in retrospect was fine with me.

The story for *Rattlers* was stitched together out of true stories about some kids killed when they stumbled into a den of snakes, a water skier killed by water moccasins, and a lady who ended up with a snake in her bathtub. One of the porn producers who also did B movies bit on this one and I got to direct it. The budget was $50,000, and it was shot in a week in the desert close to LA. We shot in a ranch house and had a snake handler managing rattlesnakes and the diamondback water snakes used around the people. Oddly, we ended up leaving there with more rattlesnakes than the trainer brought. There were no script revisions, storyboards, or even new film stock since we shot on leftover rolls the studios turned in to some guy in Burbank for a fraction of the cost. I knew two things about directing: you say "action" and "cut." Between these two words lies a movie, and Clint Eastwood who now doesn't even use these words creates masterpieces. I created shit, but it made the porn guys a lot of money and they were happy.

I wrote some other bad scripts until I realized they were bad scripts and decided to look for real writers. A science fiction book called "Close Encounters of the Third Kind" told supposedly true stories about farmers and others who had come into contact with aliens. This lent itself to low budget production and I pitched it to the producers. They were interested, but when I contacted the writer, he said he was in negotiation with the young filmmaker named Steven Spielberg about doing a film from that book. Of course Spielberg later did a film with that name but nothing in the film was out of the book. I actually took my resume into Spielberg's Amblin Entertainment on the back side of the Universal lot, but ended up being rejected because I was a B-movie maker, which seemed to be my destiny. Later I read that Spielberg surrounded himself with film school graduates because he never went to film school himself. Although I was making more money now on film projects, I still didn't take it too seriously and kept my feet on the ground remodeling houses in LA. I think it was Mick Fleetwood or some musician grounded in reality that said "Don't quit your day job." And yes, even though I was tired of looking at those dirty feet, I still shot porn. The people in them and the crew were not bad people, but the producers were exploitive, interested only in money, and generally not nice people you would hang around.

At this time, I had an agent who would pitch things to the studios and other places, but I didn't realize he had a woman and a cocaine problem that kept a few deals from happening. As I got closer to the studios with deals I learned how important politics and lawyers were. The producer of the classic film *Halloween* stopped me at the door before the pitch meeting at Orion Pictures to ask me again what the bottom line budget was. Suddenly inside the room the budget notched up by $300,000, which obviously was going into his pocket for doing virtually nothing and getting a credit for producer or co-producer. I read a lot of scripts, but only ones that could be made on a low budget. I had one deal at the table of a producer named Bruce Cohn Curtis who was related to Harry Cohn, the founder of Columbia Pictures. He made decent films with bigger budgets and somewhat "name" stars so I thought I was getting closer to what I really wanted to do. This deal ended when Bruce suggested one of his writers do a rewrite on the script. The screenwriter was a first time young writer who I told before the meeting, "Keep your mouth shut and just take the check to the bank." Of course he opened his mouth when Bruce mentioned a rewrite and the meeting ended up with the two of them insulting their mothers. In Hollywood, like in life you can't lament over the deals gone south or when someone steals something out of your screenplay, cheats you out of money or reneges on something they promised. You just say one word: next.

I felt I had reached the low point one day when I drove into Rogers Corman's lot near the beach in Venice with the script called "The Prison Women of Theta Planet." To get to his office, which was the size of most people's bathroom, you had to wander through props and set pieces from some of his old films, like *Little Shop of Horrors* (the story I heard is he made it because weather rained out another film and he had actors, a crew and film). That little film went on to become a Broadway play and then a major studio film He was pacing around in his office thinking of something and I left the film script on the desk, hoping we he would call me back excitedly because I had written it with his production efficiency in mind. The spaceship set was already on the lot and the actresses had been used in his other films and were available for almost no money. To many people, Roger may have seemed like a crazy man and his studio looked more like a junkyard compared to Warner Bros. or Paramount, but I don't think he ever lost money on a film. There's probably no other film producer in history that can say that. He kept his budgets low because that kept the risk low. He knew what even a bad film would yield at the drive-in circuit, subtracted the advertising and distribution costs and kept his budgets well below that figure. At the time he was making 90-minute features about space or women in prison, so I figured he'd go for the prison women in a spaceship concept. Either he was on to the next concept, didn't like the idea, or the script got lost as they often did even when I gave them to my agent. Roger could have been a Spielberg, but somehow had an addiction to making either low-risk profits or B movies, because after making hundreds of films, [in 2012] he made a larger budget picture it was called *Attack of the 50 Foot Cheerleader* (we have to love Roger but I don't think that's a title Spielberg will be using).

Making movies is 10% art and 90% business and Hollywood is run by lawyers and accountants. Most don't have a clue what makes a good film but are trying to copy what made money last week. I had to write or find stories that fit a safe market for film producers and distributors. They normally know they can make their money back from video sales if the budget is low enough and production quality high enough. Tony Crupi wrote the *Deadly Intruder* script that fit this format. What I liked about the script is that all suspicion was thrown onto the outcast character played by Crupi, rather than the good-looking Chris Holder. *Deadly Intruder* begins with an escaped from a mental institution and murders in a community apparently committed by the escaped.

I did get a deal to make *Deadly Intruder* and the distributor knew they would make their money back just off the foreign market. One year at the Cannes Film Festival I got to see where the money actually came from. As buyers from different countries came through the distributor's fancy hotel suite in Cannes, a check mark was placed next to each country committed to buy the film. When enough money was committed to produce the low-budget film, it was a go. I also learned about backend deals that would cheat me out of my percentage by lowering the apparent income of the film. They would take prints and sell them to smaller countries off the records or trade for art or lavish vacations they or their families could use. These guys probably taught the Enron executives how to do business.

*Deadly Intruder* was shot in the Los Angeles area in about 10 days on a budget of about $150,000. This means shooting about 10 pages a day, a far faster pace than most films so you only get a chance to do one or two takes with the actors. I knew I wasn't making great films or even good films, but the B movie world was a perfect gym for building filmmaking muscles until I could find a real story and a real director. Making films on a low budget is grueling work often with 14+ hour days and if you're the director a couple hours after that going to the lab to check your dailies. We had to bail Danny Bonaduce out of jail on a cocaine bust so we could keep shooting. He trained for many years in martial arts and was very helpful in choreographing action scenes.

Why we chose Stuart Whitman is an interesting story. Being a very low budget film all actors had to work for scale (which was at the time about €100 a day or less). The distributor always wants you to have a recognizable name and we had chosen Christopher George [1931–1983], an aging handsome actor with a gravelly voice who starred for several years in a popular action show called Rat Patrol. A week or so before we began shooting I got a call from his agent saying there was a problem. On these low-budget shoots you always arrange your schedule as much as possible around the most expensive item which in this case would be our sheriff played by Christopher George. He only had a day or two of work and didn't feel we need to rehearse or even meet him, as long as he showed up for filming. In Hollywood there are hundreds of jokes about how heartless lawyers and agents are, but when the agent told me matter-of-factly that Christopher had died, I was shocked. Even though I never met the man I had far more grief than the agent he had probably had for many years. I also realized that we needed a sheriff, and soon.

There is of course, a long list of aging somewhat handsome actors with a gravelly voice and recognizable name. Stuart Whitman was one of those former leading men whose phone was not ringing as often for parts as it used to, so he agreed to the salary and he was our new sheriff. One thing I would advise new filmmakers, or any filmmaker is to do your homework. You will more likely find most actors in a bar than in a church, but once Stuart showed up slurring his words a bit I got a little worried. I had heard stories about actors like Jan Michael Vincent where the crew had to prop him up for filming, but Stuart seemed quite functional. His part was not going to ever be considered for an Academy Award, so I asked him if he had his dialogue down, and he replied in his deep gravelly voice, "No problem." Like many actors he veered from the script here and there, but after a take or two from two different angles I felt we had all we needed and he went home … or back to the bar. I'm sure there are many stranger casting stories than this, but to me every day of making a low budget film is a great adventure.

Low-budget films are like boot camp for everyone involved because you work long hours but learn a tremendous amount. You know at the end of your work there will be no Academy Award for you, but if you do your best there may be another job. When *Deadly Intruder* was screened, it looked very jumpy and the actors and crew in the audience were all turning to look at me to see what happened. I found out that the producer who oversaw the editing had left off the beginning and end of each scene which I call "breathing room." Without that a door closes and suddenly the person jumps out of the next scene, but if you linger on the door a second it makes a smoother transition. I had to go back into all the scenes and physically edit in a few feet of beginning and ends to the scenes to make the film flow smoothly. This took some time but it helped me understand editing better, which is an under-appreciated craft in filmmaking. There was no editing software like we have today but rather a clunky upright machine called a Movieola that sounded like a machine gun as it fed 35mm film and soundtrack through its gates which often jammed and broke the film.

After *Deadly Intruder* was done I had to go back and have meetings with producers trying to do my next film. This takes far more time than actually the film itself. I had to walk away from one project that was to be shot in Mexico. The producers were trying to cut the budget for stunt coordinating so they could put more money in their pockets. I told them someone was going to die on the film and I didn't want to be involved. In 1986 the tax laws were changed restricting what investors could write off of their taxes. This completely changed the film industry and most budgets began to come from Wall Street partnership ventures with large budgets and big stars. This made small pictures harder to finance and get distribution for.

While I realized I was not a great film director, I was getting a reputation as a guy who could shoot a lot of pages in a day. I had an offer to move to Vancouver, Canada, and become a union director there. It was like going back into a time warp where there were no sleazy producers, backstabbing agents and attorneys and someone's word was their bond.

The average productions were only shooting two or three pages a day and my average was now about 12. Because Vancouver has weather like Seattle where it's often overcast and you don't have to light exteriors to match the blazing LA's sun, I figured I could get my pages per day up to about 17. While friends applauded me for leaving LA with its smog, cocaine addiction and attitude, I was not welcomed by the members of the Directors Guild in Vancouver. There was not that much work and they didn't want some hotshot LA guy taking their gigs so they complained to the president and put a huge crimp in my access to jobs. Meanwhile, my wife who always wore shorts in LA was going crazy from lack of sunshine and started drinking heavily.

I got a call from Sandy Climan, who for some reason liked my work in LA and offered me a job producing at a new studio they were starting. When he asked me where this new area code was I told them I had moved to Vancouver and at that point was sorry I did because I had to turn down the job. First the wife left, and eventually I returned to LA to shoot another $50,000 film called *Dirty Business* [1986] that was distributed in Europe and I haven't seen here in the U.S.

I came across a stylish action script called "Black Cat Run" written by a man named Frank Darabont who knew more about the writings of Stephen King than probably even Stephen King. His script was basically a chase across the desert with little dialog, and lent itself well to my low-budget format. I found it had been optioned by Freddie Fields, a producer at MGM. Looking back I should have called Mr. Fields up and said, "Hey I'm a director and I can shoot a dozen pages a day, so let's go make this movie." Instead, I gave up on it and looked for another script. The writer, Frank, went on to write and direct *The Shawshank Redemption*, one of my favorite films.

The movie business is very stressful and you don't sleep well or eat properly. Like many American men in their 40s, I had a heart attack. It wasn't a major one, but to me it was a wake-up call to get out of this crazy business. I began to read books about health, changed my diet and decided to have a less stressful life. As a kid I worked on a farm, did construction, painting and window cleaning. I began to fix up homes that were run down, making them look like new homes, making good money without having to deal with lawyers or accountants. This market did very well for the next 20 years until it finally crashed in the U.S. in 2009 with many people actually losing their homes. I ended up being one of those people. Going back to where I started as a kid I picked up a paintbrush and squeegee returning to painting and window cleaning.

**A recent photograph of John McCauley (Director/Executive Producer) (courtesy of John McCauley).**

To many people this may sound like a sad story going from movie director to window washer, but all those years I was doing physical work I listened to hundreds of audio health books and learned to reverse my heart disease. I went back to school and got a master's degree in nutrition since three out of four Americans are overweight or obese and heading towards heart disease and diabetes at a rapid rate. This is breaking the American healthcare system and it will soon collapse. I'm now 71 years old and my high cholesterol and blood pressure are now at teenage levels. I don't need medications and don't suffer any aches or pains, so life is good. I train three days a week at a boxing gym, and although sparring with 20-year-olds may not sound like the healthiest thing, it's a great workout and a lot of fun. If I were still working in Hollywood under all that stress eating what I ate I would probably be dead now rather than stronger than I used to be.

I never went to film school, but at our fingertips are hundreds of writers, actors and directors doing commentaries that give us valuable information about the art of moviemaking. I feel like a minor league baseball player who came within inches of getting into the major leagues. Although I never got to the big stadium, at least I got to play the game and still have a pretty good arm. I don't have a lot of money but along the way I've learned the secrets of good health and also gathered a few stories that would make those inspiring movies I always wanted to make. My story shows that anyone can make a film and even though I don't count on another movie deal, it is still possible, and I actually have the rights to a great story but don't want to write or direct myself. I'm older now but, we are not at the end titles yet.

## Chris Holder
### ("Bob")

*Deadly Intruder* was the first leading film role I had done to that point, but not the first [role I ever had]. I had done some supporting roles in films, and was starring in the American soap-opera *The Young and the Restless* when *Deadly Intruder* was shot. I went on to star in three other "soaps" (*The Edge of Night, Another World* and *All My Children*), as well as other films and TV series. In 1993 I started teaching acting at the Ivana Chubbuck Studio, which I still do today.

One of the most interesting and challenging things about playing the "psychopath" in *Deadly Intruder*, was that he needed to seem quite likeable and genuine. The women in the audience needed to think, "hmm, I'd like to meet a guy like that!" Right up until they realized that he was actually too good to be true, and in fact, very dangerous.

I auditioned for John [McCauley], Bruce [the film's producer/editor Bruce R. Cook], and Tony [Crupi], along with many other young actors, and was awarded the part. Most of my scenes were with Molly Cheek and Danny Bonaduce. I met Stuart Whitman briefly and that was fun. All in all I'd say the shoot went smoothly. I got along, and worked well with Molly and Danny. It was clear that Danny had some substance abuse problems going on, but as I remember, when it was time to work, he was ready to go. Molly was cute and fun, making it easy to develop some chemistry with her. Of course, my character tries to kill hers later on, so that put a damper on the romantic vibe they had.

The movie was mostly shot at night and over the weekend so I was able to keep my

*The Young and the Restless* schedule. Which was a good thing as none of the actors were getting paid much, me included. But we were treated and fed well so a nice experience all in all.

John and I got along fairly well. He allowed the actors some freedom with the dialogue, which helps the actors interact in a more relaxed and believable way. He was an easygoing type of guy who listened and was open to suggestion. He knew what he wanted and that he wasn't making an "Oscar" contender, so that kept things pleasant.

*Deadly Intruder* was a direct to video release. But there was a "premiere" of sorts at a theatre in Westwood, a trendy area next to UCLA. Everyone showed up and we were all excited to see the movie! However, we didn't know then that the editing wasn't fully completed. When the scene came up where my character, having just thrown Danny Bonaduce's character through the television set, was supposed to have memory flashbacks to when he actually killed all those people, but they had not yet, nor am I certain ever were, edited into the film. So there I/he was, crazily snapping my head back and forth "remembering" his murderous deeds for all to see … minus the deeds. Although it was an embarrassing moment for me at the time, it's something that probably adds to the cult film "humor factor" now.

When we had finished shooting *Deadly Intruder*, and especially after the screening, I doubt that any of the cast or crew thought that the film would achieve the sort of horror film cult status it has.

When I lived in New York working on *All My Children*, I went into a video store, yes … an actual video store, not only to find the movie's poster prominently displayed, which I bought and still have, but the movie was playing at that very moment on the store's monitors. I distinctly remember thinking to myself … "Well I'll be damned!"

# *Death House*
## (1987, U.S.A.)

*Genre:* Horror; *Director:* John Saxon; *Writers:* Devin Frazer, William Selby and Devorah Cutler-Rubenstein as "Kate Wittcomb"; *Cinematographer:* John V. Fante; *Editor:* Fred Roth; *Special Makeup Effects:* John Goodwin & Ron Wilson; *Special Effects:* Richard Zarro; *Producer:* Nicholas M. DeMartino as "Nick Marino"; *Associate Producer:* Nancy Paloian; *Executive Producers:* Salvatore Richichi, Marty Mazza and Barry Gottheimer; *Production Company:* Nick Marino Presents; *Cast:* Dennis Cole (Derek Keillor), John Saxon (Colonel Gordon Burgess), Tane McClure (Dr. Tanya Kerrington), Michael Pataki (Franco Moretti), Anthony Franciosa (Vic Moretti), Ron O'Neal (Tom Boyle), Howard George (Head Guard Raker), Alex Courtney (Warden Hagen), Eric Foster (Luke Hagen), Newell Tarrant (Dr. Chaney) and Rickey Pardon (Hector Morales)

    The CIA secretly carries out non-authorized studies on a genetically modified virus using prison convicts as guinea pigs. The convicts who volunteer obtain privileges and commutation of their sentences. The experimentation doesn't have the desired results and the convicts who tested the virus become cannibal zombies. The prison is quarantined and the young female doctor, who had worked on the tests, is called upon with the hope she can save the situation. A man who was a driver for a mafia boss, unjustly convicted for the murder of his boss' lover and free from the infection, helps the doctor in facing the hordes of hungry zombies.

## Devin Frazer
## (Writer)

    Before *Death House*, I was freelancing as a script consultant. One person who used to utilize my services now and again was a producer named David Permut. David has had a very long and successful career in Hollywood. While I didn't know him well, I never saw him be anything less than warm, upbeat, and generous. He probably smiled more than any other producer I've ever met.
    David was acquainted with Nick Marino. Knowing I had written a few scripts, he made the introduction (this was before I had anything bought by a studio). Nick hired me, and I brought in William Selby, a friend, to co-write. William is what people call an "old soul." There was a warm wisdom about him. I was ambivalent about working on a super low-budget horror film, but I was aware that more than a few Hollywood writers and directors started in that genre, so I thought, why not give it a go?
    Nick was a colorful character, to say the least. He was big, fun, opinionated, had a

strong NY accent, and I could see central casting typecasting him as a friendly mobster. He wasn't in the mob—he just had a bit of that aura, if, that is, the mob was a fun group of guys. He always seemed to have a few very pretty young girls crashing at his house.

Although William and I wrote the first draft of the script, later Nick completely rewrote parts of it, and he brought in "Kate Wittcomb" [Devorah Cutler-Rubenstein] who rewrote the rest under Nick's guidance. None of my original material was left over. I didn't agree with the directions Nick took it, but no writer likes to be rewritten—and it happens with the majority of scripts in Hollywood (it's just part of the business). But, believe it or not, I wasn't upset. It wasn't the kind of project I had my heart in, although I had done my best. And Nick had lived up to his contract with me and had always been straightforward. So, no complaints.

I visited one of the sets in Los Angeles, and there I had a sad experience. I learned that the lead actor was Dennis Cole [1940–2009]. I had met Dennis a few times, several years earlier. At the time, he was a very prominent soap actor, and had been for many years. With stunning good looks, a great smile, and a love of his craft, it's easy to see why. Although he was quite famous (in the soap opera world) and very successful, you'd never know it because he was always quite humble, and treated everyone as an equal. He was a truly likable guy. But to see him in this horror film, with its tiny budget, made me worry about his career. I was embarrassed for him, knowing of his past successes.

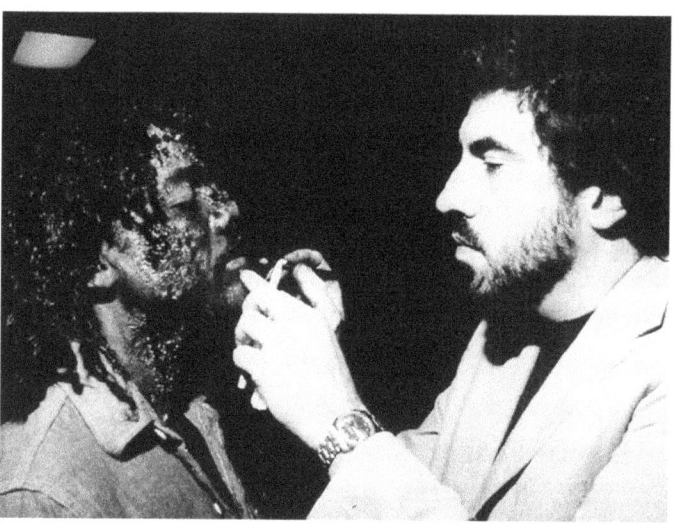

**John Goodwin (Special Makeup Effects) touches up one of his zombie creations for** *Death House* **(courtesy of John Goodwin).**

As far as I know, *Death House* was never released in cinemas. I never saw Nick nor Dennis again after that. Nor did I ever see the final film: since nothing I wrote remained in the script, I had no particular interest in it. William went on to write a wonderful script, that was unfortunately stolen by New Line Cinema. They made some changes and released it under the title *Frequency*. *Frequency* [2000, Gregory Hoblit] doesn't bear William's name, but I heard New Line ended up paying him a pile of cash to compensate him for the theft.

## William Selby
### (Writer)

I was an illustrator for many years, mainly advertising, but also painted covers for *Famous Monsters of Filmland* and *Heavy Metal* magazines (www.billselby.com). My big dream was to write for film and television, so in 1986 I moved from Ohio, where I was born and raised, to Los Angeles. I immediately took a screenwriting class at the American Film Institute and began writing spec screenplays in the horror and science fiction genre. To support myself, I took jobs doing matte painting and production design (my first screen credit was as a production designer on the remake of *The Blob*), and working in the transportation department of Hollywood Community Hospital. I spent a little over a decade trying to get several projects produced, and although I wound up either selling or optioning five screenplays, no feature films ever got the green light. I did, however write an episode of *The New Twilight Zone* that was produced in 1988, "The Hellgramite Method" starring Timothy Bottoms.

I relocated to San Francisco in 1998, where I've worked as a freelance graphic designer and writer. In 2010 I wrote and designed "Monté: King of Atom-Age Monster Decals" for Last Gasp Publishing. I've also had short stories and essays appear in numerous publications such as the 2009 Scribner's anthology "Morbid Curiosity Cures the Blues," and have written two plays which have been produced here in San Francisco, both horror plays in the grand guignol style: "The Laboratory of Hallucinations" and "Headhunters." I'm currently writing a science fiction novel about life after death.

Devorah Cutler and I were brought onto the project by Devin Frazer. Devin heard that porn producer Nick Marino wanted to make the leap from porno films to horror films, and was looking for a screenwriter who was familiar with the horror genre (like me). Devorah, Devin and I drove up to Nick Marino's house in the Pacific Palisades to meet with him. Marino—short, paunchy, balding and cocky—seemed like a typical wise-guy type from the Bronx, complete with accent and gold chain necklace. His furniture looked rented, and there were a couple of young porn "actresses" wandering around inside and outside by the pool. His "home" appeared to mainly function as a convenient place to shoot porn. I liked porn, so his setup didn't bother me at all. In fact, I sort of admired Marino for aspiring to break free from skin flicks and go legit.

I mainly remember that Marino had access to the abandoned prison in downtown LA [Lincoln Heights Jail] for 19 days and therefore needed a script in less than two weeks to take advantage of the only time the prison would be available. So, with the location already set we had to come up with a story centered around a prison. I came up with the concept of government experimentation on death row prisoners going terribly wrong. Neither Devorah, Devin or I knew much about prison life, but Marino did, and was more than happy to fill us in. We were told that John Saxon, a supposed friend of Marino's, was attached to direct (his first shot at directing) and co-star. Another of Marino's acquaintances, Anthony Franciosa [1928–2006], had also agreed to co-star. These were the only two people attached up front that we were told about.

After being given just two days to come up with a story, we were invited to John Saxon's house to pitch our idea. John Saxon was a class act all the way, very friendly, putting us at ease. He and Marino made suggestions (I recall Marino telling us we were stupid for not knowing guards don't have guns in prison). Unfortunately, I knew we were screwed when Marino insisted we had to have a secondary plot line involving the mafia (his favorite film was *The Godfather*). The story meeting lasted perhaps 3 hours. When it was over Marino said he'd pay us $10,000 for writing the script. He also told us he needed the finished script in nine days or we wouldn't get paid. This was fine with me. I'd only been in LA a year and thought it'd be a great learning experience. And what the hell, I'd already gotten to meet John Saxon.

The writing of the script was the literary equivalent of running a marathon in hell. For the first day or two, Devorah, Devin and I worked at the computer together. By the third day I requested that Devin let Devorah and I work on the script alone. Too many cooks. Devin agreed to let us do the writing, and he'd just check in periodically.

Devorah and I worked well together. By the time we hit page 60 of the script, I was doing most of the writing, and she was refining and polishing what I wrote. We managed to hit the nine-day deadline, and I wasn't thrilled with the result, but it was what it was. We called Nick Marino and told him we'd finished. Discovering that Nick had a dicey history with paying his vendors, I was afraid we wouldn't get our money, so insisted that we'd only deliver the script when we were paid with a cashier's check. Marino was furious with me, but paid us up front. He also banned me from any further involvement with the project, including no set visits. Devorah was able to eventually smooth things out with Nick, volunteering to work on the film as a production assistant. She finally finagled to allow me to visit the prison set in downtown LA on the final day of shooting. Relations were strained between Marino and myself, but we shook hands and made up after I apologized.

I recall that in the middle of writing the script Devorah and I somehow got involved in making casting suggestions. I was pushing for Clare Kirkconnell (co-star of the TV series *The Paper Chase* from 1984–1986) for the female lead, and actually delivered pages to her at her Hollywood home. Despite the questionable quality of our material, she was gracious enough to come into the *Death House* production offices the next day and read. Marino chose Tane McClure instead. Considering the gratuitous nudity added to the film in post-production, I'm grateful Clare Kirkconnell wasn't chosen. Tane McClure running naked through a field takes the prize for the most unnecessary display of nudity in horror film history.

Marino was never able to find theatrical distribution for the film as far as I know. He did, however, throw a cast and crew screening at the Director's Guild Theatre in Hollywood, followed by a party. I still have my black *Death House* T-shirt given away at the cast party, which has an illustration of the zombie chef holding his meat cleaver saying "Don't touch my Twinkies!"

I was totally surprised when the film was renamed *Zombie Death House* and released by Fred Olen Ray [Retromedia] in 2004. I tried watching it again but it's so awful that I never made it all the way to the end. To this day, I'm embarrassed by it. In fact, I've been with my wife for 15 years and only told her about it this week. I've always been grateful that I was able to "recover" from my *Death House* experience, and write a decent episode of *The Twilight Zone*.

## Devorah Cutler-Rubenstein
### (Writer)

Devin Frazer and I had been collaborating on projects, two of which were under option by Interscope, both in the fantasy genre. Devin told me about Nick Marino, we met him, along with Bill Selby. During the meeting Nick mentioned that he was looking for a director

Devorah Cutler-Rubenstein (Writer) on set doing rewrites that came up from Nick Marino and John Saxon (courtesy of Devorah Cutler-Rubenstein).

and actors to star. I brought the project to John Saxon, who was in my directing class at UCLA where we were studying with Ted Post (*Beneath the Planet of the Apes, Go Tell the Spartans, Dirty Harry*). I said, "John, you want to direct a feature, right? Here's a script and they want you to star as well. By the way, if you do this, I must be your assistant, I need the credit and experience to see how it's all done." He smiled, took a look at the script and the rest is production history. I had just completed a WGA project, and the salary Nick was offering was below scale, however he said he would make it WGA retroactively, so I signed on with the hope that would happen. I knew the experience of working with John Saxon on his first feature would empower me as a director.

*Death House* was the first politically inspired "Virus" film, which I know of. Government was messing with prisoners to create warriors and the virus mutates. The virus mutates when one of them gets electrocuted on the same weekend that a whole bunch of people are in the prison. There's a lockdown while people are becoming zombies. Some folks try to escape, most folks don't make it before the government swoops down and blows up the joint. Kind of cool conspiracy film.

The three of us came from anti-establishment 1960s–1970s rebellious "don't trust the government" mind-set. I had grown up consuming Ray Bradbury, and Bill Selby was a horror devotee. Devin and I went to the same high school and had started a number of human rights organizations to change the planet. What more inspired way to look at the big bad government using inmates to test a virus? I believe Bill had the idea, but not sure, as I had been working on a TV show about police brutality. We all were primed to do something important, even if the money sucked, the deadline was impossible and the dubious nature of who was paying our salary. I liked Nick. He was a bit gruff but charming—especially his desire to make a great film. He was a little like the director/producer from Boogie Nights. Meetings took place at an Italian restaurant on the corner of Venice Blvd. and La Cienega, which is not there anymore. It was classic old school behind the scenes. The owner of the restaurant was the principal financier of the movie.

Getting a viable composite cast of A and B players helped get the film green-lit. For instance, it was a thrill to get Tony Franciosa as the mob boss, and brother to the mob boss inside, portrayed with intensity and panache by another one of John's actor friends, Michael Pataki [1938–2010]. I believe that it was his and John's idea (not sure if we the writers came up with this) that the inside prison mob boss was portrayed as gay. Years later I met Chris Franciosa on *Never the Same: The Prisoner of War Experience* [2013], and we discussed what an amazing actor his dad was. One of the challenges with Tony was he could not memorize, so we hid his lines in loaves of bread, practicals on set and other locations. He was method and he preferred it that way.

The funniest thing was Nick was watching classics during the filming—my guess either John asked Nick to be more film literate, or Nick himself really wanted to make the best film. I only heard the story from Saxon that Nick would come to the set every morning with his morning coffee, after seeing a film like *Scarface* and say, "Could you please make it more like … (whatever film he just saw the night before)." If he had just seen *The Graduate* or *Gone with the Wind*, the direction of the film he would encourage John Saxon to go would be of the last film he saw the night before. John was polite about it all, but I have to say it was amusing as well as admirable. The script was already locked, we were in production, and the tone was set. So to mention another genre or some scene or approach … well—no comment. But it was also admirable because Nick was hands-on, and he was just kind of sweet because he was trying to make a classic. It was always Nick's intention to create a great film.

*Death House* was a great experience, and gave me confidence and set wisdom that I applied to my next television, feature and theatre experiences. I am grateful to John who included me in most of his decisions, and to Nick who gave, Bill, Devin, and myself our first shot!

## John V. Fante
### (Cinematographer)

Working with John Saxon was a great pleasure for me. He was a real gentleman and quite humble about his long and successful acting career and status as a movie star. Several times, when we were together in public, people would come up to him and say hello and ask to shake his hand or get an autograph, which he was happy to provide. On the set, he was very open to ideas and depended on me to help him visualize the script. Since he was both the director and the lead actor in the film, we developed a trust that helped both of us do our work. Ultimately, he made the decisions with the actors in how to play the scenes. Since he was a veteran actor working with other veteran actors, e.g., Anthony (Tony) Franciosa and Dennis Cole, he had a rapport with them and their respect, which was key to getting good performances.

Nick Marino (Producer) and John Saxon (Director/"Colonel Gordon Burgess") (photograph by Abe Perlstein; courtesy of Nick Marino).

There was an interesting dynamic between John Saxon and Nick Marino. Both had grown up in and around New York City and, while John Saxon had been a Hollywood star for many years, Nick had come out of the soft core porn industry to make his first legitimate feature. Saxon and several of us wondered about Nick and his New Yorker friends who would come to the set. They didn't look or sound like your typical LA film producers and on one occasion I recall, John Saxon, tried to make small talk with one of Nick's NY Italian associates, a swarthy character named Salvatore [Salvatore Richichi]. Saxon asked him if he had been in the movie business for very long. Sal replied like a character out of *The Godfather*, "not exactly," and made it clear in his body language that he didn't appreciate the interest in his background. We never asked Sal anything after that and kept our distance, but John Saxon and I shared a good laugh about it after we finished the film and said, "We dodged a bullet." Later, after we had wrapped production, Nick Marino revealed to us that when he was 13 years old he discovered that his own father was a hit man for the mafia in New York. Nick didn't elaborate, but one can only assume that Nick's circle of friends was not your typical film crowd. Despite his mysterious and colorful past, Nick was an effective producer and managed to assemble an impressive cast and crew for *Death House* and held a premiere screening of the film at the Academy of Motion Picture Arts and Science.

# *Edge of Sanity*
## (1988, U.K.)

*Genre:* Horror; *Director:* Gerard Kikoine; *Writers:* Ron Raley & Jerry Felix and Harry Alan Towers (uncredited) & Gerard Kikoine (uncredited); *Literary source: The Strange Case of Dr. Jekyll and Mr. Hyde* (novel) by Robert Louis Stevenson, 1886; *Cinematographer:* Tony Spratling; *Editor:* Malcolm Cooke; *Special Effects:* Ian Wingrove; *Producers:* Harry Alan Towers and Edward Simons; *Associate Producers:* James Swann and Maria Rohm; *Executive Producer:* Peter A. McRae; *Production companies:* Allied Vision and Hungarofilm; *Cast:* Anthony Perkins (Dr. Henry Jekyll/Jack "The Ripper" Hyde), Glynis Barber (Elisabeth Jekyll), Sarah Maur Thorp (Susannah), Ben Cole (Johnny), David Lodge (Detective Underwood), Ray Jewers (Inspector Newcomen) and Jill Medford (Madame Flora)

*Edge of Sanity* is a curious adaptation of Robert Louis Stevenson's famous novel "The Strange Case of Dr. Jekyll and Mr. Hyde," which also incorporates the almost contemporary events of Jack the Ripper. Surprisingly, what transforms the respected Dr. Jekyll into a maniac murderer of prostitutes is not the classic potion obtained thanks to crazy chemical experiments, but a mixture of ether and cocaine, discovered by Jekyll while studying a new anesthetic. The massive use of drugs aggravates the psychic balance of Jekyll, already precarious because of a childhood trauma that still haunts him: discovered while he was spying a prostitute with a client, he was punished by the man while the woman mocked him. Jekyll befriends a hustler who introduces him in a high-class brothel where he meets a prostitute with similar looks to those of the one he saw as a child and who becomes his obsession. As the blood continues to flow, Jekyll's wife and Scotland Yard start to have serious suspicions concerning the author of the crimes.

After *Edge of Sanity*, between 1988 and 1989, the producer Harry Alan Towers (1920–2009) made a series of adaptations of Edgar Allan Poe's short stories: *Buried Alive*, *The House of Usher* and *The Masque of the Red Death*, in that order. I asked Ron Raley, Jerry Felix, and Gerard Kikoine, to continue their stories after *Edge of Sanity* right up to *Buried Alive*, which was the first film of the Harry Alan Towers' Poe Cycle.

## Ron Raley
### (Writer)

I was working at Cannon Films as an executive story editor when I first met Harry Alan Towers [1920–2009]. He had several projects that were being produced and/or distributed by Cannon. In the fall of 1987 he asked me to suggest a screenwriter for a film he wanted to do with Anthony Perkins [1932–1992] based on the "Jekyll and Hyde" story. I recommended a former colleague at Cannon, Jerry Felix.

Jerry had not begun writing the script when I left the job at Cannon so I suggested that we write it together. Jerry agreed. Harry Towers and Anthony Perkins both wanted the script to be literate but sensational. Harry encouraged us to "borrow" the Jack the Ripper elements and to add the cocaine usage. Jerry and I thought it was all great fun and we dived in. We laughed a lot. I recall that we usually would write a scene by ourselves then go over and edit them together.

We knew from our experience working with Harry that he was primarily interested in the "naughty bits" and so we weren't really surprised when he brought Gerard Kikoine on as the director. Kikoine had previously directed soft core erotic films in France. I was not in Hungary for the shoot but we heard it was pretty hysterical: Kikoine didn't speak English very well, the Hungarian crew didn't speak English or French and the British cast (other than Perkins) were pretty much on their own.

I know that Harry had high hopes for the film primarily because of the Anthony Perkins name. Even though *Edge of Sanity* (I have no idea where that title came from—our early drafts were titled "Jekyll and Hyde" as I recall) didn't make much money, Harry hired Jerry and I to write *Buried Alive* based (sort of) on a story by Edgar Allan Poe. In the screen credits Poe's name is misspelled as "Edgar Allen Poe." Jerry and I decided to change our names on the credits as well ["Stuart Lee" and "Jake Clesi"]. That film's only other claim to fame is that it was the very last film that John Carradine [1906–1988] ever made. He died a few days after the shoot.

Harry then asked us to write another script for Anthony Perkins, "Dorian" based on "The Picture of Dorian Gray." We worked with Perkins more closely on that script. He said, "You fellows write a lurid script and I'll provide the lurid name to sell it." He also said, "I hope half the audience walks out saying, 'now they've gone too far!'" Sadly, Perkins died before the picture could be made. The script was re-written by someone and later produced [2003, Allan A. Goldstein] with Malcolm McDowell playing the part we wrote for Anthony Perkins. I wrote another script for Harry Towers, based on the Fu Manchu character, that was also to star Anthony Perkins but that one was never made.

Harry Alan Towers was a "character." He always wore a herringbone jacket and with his shock of white hair and polite, almost deferential manner, he reminded me of a white rabbit, popping up unexpectedly, scurrying about, always industrious and extremely easy to work with. He had a very "lurid" reputation and not just because of the sleazy films he made but in my dealings with him he was rather gentlemanly. Of course, he still did owe me money when he died.

# Jerry Felix
(Writer)

I was working as a creative development executive at Cannon Films when I first met Harry Alan Towers. I was assigned to oversee several of his projects to be sure the creative elements were as close to being production-worthy as possible for the type of genre pictures he was making. As I worked with writers and scripts for his projects, he came to trust my storytelling and story-editing instincts. After I left Cannon, Ron Raley was still working there and put forth my name as a possible writer for the "Jekyll and Hyde" film Harry was trying to put together. After Ron left Cannon, I asked him to join me as writing partner on the script.

It was what they called the "Go-go" days for awhile because it was during a phase of rampant film pre-sales (the financial "art" of paying for the film before it is made by securing contracts from distributors in various foreign territories for the right to release the film there). Harry Alan Towers seemed to be a master at putting together financing from investors in various countries who were getting tax breaks for their investments. It is something I never understood, so I cannot speak to how this was done or what exactly was done in any authoritative way. It seemed to take a person—like Harry—who knew international film financing, the players involved, and who could keep up with the ever-changing tax advantages and laws around the world.

I didn't meet Harry until I was working at Cannon. He was elderly then—or seemed so—an impish grey-haired man who would pop-up from time to time, having just slept on a plane for six hours or so. He seemed to have boundless energy. He also had a positive demeanor when dealing with film executives or creative sorts. He seemed to know every euphemism for bad filmmaking. When the draft of a script was inferior, he would say the writer had done "a yeoman-like job"; or when the final product was poor because of the directing, he would speak of "perhaps having put a misplaced trust" in the person he had hired. In-the-moment translation of his idiomatic language was not difficult. Because I got his lingo, I felt he was always direct. Sometimes he was just forthright. Working on an Italian sword-and-sandal action piece [*Warrior Queen*, 1986, Chuck Vincent], he did not mince words with the writer [Rick Marx] on what was still needed, "You know ... a little bondage, a little nookie." His directness worked to his advantage in dealing with people. His decisions and demands (as I witnessed them) were always pragmatic.

It was the late 80s when I first met Harry, and it was the very beginning of the cell phone. My most indelible images of Harry were the times he appeared after his wife had presented him with this brand new invention. Harry Towers, five-foot-something, hauling around a huge electronic black box that seemed about half his size—handles, black coils, handset and antenna protruding from all around it.

*Edge of Sanity* was Harry Towers' concept to do a mash-up of *The Strange Case of Dr. Jekyll and Mr. Hyde* with Jack the Ripper. Therefore most of the creation of the narrative became a problem-solving exercise (as it did with *Buried Alive*). Harry was quite focused on the blueprint for titillating and graphic opportunities (including the slasher scares, this still being the heyday of franchises like *A Nightmare on Elm Street* and *Halloween*). He gave us his copy of *Fanny by Gaslight* [1944, Anthony Asquith] as background for the Victorian prostitution underbelly in London. As writers without a strong draw to any of these genre aspects, we were determined to give it some more solid narrative underpinnings. My own research added digging into the "new" Freudian psychology of personality that was so shocking when it was first being published and spreading in the West. I was interested in how it seemed to be reflected in the Robert Louis Stevenson novella, although I can't remember my conclusions. Beyond that, once we had done our research, it threw ourselves into having fun with all those genre demands and seeing how effective and sharp we could make the turning points using those idioms. Another inspiration was knowing that we were writing for Tony Perkins. At this point in his career, he fully understood how he would use his persona to bring the role to life. And he was a willing player ready to dive it with full commitment. Being a true fan of his talent from his earliest (pre–*Psycho* days), I was able to hear his voice and visualize his behavioral traits and quirks both with its earlier natural expression and later engrained mannerisms—the halting speech, the darting glances, etc. He was still a master of expressive internal acting, so being able to write for him with a lot of subtext and leaving a lot unsaid was a gift. Once the plotting was concocted—and I use that word quite deliberately—we were able to construct the scenes with great relish. In several conversations with Tony, he gave us notes. I cannot remember specifically what they were, but I do remember that they were smart, character-centered concerns.

Once the script was turned in, everyone but Ron and I was off to Budapest. We never met Gerard Kikoine, but he and Harry ran with it. They did a fair amount of rewriting. Harry knew his markets, and they infused it with the enhanced erotica and heightened sensationalism that they felt would make it a theatrical and post-theatrical financial success.

On the *Edge of Sanity* set: Anthony Perkins ("Dr. Henry Jekyll"/"Jack 'the Ripper' Hyde") and Gerard Kikoine (Writer/Director) (courtesy of Gerard Kikoine).

*Buried Alive* was written fairly quickly. Again, it was Harry's concept. He was making film based on Poe works. I guess he wanted to take all the leftovers and funnel the motifs into one film. This was also a creative problem-solving exercise for Ron and me. In addition to using Poe motifs, he wanted to use the production constraint of one location. One large old house. A girl's school would provide lots of opportunities for young women in jeopardy. The idea of them being scantily clothed at times during the scenes may have played into his thinking in terms of marketing, but I don't remember that being overtly discussed. He did want a headmistress character or older female lead, which was going to provide him the opportunity to cast an older actress with marquee value. I believe that evolved into a younger woman [Karen Witter], and he began wanting to create parts for older men [Donald

Pleasence, Robert Vaughn, John Carradine] who could provide some name value for sales to international territories and video. This was intended to be shot in Canada. Both Ron and Harry were Canadian citizens. However, when we were told that the financing was going to come from South Africa and that the film was going to be shot there, Ron and I decided to use pseudonyms (because of apartheid still being the law there at that time).

## Gerard Kikoine
### (Writer/Director)

At the time, I had a production company, Gold Productions that I had created with a gentleman called Wilfrid Dodd, who was 20 years older than me. Wilfrid was a foreign distributor and knew Harry Alan Towers. We met Harry at Cannes. He was introduced to me in 1983—I had finished with porn movies and Harry said to me, "Hey, Gerard, I've seen two or three of your movies. I've got a contract at Playboy Channel for a movie called *Frank and I*. We've got an IOU from Playboy, $350.00 dollars at the delivery of the film." So Harry gave me the script but it was like climbing Mount Everest because it was set in the 1800s in England and it was also shot in the suburbs of Paris and Cabourg, a town near Deauville (Normandy). The main male actor was Chris Pearson, a Brit. *Frank and I* [1983] was his only film.

Then I shot *Dragonard* [1987] and the sequel *Master of Dragonard Hill* [1987] in Africa. It was fantastic. I had a big crew (there were 80 of us) and we had a crane—everything that I needed. We were working for Cannon Group, Menahem Golan & Yoram Globus. The movie was set in the 1700s on the islands. Oliver Reed [1938–1999] played a kind of Torquemada character. He was always drunk but we got along because I know my job. I divide my movies, which means that every sequence you see in the film is planned and this is a thing that Oliver Reed appreciated. Then I tried to enrich the technique (actors are a bit like musical virtuosi: the more complicated the score the more they enjoy themselves and are happy). Oliver and I got along fine. Lots of laughs. Sometimes we dined together, and he was a real powerhouse. The first day of shooting, Oliver arrived drunk, completely legless…. I had to take charge of the situation. He had emptied the hotel mini-bar, and had taken the mini bottles of whisky and vodka to his motorhome.

Shortly after *Dragonard* and its sequel, I was about to shoot "Treasure island" with Oliver Reed as Captain Hook, but it never happened and Harry offered me *Edge of Sanity*. Only a small part of the film was shot in England, the rest in Hungary. After reading the script, I wanted to change some things. In the original script, the main character, Dr. Jekyll [Anthony Perkins], dies and I asked if it could be the other way around: he kills his wife [Glynis Barber]. In the original script the wife was pregnant and he commits suicide. So, they told me, "Okay, he kills her, but she won't be pregnant." We agreed and the script was changed. It was a great moment with Tony Perkins. I met him the first time at his home in LA. We got along very well. Tony called me "my Dad" and I called him "my Diamond." … Then I made *Buried Alive*. It was shot in South Africa with Donald Pleasence [1919–1995], Robert Vaughn and John Carradine. They were fantastic, we got along very well. Donald Pleasence was exquisite; he spoke French, very enjoyable! John Carradine was already very sick, and Robert Vaughn was a lot less friendly compared to Oliver Reed.

Avoriaz Fantastic Film Festival 1989. Anthony Perkins ("Dr. Henry Jekyll"/"Jack the Ripper Hyde"), Gerard Kikoine's wife Kat and Gerard Kikoine (Writer/Director) (courtesy of Gerard Kikoine).

The budgets of *Edge of Sanity* and *Buried Alive* were not very big, I guess around $1-$1.5 million, at the most $2 million. The films were done in a very professional manner—for both movies we had 2 months to prep and 3 weeks to shoot. As Harry had great trust in me, I got what I asked for. Harry was very professional. It's true that he could be a bit tight and didn't let anything get out of line, but I always finished in time and within budget, so he was always happy. Harry was full of kindness, funny and loved women. He was always very protective towards me. I stayed in his apartment in London; he allowed me to prepare various movies there (like *Edge of Sanity*).

## Sarah Maur Thorp
### ("Susannah")

I was a fully trained actress, fresh from a 3 year acting degree course at a revered London drama school (I qualified at the end of my final year with "distinction"). I quickly got a good agent and started working in theatre, doing musical comedy and classical theatre, which were both strengths of mine. My training had been mainly theatre based—British drama schools in those days didn't give you much experience in film or TV. It was very much a theatre based training, as it was considered more important to understand the techniques of theatre and the demands it places upon the actor. It was considered that if you could act in the theatre you could do anything. That's a really limited vision as far as

I'm concerned, and probably why American actors/actresses are often so much more natural on film, screen work is the key to their training. Back in the '80s, "film" was almost considered a "dirty word" and unattainable, at least it was at my drama school. Ridiculous when you think how TV and film dominate today, and how the two techniques differ enormously in skill sets. Theatre is about a slightly larger than life performance in order to reach your audience, and film is more about "being" and "thinking" the character rather than acting it (the camera can almost read your thoughts). To rephrase, you really don't need to act in film: you just need to be. Whereas in theatre the skill is about reaching an immediate and physically larger audience. That was my first problem! I was never taught to "film act" properly! Which is partly why I was so embarrassingly appalling in Edge of Sanity!!!

The *Edge of Sanity* audition/screen test was my first film opportunity. I was at the time appearing in theatre in a classical comedy, "The School for Scandal" when my agent rang me to tell me I had the screen test. I was over the moon! When I got my first screen test for *Edge of Sanity* I was beside myself with excitement. I knew Anthony Perkins was in it and was absolutely star struck! Likewise, when I also found out that Glynis Barber was in it, I knew it would be a respectable and interesting film opportunity, and when I was actually offered the role, well, I felt I was "on my way." I really was thrilled. How wrong can you be? The screen test involved me and a stand-in for Anthony Perkins, opposite whom I read and played the scene. It seemed to go well, and afterwards I discovered they chose me because I was the only actress who had played the character of Susannah as a strong woman—challenging Perkins' character and attempting to fight him, rather than playing her as a victim in the scene. I think they liked my feisty approach. It was instinct on my part—I didn't really have a clue how to act on screen at that time! I understood that I would be required to do a few topless scenes which my agent and I were agreeable to: I was playing the part of Perkins' character's key "prostitute obsession," so it was understandable ... or so I thought. And if it was playing opposite Anthony Perkins, I felt convinced it must be ok. A young fresh actress didn't often get the chance to work with such an eminent, famous and respected actor.

However, I soon realized what a horrible mistake my agent had made for me! What appeared to be a strong story line soon got lost amongst frequent, freshly written scenes of a "blue," light-porn type all of which were slipped, every evening, under my hotel door for me to learn in time for shooting the next day. I was truly upset—devastated in fact—I am no prude but I had had no idea my agent had got me into what was fast turning into a "blue" movie! Some of the scenes I was asked to do—for example the nun worshipping, topless in the bordello, and a scene involving me sitting astride someone (Anthony Perkins? I genuinely can't remember as I have blocked it from my mind as much as possible, although unfortunately some of those scenes I just can't forget!) and cackling loudly, topless and with crazy hair everywhere—oh Lord, I thought they were horrific, gratuitous scenes and bore no resemblance to the film I thought I was signed up for. I was truly terrible in that film because I just didn't want to do it, and couldn't act for the camera as I was just too miserable. *Edge of Sanity* brought me a lot of embarrassment for many years after.

One might ask why I didn't go to the director Gerard Kikoine and producer Harry Alan Towers and talk to them about it? Maybe explain to them that I had thought it was to be a new and challenging version of previous Jekyll and Hyde films, not a blue porn version. Well, I did go and talk to them! But I was taken aside by H.A.T. and told in no uncertain terms that if I kicked up a fuss or refused to do any of the scenes, causing disruption for the film schedule and crew, Harry Alan Towers would personally see to it that I never worked in the film industry again! I was very young and I believed him.

I was very upset and terrified that he could so badly influence my career and end it as quickly as it had begun. I only wish I'd been braver and had stuck to my guns and refused to do it. *Edge of Sanity* was the worst thing I ever did professionally, and I was just miserable! Even Glynis Barber apparently had strong words with the producer saying she didn't want to put her name to such a film, and that it was pretty disgusting, which I like to think proves that it was not just me having tantrums over it. However, I suppose it did lead to two further films for me [*Ten Little Indians* and *River of Death*], both negotiated carefully by my agent to ensure I'd never be put in that semi-porn position again. But I still wish to this day that I had not been made to do that film, and although I find it quite funny now, it's still embarrassing for me if I know that anyone who knows me has seen it. It was not my finest hour!!! I was so deeply embarrassed by it I was unable to act it well, and it remains a blot on my memory!

I'm very honored to be able to say I have acted with the late, great Anthony Perkins. He was a true professional, and very inspiring—but he was in a very strange stage of his life. I believe he already knew he had AIDS (or at least maybe he was actively bi-sexual by then) and after first meeting me and being incredibly gentlemanly and friendly and warm towards me, he then refused to come out of his caravan or hotel room for the rest of the duration of the filming schedule, unless he was filming, or to even speak to me in case it "ruined his perception of the character of the prostitute and his relationship with her" or something like that. I was bemused and often couldn't help thinking, in the words of Sir Laurence Olivier, "Why not just try acting it, dear boy?!?"

As I said before, after our first meeting which was very friendly and enjoyable, Anthony Perkins became very aloof—deliberate on his part I think, to help him work with his character. I spoke to him very little during filming. He was not easy to work with because he wouldn't rehearse a scene or even discuss character/approach etc. Method acting is an excellent form of acting, and some of the greatest actors work in this way, but it can be a little tricky if your co-actors are not used to this style. I went with it, but as I mentioned before, was so wrapped up in misery at having to play such suggestive and semi pornographic scenes that I didn't find it very helpful. I certainly couldn't ask him for help or guidance. He was not in that head space.

Later his wife and children came to the set and stayed for a day or two, and he seemed proud to introduce them to us. His wife was very attractive and he seemed proud of her and them, yet I have a feeling he was already in the grip of AIDS (or possibly under the influence of drugs?) by then—he was painfully thin and seemed really "wild" eyed. It's only my opinion, and I have nothing to back this up with. He was an interesting man. But he also seemed a bit tragic. I think he died a few years later. All the above is only how I saw it. I neither knew the true facts nor asked about his personal life—it's just how he seemed to me at the time.

I remember Glynis Barber was somewhat cold towards me. I have no knowledge of her as a person as she did not choose to "hang out" with any of us lesser known actors, and kept herself very much to herself. She probably imagined we were all porn stars or inexperienced, untrained actors and thus didn't bother with us unless she had to. I do know that she was as unhappy as I was at the way the film was progressing, and she once took me aside and told me I shouldn't be lowering myself to do those scenes and that I was weak not to walk away. I agree with her. I was weak, but at 23 I didn't dare to rock the boat, being fresh from drama school, working with one of the world's best known actors and being threatened by the producer. I would have liked to have got to know her as we were the only two actresses there for any length of time together, and it would have been nice to have an ally or friend on set, but she was ungiving. I'm sure she's a great person, but she did not show me that side of herself.

Ben Cole was a lot of fun at the time, and we had fun together. We later went on to do a theatre tour in the Far East together, *The Importance of Being Earnest*, in which I played Gwendolen and I think he was Jack (Earnest), my love interest in the play. We became friends and spent quite a lot of time on set together. I enjoyed Ben's company and we would eat dinner together and hang out in Budapest sometimes, going for dinner or whatever. Film sets are enormous fun, all absorbing and fascinating, but they can also be lonely places if you are unhappy in your work or far from home. I was both, and Ben was a help to me at the time.

I spoke very little to Gerard Kikoine. Someone told me that he was originally a porn film director and that he had wanted to get into directing more mainstream, popular films and so had taken this opportunity to make his break from his porn past and do some serious film work. Sadly, it seems that he could not leave his love of porn behind him, and although I'm not saying *Edge of Sanity* was a proper pornographic film, it certainly had elements of it. As my source told me, "Once a porn director, always..." Anyway, I don't think he did a very good job of leaving his old style behind him!

I was excited to attend the premiere—who wouldn't be? I think I had somehow managed to make myself believe that it would all be all right and that my performance and soft porno scenes weren't as hideously embarrassing as I'd thought they were. I think I hoped for a miracle and that some of the more weirdly sordid scenes might have been left on the cutting room floor. Sadly, not so—I attended and gradually slipped down in my seat and wanted the earth to swallow me up! I was distraught at the finished film and my scenes and performance in them—I was just too ashamed to act properly in them, and too self-conscious to be able to make a good job of the work. Mortified is not the word ... my agent was very apologetic to me, saying she would never let me get drawn into such a film again. And that's it—I drew a line under it, and moved on.

## Ben Cole
### ("Johnny")

I trained at the Drama Center in London and graduated in 1983. I spent a few years in theatre and *Edge of Sanity* was my first leading film role. I was always wanting to be a film actor, but there were only a few roles for British actors at that time. During the 80s film in the UK was at an all- time low so I tried to get a few low budget film roles. My agent told me that Allied Vision was making a series of horror films selling 400,000 video copies for £2,000,000—they would make the film with a big star and cast the rest of the roles from up and coming actors.

I had an audition with Gerard Kikoine and he was very kind. He asked me to act the first meeting scene with an actor standing in for Anthony Perkins. I knew that we had a good connection—after the audition Gerard was smiling and I thought I had a chance. It was lucky as I am 6 ft. 2 inches tall and many roles I had been auditioning for I didn't get because I was too tall. But Anthony was 6 ft. 2 inches tall too … so I was in with a chance.

The script was, on first reading, very sexy and had a scene where Susannah [Sarah Maur Thorp] and my character and Mr. Hyde had sex together, which as a young actor I didn't think added to the film. When I was offered the part I asked to discuss the script with Gerard which he kindly offered to do. When we met and I asked him why there was so much sexy scenes in the script and that the one where we had group sex offended me, he immediately said he would cut that scene and I was happier.

Hungary was very interesting at that time as the Russians were still in control of the whole country with a circle of no-man's-land around the city. We could not get fresh vegetables in Budapest for love nor money. Fresh fruit was impossible. I remember that the producer brought me a few bananas and I stood on the steps of the hotel eating the fruit, but had a queue of people from the film asking me for a taste as they had never eaten a banana. In fact I think I gave away all the bananas as I felt sorry for all the people queuing for a bit. We filmed one scene in the loft of a building where the SS in the war had built a concrete slab in the middle to interrogate their prisoners. There were bullet holes in the slab and inside this dome-like structure was like being inside an old sailing ship.

I met Anthony Perkins when he was shooting the London scenes around Chelsea in London. He was very kind to me saying that he would look after me as Gregory Peck had done on his first movie. Gerard also suggested that I bleach my hair very blond for the role which I was happy to do. I remember my first scene with Anthony. I was very nervous and asked him if we could walk through the scene early to get my confidence. He was very kind and agreed. We began walking and rehearsing the dialogue on the street where they were going to shoot. I have no idea how long we were rehearsing but we turned around and Gerard had the crew lights and camera ready to shoot. I suppose they wanted to capitalize on the fact that we were ready to shoot.

Anthony was amazingly kind and happy to hang around with me on and off set. He told me amazing stories about Laurence Olivier and John Gielgud on tour with *Hamlet*. Anthony was working with his touring company at the time and Olivier was getting great reviews for his Hamlet but when Gielgud swapped his role of Laertes he got bad reviews. Gielgud was very jealous of Olivier and one evening they were in Olivier's hotel room on the 5th floor and were arguing about who played the best Hamlet. Gielgud—who was immensely strong—grabbed Olivier and held him out over the balcony in his outstretched arms and asked Olivier to give him a good reason not to drop him to his death below. Olivier turned to Gielgud and said that he didn't have a good reason and Gielgud pulled him back and set him down in safety. Perkins was very relieved to see that murder had not been committed that evening.

Glynis Barber was not a well behaved actress, very nervous on set and always keeping the crew waiting as her hair was not right. One scene I was directed to throw her to the ground and threaten to rape her. She was very nervous about getting blood all over her costume as they had to shoot another scene before the end of the day. So I came up with the idea of being a dog and when she fell onto the ground I would lick her face then there was no risk of blood on her costume. So I told her to just close her eyes and it would feel like being licked by a dog. This she did and the scene got a big applause from the crew.

Sarah [Maur Thorp] was great—it was her first movie too. So we were good friends and it was hard for both of us coming from a background of classical theatre to be thrown into a crack induced love scene on our first day...

It was fantastic working with Gerard Kikoine. He was kind and sensitive and seemed to know how to direct each actor according to their own needs. I was nervous of the sex scenes so I gave Gerard a Joker card from a pack of cards and said that he could show me the card any time he wished and if I didn't have my Joker card on me then I would have to moon him (show him my naked bottom). The same goes for me too. My first time on set I had left my joker card in my caravan and arrived on set to do the sex scene and he immediately showed his Joker card so I had to moon him. After that I had no nerves.

Harry Alan Towers was feared by all the cast and crew and was not a good man—very fat and old and tired. He seemed to treat all the girls as sexual objects and offered many of them parts in return for sex. I remember sitting on the boat at the wrap party and Harry sat next to me. I was protecting Sarah from him as he was trying to get her to go to Hollywood with him but he was a little amorous towards her. He turned to me and said that he was too old to care about actors anymore. I had only met him on set once and then he stood next to me and farted during a sensitive emotional scene. I wanted to throw him over the side of the boat! He told me about being a producer around Marilyn Monroe and confessed to me that she had died in one of his whorehouses where she had many friends, so the CIA had visited him and told him to get out of the country for 12 years or they would pin her death on him. So he went to Europe and produced movies there.

There was the cinematographer Gerard Lubo on *Edge of Sanity*. I became fascinated with his work and loved Tony Spratling's lighting from very old mirrors found on set. One evening I knocked on the cinematographer's hotel door and asked his story. Gerard Lubo told me an amazing story about a few years before. When he was a young cameraman he was asked to shoot some documentary style footage of the Algerian war. So they went undercover and got caught and sent to prison for spying on behalf of the French government which was not true. Whilst he was serving his 14 years in prison he lost his house and wife but studied mathematics and passed his degree in a few months. The head man of the prison was a maths teacher and saw his exam. He had a good talk with Gerard and got him 7 years off his prison sentence. Gerard was a great inspiration to me. I got a first chance to look through the lens of his camera and I was hooked. Now I am a cinematographer myself, and owe a lot to his inspiration. I would hang around him on days when I was not on set and ask him lots of questions, the answers to which I still use! (www.bencolecinematographysite.com).

# *The Evil Below*
## (1988, U.S.A./South Africa)

*Genre:* Horror; *Director:* Wayne Crawford; *Writer:* Arthur Payne; *Cinematographer:* Keith Dunkley; *Editor:* Micki Stroucken; *Visual Effects:* Opticals Irene; *Producer:* Barrie Saint Clair; *Executive Producers:* Wayne Crawford, Andrew Lane and Joel Levine; *Production Company:* Gibraltar Entertainment; *Cast:* Wayne Crawford (Max Cash), June Chadwick (Sarah Livingstone), Ted Le Plat (Adrian Barlow), Sheri Able (Tracy), Graham Clarke (Ray Calhoun), Liam Cundill (Calhoun Junior) and Gordon Mulholland (Max Cash, Sr.)

A group of adventurers, seeking a mythical underwater treasure, face a diabolic force that protects an ancient Spanish galleon. In 1989 there was great trepidation for the release of two sci-fi/horror blockbusters, which took place in the ocean depths: *The Abyss* by James Cameron and *Leviathan* by George P. Cosmatos, not to forget *Deep Star Six* by Sean S. Cunningham. Independent producers didn't waste time and took the bull by the horns. Three low-budget underwater horror movies were made in 1988: *The Evil Below*, *Lords of the Deep* by Roger Corman and *The Rift* by the Spanish director Juan Piquer Simon. *The Evil Below* was produced by Gibraltar Entertainment, the newborn company of Wayne Crawford & Andrew Lane, the duo creators of *Night of the Comet* (1984).

## Arthur Payne
### (Writer/"Fisherman")

I studied film at University of New Orleans. My first movie experience in Hollywood was as a production assistant on *Night of the Comet*. My first TV work in Los Angeles was as a production assistant for a girls' rock and roll band called the Go Go's. I believe they were the first girls band (played their own instruments) to have a number one hit on the Billboard charts in America. Their singer, Belinda Carlisle, would also go on to enjoy success as a solo artist. I was later to reunite with one of the Go-Go's on a movie called *Bill and Ted's Excellent Adventure* with Keanu Reeves.

I originally met and worked for Wayne Crawford and Andy Lane on a movie called *Barracuda* [1978, Harry Kerwin] which was shot in Miami, Florida. Little did we know at the time, that movie, years later, would have a strong influence on the making of *The Evil Below*. Wayne learned to scuba dive for *Barracuda*, an important skill used again in *The Evil Below*. *Barracuda* gave us the confidence we could tackle the ambitious underwater requirements called for in *The Evil Below*. It taught us how terror and suspense could be played out effectively and production value gained by working beneath the waves. And, it also influenced us to throw in the fish attack on the diver except, in this case, it was under the control of the dark power of evil carried by that ship, now lying in its watery grave, and its guardian residing on the island.

Some time after *Barracuda*, I went out to Los Angeles where I reunited with Wayne and Andy and traveled to Africa to help make an action film called *White Ghost* [1987, B.J. Davis]. Wayne had starred in an international movie called *Jake Speed* [1985, Andrew Lane] and some of it was filmed in Africa. He fell in love with it over there and met an expatriated English producer who shared his dream to make more films in Africa. Barrie St. Clair, who was now a citizen of South Africa had made a really good film there called *Zulu Dawn* [1978, Douglas Hickox]. So they put together financing to make movies in Africa through Gibraltar Entertainment which was the company owned by Wayne and Andy and an attorney named Joel Levine. One of these films turned out to be *The Evil Below* and a lot of it was shot on the Natal Coast of South Africa which is very lush and scenic. I think for a low budget movie it had to be some of the most beautiful locations ever used in a horror movie.

I had grown up on the Florida Coast of the United States and had always been attracted by the history and stories of the explorers and adventurers who came there looking for treasures of various kinds (usually gold) and a spring water that was reported could provide eternal youth once you drank it. Yes, a famous Spanish explorer actually came to America looking for this new-life giving water and was eventually killed by Indians living on the West Coast of Florida. Anyway, I also used to hear about, and was intrigued by, a treasure-seeking group that was based in Florida that was always looking for Spanish galleons that were sunk in storms in Florida waters. Also just this world of the underwater was fascinating. I used to love snorkeling in the ocean there and watching the TV programs of Jacques Cousteau. And I loved horror movies, especially Hammer films, so when Wayne came to me with some ideas that would have this setting, I was very enthusiastic. I started making an outline for the script and then went to Africa with Wayne and finished fleshing it out. Wayne, I believe, had read somewhere about particular groups that had fled Europe for various motivations, and it wasn't always the dream of wealth or religious freedom. I really can't remember if he had read something about some heretic monks that set sail for the New World, or he had dreamed that up as an extension—but that idea was his.

We also loved the movies of Humphrey Bogart and *The African Queen* so I think the idea of the expatriated American boat captain [Max Cash] grew from that. We wanted an active and passionate woman lead character, so an adventurous lady [Sarah Livingstone] with dreams of finding a lost treasure in an exotic location came to life. And so, like in *The African Queen*, the leading lady had to seek out help from a boat operator to achieve her goal (obviously for different reasons). There is also an homage to *The African Queen* at the end of *The Evil Below*. Peter Yates' *The Deep* also had influence and some parallels in creating *The Evil Below*.

I know it is odd that the few movies I have mentioned so far as having influence were not really horror movies, but there were horror films that did have some effect on writing or inspiring *The Evil Below*. John Carpenter's *The Fog*, for example. A small costal town that has some old ship haunting it in a sense. Supernatural danger that lays out there in an old sailing vessel in the water near their homes that given the right or wrong conditions or provocations can mean fear and death for visitors or members of the community. Also, *Angel Heart*. The idea of the Devil going about his business in human form in nice clothes instead of some hideous looking monster or creature with horns. And of course one almost can't think of doing any underwater horror movie without at least a moment's reflection on *Jaws*, the best known of them all.

There are very good memories of the movie and, like on all productions, there are/were also some frustrations and obstacles. One thing I remember that was a big problem was with the underwater filming. Of course that is always something of a problem and the reason some studios and production services have built large water tanks to shoot in a more controlled environment. We did not have a tank available to us although some close-up work was finally done in a large water exercise pool built for horses. We had to move the large Spanish Galleon wreck all over the place. It was trucked out to the coast of South Africa but the surf was very strong and the visibility terrible near the shore, and a storm headed our way so it was trucked back inland with plans to shoot in a river. We filmed a bit more there in a river but the bottom of the river was rather shallow and sand and silt would get stirred up in the water which allowed only a short filming window. Then you had to wait for the sand to settle so you could film for another very brief period. Also the river was not very clear to begin with. Finally the ship wreck was taken apart and shipped to the islands of Mauritius which had beautiful clear water and reefs that protected the area we worked in. Of course whenever you do underwater work it has its limitations with work time for actors and camera and support crews but Mauritius was like a dream after the previous underwater experiences. When we would go back to the beach hotel at the end of the work day and sit outside and have drinks saluting the sunset and telling stories of the day, it was magic. I believe at that time, "La Isla Bonita" was a big musical hit by Madonna and the hotel would play it constantly because it sure fit Mauritius.

It was very interesting to see the divers coordinating their work and communicating with the actors. I am sure now days the divers would be communicating electronically, but back then they used to write things on slates and have the others read it down there. Unlike on land, they could only work for certain periods of time, both because of air supply and having to come aboard the support boats to rest. It was fun work in some regards for them, but it was also hard work and tiring as well. We would return to land for a while, have lunch and rest and then go back out. Toward sunset we would return to the hotel on the beach. This setting was already fantastic and it became simply magic after a couple of sundowners. Plans would be made for the next day, then there would be wonderful food, often cooked out on fires, and we would start all over again the next day.

I believe *The Evil Below* was my first script and it was a wonderful experience. What a location and subject matter to work with! To this day, even though I have had various experiences in making movies from different job and creative positions, I still enjoy writing the best. It is then great to see how it all comes to life in the film itself. Some of the script is always what you would expect or hope for—other elements can be disappointments—and once in a while something turns out better than you imagined (that is somewhat rare, but it does happen). Usually in your mind you create/picture the perfect visual scenario and it is often hard to create that exactly on the screen. But it is also wonderful to see a director and cast and crew all come together to give the script "being" their own collective creative way.

# *Ghost Town*
## (1987, U.S.A.)

*Genre:* Horror; *Director:* Richard McCarthy as "Richard Governor"; *Writers:* David Schmoeller (Story) and Duke Sandefur (Screenplay); *Cinematographer:* Mac Ahlberg; *Editors:* King Wilder and Peter Teschner; *Special Makeup and Creature Effects:* Mechanical and Makeup Imageries, Inc.; *Special Effects:* Eddie Surkin; *Producer:* Timothy Tennant; *Executive Producer:* Charles Band; *Production Company:* Empire Pictures; *Cast:* Franc Luz (Deputy Langley), Catherine Hickland (Kate), Jimmie F. Skaggs (Devlin), Penelope Windust (Grace), Bruce Glover (Dealer), Zitto Kazann (Blacksmith), Laura Schaefer (Etta), Michael Alldredge (Bubba) and Blake Conway (Sheriff Harper)

While investigating the disappearance of a girl in the middle of the American desert, a young deputy sheriff finds the tombstone of a sheriff who had been buried in the sand. Before decomposing, the sheriff's skeleton emerges from the grave, grabs the man's hands and gives him his badge. The deputy finds the missing girl in an abandoned town from the Wild West days, inhabited by ghosts and they both have to face the ghost of an infamous outlaw and his posse. The deputy's mission is to defeat the ruthless gunslinger once and for all, vindicating the sheriff and finally giving peace to the souls of the town's inhabitants, all killed by the outlaw.

## David Schmoeller
### (Writer)

*Ghost Town* started as a title and the poster artwork, which is how many of the films of that period came about. Charlie Band probably came up with a basic idea, "Let's make a film about a haunted ghost town."

I don't remember if I wrote more than a treatment. Maybe I wrote a first draft but when I read the IMDB synopsis of the final movie, I don't remember writing ANY of that story, in treatment or screenplay. (Not that there is anything wrong with what they did. I've never seen the movie.) So, the team who came in probably threw out most of whatever I wrote and just made their own movie.

Originally, I was going to write and direct *Ghost Town*, but *Catacombs* [1987, David Schmoeller] received a green light to shoot in Rome—and I just couldn't be in two places at once.

## Duke Sandefur
(Writer)

[Author's note—I asked Duke Sandefur to shed some light on "Subterraneans," his second project for Empire Pictures, following *Ghost Town*. I discovered that "Subterraneans" is not really an unproduced movie. Do you remember the 1991 vampire movie *Subspecies* directed by Ted Nicolaou? Well, nothing was left of the original project but the prefix "Sub." I was about to forget … of course I could not have ended the interview without some questions concerning his unproduced screenplay "Nightcrawler."]

What I can claim as unique in my life is that I was surrounded by fabulous writers from a very young age. I learned my craft from people I admire greatly like John Hawkins, Gerry Day, Jack Sowards, Joel Murcott and many others—and my own father, B.W. Sandefur. My mother, Jean Sandefur, was the horror fan…

My first credited television episode was *The Amazing Spider-Man*: "Escort to Danger" [1978] for CBS back when I was in college. That episode was written, in part, to satisfy a requirement for a writing class that I failed anyway! Odd, but I never thought at the time to just quit school and pursue screenwriting, which is what I should have done. I continued to dabble in both writing and school until the offer of a staff job on a *Dukes of Hazzard* spin-off forced the point. It was decades and many, many episodes before I went back to college to finish my degree.

Somewhere in there, my father and I, influenced in part by my mother's love of "scary movies," put our heads together to write a manageable (read: cheap) horror/action movie called "Nightcrawler" [1985]. We locked ourselves in a beachfront duplex and composed that script in very short order. It was a lot of fun. We laughed, we fought, we drank, we wrote a screenplay.

"Nightcrawler" is an action-horror story of a young engineering professor, Gage, who comes into possession of a wrecked motorcycle. Over the course of days, the issue of possession becomes less clear as our young professor is swept into a very dark tale of vengeance. There is a ghost in the machine—a ghost with an agenda—the ghost of Nightcrawler, an outlaw biker who was betrayed and killed in the worst possible way. Against a backdrop of bikers, drugs, violence and murder, Gage's own life disintegrates as he transforms—not into Nightcrawler, but something else—something more. Gage's planned wedding, pending tenure at the university and all the trappings of his "normal" life are a fading dream as the nightmare becomes real. My father and I had discussed doing a dark "vengeance from the grave" story. We wanted to take a regular guy and pull the rug out from under him, leaving him virtually defenseless unless he gave himself over to the curse. Moreover, we wanted the dark adventure to be enticing to him, a realization of that universal fantasy of being tough, strong and able to do nearly anything. Consider the way that Jessup was drawn nearly to his own doom in *Altered States*. Or young Arnie in John Carpenter's *Christine*. That's what we wanted on a more subtle level, more sexual, more violent and more frightening. Beyond that, we had discussed the look of Michael Mann's *Thief*—exceedingly dark with available light—lots of sparks and metal and fury. The name Nightcrawler was from an actual person, but that's another story.

"Nightcrawler" has been optioned a handful of times. The movie was set for production

[1985] with Samuel Z. Arkoff. Louis, his son, was active in putting the whole thing together and was quite taken with the script. Dwight Little [*Halloween 4/Bloodstone/The Phantom of the Opera*] was set to direct. I was very much looking forward to seeing this one on screen. It's a serious character study within the framework of a horror movie. We saw a bit of that in *Amityville Horror*, Sam's most successful feature film, and I think the motivation to go deeper was there. Alas, this project was a near miss and never reached the camera. Over the years, I've gotten a lot of work from this script. It's a visceral read and it leaves a lasting impression. I'm about halfway through a major rewrite of the screenplay with a dramatic refocusing of the protagonist. Maybe we'll get to see it after all.

My literary agent set up an appointment for me to meet with Debra Dion of Empire Pictures. She had read "Nightcrawler" and I assumed she wanted to discuss producing that movie. That was the first time I met Charlie Band, but only in passing and he revealed that his goal with Empire was to produce "2000 films by the year 2000!" They damn near did it. I was prepared for that meeting, I really was. But when I met Debra, I almost forgot why I was there. I found her magnetically attractive, absolutely charming, exceedingly considerate and on top of the material. She knew "Nightcrawler" better than I did and I believe she would have liked to make that movie, even if it was somewhat outside the Empire model.

But there was another piece of material on her desk: *Ghost Town*. David Schmoeller had written the screenplay. Debra asked nicely (which may have been her way of insisting), if I'd be interested in doing a "polish" on *Ghost Town*. Of course, I said that I would. I was in a trance.

Reality Strikes: *Ghost Town* was very far from being camera-ready and it needed far more than a polish. I had nothing to do with David Schmoeller's draft, so I can only imagine what went on during the process. Empire Pictures was like wartime filmmaking back then—get in, get out, move on—so, who knows? David has written enough good material since that I think he'd probably admit that the version of *Ghost Town* I was asked to address was not his finest work. I've only had the opportunity to speak with David once—or maybe twice—and I'd love to sit down and talk about *Ghost Town* with him some time.

I generally have a very light touch when rewriting another writer. Writing screenplay is difficult. Writing story is next to impossible and potentially life-threatening. Thus, I have the utmost respect for anyone who can get through a story and a script and live to tell about it. In the case of *Ghost Town*, I did my best to conserve the original concept, but I set the script aside. It was full of shadowy ghost things that pop up everywhere and I didn't know what the hell was going on. There wasn't enough time to polish or rewrite. It was much faster and more efficient to use the general structure and just write a new screenplay. The final credits on the release reflect that properly: Story by David Schmoeller, Screenplay by Duke Sandefur.

This was many moons ago and I don't remember every facet of the process, but a couple of things come to mind. For one thing, there was a lot of subtlety in the screenplay that never made it to camera (which often happens, but particularly in this case). Resources were limited in terms of both money and time. If I'd known how that would all go down, I would have aimed a little lower in the first place. In the end product, certain elements seem patchy because the arcs weren't complete. This is something that happens.

Unique to this movie at the time was that our Sheriff carried a .454 Casull five-shot revolver. It was expensive, rare and difficult to obtain and Empire's armorer got one! The five round capacity of this weapon was key to a moment in the script that didn't play out fully on screen. There was also a scene on paper in which he fires on some ghostly bad guys and there are huge impacts on the wall beyond before the phantom outlaws realize they've been shot. Very easy to write, but difficult to film! I think they tried, but again, it wasn't fully realized. I still have a belt buckle from Casull that they gave me for including their magnificent revolver in the movie. After I eventually fired one of these hand cannons, I felt kind of bad for the actor. It had to kick like a three-legged mule, even with blanks.

Close to production and toward the end of my involvement, I had a contentious meeting with "Richard Governor" [Director] and Tim Tennant [Producer]. They were facing their own reality of having to shoot this film in a span of fourteen days or so and their anxiety was showing. I do not remember the subject of the "discussion," but I do remember clearly how it ended after a couple of hours in a hot, uncomfortable room in Hollywood. I had had quite enough of these two guys. I could smell the tension in the room and it was contagious. There wasn't enough light or space. Tim Tennant says to me, "Duke, what do we have to do to make you see this our way?" I stood, straightened my collar, collected my materials, picked up my Blackwing 602 pencils, looked to each of them, allowed a moment to pass, and said: "Blow me." Not that I'm particularly proud of that, but it was one of two times I've lost my composure concerning a screenplay. I caught Debra outside the building and apologized to her, in case I upset the gentlemen. She laughed, but I could tell it was one more challenge than she probably needed that particular afternoon, on the eve of production.

I also worked on "Subterraneans" [1987] for Charles Band. I've seen posters, some with credits included, for movies that were never made, or were made under different titles (including "Subterraneans,"). Charles Band used to mock up the posters and go shopping for backers, particularly in Milan. It was a great strategy and it worked repeatedly. A poster gives a project credibility, even where there may be no other substance at all.

First, Charlie Band had a theory (probably right), that any creatures in a movie that were shorter than the seat cushion of a movie theater seat contributed to viewer anxiety. That's why he did a lot of films with little puppets and toys and creepy short things! The story of "Subterraneans"—my version—had to do with a society of little creepy things living below the surface. They were released upon a small town (a production consideration), after a big civic event was held to dig up a fifty-year-old time capsule. The recovered capsule was empty, though it had been set in a concrete vault. Viewed from the point of view of the Subterraneans, this was the fulfillment of a prophecy of sorts, as their society had incorporated many things found in the time capsule, which they had raided decades before. What ensues is mostly partially clothed ladies being carried away and dragged into the underworld by little creepy critters with an agenda. It was really fun to write and I'm sorry it wasn't produced in that form. A number of films came later that featured similar themes—small things raining havoc in the community: *Gremlins, Critters*, etc.

I wasn't involved with any other Empire or Full Moon projects, no matter how I tried to get back into that circle of maniacs and fiends. I don't regret a minute I spent with these folks and if called upon, I'd go write another creep show with them in a minute!

## Richard McCarthy
### (Director)

[Author's note—I think I am the first person to reveal the identity of "Richard Governor." After almost 30 years I am pleased to introduce you to the real director of *Ghost Town*, Richard McCarthy.]

*Ghost Town* represents one of the worst choices I have ever made in my drive to make quality feature films. I was directing commercials in the U.S. at the time, and in 1982 had won the International Commercial Directing Clio Award and I was in the final stages of getting my film "Copycat" the go ahead by MGM.

Tim Tennant (line producer) put me up to Empire Films as the director of three low budget films. The first was *Ghost Town*. The budget was $1 million two hundred thousand and it needed to be shot in 24 days (with the loss of the first day due to a terrible storm, the shooting days were actually 23).

I was selected due to my many awards for commercials, and the Australian special *The Benny Hill Show*. Benny was a famous British comedian with a regular TV series and he had asked me to direct the Australian one hour special [*Benny Hill Down Under*, 1977] due to my name as a comedy director. I'd won the Australian Commercial Director's Award for six or seven years in a row (and named Director of the Decade by the top Broadcast magazine) and topped that with the International Clio where I edged out Ridley Scott for that gong.

So the task of filming a feature like this with stunts and cheap special effects (I still cringe at the skeletal and ghostly sheriff who rises from the grave) in a few days over two weeks, was daunting to say the least. The film was originally meant to be shot at the De Laurentiis studios in Rome, Italy, using the sets that were used by Sergio Leone for *The Good, the Bad and the Ugly* and other spaghetti westerns. But with only two weeks to go the producers decided it must be shot in Arizona. I was later to discover that they were in deep financial trouble and this allowed them to save money without increasing the budget or production time.

The big problem for me (and my cameraman) was that we both belonged to two strong guilds. I was a member of the Director's Guild of America, so while shooting in Rome would have taken the film out of DGA jurisdiction, by moving the production to Tucson, Arizona, where there was already a western "set" town (some miles out of the main town), we stepped into Director's Guild territory and their requirement that no guild member could work within a non-union production at risk of huge fines including the entire directors fee. Now this was not that big—only $60,000—but I needed the money and decided to risk it. At the end of the second week the producer came to us and told us that the DGA was alerted to the production and intended visiting the set, so a pseudonym could be adopted to avoid the penalty to ourselves and the company. This is when I made the awful decision. Instead of risking it, I accepted their urgings and adopted the pseudonym with the name the crew called me: "The Governor." So I became "Richard Governor," trusting that the next two films for Empire would enable me to correct that name.

Well the rest is history. After fighting with the old man who was the executive producer and owner of Empire Pictures for the quality I'd planned for the film, both in the editorial and the sound, I lost both battles. Faced with only two weeks and a few days to film a horror film, I chose to do what was done in *The Innocents* (*Turn of the Screw*) and use sound to create the horror.

Charles Band interfered terribly and rushed through a re-edit of the film when I was in Australia for Christmas. I returned and restored much that the fool had cut out, but he insisted on doing the mix himself. With a restricted budget and a short shooting time, I intended sound to carry much of the horror. So I'd supplied sound sheets to the studio. These were ignored, so for example when the Deputy steps into the jailhouse when he first arrives in the town, sound was intended to drive the scene—or at least it was supposed to. You can notice he looks up as if he has heard something upstairs. That something was the sound of something being dragged across the floor and the sound of women wailing as if they were being tortured. This sound draws him to the cells where he finds the skeletons of the women. For some unexplained reason Charles Band cut most of that sound out and in so doing disempowered the scene. He did this throughout the film removing the constant whispering of the trapped townsfolk, the laughter and sobbing of children and thus took away a great deal of suspense and horror.

*Ghost Town* opened at the Chinese Mann Theatre and ran for a couple of weeks. I received a good review in *Variety*, and Richard Governor was praised for creating "verisimilitude." The following two films were never made and I came to realize the enormity of my decision. No one in Hollywood could find Richard Governor, and I was to find out many years later that producers, impressed that a film could be shot in such a short time, wanted me to direct their films. As it turned out due to my anonymity, *Ghost Town* was my only feature film, and despite my many awards for commercials, I feel that my crazy decision to create Richard Governor was a fatal blow to Richard McCarthy and his dream to make it big in Hollywood.

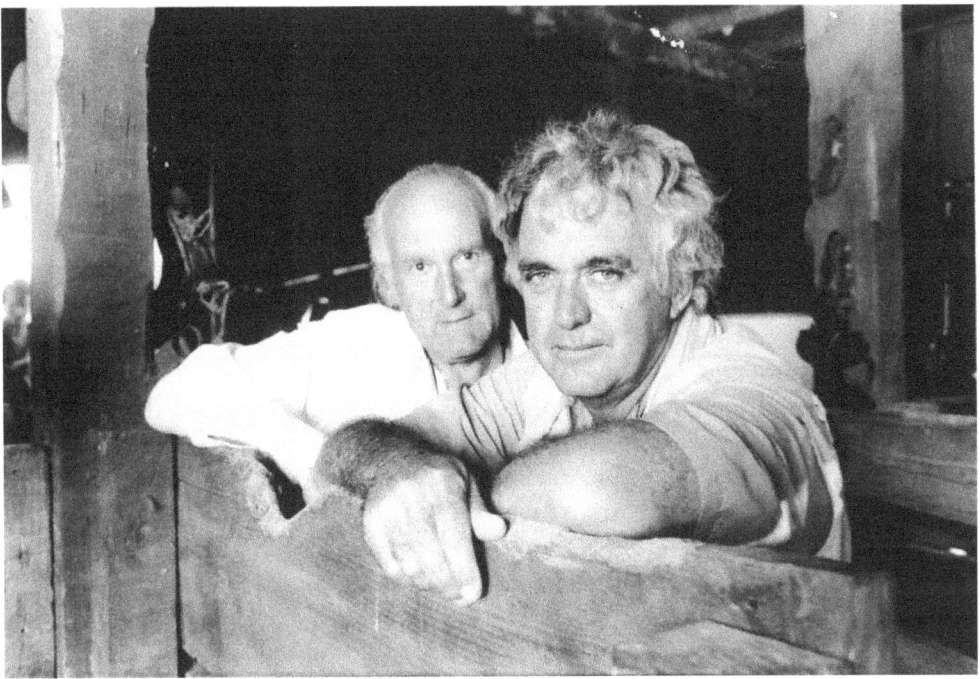

**Mac Ahlberg (Cinematographer) and Richard McCarthy (Director) (courtesy of Richard McCarthy).**

In distant hindsight, now I recognize that if I had ignored the damage the studio predicted and demanded they keep my name on the film—as I found out later Mac Ahlberg [1931–2012] did after he had a change of mind—*Ghost Town* would have given studios the confidence to offer me other films. Yes a foolish and career-changing decision indeed that I'll always regret.

## Michael Deak
## (Special Makeup and Creature Effects— Mechanical and Makeup Imageries, Inc.)

*Ghost Town* was about a 4 week shoot in an existing ghost town about an hour's drive from Tucson. It was in the middle of nowhere and there was nothing around except a gasoline station near the main highway. It was the first (and only) western I worked on. I am a big fan of westerns (*The Wild Bunch* is probably my favorite movie) so I was looking forward to the opportunity. I convinced the armorer to let me wear one of the prop gun belts with a six shooter so I could practice my fast draw when I wasn't needed on set.

John Criswell handled most of the effects of Sheriff Harper's skeleton [in flashbacks the sheriff is interpreted by Blake Conway]. It was very elaborate. Production dug a big hole in the ground and covered it with a fake surface. John was in the hole and puppeteered it from underground. They had a fan to blow air in the hole so he could breathe. We were on the surface and covered the puppet with a thin layer of dirt so it would appear to pop out of the ground. I think there was even a separate mechanical puppet hand that could grab the actor.

We also had a full body puppet of Jimmy Skaggs [the outlaw] for the ending where the Sheriff throws his badge into Jimmy's forehead. The dummy was to fall back, the chest open, and a lot of black snakes came out. There was a guy who handled the snakes, harmless garter snakes about 2 feet long and we (MMI crew) supplied the black slime to cover them. (We used tinted methylcellulose, a food thickener. It seems every monster we did at that time was covered in it!) We filled the puppet body with snakes and slime, "action" was called, the body fell back, the chest opened … but no snakes came out. We shot that scene at night and it gets much colder in the desert at night, so the snakes being cold blooded were not that active. After a few seconds they stopped filming and during that short time, the snakes could sense the warmth on the ground from all the movie lights and all slithered out of the body and tried to escape in the desert. The snake handler and the MMI crew rushed to grab all these snakes before they got away. This happened exactly the same on the second try and we all rushed into the desert night to grab the snakes. Sometimes in the heat of a situation you forget yourself.… I do NOT like snakes at all, but at the time all I could think of is to make the effect work and we needed the snakes. Halfway through gathering the snakes the second time I had a sudden realization.… I was in the desert, at night in partial darkness, which was filled with all kinds of other snakes including rattlesnakes and here I am grabbing anything that moved. I looked at the two handfuls of snakes I had already gathered and said "What the hell am I doing!?!," quickly tossed the snakes toward the body and excused myself from the snake hunt for the rest of the night.

I also handled most or all of the blood effects on that film. I remember making "collapsible" nails for the Sheriff's crucifixion, a bleeding pitchfork for killing the Blacksmith's daughter [Laura Schaefer], bullet hits, etc. I also helped rig up a gag on one of the actors who was an amputee with a missing arm. We made a fake arm holding a gun that was shot off with squibs from the pyrotechnic guys.

Mostly I remember that very little of the actual movie dealing with the Jimmy Skagg's character was shot in the first 3 weeks, but a lot of atmospheric and arty type stuff. Our make-up crew (Greg Johnson and Scott Coulter) would put Jimmy in that make-up almost every day and most of the time he was never filmed. Everything was rushed into the last week and we ended up working 20 hour days to try and finish the film (that gave us 4 hours off, and it took 2 hours to drive to the hotel and back, so we all were exhausted at the end).

Bruce Glover played the blind man [Blacksmith] in the film. I was thrilled to get to work with him having been in so many cool movies (*Diamonds Are Forever*, *Walking Tall* to name just a few). I always try to be professional but occasionally I would get to talk with him between filming about his past work and he seemed to be okay with that. One day, Greg Johnson was putting in the white contact lenses that Bruce wore, when a wardrobe girl (I am pretty sure she was an inexperienced local hire) came by and started powdering Bruce's costume with dust and the dust got in his eye under the contact lens. I was in the make-up trailer when this happened so I didn't know what was going on when Bruce burst into the trailer, holding his eye and yelling in pain. Greg quickly explained what happened (I knew Greg was very responsible and none of this was his fault), but Bruce refused to let Greg take out the lens. I tried to calm Bruce down and he eventually let me take out the lens. Someone from production came in to find out what happened and I suggested they take Bruce to an eye doctor to have him checked out, which they did right away.

Soon (I don't remember if it was back in town or if there was a production phone on set) I started getting calls from Los Angeles—MMI head John Buechler called to find out what happened as did I think Charlie Band directly. I called the doctor that treated Bruce and asked how he was. The doctor said he had a scratched cornea. I panicked a little and asked how serious this was. The doctor said, he'll be okay, he just shouldn't wear contact lenses for the next 24 hours. Relieved, I called production and Los Angeles to let them know everything was going to be okay. That night I noticed Bruce at the hotel bar, seeming to be having a good time, but half his head was in a very dramatic looking bandage.

The next morning I went up to Bruce (with no bandage) and explained the situation, that my crew was very careful but it was an unfortunate accident, we'll make sure nothing like that happens again and I and the crew were very sorry that he had to go through that discomfort. At that point, I was a little startled by his dramatic reaction (I am paraphrasing here not remembering the exact words), but he told me, "You, you're okay, you are the only one to come up and apologize to me. I may be an older man but I know ways to hurt people, I know how to break kneecaps and I know how to kill a man with just my thumb…" and so on. Maybe he was just getting into character or letting off steam, I'm not sure, but from that point on, he didn't wear the contact lenses again and our conversations were limited.

## Franc Luz
### ("Langley")

After the national tour of the Broadway show *The Robber Bridegroom* with myself in the lead role, my soon-to-be wife Barbara Marineau in the female lead (she sang beautifully), and John Goodman (yes, THE John Goodman) in the lead "bad guy" role (he absolutely stole the show, he was brilliant), I landed my first Broadway show, *Whoopie!* when I was 26 years old. I played a Dartmouth educated American Indian (couldn't do that in today's paralyzing politically "correct" climate!), and I was the young romantic lead. I received excellent reviews and soon after, successfully auditioned for, and was cast in the long running soap opera *The Doctors*, for which I was nominated for an Emmy Award as "Best Lead Actor" in daytime. After *Whoopie!* ended its Broadway run, I shot the scene in my first feature film *Voices* [1978]. I loved the experience and vowed that I would work more in feature film going forward. I went on to do another soap, *One Life to Live* and soon after was cast in *Little Shop of Horrors*, the long running, mega-successful Off Broadway show, for which I received a NY Drama Critics Award for "Best Supporting Actor" in 1982. The three main leads (myself, Ellen Greene—who went on to do the movie—and Lee Wilkof) opened in the Los Angeles production (I think it was 1983). We were an instant smash success and from that exposure, and momentum, I went on to have the long "on camera" career detailed, for the most part, in the IMDB website—including *Ghost Town*.

*Ghost Town* was an important casting for me, as was *The Nest* [1987, Terence H. Winkless]. I knew that film careers such as Jack Nicholson's, Barbara Hershey's, and many others were birthed in the cult "B" movie market, and I always knew that every bit of success that I enjoyed would have to be earned the hard way, and by paying my dues by coming up from the bottom of the ladder, and I was also fascinated, and loved many "B" movies, and was thrilled to be a major player in some.

I had been complaining to my agent that I was sick and tired of being cast in the "Yuppie" roles I was stuck in, in Hollywood films and TV. It was certainly my bread and butter, and I earned a lot of money playing everybody's boyfriend on TV—Jane Curtain's guilty younger love interest in *Kate and Allie* (my episode won the Emmy as "Best comedy episode of the year"); Pam Dawber's BF in *My Sister Sam*; Patricia Kalember's BF in *Kay O'Brien*; one of Meg Ryan's BFs in *When Harry Met Sally*; Dr. Beverly Crusher's BF in *Star Trek: The Next Generation*; and numerous others.... I so badly wanted to break away from the "Yuppie BF" stereotype and play everything from "bad guys" to "action adventure" leads. I had manufactured an entire career out of nothing but some talent, strong work ethic, and determination. I never believed in placing limits on myself (I knew that there's plenty of others who would do that). In many ways, I was naive, which actually helped me.

I later learned that when in a "two shot" with major stars like George Segal, Pierce Brosnan, Marlon Brando, Johnny Depp, even David Hasselhoff, that they ALL had enormous, powerful craniums (big heads), and in two shots, or publicity photos next to these stars, I looked like an "attractive" supporting actor, not a film star. My long-time agent, Judy Schoen, was correct all along. She had a theory, she called it her "Richard Burton Theory of Film Stars." She had noticed, when a young agent, upon meeting Richard Burton at some event, that he had a shockingly large head. She later realized that all movie superstars (Paul Newman, Marlon Brando, and others) all had this characteristic in common. She believed this conveyed strength in close-up shots, on camera, and distinguished them from many other actors in the same film, or TV show, who played supporting roles. I now subscribe to Judy's "Big Head" theory as every major star I've worked with had this characteristic in common. Judy labeled me (in a business that lives by labels) a "character lead," as opposed to a pure character actor such as say, a John Candy. She believed I could play both leading men AND character roles, but that it was unlikely that I would become a film star, in the classical sense, such as the aforementioned stars. She was absolutely right! It was a blessing (wide range of roles available to me), and a curse (every young boy and girl fantasizes a star's life)—but Judy's job was to be a realist, and have a deft eye for matching her clients to the right roles.

My experience with Catherine Hickland has to go down as, perhaps, the greatest surprise of my personal, and romantic life. I was a product of NY theatre. I was a fully vested, celebrated NY theatre actor. I had "cred" (street slang for credibility). We tended to look at the "pretty people" who came from "pretty actor" backgrounds like modeling and soaps, such as Catherine Hickland, as lucky that they were born so stunningly beautiful, because they had a paucity of talent and "chops" (slang for hard, real skills, theatre background, and superior talent). In other words, I was probably a bit of an elitist, in large part because it was hard earned, and I thought gorgeous people like Catherine, had it all handed to them on a silver platter. I was already "on set" when Catherine pulled up in her car to begin shooting. She was in a black corvette with license plates the read: "MEHAPPY." My blonde bubble-head-shallow person-alarm went off and I immediately thought "Oh, oh," somebody was casting with their dick, and not their interest in having a serious actress, with chops, to play the female lead...

I got a valuable life lesson here. Catherine was immediately fun, enormously likable, and extremely sweet and generous in every way possible. She made an effort to establish a congenial, personal relationship with everybody in her sphere, and ... I gradually started falling for her—hook, line, and sinker (American slang for TOTALLY). We started hanging out with each other and I realized, pretty quickly, that I wanted to get to know her better. Much better. She also was very professional in her approach to work. She always knew her lines, was going for deeper stuff in scenes than I thought she was capable of going to. I loved working with her, and after the shoot ended we began seeing each other in Los Angeles, where we both lived. At the time, I had a wonderful cottage in Malibu, overlooking the Pacific Ocean (lived on the same street as Ed Harris, Madonna, and others). Catherine and I went on to have a glorious few months of an affair, and before I knew it, I was starting to seriously think that I wanted to marry Catherine. After my experience with Barbara (WONDERFUL person, and exceptional musical theatre talent) ended so poorly, and my longest relationship (9 years with Valerie Mahaffey, whom I had met on *The Doctors*) had just ended, I was as far from thinking that I would ever want to marry again as a person could be. Then ... BAM! "MEHAPPY" stole my heart. However, on one of our lovely walks on the beach one night when I talked about taking the relationship further, Catherine shocked me by saying that she could never marry a man "who didn't accept Jesus Christ as his lord and savior." I was stunned. I am a long-time atheist, and I knew what she was asking for was an impossibility for me. Our relationship, which began in the desert of Arizona, ended that night, on that stretch of beach in Malibu. I am still vaguely saddened by it as I have never considered marriage since.

The other actors in *Ghost Town* were all wonderful actors, including the locals hired to play the smaller roles. "Richard Governor"—always knew that was a pseudonym but never learned his real name!—cast this picture very well. Jimmy Skaggs [1944-2004] is an EXCELLENT actor, and I was thrilled to work with Bruce Glover as he was a cult icon from the early Bond movies, and other things I had seen him in. I loved our scene on that dusty front porch. He wore these opaque contact lenses to give him that creepy look and he put up with the discomfort and danger of inserting those hard lenses because he was committed to his craft and the best possible performance. He was wonderfully idiosyncratic, and a great example, for me, of a committed actor with an exceptional work ethic. Jimmy had that, as well, as did all of the cast as I recall.

Inspired by tales of actors who had done their own stunts (like Steve McQueen, and others), I had worked exceptionally hard in the gym to be super fit for this shoot, and was prepared to do as many of my own stunts as possible. I ended up with numerous injuries, some, at the time life threatening. They forgot to bring the harness to hang me in the hanging scene, and to save time and protect the budget, I agreed to do the hanging scene without it. It all went very well in rehearsal so we went ahead and shot it. Unfortunately, for me, the stuntman in charge of pulling the rope up, got too caught up in the moment, pulled way harder than he had in rehearsals and the rope slipped completely through my fingers and I was actually hanged, briefly. Brief, or not, it bruised my trachea and there was a serious risk that it would swell shut, so I was closely watched and shut down for the rest of the day's shooting. Most of my injuries were created by stunt men, who were also dedicated, passionate individuals about the quality of their work, would get more carried away, and intense in the actual shooting scenes than they had been in the rehearsals. I, quite literally, had "skin the game" in that shoot.

One enormous negative that I carry with me, even to this day, occurred from that shoot. In one scene, I was under a porch with the bad guys running all around and above me on the porch, with the effect of explosions and fires going on all around me. To achieve that effect, they placed me under this porch by removing the floor boards, inserting me into the crawl space, then nailing the boards back in, trapping me in this crawl space. Then they used a dangerous, powerful chemical, called "A/B smoke" to create the smoke in the scene. The wind shifted and a powerful blast of that chemical wafted into my crawlspace and I was nailed in like a coffin with no escape. I developed, from that unfortunate scene, a case of claustrophobia, which remains with me to this day.

Richard Governor seemed like a crazy, high energy, highly sexed, charismatic guy with a strong Australian accent, therefore exotic in some way. At the time, I was not sure that he had complete control of his set, but I've since learned that NO ONE ever has COMPLETE control of any set. In the end, he produced a surprisingly handsome, well shot movie on a relatively small budget. So, he definitely had skills.

An update on my life now—I split my time between NYC and various other places that I have experimented living in (such as in the middle of the high desert in CA, on a lake in a Massachusetts/New Hampshire forest area, etc.). I acquired a taste for adventure from my adventurous life as an actor, and I still have an appetite for it. I stopped pursuing my acting career about 12 years ago, due to various influences. I had hit an awkward age at which there was a paucity of work for me; I had lost my conditioning and ability to carry a Broadway show (my "chops") from not doing it for decades; my agent died, and I had no desire to look for another, especially in my least desirable age bracket and least hirable stage of my career. Also, I was just exhausted from 30 years of chasing work nearly every week of my life. I am, however, considering a "Chapter Two" in my career as I have hit a more cartable, and marketable age. We'll see how that goes over the next year, or two.

# *Ghost Warrior*
## (1983, U.S.A.)

*Genre:* Sci-Fi; *Director:* J. Larry Carroll; *Writers:* Tim Curnen and David Carren (uncredited); *Cinematographer:* Mac Ahlberg; *Editor:* Brad Arensman; *Special Makeup Effects:* Robert Short; *Special Mechanical Effects:* Roger George; *Producer:* Charles Band; *Associate Producers:* Mieko Bercovici and Gordon W. Gregory; *Executive Producers:* Albert Band, Arthur H. Maslansky and Uri & Efrem Harkham; *Production Company:* Empire Pictures; *Cast:* Hiroshi Fujioka (Yoshimitsu), John Calvin (Dr. Alan Richards), Janet Julian (Chris Welles), Charles Lampkin (Willie Walsh), Frank Schuller (Detective Berger), Bill Morey (Dr. Carl Anderson), Andy Wood (Dr. Pete Denza) and Robert Kino (Prof. Takagi)

In feudal Japan, a samurai falls into a frozen lake during a battle, while defending his beloved princess. His body remains hibernated for three centuries until it is shipped to a laboratory in California and brought secretly back to life by cryosurgery. The samurai escapes from the lab after killing one of the guards who had tried to steal his sword, and ventures out onto the streets of Los Angeles. Although the setting is now in current times his code of honor has remained true to his period. The samurai is chased by the police because he has broken the laws of the twentieth century and the scientist who revived him wants him dead to conceal an experiment that was to remain secret. Only one doctor is on his side. Disoriented in a chaotic modern metropolis, and with the princess he loved now lost forever, the samurai still has a way of making justice.

## Alan J. Adler
### (Writer, "Frozen Shogun")

[Author's note—Few people probably know that Alan J. Adler (*The Alchemist, Parasite, Metalstorm,* etc.) was also about to write *Ghost Warrior*. I asked him for information concerning the origins of "Frozen Shogun." When *Ghost Warrior* was made he had stopped working with Charles Band.]

Charles Band and I created this project. My original joke working title was "Frozen Shogun." I believe I wrote the original treatment then someone else wrote the screenplay and made it work. I liked the way it turned out—more serious than I envisioned it. I always wanted a scene where the samurai cut off someone's fingers with his sword in a sushi bar and a hapless customer ended up with a finger in his miso soup. Maybe that made it into the film—I only saw it once decades ago! I still have the original press kit we created that opened up like a broken piece of ice to display the warrior inside!

## Tim Curnen
(Writer)

[Author's note—I couldn't waste the chance to ask Tim Curnen about the story behind "Beasties," the movie that could have been the debut as director (before *Pumpkinhead*) for the wizard of special effects Stan Winston (1946–2008).]

Ed Pressman knew some of my previous writing [*Forbidden World*, 1981], and I believe he was looking for a way to involve me in some of his own projects. Ed introduced me to Stan Winston and Albert Band [1924–2002].

Before I was hired, Albert Band and Ed Pressman had commissioned a horror script, and Stan had designed and built a magnificent, very large, dragon-like creature for that film. But, as often happens in movies, they decided not to produce that script. Stan wanted to try something less brutal for his first film and wanted to start over with a more family-friendly story. But, he still had this huge creature in his studio to deal with. That's where I came in.

Stan took me out to his studio (still a fairly small operation at that point) and showed me the creature, asking if I could build a story around it. In the course of our discussions, he showed me a series of other creatures he had designed—wonderful gnomes and trolls—that he said he'd always wanted to use, but had no story for. So, that became my mission—to come up with a family-friendly story that used the monster and the other, smaller creatures as well. And "Beasties" [1983/1984] is what I came up with.

"Beasties" is about a father and his young son (named Matt, after Stan's own son Matt) who move into the boy's grandfather's house in the woods after the death of the boy's mother. The father is embittered, mourning the death of his wife, and the young boy was feeling the strain of that. In time, a number of "invisible" creatures (a humorous gathering of Stan's gnomes) begin to appear to the boy, who delights in their company. The boy can see them, but the father cannot, and soon the father becomes concerned that his son is emotionally disturbed and takes him to see a psychiatrist, a lovely woman who lives in the village. The boy knows the creatures are real—even if his father can't see them—and in time convinces the psychiatrist of that. The creatures want the boy to help them save their domain (a wondrous fantasy world which they allow the boy to see) from the local mogul who is trying to buy the land from the boy's father, planning to turn it into a shopping mall. So the creatures, and Matt, and eventually the psychiatrist, join together to convince the father to keep the property and save the creatures' world. In the process, the father is brought out of his despair, and father and son and the beautiful psychiatrist (and all of Stan's creatures!) live happily together ever after. (There's more to it than that, of course, but that's the gist of it.)

My main sources of inspiration for the script were Stan and his creations. Stan was alive with ideas, and had clear attitudes about the essential character of each of the creatures he created. Stan had at one time attempted to write a script himself using the characters, but abandoned it. We had many, many discussions before I sat down to write the script. Stan and I were also great fans of the artwork of Bernie Wrightson, whose illustrations helped to enliven our discussions.

Stan wanted to film it himself as his directorial debut, and ultimately (and unfortunately) that became part of the problem in getting it produced. There was a lot of interest in the script within the industry, and several studios seemed willing to take it on—but they wanted someone more experienced to direct (though they were more than eager to have Stan create the creatures). That was a deal-breaker for Stan, which was certainly his right. So, they were at a stalemate. In time, Stan's business grew enormously and he moved on to other things.

Stan made his directorial debut with a less challenging story, and "Beasties" languished on the shelf. It's too bad—Stan's preliminary work on that film was wonderful. (The models they made of the creatures were extraordinary!) Stan was an enormous talent and a great pleasure to work with. "Beasties" was a great working experience for me, and I've always been disappointed that the film was never made.

The work I did on "Beasties" led directly to my being invited to write *Ghost Warrior* [which was titled "Swordkill!" at the time]. Albert Band, one of the producers attached to "Beasties," was a big fan of that script. He recommended me to his son, Charles Band, who, with his father, had founded Empire Pictures, a prolific production company of B films at the time. I became involved with that script when Charles Band telephoned me to discuss his ideas for "Swordkill," with the hope that I would write it—as always, the ideas for his films started with him. I was interested and called my agent, Peter Turner, to discuss making a deal. My agent sounded amused, and asked if I had seen *Daily Variety* (the Hollywood trade newspaper) that day. I took a look and discovered that Empire Pictures had already run a full-page advertisement for "Swordkill," complete with spectacular poster design and announcing the start of principal photography in only a few weeks. The impression was that the film was about to start shooting. (Though they didn't have a script yet!) This was typical, I think, of Charles' self-confident marketing. I decided to go ahead with it and wrote the screenplay. (Very quickly, to be sure!) Somewhere in the process I was introduced to Larry Carroll, who directed, and the result was *Ghost Warrior*.

*Ghost Warrior* was made very quickly on a low budget. I'm a fan of samurai films, and I did a lot of research on the "way of the warrior" while writing the script, which went quickly into production. *Ghost Warrior* was mostly shot at various locations in Los Angeles. The snow sequences at the start [the duel engaged by Yoshimitsu to protect his princess] were shot at Mammoth Lake, a ski resort north of Los Angeles, and the confrontation at the lake at the end [between the samurai and the scientist who brought him back to life and the police] was shot at a local Los Angeles reservoir. The samurai gear—the saddles, armor, swords, etc.—were shipped to us from a film studio in Japan (as I recall), and arrived smelling of horse urine, which was used to preserve the leatherwork, and which smelled so bad that we almost had to close the production office the day they arrived. One of the pleasures of working on this film was working with Hiroshi Fujioka, a well-known actor in Japan, but little known in the U.S. at the time. One day while we were shooting in downtown Los Angeles a passing busload of Japanese tourists suddenly came to an abrupt halt and all the tourists rushed out. They had recognized Hiroshi and swarmed around him, wanting pictures and autographs. It was a real lesson to the film crew, I think, as we had no idea how famous he was in Japan. Hiroshi spoke little English, so most of the directing had to be done through an interpreter (a difficult challenge for both Larry and Hiroshi), but Hiroshi took his work seriously, and brought a lot of quiet dignity to the role. He was expert in the martial arts, and I think rare among martial arts actors, as he could do the sword work himself using real swords (which are alarmingly heavy), though for safety reasons he generally used prop swords in the film. He practiced his sword work daily on the set with a master teacher, who also appears in the film. The production gave Hiroshi a top-grade samurai sword—a real collector's piece—as part of his contract.

## J. Larry Carroll
### (Director)

I and some of my film school friends formed a production company (Shootout) in Austin. We were involved in making documentaries, industrials, TV commercials, etc. I produced, directed, and edited a number of these projects, one of which was a documentary that won an award at the New York Film Festival. Ted Nicolaou was one of those film school buddies along with Courtney Goodin and Daniel Pearl.

David Schmoeller, who I knew from film school, had been in Hollywood for a couple of years trying to get a mainstream project going. I suggested we collaborate on a low budget horror script which eventually became *Tourist Trap* [1978, David Schmoeller]. David's agent tried to set it up with John Carpenter, but I didn't like the deal. I wanted to put the project together myself so David could direct and I, produce. David's agent, Marty Shapiro, was pissed when I went over his head and made the deal with Charles Band but I think he was okay with it after we got the film made (sometime later, around 1988, I signed with Shapiro-Lichtman and they represented me for many years). I met Charlie when I was working as an assistant editor on *Dracula's Dog* [1976, Albert Band] with his father, Albert. I was working with film editor Harry Keramidas and Albert kept me on after the cut was finalized to shepherd the film through completion to the final print.

I brought Ted on as the editor for *Tourist Trap* and he has since worked a lot with Charlie in various capacities. As I recall, *Vortex* [1979, John "Bud" Cardos] was in development while *Tourist Trap* was in post. Wayne Schmidt and Steve Neill developed *Vortex* [a.k.a. *The Day Time Ended*]. I don't remember if they had written the original script on spec or not. Charlie hired David and I to do a quick rewrite which we did over a long weekend. Happily Wayne and Steve were cool with our revisions which was good because I liked them both. As for *Tourist Trap*, when I submitted our spec script to Charlie, his assistant, a great gal named Bennah Burton [1946–2006], read it and liked it. She made sure our script was always on top of Charlie's to-be-read stack. This went on for several weeks until Charlie finally gave in, read the script, liked it and the rest, as they say, is history. At Charlie's request, we rewrote the script to give Slauson (Chuck Connors) telekinetic powers. Before that, his "traps" were all diabolically mechanical in nature; a "real" Tourist Trap.

*Ghost Warrior* was my first (and only) movie as a director, but I had a bit of experience directing documentaries, industrials, TV commercials, etc., before I came to Hollywood. My directing the film was Debra Dion's idea. She sold Charlie on it then they brought me in. Debra was my assistant on *Parasite* [1982, Charles Band] as well as the Tom Petty music video "You Got Lucky" and a good friend.

"Swordkill" was a concept from Charlie & Albert Band. There was a one sheet (poster) before the film was made. I worked with Tim Curnen as he wrote the script. I don't recall if he had begun writing before I came onboard but I did work with Tim on various drafts. I don't think I have ever revealed this in an interview before, but my future writing partner, David Carren, did an uncredited rewrite at my behest, focusing on some problematic scenes.

Albert Band, bless his larcenous heart, had read a book called "The Far Arena" [1979, by Richard Sapir] about a gladiator who was somehow frozen then revived in modern times. He and Charlie liked the basic idea and decided to use the classic (hoary?) freezing-to-travel-through-time device with a samurai warrior. Tim Curnen was deep into the scripting process when we learned about the source of the Bands' inspiration. This came about when Albert wanted us to read the book for "ideas." We were horrified and as I recall Tim refused to even look at the book. I think I read the book myself prior to shooting to try to avoid any plagiarism, unintended or otherwise. I don't remember a great deal about *The Far Arena*. Maybe *Ghost Warrior* would have been a better movie if we had lifted the script from the book like Albert wanted.

Mieko Bercovici was instrumental in the involvement of Hiroshi Fujioka. Mieko had been involved with *Shogun* [1980] where she met her husband, Luca Bercovici. Luca, who was trying to get *Ghoulies* [1984] off the ground with the Bands, introduced us. Mieko then worked with Debra Dion to come up with a very short list of Japanese actors. Then Mieko and I went to Japan to audition them. I knew Hiroshi was the right guy the minute I met him. Mieko was also instrumental in acquiring authentic props, wardrobe and some of the supporting cast like Toshishiro Obata. Hiroshi and I exchanged Christmas cards for a few years, but I lost contact with him some time ago.

Early on, an unknown American actor was proposed for the part of Yoshi. I was dubious, but agreed to meet with him. Afterwards I decided he wouldn't work for a variety of reasons. The actor was Steven Segal. *Ghost Warrior* would likely have been his first starring role.

The schedule including pickups was about six weeks. The snow sequences in the beginning of the film were shot in Mammoth after principal photography. The interior of the ice cave was on a stage in LA. The location for the fight with the gang [Yoshimitsu is involved in the rescue of an elderly man] was the old Pan-Pacific Auditorium. In its day it was one of the finest examples of the streamline moderne style in the country. Sadly it was pretty decrepit by the time we were shooting there. Intensely weird (and filthy) inside. It burned down a couple of years later. *Ghost Warrior* was one of the last times it appeared on film.

We cast two Japanese American actors for the discovery of Yoshi's frozen body in the ice cave. We had our Japanese consultants work with them on the dialogue as neither actor spoke Japanese. The Americans' mispronunciations must have been pretty outrageous as the Japanese literally wound up on the floor, laughing.

During the film's climax, Yoshi is shot and falls over a cliff. However, on the first take when Hiroshi is shot, he staggers and falls over backwards and lay dead still. I was surprised because Hiroshi usually understood my direction. Then I realized he actually collapsed because he was so ill and exhausted. Hiroshi was a real trooper—but should have been at home in bed.

I recall meeting Uri and Efrem Harkham [the Executive Producers on *Ghost Warrior*] only once before we began shooting. One kind of funny incident came about because the Arkhams were in the clothing business and had their own line of jeans. There is a moment in the film when the newly awakened Yoshimitsu encounters a TV and is stunned by the images of a jeans commercial. We originally had a really outrageous, visually stunning Levi commercial for said images but because the Arkams had their own line of jeans, we wound up using one of their not-so-stunning commercials. Supposedly the Harkhams sued Band in 1988, but I didn't hear about it until many years later. However, I question whether there was a lawsuit as I was never deposed.

In hindsight, the story would have been better if we had used time travel instead of freezing to bring Yoshi into the present. If the samurai had been brought into our time by an accident during a time travel experiment, then the Chris Welles character [the girl who helps Yoshi, interpreted by Janet Julian] and the scientists would have been working against the clock to find Yoshi and return him to his own time. And there would be a happy ending when Yoshi returned in the nick of time to save Princess Chidori.

For me personally the film was a watershed moment. Like everyone who graduates from film school, I wanted to be a director. I worked toward that goal for the better part of five years. But when I finished the film I thought, "Huh. That wasn't what I thought it would be like." But what I really enjoyed was working with Tim and David on the script. So I dedicated my energy to building a writing career. Something I have never regretted. That said, people weren't exactly knocking down my door with directing offers. Plus I had a new daughter and I didn't want to be away from home as much as film career would require. Like I say, I have never been sorry I focused on my writing career after *Ghost Warrior*. Wish I had done so sooner.

# *Hunk*
## (1987, U.S.A.)

*Genre:* Fantasy/Comedy; *Director:* Lawrence Bassoff; *Writer:* Lawrence Bassoff; *Cinematographer:* Bryan England; *Editor:* Richard E. Westover; *Special Makeup Effects:* Thomas Wayne Schwartz; *Producers:* Mark Tenser and Marilyn J. Tenser; *Associate Producer:* Steven J. Wolfe; *Production Company:* Crown International Pictures; *Cast:* John Allen Nelson (Hunk Golden), Steve Levitt (Bradley Brinkman), Deborah Shelton (O'Brien), James Coco (Dr. D.), Rebecca Bush (Sunny), Robert Morse (Garrison Gaylord), Cynthia Szigeti (Chachka) and Avery Schreiber (Constantine Constapopolis)

A goofy computer programmer makes a pact with the devil and his charming agent, before being transformed into an irresistible hunk. The agreement allows for a trial run and if at the end of the time agreed the young man is satisfied with his new life, he will surrender his soul to the devil forever. It is a rocking summer for the young man who quickly becomes the idol of the beach whom no woman can resist. Under the features of the beautiful psychiatrist to whom the boy confides his incredible story is still the agent of the devil who has to be careful not to fall in love with him: in the last hundred years, she has not provided the devil even with one soul and if she does not fulfill the contract she will be fired.

## Lawrence Bassoff
### (Writer/Director)

First of all, I want to say how grateful I am to Mark Tenser (Chief Executive/Producer) and Marilyn J. Tenser (Producer) of Crown International Pictures for giving me the opportunity to write and direct two feature films for them: *Weekend Pass* [1983] and *Hunk*. Their experience and guidance made them marvelous to work with and we really had a great time making the films.

I was born in New York City, in 1951. I was movie mad for as long as I can remember and my parents' love of movies stoked my interest. A babysitter took me to see a double feature every Saturday and sometimes I'd go to a movie that same night with my parents. My grandmother took me to Manhattan to see blockbusters like *The Seventh Voyage of Sinbad*, *Ben-Hur* and *El Cid* at classic palaces like Radio City, the Roxy, and the DeMille. *The Vikings* (1958) with Kirk Douglas also really blew my mind and was my favorite movie for years. New York local television was playing off great films from all the studios seven days a week: *King Kong*, *Gunga Din*, and *Captain Blood*. Bodybuilder Steve Reeves was another boyhood favorite in *Hercules Unchained*, *Morgan the Pirate* and *Thief of Baghdad* (I later became quite friendly with Steve after I interviewed him for the *L.A. Times* in 1976). I saw every 007 film as released.

I finally got to apply my love of movies when I attended Cornell University in Ithaca, New York, from 1969 to 1973. From my first semester I started writing film reviews for the school newspaper, *The Cornell Daily Sun*. I wrote reviews for four years and became review editor my final year.

This identification with movies led me to move to Los Angeles in 1973 to attend the University of Southern California Law School—I hoped to be a lawyer in the movie business. Across campus, however, was what is now called the USC School of Cinematic Arts and I soon transferred there and studied film production where fellow directors Albert Magnoli (*Purple Rain*), James Foley (*Glengarry Glen Ross*) and Kevin Reynolds (*Waterworld*) were also learning at the same time.

I wrote and directed a comedy short there in 1980 called *Today, I am a Man ... I Think*. It was a satire about a Jewish boy whose parents are giving him a "Star Wars" themed barmitzvah and how he learns to endure it with dignity with the help of his traditional grandfather. The film was shown at the Academy of Motion Picture Arts and Sciences Student Film Awards (2nd place in the Western Region), the Los Angeles International Film Exposition (Filmex), the Writers Guild of America and the Screen Actors Guild of America. From there I was able to secure an agent and manager. I started writing feature screenplays as soon as I left USC in 1981.

I also studied extensively in the theatre in hopes of improving my directing of actors. The first class was beginning acting at the Melrose Theatre in West Hollywood. The teacher was actor Paul Mantee, the star of the cult sci-fi movie *Robinson Crusoe on Mars*. I later studied improvisational comedy at the Groundlings Theatre in West Hollywood, a place which has produced Pee Wee Herman, Kathy Griffin, Melissa McCarthy, Elvira, Jon Lovitz and many others. A great opportunity to study with legendary Lee Strasberg arose in 1981–1982. I studied acting, directing and Shakespeare with Lee in Los Angeles and New York. He was extraordinary. Other esteemed acting coaches I studied with included Stella Adler (for script interpretation), Jose Quintero (director of classic Eugene O'Neill productions on Broadway with George C. Scott and Coleen Dewhurst), Nina Foch (Academy Award nominee for *Executive Suite*) and Robert Lewis (former Yale drama professor of Meryl Streep and a renowned character actor in his own right).

I did take a break from film school when I won a training job at Warner Bros. in advertising and publicity in 1977. I worked in all the departments for about 16 months, became a member of the Publicists Guild and then left the studio in 1978 to go back to USC. I paid my way through the rest of USC by working on advertising campaigns for many studios and movie ad agencies. Films I worked on included *The Gauntlet, Someone Is Killing the Great Chefs of Europe, Hooper, Somebody Killed Her Husband, Tom Horn, The Champ, Time After Time, 10, A Little Romance, Let's Do It Again, The Goodbye Girl, Crossed Swords, The Octagon, Zulu Dawn, Girlfriends, The Main Event, American Success Company, Fame, Dreamer, The Big Fix, French Postcards, Honeysuckle Rose, Avalanche Express, California Suite, Agatha, Winter Kills, It's Alive!, Golden Girl, Hide in Plain Sight, Capricorn One, Swept Away, Our Winning Season, Nijinsky, Goin' Coconuts, Boulevard Nights, Americathon, Promises in the Dark, An Enemy of the People, When Time Ran Out* and many others.

I also wrote freelance articles for the *Los Angeles Times* and *Los Angeles Free Press*. I interviewed Sylvester Stallone, Randy Quaid, Steve Reeves, Clayton Moore (*The Lone Ranger*), Rory Calhoun, director Claudia Weill and others.

After completing film school, I decided to concentrate on comedy. I wrote a sample screenplay called "Teen Tour," a raucous road movie about teens touring famous American tourist attractions. My agent and manager arranged screenings of the USC short and began circulating "Teen Tour."

While they did get me many meetings, I got the job for *Weekend Pass* through my advertising work. When I was at Warner Bros. I had met a graphic designer named Cheryl Poindexter. After I left the studio, we began working together and she suggested me to Mark Tenser at Crown. She had worked on a number of Crown movie ad campaigns. Mark screened the USC comedy short and had me come in for a meeting in 1983. I then submitted "Teen Tour" as a writing sample and Mark offered me the chance to create a story for *Weekend Pass*.

*Weekend Pass* was totally Mark Tenser's idea. He felt there hadn't been a "service comedy" in a long time and that uniformed comedy did well. *Police Academy* had just been a big hit. Mark suggested having three sailors racing through a final wild weekend in Los Angeles while on their way from basic training to their first deployments. I suggested adding a fourth sailor and away we went setting the four interlocking stories of the sailors against a montage-laden, music-packed visit to all the great tourist attractions of Southern California. *Weekend Pass* became one of the top-grossing independent releases of 1984. It was played-off around the U.S. and sold into many foreign markets. The Vestron video release received an "RIAA Certified Gold Video Award" for sales of 50,000 units.

After making *Weekend Pass*, I discussed several other projects with Mark Tenser. These were concepts he was already considering: *My Chauffeur* (which was called "Limo" at first as I recall) [eventually written and directed by David Beaird, 1985], *Cavegirl* [eventually written and directed by David Oliver Pfeil, 1984] and, later, *My Mom's a Werewolf* [eventually written by Mark Pirro and directed by Michael Fischa, 1988]. He'd had the title "Hunk" for some time and may have had some artwork for that.

Mark asked me to come up with a story concept for a handsome Adonis and set it at the beach. It took awhile but I worked out a Faustian approach to the story—that a nerd would sell his soul for the summer to the Devil for the chance to become a peerless playboy and man of the world. This freed the title from the usual beach movie hijinks and gave us much more to play with dramatically and comedically. I also added a then-prevalent "yuppie" theme which made the supporting characters more than the usual parade of beach beauties and bohunks. Certainly the story has echoes of *Damn Yankees* and *Bedazzled* but the setting was novel. I wrote a very short treatment and Mark accepted that approach and I then wrote a longer treatment and the script.

*Hunk* was much simpler production-wise than *Weekend Pass*. The key thing was finding a beach house where we could shoot interiors and exteriors. That is the production basis of many beach and haunted house movies—find one location where you can shoot as much of the film as you can.

—Beach house ... We found a beach house on Paradise Cove, a strip of beach north of Malibu which has been the scene of many beach movies. The house was a bit small but it had a roomy deck on which we shot many exterior scenes. Because the bathrooms in the house were hard to light, we "built" an exterior bathroom with a sink and shower right on the beach for the opening montage and other scenes. The house had nautical dècor so we jazzed that up and used it. The gated driveway to the house was actually shot in Malibu at a different private home. We also shot at a private ocean view home owned by actor Paul Mantee.

—Beach club ... The exterior beach scenes were also shot in Paradise Cove. We dressed the beach and filled it with extras. Director of photography Bryan England did a top job of lighting the rocky bluffs of the cove for the climactic night scene when Hunk is given the key to the city of Sea Spray.

—Night club ... These sequences were shot in the restaurant at Paradise Cove. Our production designer, Catherine Hardwicke (who later directed *13* and *Red Riding Hood*) covered the walls with fabric to give it a fantasy undersea atmosphere. Our best prop in this scene was a living one—a live mermaid played by Andrea Patrick.

—Constantine Constapopolis computer offices ... We got a lot of production value shooting these scenes in a phone company office in Pasadena, California. They had a big computer board with lots of colored, flickering panels which we used to great effect and at no extra cost.

—Dr. Sunny Graves' office ... This was a vacant office space in West Hollywood, California. What was nice was the high ceiling which allowed us to get a marvelous high angle shot of the office. It gave the film a rich start.

—Helicopter shots ... For the opening montage, we were able to secure a helicopter and did several days of shooting. We shot Hunk driving up the Pacific Coast Highway in his red Maserati. Another day, we did copter shots of him driving his car in Beverly Hills and were flagged by the local authorities for flying too low but we still got the shots.

Since the film had a "before" and "after" aspect, it was crucial to find two very good but very different actors to play Bradley Brinkman and Hunk. John Allen Nelson was outstanding in our auditions and he trained and dieted to get his body to peak perfection. Steve Levitt, as the nerdy Bradley, was so opposite—a comedy character with red hair and a self-deprecating sense of humor. A favorite scene in the film is when they both appear on screen at the same time in the scene where Bradley "escapes" from Hell to warn Hunk about the devil-of-a-deal he has made.

Deborah Shelton was always a top choice to play O'Brien, the Devil's soul searching minion. Deborah is a great beauty inside and out. A former Miss U.S.A. who had appeared in the *Dallas* TV series and Brian De Palma's *Body Double*, Deborah was a total delight to work with—down to earth, serious about acting, friendly to all.

I don't remember anyone but Academy Award nominated actor James Coco [1930–1987] being considered for the role of Dr. D. He read the script in New York and agreed immediately. It was his last film and, alas, he never saw a frame of it. I adore the scene he plays in a Nazi uniform when he is warning O'Brien about falling in love with Hunk. It's the best scene I ever wrote and the two of them played it to the hilt.

Hilary Shepard had appeared in *Weekend Pass* and returned to work with me as one of the bitchy beach yuppies. Cynthia Szigeti, who played the local gossip, Chachka, had been my comedy instructor at the Groundlings and I wrote the part with her in mind. Comedy veteran Avery Schreiber was ideal casting as Constantine Constapopolis—he had

**John Allen Nelson ("Hunk Golden"), Lawrence Bassoff (Writer/Director) and Deborah Shelton ("O'Brien") (courtesy of Lawrence Bassoff).**

so much comic technique that you never knew what he was going to do next. Rebeccah Bush did a fine job as O'Brien's alter ego, Dr. Sunny Graves.

Because *Hunk* is a fantasy, we had a few trick shots to pull off in the scene where O'Brien "molds" Bradley's new body while he sleeps. We shot Deborah Shelton in slow motion against a black background and later superimposed this over the shot of Bradley sleeping so it looked like she was in the room in spirit form. The big joke in that scene is where she makes his crotch grow. We interviewed several special effects companies and finally found the right people to use molded rubber to give Hunk enhanced biceps, pectorals and an up-growing crotch.

The 1-sheet poster utilized a special shoot with the four principal actors—Nelson, Levitt, Shelton and Coco. It shows Levitt jumping through a mirror and coming out the other side as Nelson—basically dramatizing the before and after concept of the film. When

RCA-Columbia Home Video bought the film they shot a new cover with more typical beach-movie-type art.

Music for *Hunk* came from two sources—composer David Kurtz and the team of John and Robbie Baer. For the title song, "Real Man" (written by John Baer) we brought in famous saxophone session player David Woodford ("The Heat is On" from *Beverly Hills Cop*) to do a sax solo over the credits. David Kurtz did a fine job blending the scenes together musically.

I later wrote the original screenplays "Hollywood Heroes," "Forbidden Television" and "Don't Make Me Over." In 1994 I realized another lifelong movie dream and established a movie book publishing company, Lawrence Bassoff Collection, Inc. I wrote and published a trilogy of movie poster books—"Errol Flynn—The Movie Posters" (1995), "Crime Scenes—Movie Poster Art of the Film Noir" (1997) and "Mighty Movies—Movie Poster Art from Hollywood's Greatest Adventure Epics and Spectaculars" (2000).

That all sprang from a twenty-year hobby I had of collecting vintage movie posters. The books were very successful, selling a total of 31,000 copies. I have also exhibited movie posters and related memorabilia at the Los Angeles County Museum of Art (Made in California), USC School of Cinematic Arts (an exhibition for John Wayne's centennial birthday), and the Art Gallery of New South Wales, Sydney, Australia (numerous lectures and shows including Errol Flynn, adventure epics, and film noir).

# *The Lamp,*
# a.k.a. *The Outing*
## (1986, U.S.A.)

*Genre:* Horror; *Director:* Tom Daley; *Writer:* Warren Chaney; *Cinematographer:* Herbert Raditschnig; *Editor:* Claudio Cutry; *"Lamp" and "Genie" designed by:* Barbara Anne Bock; *Special Makeup and Creature Effects:* Reel EFX; *Visual Effects:* Technomagic Film Effects (Hollywood Optical Systems); *Producer:* Warren Chaney; *Associate Producer:* Deborah Winters; *Executive Producers:* Fred T. Kuehnert and M.N. Sanousi; *Production Company:* H.I.T. Films; *Cast:* Andra St. Ivanyi (Alex Wallace), Deborah Winters (Eve Ferrell/Young Arab Woman/Old Arab Woman), James Huston (Dr. Wallace), Scott Bankston (Ted), Mark Mitchell (Mike), Andrè Chimene (Tony), Damon Merrill (Babs), Barry Coffing (Ross), Tracye Walker (Gwen), Raan Lewis (Terry), Danny D. Daniels (Dr. Theo Bressling), Hank Amigo (Harley), Brian Floores (Max) and Michelle Watkins (Faylene)

The year 1893: The entire crew of a ship bound for Galveston (Texas) is slaughtered by an evil genie, who dwells inside an old lamp from the Middle East. A young girl takes possession of the lamp and of a strange bracelet and takes the two objects away with her. We come to 1986. Three young robbers burst into the home of an elderly woman and brutally kill her with an ax. Unfortunately for them, the woman has the lamp described in the prologue of the film in custody, and the three thieves are slaughtered by the genie. The lamp, which was found by the police on the site of the massacre, is transferred to the local natural history museum. The daughter of the director of the museum, who wears the bracelet, unwittingly expresses a fatal desire against her father, who, following the death of her mother, starts seeing her teacher. Possessed by the spirit of the malignant genie, the girl convinces her friends to spend a night in the museum. In the building the genie abandons the girl's body to satisfy his thirst for blood and to fulfill the wish of his new master, the girl wearing the bracelet.

## Warren Chaney
## (Writer/Producer/2nd Unit Director)

*The Lamp* was intended to be "part satire" of the "horror genre" at the time and a variant of the "Genie in the magic lamp" story. As a youngster, my mother read me the story of Aladdin from a "grade-school" primer. In it, there were drawings of the "jinn" or "genie" and I can remember thinking that it would be terrifying if one actually met one of these creatures. Naturally, I made a point of seeing all the Aladdin films as I grew up in the 40s and 50s. *The Lamp* (in my mind) was Aladdin's—only instead of a genie granting you your every wish, you and a genie that made you careful of what you wished for. This was the reason for the opening scenes which depicted the "cargo" as Middle Eastern in origin. I knew that there was also a Chinese version of Aladdin but I chose to stick to the Arabian form. The original theme of the movie was supposed to have been: "*The Lamp … be careful of what you wish for!*" As I recalled, one of the Skouras film's releases had: "*The Lamp … don't rub it the wrong way!*"

With the advent of London's Hammer Films, the horror genre found new life with continuing reincarnations of Peter Cushing's Frankenstein and Christopher Lee's Dracula … not to count the mummy, the werewolf and other such films. Like many young people, I was drawn to those films but never wanted to film one. However, when I produced the film *Aloha Summer* [1984], I hired my friend Tommy Lee Wallace to direct. Tommy had been the editor and art director on the first *Halloween* and had directed the 3rd one. Many of John's [John Carpenter] crew worked for me on the shoot and we spent many hours talking about their film and how they managed to squeeze out such a successful film on such a low budget. At any rate, it started me thinking about doing a horror pic but I wanted to do something different. By 1983 there were already dozens of copycat pics from the Friday the 13th series to multiple Freddie Krueger, *Killer Shark* and *Fright Night* films.

It seemed to me that the goal of most horror films was to kill as many dislikable teens as it could in 86–94 minutes. So, after I'd shepherded *Aloha Summer* through its distribution, I sat down one night at a typewriter and began to bang out *The Lamp*. A few months earlier I'd been in Milano for its annual film festival and had an opportunity to tour one of the large museums that are there. It occurred to me that no one had ever shot a horror film in a museum before—and given the right ambience, it could be very creepy. So, I combined the genie with the museum and developed what I thought was a good fit. For the first 50 minutes, the genie is unseen and the viewer is aware of it only through the use of POV shots. I wanted to do a satire of the genre so I used three "hicks" (*The Texas Chainsaw Massacre*), disobedient teens (*Friday the 13th* and *Jaws 3, 4, 5, 6*, etc.), and the parent that doesn't get it (*Halloween, Jaws, Fright Night*, etc.). At the time, many horror films always had an old codger, or professor type who knew

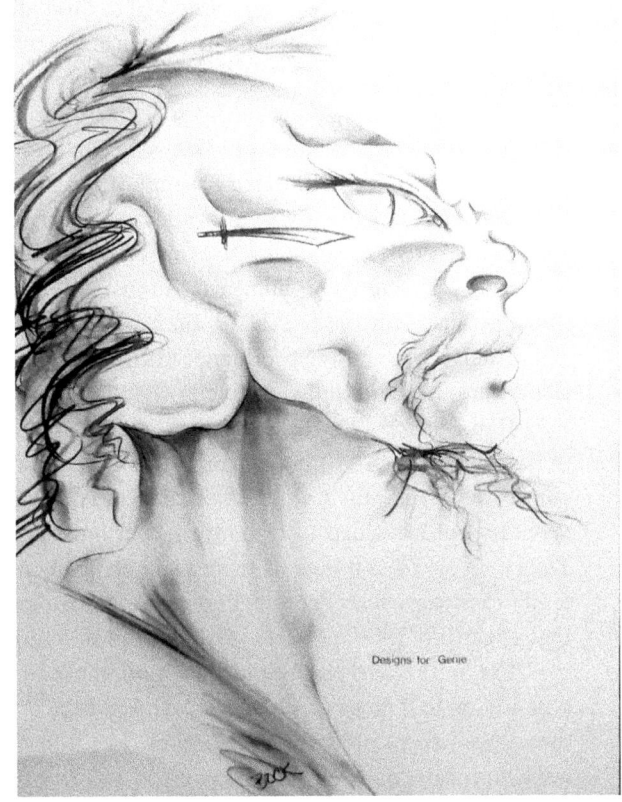

**One of the preliminary designs for "The Genie" (courtesy of Barbara Anne Bock).**

there were "creatures" about (*Dracula's* Van Helsing or *Halloween's* Dr. Sam Loomis). Instead, I decided to make the character a "woman" and instead of a learned professor, a learned high school teacher [Eve Ferrell, played by Deborah Winters] that knows martial arts. Now, keep in mind that the "women as heroes" films hadn't been made and wouldn't occur until near the turn of the century.

I'd always loved how there are "characters" so oblivious in horror films that you wonder how they made it this far hence my early use of the "two detectives" [Detective Charles and Detective Adams, played by Warren Chaney and Blue Deckert] freely handling the lamp while squabbling over what's for lunch, "chicken or pizza." Later on we've got the "singing guard" [Roy Alan Wilson], and the other museum guard [Coy Sevier] killed by being stuffed with JujyFruits (in the U.S., this candy was a favorite in most movie theatres and hence my use of it to "kill" one of the film's victims). Now even with the satire, I wanted to keep the film creepy. I remember one night in Hollywood, I'm pecking away (no word processors then) and it's rather late. I'm writing the scene where the "old lady" is killed in a "double axe murder" (meant to parody the plentiful axe murder films) and actually spooked myself when I wrote the scene.

At the time of writing, I'd just come off of *Aloha Summer* which was for the time a large budget film, and I wanted to do a low budget film. I didn't want to do one too low else you have to write a film that defies the odds but I didn't want to do a 20 million dollar film. Can you believe we're spending $80 to $100 million now? Sheesh. The average cost of a Hollywood film then was in the $6–12 million range (*Star Wars* was $9 million), So I aimed to write something that could be shot for 1.5 to 2.5 million. You can, but it's hard to lose money at that scale providing you shoot something that gets distributed.

My screenwriting time was 5 days. I didn't want to give it to the studio then else they would have thought I'd hurried through it. So, I put it on a shelf and waited a few weeks then delivered it. The production house shooting the film was H.I.T. Films (*Buddy Holly Story*, *The Aurora Encounter*, etc.) owned by an Arabic group from Kuwait. The president was a nice man named Mohammed Sanousi. Interestingly, the CEO for *Halloween* was from the same area, Moustapha Akkad. Both were executive producers on their respective films. The American executive producer with the company was a fellow named Fred Kuehnert, also a very nice and quite capable individual.

Tom Daley [?–2014] was a friend of mine that I'd met on *Aloha Summer* while filming in Hawaii. Tom was originally from Austin, Texas, and had directed a number of successful commercials and music videos (which were fairly new back then). He hadn't directed a feature film but I decided to give him a flyer on this one. In retrospect, directing a film like *The Lamp* on a low budget is trying and probably unfair for a first time director. They will tend to become overly dependent on the cinematographer whose primary emphasis is often that of getting "nice" pictures—as opposed to telling a story.

The film's actual budget was $1.6 million but by the time the production house and studios add on to it, it was around $3 to $3.7 million—about a third of the average film budget then. But, I spent only $1.6 on the film. The film had a 6 week prep time followed by a 5 week film shoot on location in Galveston and Houston, Texas, and another week of filming in Hollywood. This was followed by 90 days of post-production, also in Hollywood.

As a side note, the film was originally scheduled to be shot in L.A., using the Natural Science Museum by the Tar Pits and Marina Del Rey—dressed for the 1890s Galveston segment. It just so happened that representatives for the Texas Film Office were in LA pitching their state and the savings that could be incurred by relocating the filming. I found several sound stages in Houston and wonderful locations in Galveston not to count Houston's Museum, and decided to change locations. The savings knocked at least $500,000 off the budget. My budget for "location fees" went from $80,000 to $415, for example. This gave me more money to put up on the screen and as the studios saw it—more money to pad their budgets with to line their pockets.

CGI didn't really exist at that time as we have them today. The "effects" that were added in post were mostly "animation" such as the glow around the genie, the lamp clicker, smoke enhancement, etc. I knew and liked David Hewitt [Technomagic Film Effects/Hollywood Optical Systems], very much. He worked with us in post-production and some of the animation effects that were added, were his. David was a few years older than me, but being young at the time, we struck it off pretty good. He had also been involved with "stop-motion" animation and I was very tempted to go that way with the genie. Eventually, budget limitations and time overtook us, so I continued with what we had.

For the genie, I wanted to avoid the guy in make-up and smoke so I used an LA company called Reel EFX to build a large latex figure. The genie was huge and towering, and it was creepy. It was very well constructed—when I left LA for Houston, it worked fine. But something happened between there and the filming. The creature could have been

**Final design for "The Lamp" (courtesy of Barbara Anne Bock).**

damaged in shipment, I don't know. Very few of the genie's effects worked as they were supposed to. The eyes wouldn't move and there were problems with the fingers. So, Tom Daley filmed the genie in quick-cuts. Everything else that Reel EFX did for us from the Lamp itself to the body in the pool [Brian Floores, cut in half by the genie], worked great.

There were some longer shots of the genie that were cut out of the original scenes but later reinserted by the studio. My belief has always been that the "less you show" the greater the fear since people worry about what they can't see. I wanted to film much less of the physical genie; Tom wanted to film more of the creature and so shot a great deal more footage in production. When I did the final edit however, I cut much of it out but as fate would have it, both distributors [Skouras Pictures and TMS] agreed with Tom and edited much of it back into the picture. I have always believed that when you are filming creatures "less is more," but given the success both distributors had with the film, it's hard for me to argue against them.

*The Lamp* was the title of the film as sent to distribution. H.I.T. Films separated U.S. domestic from overseas and so "two films" were born: "The Lamp" and "The Outing." Skouras Pictures took the pic as *The Lamp* and released it in theaters in the overseas markets; TMS (The Movie Store) was the domestic distributor and wanted to cut 18 minutes out of the film in order that it could run "one more time" in the theaters. The original film ran 102 minutes but after their cut, it was reduced to 86 minutes. Now, their method for editing left a lot to be desired: they merely took a pair of scissors and cut 18 minutes off the front end; they tacked on some "cheap" credits and ripped off some of John's music [John Carpenter] and they had a pic that would run 4 or 5 times per day instead of 3. Reviews for the original were pretty good; reviews for *The Outing* were much less so—and I agreed with the critics.

Five scenes were cut from the opening of the film. The opening scenes set the picture up to be a "tall tale"—there was considerably more detail about the ship, its cargo, and what happened on the way over (however, there were no hints as to the cause … you heard the screams and the helmsman lashing himself to the wheel). In a later scene (cut from the movie), one of the hoods [played by Hank Amigo, Brian Floores and Michelle Watkins] while delivering groceries, hears the old lady talking to the lamp. It occurred prior to the scenes where she was killed. That scene set up the "killers," her, and her mystical aspects which is misunderstood by the thugs as her having a lot of money. When the scenes were cut, the picture opened in what was probably the poorest directed segment of the film: the scenes with the hoods in the van, on the way to the old woman's house (if I had known this, I would have destroyed that part of the print). As a consequence, there was no "logic" to the film's story from that point forward.

The end of the movie was trimmed (some 3 minutes). The museum director's daughter [Andra St. Ivanyi] was being taken to a local hospital (explained by Detective Charles). Given the circumstances of the killings in the museum, the police are keeping her under guard. The teacher [Deborah Winters] remains to answer questions. There is a scene of a delivery truck delivering cases of soda. When the driver handles the cases, the bottles jingle, producing the sounds of the "evil-bracelet." What was cut earlier was a quick scene early in the film when the driver is doing the same thing as the kids enter the museum. Andra St. Ivanyi looks at the truck and then at her bracelet. At the close of the film, the same thing happens, only now it's a deathly reminder the girl of what happened. What was cut in the final scene was the close up of the bottles clinking together and making the bracelet sound.

At the same time, the picture had been given a "PG 13" rating and the distributor wanted a harder "R" rating so they looped in a ton of "language" not present in the original screenplay or film; "4-Letter" words were dubbed in—sometimes, I heard the language without ever seeing the actor's lips move!

At the time, I was filming in the Channel Islands and then spent several weeks in London, so I was unaware of the changes till I returned to the States. Now all this being said, both films ending up earning large dollars considering the amount it took to make it. Go figure? *The Outing* eventually went to video tape and had an excellent release and then was bought out by USA Network for 5 years of screening. The last time I saw a clip it was a late-night showing at 2 a.m. on a screen with a couple of robots talking to the screen.

I had thought of a sequel and the end of the genie does leave that hanging. However, about 7–8 months after the release, the film's production company (H.I.T. Films) sold to a Kuwait film company and I lost touch with them. The second screenplay had been contracted for, but I never got beyond a screen-treatment for them. The tentative title of the screenplay was "Legacy." As I recall, in the sequel, the lamp is discovered many years later in the discarded ashes from the furnace [where it had been thrown away by the girl at the end of the film] with an assumption made that the "relic" was there by mistake. After an initial "evil encounter" the lamp becomes part of a new Arabic exhibit and goes on tour, stopping at one point at the Smithsonian, where it finds another "handler" who is the daughter of a U.S. Senator. I reckon this sounds sort of like "Mr. Genie Goes to Washington," right? The film was to have been entirely recast. Those in the current cast at some point tried to contact both the original characters, but discovered that the teacher was dead and the [museum director's] daughter committed to an asylum. That's about as much as I can remember. Tom would not have been the director as I wanted to take the film in an entirely new direction. He and I had discussed it and he was in agreement with me.

[Here are some stories from the filming…]

—One of the extras I'd hired to play a museum guard was an actor named Roy Alan Wilson. One night during a break in filming, it was very quiet in the museum when suddenly I heard the most spectacular operatic singing. Roy was in the central part of the museum singing a passage from Mozart's "Le nozze di Figaro." It was eerily beautiful and since I wanted humor and satire in the film, I set up a camera on the spot and filmed the sequence. In the original film, at its very end, Roy concludes the song and takes a bow. Unfortunately, when they were shortening the film this was cut along with the opening scenes. What the studio ended up with was a series of parodies that no one in the audience understood because the set ups for the "tall tale" were taken out, before during and afterwards.

—There was one scene toward the end where my wife Deborah Winters (in her character) is grabbed by the genie. So you had this big hand around her throat, tons of smoke and blowing fans going. On "action" she was supposed to scream, and she did. On set, it looked and sounded very good, so no retake was done. However, in the dailies, her voice didn't sound right. Tom thought that he'd made a mistake so later on he had the scene reset and did a retake. Same results! This went on for 4 more setups and retakes during the film. He had Deborah lower her voice, raise her voice, do it louder, soften and even in between. It never came out right. Tom and I decided during the edit to cut the scene, but in the distributor cut, in both cases, it was added back in. Much later on we learned that our soundman was using a specific kind of mike for that set, one that he wasn't using for the other scenes and for whatever reason, Deborah's voice was recorded in a higher tone. Go figure. Must have been the genie at work.

—My younger son Jason (who was 6 at the time) was deathly afraid of all horror films, even those dating back to the 30s. Of course we never encouraged him to watch them so that's understandable. One day I took him to the set to see the "big genie" that he'd been afraid of when he watched one of the dailies. Once on set I held his hand, showed him the set and then went to where the genie was positioned. I carefully pointed out that he was nothing more than a large robotic puppet that wasn't working. This encouraged Jason enough that he walked up to it and as he approached, the thing fell forward. To a 5-year-old it appeared that the genie was lurching for him. So much for the "lesson" on Hollywood fakery.

As I look backward on *The Lamp* or its stepchild, *The Outing*, I was shocked that it made the money it did and had as long a run as it had. It developed a cult following such that when Roy Alan Wilson was on vacation in London, he was shocked to discover that many recognized him as the singing guard in the museum. In fact, the ownership of the hotel he was staying at would not accept payment for his stay. In 1997 or 1998 *The Lamp* was inducted into the Cult Film Hall of Fame—and I never added that to my resume! Then it was parodied in a comic version and sequel that did well in box office titled, *Night at the Museum* [2006]. Milan Trenc's book "The Night at the Museum" [1933] had first conceived of using the similar concept that had influenced him but more fancifully so. They named the "night guard" [Ben Stiller] Daley! A nice touch, I thought.

Tom Daley passed away in Hawaii in mid–2014 and that was a sadness to me. He was a little guy with a wonderfully happy personality. If there are such things as leprechauns, then Tom is one of them. He was imminently easy to work with and did well under pressure. We were often pressed for time in our shooting schedule so when filming fell behind, he never minded that I would go off and do 2nd Unit work to get us back on schedule (I directed several of the scenes in the museum as well as the night-time scenes outside of the museum). His goal was to shoot a good picture, however it needed to be done. Too often in this business, you work with someone day and night for months on end, and the picture ends … the shoot is over … and the film is finished. Afterwards, you may never see or hear from that person again. Tom was not such an individual. From our first encounter on *Aloha Summer* until his death, he went out of his way to stay in touch. Everyone that knew him, misses him and his passing has left a "hole" that will remain empty. He was a good friend to all.

I ended up spending a quarter century in filmmaking and enjoyed all of it. While I did direct some much higher budgeted films (*America* with Charlton Heston and *Behind the Mask* with Deborah Winters), I always had the most fun on the smaller films. In an industry where job security is nonexistent, that approach kept me working nonstop until I retired from film and television in 2005. I intended to stay retired but the old curse holds true, "writers must write and directors must direct." So, at age 73 I'm finding myself writing a new screenplay and getting ready to direct a couple of new films. Go figure! Oh well, I will retire later.

## Barbara Anne Bock
### ("Genie" and "Lamp" Designer—Reel EFX)

I retired at age 40 and now reside in the Northwest. I graduated from California Lutheran College in 1979. I earned a BA in Fine Arts. I worked a few odd jobs in the newspaper field after graduation. Then one night I went out partying with some friends and met Martin Becker [1955–2004] and his whole company, Reel EFX. We met in a restaurant by chance. We all hit it off and they gave me a job the next week. Reel EFX was based at Raleigh Studios in Hollywood, it is right across the street from Paramount Studios. Honestly I think I was the only one who could draw fast on staff! I had a heavy graphic background. All the boys were phenomenal sculptors.

I did a few versions of the Lamp and Genie. The director just picked one. I always liked to draw mythical beasts. The Lamp is kind of based on sex. The two dragon things are having a good time! I know Chris Biggs sculpted the Lamp alone. The Lamp stayed pretty much the same during sculpture. Brian Wade, Chris Swift and Gabe Bartalos sculpted the Genie. It changed (for the better!) from the original sketch. They made it look great. It was about 10 feet tall and massive.

## Gabe Bartalos
### (Special Makeup and Creature Effects—Reel EFX)

Martin Becker used to run a company called Reel EFX. They specialized in pyro techniques, rain machines, fire bars, etc. They were known as a Physical Effects shop. They were wisely located on the Gower Studios lot and would get much of the work that went through there. Martin's right-hand man and chief mechanical designer was Jim Gill, who now with his wife Susan run Reel EFX. They were offered *The Lamp* and instead of having the special make-up effects done elsewhere, they took on the whole account—including the construction of the large Genie. I heard that they were hiring and presented my portfolio. I knew they needed someone who was comfortable applying prosthetics, that is one of my specialties.

One of the first tasks was to create the look of the genie. This job went to Barbara Bock, a great illustrator and designer. She drew inspiration from all sorts of animals and used her imagination on the face. I remember her saying she used Arnold Schwarzenegger's back as reference for the genie's muscular back. Some of my fondest memories of the shoot was the construction of the amazing genie and operating it on set. The sculpture, giant fiberglass molds and even foam fabrication was accomplished in Los Angeles at Reel EFX. We then trucked everything down to Huston, Texas, and set up a temporary work space. The genie was revealed in pieces, so we assembled him in sync with production. The first week just the arm was needed to burst through a wall, so Jim built an articulated aluminum armature that was inside the creature's arm. I then painted the skin using a combination of rubber cement paint that was airbrushed on and complimented by hand painting details in PAX paint. By the time the full genie was needed, we were ready, and it was pretty impres-

**Gabe Bartalos (Special Makeup and Creature Effects) on set preparing a stunt woman and the genie (courtesy of Gabe Bartalos).**

sive. The entire genie was mounted on a riser arm attached to a heavy weight dolly. Mounted on the sides of the dolly were the long controllers for the arms, torso rotation and head movement. Under the genie where his waist ended, we attached a cheesecloth pouch that had huge amounts of smoke pumped through it so it looked like the genie was floating on this column of smoke. When we pushed him through the museum at "high speed" with all of us on the dolly manipulating the creature, it was a real thrill—this was making a monster movie!

"The reanimated mummy" was an effect that I tackled. I began by getting a store-bought medical grade skeleton. I then molded its face and created a cement "positive" which allowed me to sculpt on new features. I gave the illusion that the eyes had dried into their sockets, that the skin collapsed around the bones' high points, and that the overall texture was dried and decomposing. I then molded my facial sculptures and ran them in foam rubber. These pieces I now was able to apply to the skeleton's face, custom made prosthetics for a skull! I added stringy white and grey hair and painted the whole skeleton with parched colors (a lot of grey and umber tones). At the same time Jim was working on the waist of the skeleton. He installed a cool pneumatic rig that allowed the skeleton to sit up on its own when activated. He also added a mechanism inside the jaw, so it could chomp down on one of the students' fingers. For this effect I made a fake hand that had a blood tube concealed inside of it. In closeup you see the "Mummy" bite down on the fake hand and pierce the finger. In the wide shot it was the real actor [Scott Bankston] with his finger bent back with a prosthetic stump attached and plenty of flowing blood.

I did most of the on set gore effects. There is a scene where a lovely young lady [Damon Merrill] gets attacked by snakes while she takes a bath. I was tasked with applying nine different prosthetics to her entire body that simulated the snake bites. Right before cameras rolled, I added fresh blood dripping from the puncture holes and spritzed it with water. The added water over the blood made for a very real "bloody wet look." One of my favorite effects was the "Night Watch-Man" character that is established as a junk food over-eater. I created a "wrap-around" prosthetic that gave the illusion that mysterious forces have slammed copious amounts of food down his throat. Once I applied this burst neck prosthetic, I placed various hard candies in the open wound: Smarties, Mints, Twizzlers, etc. Good fun.

## Andra St. Ivanyi
### (Alex Wallace)

I was a student at the university when we shot *The Lamp*, although I dropped out for one semester in order to make the film. I graduated with a degree in Radio/TV and Film in 1989. My husband and I married later that year. I went to the audition as a kind of a joke—a fun thing to do one evening. I spent time with a number of actors in the university's theater department, and they asked if I wanted to go along to audition as an extra. That's all that first audition was supposed to be: a good time with friends. I recall that the dynamic in the room became serious very quickly. After all, these were serious people making a film auditioning acting students who desperately wanted to work. So I stopped goofing around very quickly and paid attention.

A few days later, I was invited back to audition again, this time for a speaking role. I didn't have an agent or a resume. Of course no one had cell phones back then. So I came home from classes to hear a message on my answering machine. My first reaction was one of discomfort. How could I tell the others that I was invited back and they weren't? The auditions continued for several weeks. Deborah Winters, who starred in the film and was the wife of producer Warren Chaney, coached me and several others with intensity and care. I don't remember ever meeting any other young women auditioning for the role of

Alex, but I do remember running scenes with several actors who were hoping to be cast in the role of my father [the part eventually played by James Huston]. During my favorite audition, Deborah profusely apologized before making her last request. I braced myself: what on earth was she going to ask of me?!? She asked me to become hysterical, to scream and cry. I did. I went all out, throwing myself around that little room until they told me to stop. And then I was told I had the part.

I enjoyed getting to know James Huston, who was a Boston actor with a terrific sense of humor. We listened to the same music and cracked jokes to pass the time; once we became so bored waiting for the lights to be set up that we rehearsed our first scene in the museum with different accents, or with me as the father and he as the daughter (as one can imagine, it passed the time and kept us laughing). I became closest to Damon Merrill during shooting. She was such a lovely young woman who grew up in hardship but had the most wonderful heart, and I marveled at her generosity. Unfortunately, I've lost touch with them both, but I remain in contact with Deborah Chaney (who took all of us younger/teen actors under her professional wing!) and Barry Coffing, who lives here in Southern California.

I remember spending a great deal of time exhausted. The other actors and I would try to find somewhere close by but not in the way where we could rest because much of the movie was shot at night (in the school, for example, as well as in the museum). We wandered around the museum at night as best we could, but much of it was off limits and, of course, it was a bit creepy there at night anyway with so many dark corners—and that shrunken head was a REAL human shrunken head, part of the museum's exhibits! So we would try to lie down, maybe even sleep, without crinkling our clothes or ruining our makeup and hair. But it was difficult to sleep because we were so excited to be there, to watch the crew at work, and to enjoy every minute of the shoot.

Tom Daley had a very mischievous sense of humor. He liked to play little tricks and then he giggled like a happy little boy. I liked him very much. He was fun to be with but when it was time to work, he was professional and straight-forward. He never bullied, he never raised his voice. He was totally focused on the shot. I also admired the way he and Warren worked out, in calm conversation, the usual small obstacles that always arise during shooting. Tom was a good and gentle man with a wide range of interests. I don't think filmmaking was his only passion, and that made him very appealing.

I attended the premiere in Houston. Back then, there weren't a lot of films made in the area, so it got some press coverage. I admit that I don't remember much—except my dress! I remember sitting next to my mother and hoping that she wouldn't be terribly uncomfortable with the expletive I whispered as I incinerated the genie at the end (she wasn't). And I remember watching the credits at the end, feeling relieved and satisfied, and marveling at the number of people it took to make a film. It was a wonderful experience.

After post-production on the film was finished in the summer of 1986, I finished my university degree and continued to pursue an acting career. I had some luck in New York and Florida. But I became quickly frustrated by the process, by having to wait for others to hire me—I resented having little power over my own career, and although the rewards can be tremendous, acting is a difficult life path, psychologically and emotionally. As a result of my frustration, I turned my energies into refining my writing skills and began writing short stories and plays. Soon those earned me grants and awards, and my work was published in various literary magazines. Several years later, I had a play produced off-Broadway, was nominated for a Pushcart Prize for Short Fiction, and then moved to Los Angeles in 1993, where I now work as a writer, script analyst and consultant in international film sales. I'm married to the same guy and we have three teenagers, so life is interesting! Occasionally I will be recognized (or sought out) because of my participation in *The Lamp* (and no, my kids have seen scenes of the film but not the whole movie), but it rarely comes up. It remains a wonderful memory.

# The Masque of the Red Death
(1989, U.S.A./South Africa)

*Genre:* Horror; *Director:* Alan Birkinshaw; *Writer:* Michael J. Murray; *Literary source:* "The Masque of the Red Death" (Short Story) by Edgar Allan Poe, 1842; *Cinematographer:* Yossi Wein; *Editor:* Jason Krasucki; *Special Makeup Effects:* Scott Wheeler; *Special Effects:* Greg Pitts; *Producers:* Harry Alan Towers and Avi Lerner; *Associate Producer:* John Stodel; *Production companies:* Breton Film Productions and 21st Century Film Corporation; *Cast:* Herbert Lom (Ludwig), Frank Stallone (Duke), Brenda Vaccaro (Elaina Hart), Michelle Hoey McBride (Rebecca Stephens), Christobel d'Orthez (Dr. Karen), Simon Poland (Max), Christine Lunde (Colette), Foziah Davidson (Kitra) and Lindsay Reardon (Dallon).

An elderly and eccentric millionaire organizes a fancy dress ball in his Bavarian castle inspired by the Edgar Allan Poe tale. A young journalist crashes the ball with the intention of writing an article on a soap opera diva in attendance. The party is marred by bloodshed perpetrated by a mysterious masked and red caped individual.

*The Masque of the Red Death* (that was curiously shot nearly simultaneously with the new version of the story made by Roger Corman) was the third and last film of the series of adaptations of Edgar Allan Poe's short stories produced by Harry Alan Towers: *Buried Alive*, *The House of Usher* and *The Masque of the Red Death*. In consideration of the fact that *Buried Alive* has been discussed in the chapter on *Edge of Sanity*, I asked Michael J. Murray and Alan Birkinshaw to begin their stories by commenting on *The House of Usher*.

## Michael J. Murray
### (Writer)

I went to Northwestern University in Chicago for my undergraduate work in Radio-TV-Film. I came out to USC for their MFA program in Professional Writing in 1980. After graduate school, I had a variety of jobs in the industry as a story analyst (someone who reads and evaluates scripts for producers—basically you get paid to write book/script reports). My steady paycheck came from working at Sears Service Center (ugh!) working at the parts counter in appliance repairs. It was hardly an artistically enriching job, but it paid for college, graduate school, and allowed me write during the nights and weekends while I tried to launch my career.

Anyway, in the mid 80s I started working a second job as a story analyst for Sherry Lansing at Paramount. She had a production deal there and would soon go on to run the studio. These were the heydays of *Fatal Attraction* which she produced with Stanley Jaffe so we would get every top script in town for consideration. Most were DREADFUL so it was a great training ground for me. It was during this period of working for Sears, Sherry Lansing and writing during my other walking hours, that Harry Alan Towers came into my life. Someone who I had read for put him in touch with me. He offered me $25,000 to write *The House of Usher* in four weeks. So I quit my Sears job (hallelujah!) and left Sherry Lansing and finally launched my writing career. I had no idea what I was about to get myself into! Since I started working professionally in 1988 (for Harry), I've gone on to write and produce over two dozen movies for television and cable. Some of my CBS holiday films were the highest rated TV movies of the decade 2000–2010.

I first met Harry by phone, I can't remember if he was in South Africa or England or his home in Canada (I think it must have been in South Africa because I remember getting bizarre phone calls at strange times like midnight and 1 a.m. LA time). At first, I had to wonder if he was for real—I would have nightmares that this was all a joke and I had to back to work at Sears!

We had our initial story conference by phone and he turned up in LA about a week later. I had an agent at the time, but Harry (naturally) didn't like to deal with agents or lawyers. I would soon learn that money was a slippery slope with Harry Alan Towers: bounced checks … missing checks … missing checkbooks … whatever served him so that he could avoid paying … that was the Harry way. Harry was a character from the first day I met him. He was strange and short and squat. There was no warm and fuzzy, he rarely smiled or laughed. But occasionally, he did find something amusing and he would chortle.

When he came to LA, I had sketched out the plot in a 15 page outline. I met him at the Sunset Marquis Hotel in Hollywood, where he had a suite and loved to stay. We met in the lobby and talked about the outline, he was very happy. I always loved horror films and *Carrie* was one of my favorite films from the genre. Brian De Palma came to Northwestern when I was in film school and talked about the horror genre at length. It was a perfect match for me to write these kinds of films.

I got my first payment from Harry and RAN to the bank…. The check actually cleared. I was quite happy. It was non–WGA work but I was not yet a guild member so it was okay to do. I hoped and prayed the next check would clear…

The time frame for writing the piece was punishing. The restrictions were even worse: the film had to be constructed (storywise) from the surviving sets of his last film. I remember saying to Harry, "Excuse me, but what the hell are you talking about? Surviving sets?" Well it turned out, that they burned down the set of his last film (as part of the narrative) and there were some flats, some room left at the studio. What sets remained undamaged were to be the basis of the "Usher" film. Now in film school, we had studied that "story follows character," but no professor ever prepared me for "story follows the sets." I received a list of sets and then had to write the screenplay around those locations, often using a specific actor. We knew that Oliver Reed would be in "Usher" [Oliver Reed played Roderick Usher], so I was able to customize some of it for him. It was a great training ground for me. College and grad school in film production and writing did not prepare for this kind of work. It was like being in the trenches, writing under horrid deadlines and with bizarre constraints.

I started on the script and had about three weeks left to write a first draft. It was a crazy time crunch, but very exciting for me as I was no longer working at the dreaded Sears job and while I missed working for Sherry Lansing, I did not miss writing story reports on BAD scripts. William Morris used to flood us with crap and pass it off as brilliant. Sherry was the top producer in town and it was shocking what they'd send for RUSH WEEKEND READS.

I took great liberties with "Usher." Harry didn't care. As long as there were murders and gore and a little bit of sex (the tamest sex imaginable), he was happy. And yes, an occasional fire or amputation or rodent attack made him even happier. He LOVED to talk about the ways to kill people.

The production took place in South Africa where no American actors would work at the time because of its stance on apartheid. Of course, none of this mattered to Harry. He was rolling crews and getting these movies made back to back. He told me I could use as much or as little of the original Poe material, he didn't care. Harry reported that Oliver Reed was loaded a lot of the time (I have no idea if this is true). He said that Reed got injured during the destruction of the House of Usher, cut on a piece of the set or something. I never got many details from the production. Once Harry had his script, he was off to make the movie and could care less about the screenwriter.

After we finished "Usher" and the movie wrapped (on an impossibly tight schedule), Harry asked me to write *The Masque of the Red Death*. I wanted to make the story as contemporary as possible. Some of the HAT films were a little musty when it came to plot dynamics. They were often very conventional and earnest, maybe too earnest. I figured the tabloid journalist Rebecca Stephens would be fun, interesting and offer us a little opportunity to bring in a bit of humor and levity. We never wanted to go campy, though—Harry took the horror genre very seriously as did I. When I was structuring the movie, I had to do a lot of brainstorming to come up with creative ways to kill people in the castle. I made lists of rooms, props, etc. until I settled on the ten killings in the movie. Harry would get so excited about the killings, like a kid on Christmas morning. His face would light up with glee. It was kind of bizarre. We were always hemmed in by budget constraints, but when it came to the killings, he never said we couldn't do something because of lack of funds. He was also ready to budget funds for killings! In "Masque" I had a character [Kitra] "woven" into a loom and killed. It was utterly ridiculous, but Harry LOVED it. The woman in the loom was not cheap and involved make-up, prosthetics, the building of the loom … so that was a big deal. The slasher elements had to be in these movies in order for him to sell them to foreign investors.

As we went through revisions and drafts, Harry would start to flake out about timely payments. I can't tell how many times I showed up at the Sunset Marquis to pick up a check and Harry would either not be there, have lost his checkbook, had an excuse for not paying, etc. I would withhold work, but even that didn't matter at some point.

Harry also would occasionally have me meet him in his room if he had a suite with a living room. Invariably, there would be Euro trash or Russian trash models hanging around. I'm guessing they were high class hookers. I'm not sure about the high class party, but Harry seemed to have a thing for women with accents. Some of them were actually quite beautiful. It was strange to see these Amazonian type girls with their long dark hair and crazy long legs leaving the room and saying good-bye to short squat aging Harry Alan Towers. One time, he accused one of them of stealing his watch. Another time, he accused another of taking his checkbook (a plot to avoid paying me of course). It was creepy and sad. Sometimes, the girls would leave the room and then he'd receive a call from his wife in Toronto. I never met her, but I hope she had a good independent life up there away from his nonsense and outrageous behavior.

Foziah Davidson ("Kitra") and Alan Birkinshaw (Director) (courtesy of Foziah Davidson).

During production, I was never on set or went to South Africa. I often did not hear from Harry until the movies wrapped ... weeks and weeks later. I doubt "Usher" and "Masque" were ever projected onto a screen here in the U.S.A. I think they went straight to video. I'm not sure I even own a copy of them. I think perhaps not.

After the two Poe movies, Harry hired me to write "Dance of Death" which would be a Poe-like story, freely invented by me, about a dance school and the murderous behind the scenes drama.... For the dance instructor, he wanted a big name. We meet with Richard Harris, who was an old associate of Harry's. It was bizarre to have a breakfast meeting with this icon, who must have been on hard times to even consider working with Harry and traveling to banned South Africa. We had a very civilized breakfast and talked about the character and story.... It was an absurd situation. Harris fell out of the project. I was secretly happy, I didn't want him working in Harry's crazy shop of horrors.

Then Harry somehow made contact with Anthony Perkins about playing the role. We went to Anthony Perkins's house up in one of the gorgeous tree-shaded canyons of LA. For me, he was another icon and I was rather stunned that he would even consider working with Harry. We spent an hour or two with Anthony talking about the role and the film. He had a interesting architectural home filled with rough-hewn beams and walls of glass. The main room felt perched like a tree house in the shady sycamores and oaks. His boys came in, he was a great loving Dad. Then his wife Berry Berenson, the photographer, joined the group. It was an interesting afternoon. Anthony Perkins was shy, intelligent, and very funny. I told him how much I enjoyed his work in famous movies like *Psycho* as well as lesser known films like *The Last of Sheila*, which he co-wrote with composer Stephen Sondheim. There were stories that he and Sondheim were together for a while. I assumed that Anthony Perkins was gay. Yet he assembled a wonderful conventional family around him and Berry seemed happy that afternoon. She brought in groceries, talked to the kids about school and sports. It was like every other American family, or so it seemed. But it wasn't. What I didn't know was that Anthony was sick with AIDS and would later pass away. Even more tragic, Berry was on Flight 11 on 9–11 and perished when it crashed. Their two sons were left without parents.

Ultimately, Harry never made a deal with "Dance of Death" and the project went away. Dead, I thought. I imaged it sitting on a shelf gathering dust. Then a couple years later, I got a call from a friend who just saw a movie at the video store starring Robert Englund (*Nightmare* series) about a homicidal maniac who ran a dance school.... The film [*Dance Macabre*, 1991, Greydon Clark] was produced by Harry Alan Towers. The screenplay was credited to his pen name.... The majority of the story/dialog was mine. I spent the next five years trying to sue him to get a settlement. When we finally got to depositions, I had a female attorney who was quite beautiful and he was an intimidated mess. He didn't show up with counsel and then refused to answer questions. When it went to trial, he never once showed up even after the court gave him ample opportunities to testify. Finally, the court issued a $110,000 judgment against him. Sadly, I was never able to collect a penny of it because he was a Canadian citizen and kept all his businesses off-shore. I would have had to start the process again and file in Canadian court and the attorney said I would never be able to get any money out of him.

The whole Harry Allan Towers experience left a bad taste in my mouth. But like so many other writer/actors/directors who cut their teeth in the world of cheapie independent horror movies, that's where I got my break. Without Harry, God knows how much longer I'd be working at Sears and working as a story analyst. We had just settled the 1988 WGA strike which put all the story analysts out of work immediately so I was working at Sears full time (ugh!) and feeling pretty terrible about my prospects in the business. Then out of the blue, Harry came along. It was a crazy wild rollercoaster ride, but I would do it again in a minute. For better or worse, Harry launched my writing career.

## Alan Birkinshaw
### (Director)

*Ten Little Indians* [1988], *The House of Usher* and *The Masque of the Red Death* came about because of a previous movie I was involved in as additional director for Cannon Films. It starred Donald Sutherland, and was called *Ordeal by Innocence* [1984.] When they completed the film with the original director [Desmond Davis], they decided it lacked tension and excitement so I was hired to add those ingredients. I shot about 20–25 minutes of the completed film. The same producers were involved with *Ten Little Indians* and the other two films so that is how I was chosen to direct them.

[*The House of Usher* was shot after *Ten Little Indians*.] Some opening locations were shot near London. The rest was Johannesburg in a studio mostly with a few locations shots added in. Donald Pleasence was a consummate professional and a pleasure to work with, also great fun to be with socially. Oliver Reed always knew his lines in spite of his drinking.

On set for *The Masque of the Red Death*: Alan Birkinshaw (Director) is the guy in the middle (courtesy of Alan Birkinshaw).

He was I believe dyslexic, so it must have been difficult for him sometimes to get to grips with long pieces of dialogue—especially if there were any changes. But he succeeded. Oliver had an amazing screen presence. Your eye always went to him on the screen. The sad thing is, that in his latter days, I reckon that due to the amount he drank, only 50% of his performance was there on the screen.

[*The Masque of the Red Death* was shot not long after *The House of Usher*.] It was filmed around Johannesburg [and in Germany]. Herbert Lom [1917–2012] was a pleasure to be with, both as an actor and a person. Directors and actors don't mix generally when working. But with Herbert it was different. The role, the character he played was discussed in great detail before shooting began. He wanted to know everything. And it was good. So there were no surprises. And if there were, they were good ones. Actors tend to know how they look on screen and a lot of them have a favourite angle to be shot from. In other words, "If you have the choice when shooting me in close up," they would say, "Shoot me straight on—or from the left"—etc. So on one occasion when all the cast were in the same shot and the camera tracked around the room from right to left, the three actors in question who had previously mentioned to me about their best side, all moved in conjunction with the camera so their best side was always favouring the camera during the shot!

Harry Alan Towers was a one-man production machine. His ability above all others, was to make the deal happen. And this he did superbly. He was able to piece together a production by bringing all the elements together. Many countries had their own tax shelter deals, and Harry sniffed them out. Then using his dual nationality (British/Canadian) he was able to put all the pieces together, just like a jigsaw puzzle. Agents liked him because he was always true to his word. And this way, he was able to do a block deal with an agent, taking on actors and directors from the same stable. He was also motivated by pretty women. He could guaranteed their break into movies, and it was up to them if they made that break a successful one. Some did. Others didn't. But Harry always kept his end of the deal. And at Cannes Film Festival, it was always Harry who had the most beautiful women on his arm. As a person, he was fun to be with. Life was always full of surprises when he was around. He had a great smile. A great sense of humour. And most important of all, he made things happen. Sometimes you had to be on the next movie before you received the final payment on the last one. But hey, that was Harry.

## Michelle Hoey McBride
### ("Rebecca Stephens")

*The Masque of the Red Death* was my first speaking acting job. I started with jobs in music videos and went on to doing many television commercials while I was studying and taking acting classes until I felt I was ready to find an agent and begin auditioning for film and television roles. I guess it was a combination of being prepared and tremendous luck to book a leading role in "Masque" as my first professional acting job. In fact, I was actually chosen for a smaller co-leading role in a different film but the shooting schedules overlapped so I chose "Masque."

It was one of the very first auditions that my newly acquired acting agent sent me to. I don't remember much about the initial meeting and audition but I do remember thinking

I totally blew it at the final audition screen test where I was to meet the director and be filmed as one the final choices for the role [the tabloid journalist] because I was so nervous. The whole experience was like a whirlwind since it was all so new. It was hard for me to believe that I booked the leading role with so little previous experience. It was thrilling. I remember meeting for lunch with the director Alan Birkinshaw after I booked the role at a fashionable restaurant on Melrose Avenue and feeling as if I were in a dream and it wasn't real since most people will tell you you're living in a fantasy world if you think you can make a living as an actor in Hollywood. I was 22. Alan told me my job wasn't official until I met with the producer Menahem Golan [Cannon Films/21st Century Film] who wanted to meet me in person for the final approval.

From what I remember, we shot the film six days a week. I remember being picked up for work in the dark and watching the sun rise on my ride to work everyday and being the last actor working at night. It was like I was given a crash course in how to act in a movie. Many of my close-up shots were done after the big name actors went home for the day. Somebody would be standing next to the camera reading the script so I had somebody to look at while saying my lines.

I saw very little of South Africa because of my work schedule. The only time I didn't work from sunrise to sunset was when Duncan, who's now my husband, came to visit me and I was granted the weekend off so we could spend some time together and go on a safari at Kruger Park. It was an interesting time to be in South Africa since it was during the collapse of apartheid. My hotel was in downtown Johannesburg. The week I first arrived and was settling in I took a stroll through the outdoor market near my hotel. When I told the people who were in charge of looking out after me, they were sort of shocked and surprised and told me I shouldn't be walking around by myself where I was staying, not to do it in the future and they would gladly find someone to show me around Johannesburg if I liked. It didn't seem all that dangerous to me. What seemed more dangerous and got my attention was the intense security at the airports and entrances to the finer shopping malls and public places meant for the white people. The homes I visited for lunch or dinner on my Sundays off were surrounded by tall cement security walls with rolls of barbed wire at the top. Little did I know that I was looking at the future for how things would be after 9/11.

One Sunday, Alan and I decided to see the film *Mississippi Burning* at a theater down the street from my hotel. As we were watching this film depicting how horribly white people treated African Americans in the South, I observed that Alan and I were the only white people in the audience and wondered if they would be looking at us with hatred when we were exiting from the theater. Later, as we were exiting and feeling ashamed for all the terrible things white people have done to people of other races in United States, I realized nobody seemed to even notice us.

The second filming location was in Germany, which I loved because we were filming outside in breathtakingly beautiful countryside and in ancient churches and castles instead of being indoors on the set all day. We filmed at the legendary castle named Neuschwanstein which served as a model for the Sleeping Beauty Castle at Disneyland.

I'm especially appreciative of the thorough, and patient, mentoring I was given by the director Alan Birkinshaw. During the time we were shooting the film I was akin to a barnacle on his side. My character was in so many scenes in the film that our working hours on the set were almost the same. So, we mostly drove to work and ate our meals together every day. It allowed me a once-in-a-lifetime chance as a newly emerging actor to pick the brain of a successfully working director about all aspects of making a film. He knew I felt anxious and a huge responsibility to do a good job and I didn't want to let everybody down who'd taken a chance hiring someone new like me. He taught me all the different stages of making a film, the roles and responsibilities each person has while collaborating on a film. I took advantage of his invitations to watch the dailies at the end of the day so I could learn what the editor's job is like and Alan would coach me on how I could improve. He showed me what an actor should be mindful of in order to make everyone's job a little easier with fewer obstacles to successfully complete their piece of the work. The knowledge he shared gave me surety in future acting roles because I learned how to be a truly professional actor, which fostered a sense of being a valuable team player when I was working.

For example, when working on a low budget film, you want to keep in mind the fact that it has a low budget and do what you can to help keep the costs down. I remember the goal was to successfully do each shot in just two takes since film and time paying for everyone working on the set was costly. Brenda Vaccaro joked about it once with me calling herself "two take Tessie." I did a commercial for house paint when I got back home from shooting the film. I nailed each shot in two takes, which thrilled the crew, producers and director and everyone was happy to have an unexpected afternoon off and go home early that day. I remember how great I felt about it and in my mind crediting the job well done to Alan. Another example, I learned it's important to remember how you move your head or body in a wide shot to match the same movements in shots you'll do later in close ups for smoother editing transitions. As I'm reflecting this moment, 20 or so years later, I'm realizing even more so how much effort and skillful coaching it must have taken from Alan. He never was grumpy or irritated with all the instruction I needed either. Any acting job that came my way after doing "Masque" was met with prepared confidence and ease due to the knowledge he imparted to me. I'll always be grateful.

Aside from watching a few clips and scenes in the editing room when Alan was in LA editing the film, I didn't watch "Masque" until ten years after it was released. There wasn't any official screening of the movie for some reason, or maybe I just didn't go—I don't remember. Ten years later, I was talking with a friend of mine about the movie and told her I was so nervous and sick to my stomach about watching the film when it was released that I'd never watched it. So, I was surprised by getting the video in the mail a week later as a surprise gift from my friend and I finally watched it at home. I didn't want to watch the movie when it was first released because I was sure that my acting was going to be embarrassing to watch. I thought there might be a danger watching the final product by knowing I was so hard on myself (a perfectionist) and might make me too shy, self conscious or inhibit my acting work in the future. Not that my acting was at any level close to Johnny Depp, but I remember reading in an interview he did that he never watches any of his films and it made me feel a little better about it. I often had a sense while filming "Masque" that my acting wasn't my best work because I felt stiff, intimidated and possibly a bit in over my head working with famous actors like Herbert Lom and Brenda Vaccaro and starring in my first speaking acting role. A few years ago, my kids googled my name and found comments and reviews about my work. I was pleasantly surprised to see nice reviews of my past acting work and think it's kind of funny that I had no idea I was getting such favorable reviews.

My next role in *Subspecies* [1990, Ted Nicolaou] seemed like a piece of cake after "Masque" and I felt completely confident while filming *Subspecies*. "Masque" prepared me well. We were the first Americans to film in Romania—it was just a year after Nicolae Ceausescu's regime collapsed (after he ordered his security forces to fire on anti-government demonstrators in 1989) which resulted in a whole bunch of troubles and drama trying to make a film during a volatile and sensitive time in Romania along with lighter hearted stories as well. I'm still very close friends with two of the main actors and keep in touch with the director, cameraman and wardrobe director who are all dear in my heart.

*Prey of the Chameleon* [1991, Fleming Fuller] was my last acting job before I quit acting to raise our children. I was newly pregnant while filming *Prey of the Chameleon*. I thought I might continue acting after I had my daughter by acting in smaller roles but that wasn't the vision my acting agent had for me. They really wanted me to stay on the track they'd set for me to be a leading role actress and felt smaller jobs would be stepping down from the progress I was making. I was starting to get really exciting auditions for films with larger budgets and big name actors, like one with Steve Martin (*Father of the Bride*). Five minutes before I walked into the office to read for that film, I vomited in the bathroom because I had terrible morning sickness. I tried going on a few auditions after I had my daughter, but it just felt wrong in my heart. I'm not the type of person who could have done both jobs well.

Now, I'm at an exciting place because our last child of three is about to graduate from high school and will soon be off to college leaving me free to begin the next phase of my life. I love singing and writing music in a little rock band with musician friends, oil painting and experimenting with other forms of modern art and sculpture, which I plan on studying further.... I've been watching Los Angeles' art scene steadily growing and diversifying over the last 25 years and look forward to taking full advantage by studying and eventually participating with my own work in the future. I've got many ideas for art pieces I've been figuring out how to assemble and things I want to say through art. As long as I'm getting my fix doing some sort of art in any form everyday, I'm a happy camper. I've been volunteering in hospice for the last 17 years working with terminally ill patients and families.

## Christobel d'Orthez
### ("Dr. Karen")

I started my film career in South Africa after studying drama for three years in the UK. I returned to South Africa after drama school as there was a big film boom happening in the 80s in South Africa and I wanted very much to be in film. My first part was in *Gor* [1986] as an extra and when they did the sequel *Outlaw of Gor* [1986] I was asked to play a small part. Thereafter I did *Act of Piracy* [1987] before I was asked to play in *The Masque of the Red Death*. I did not need to audition for the part of Dr. Karen, I was asked if I would play the part as I had worked with various directors who knew my work by the time "Masque" was produced. Between film roles I did a lot of theatre work and did many plays throughout the 80s.

"Masque" was very much an ensemble piece and one after the other the characters were being killed off until it was only really my character that was left. I lost my life by having my head chopped off by a large pendulum, which was very frightening as during filming the pendulum slipped and very nearly did chop my head off, so my expressions in my dying scenes were real, I was genuinely afraid—but clearly I'm still alive and well!

Frank Stallone was a real character as was Brenda Vaccaro who was a very good actress. Christine Lunde became a very close friend although we lost touch over the years. Working opposite Herbert Lom was a real treat. He was a wonderful actor and a great man and became a good friend. He once paid me a great compliment that I reminded him of a young Lynn Redgrave (Vanessa Redgrave's sister). By chance I was speaking to someone at Equity who told me that Herbert Lom had been looking for me and did they have a contact number for me—he left a lovely message on my answering machine saying he would love to meet me again (25 years after we'd worked together) so my husband and I went to have tea with him at his home in London and it was wonderful to see him again.... He died soon after aged 90, so maybe he wanted to see me again one more time before he passed away!

I left acting pretty soon after "Masque" as I returned to the UK and started to work in theatrical marketing and production for a very well known London theatre producer called Bill Kenwright. I then got involved in theatre and film casting in London working for Suzanne Smith Casting, so spent many years always involved in the world of film and theatre.

## Foziah Davidson
### ("Kitra")

I was a jewelry designer in the 1980s, and a picture of me appeared in a local newspaper accompanying a story on the investment value of gold and diamonds. A local production house (Dirk de Villiers' C-Films) saw the picture and contacted me to audition for the female lead in their made-for-TV movie called *Jantjie Kom Huis Toe* [1985]. I got the role and loved working in the film industry. I got myself an agent and worked as a photographic and ramp model from the mid-eighties, appearing in many TV commercials and magazines. In 1987 I landed the most expensive pro rata ad ever made in Southern Africa, "Sun International's Wild Coast Sun" commercial. This led to my being "discovered" by international photographer, Monty Shadow, who took me to Milan where I worked with agents Vesna Esposito and Riccardo Guy.

In the meantime, the South African government issued a subsidy deal to international filmmakers to incentivise them to make movies in our country to boost our own industry. In 1988 I was called back by my agent to audition for *River of Death* [1988] starring Donald Pleasence and Robert Vaughn. Later that year I made *You're Famous* with Alain D. Woolf. In 1989 I worked in a local television series, SABC's *Whirlpool*. Later that same year, I made a brief appearance in *Last Samurai* starring John Fujioka and John Saxon. I also landed the role of fashion designer Kitra in *The Masque of the Red Death*. In 1990 I made a local television series called *Craig en Cardo*. By this time, the SA government had stopped their subsidy programme, and the makers of B-grade foreign films stopped coming here. Work was scarce, and I went back to doing local TV shows, commercials and stills shoots for a living. In 1994, while filming a local television series called *Butterfly Dream*, I became pregnant and gave up acting to raise my boy J. I carried on modeling until about 2008/9, but never accepted another "out of town" or "on location" shoot.

In mid–April 1989 my agent, Gianna Pisanello, called while I was filming *Last Samurai* in the Drakensberg Mountains and said I should fly back to meet an English director called Alan Birkinshaw. We met at the Johannesburg Sun Hotel, and hit it off immediately. We collaborated on both Kitra's costume and her make-up. We decided to make Kitra British and I worked closely with Alan to improve my British accent. He was very patient and funny about the "South Africanisms" that sometimes slipped through.

I got on very well with my fellow actors. Working with Herbert Lom for the second time (he was also in *River of Death*) was great. He was a terribly humble man, with a sharp sense of humour. He teased me when I couldn't remember how many movies I'd made ("three or four," I'd said), and told me he'd made dozens of movies over the years, and remembered every one of them. Brenda Vaccaro was a very fine lady indeed. She was married to a young man called Guy, and we often went out for dinner together. I loved listening to her stories of Hollywood in the heydays. She constantly told me I was too skinny and tried to feed me up. Frank Stallone and I were already close friends by the time we worked on "Masque" together. I'd met him via an American actress called Cynthia Erland whom I'd worked with on *River of Death*. Her boyfriend was Frankie's agent and he was making another movie here at the time. We spent a great deal of time together and are still good friends. Frankie was always an utter gentleman who was and still is very protective of me. I appreciate and value him a great deal. Lindsay Reardon was very dear, if very intense. I liked him a lot. We had long, in-depth, philosophical conversations into the hours of the night. I still have a note he wrote me. He was a local actor married to one of South Africa's foremost Afrikaans playwrights, Reza de Wet.

Alan Birkinshaw was one of the nicest directors I worked with during my brief time in the film industry. He was patient and funny and very English in his sense of humour and his outlook on life. He was an easy director to please, and willingly worked around the shortcomings of his cast. When someone couldn't deliver whatever it was he envisaged, he'd say, "Well, let's try it another way," or he'd huddle with the DP and replan the shot from another angle. I remember when Frank and I had to do the tango on the dinner table. The dance instructor had given up on me, and Alan said, "Good grief, this girl can't dance at all! Shoot from the shoulders up!" He made a plan with good humour. A funny moment was when Christine Lunde [at the conclusion of the film, the masked killer is revealed as Colette] saw the stunt double who was to play the "Red Death." She pointed and screeched, "I'm not that big, no-one's going to believe that's me!" Alan rolled his eyes and said, "We'll fix it in the edit."

## Simon Poland
### ("Max")

Having being forced through injury to give up my dream of becoming a full-time professional cricketer, I moved to South Africa to work for a shipping insurance claims company. No longer playing cricket I entered into the wonderful world of amateur dramatics in 1983–84. It was a way to meet people. One night after a show an actor suggested my voice was well suited to radio. I auditioned and was fortunate enough to be accepted onto the roster of local radio actors. I was offered a lot of radio work, so I left my job and became a professional actor. In 1985, I moved to Johannesburg. I was lucky, at this time a lot of American films were coming over and mostly they were low production "B" movies. I love the B movie profession; as an untrained actor it afforded me numerous opportunities to understand camera, lighting and the various forces that come into play over which I had little control: production politics, acting pressures, creative conflict. It was all hugely enlightening for me. *Alien from L.A.* [1987] was my first feature film and I auditioned for Albert Pyun. I think I have done four or five films for him. I think Albert is one of the most fascinating people I've ever met. He is a wonderful director, who has a gift for completing his movies done on time and under budget.

*The Masque of the Red Death* was fascinating for being able to work with great actors like Herbert Lom, Brenda Vaccaro and Frank Stallone. Herbert Lom was an old school actor. He used to practice the alphabet every day in his caravan for projecting and warming up the voice. We had a technically difficult scene together. There were various choreographed camera movements in a small space and the director wanted to shoot the scene in one take. I seem to recall a myriad different strips of coloured tape plastered over the floor indicating the marks we had to hit. Herbert loved to meticulously prep his way round each scene with an awe-inspiring attention to detail. When we filmed the scene, it didn't quite go according to plan (a few things didn't fit into place)—but we played the scene out. Afterwards, to my astonishment, Herbert came up to me as we were leaving the set, and said, "Simon, I really enjoyed it, but it didn't go as we planned, do you think we'll be all right?" I was stunned. Here was an actor who had done a far greater number of films than I could ever hope to do, who had starred in more historically important films than I could ever dream of doing, asking me (an actor with a CV of 4 films!) for support. I replied, "Yes, Herbert, it was fantastic ... and often when things happen by accident the camera captures something that cannot be captured if it has been rehearsed." So that was a sweet, bizarre, surreal moment. Herbert was charming. A wonderful role model ... an unselfish and modest actor always professional.

Work has been tough since I came back to England, I cannot lie. I won a lead in a film about George Orwell's "Burmese Days," playing George Orwell—sadly it never got made. That was a huge blow to me. That's now close to 25 years ago, but I keep believing in my passion for this creative world.

# *Munchies*
## (1986, U.S.A.)

*Genre:* Horror/Comedy; *Director:* Tina Hirsch; *Writer:* Lance Smith; *Cinematographer:* Jonathan West; *Editor:* James A. Stewart; *"Munchies" designed by:* Robert Short; *Visual Effects:* Roger George; *Producer:* Roger Corman; *Co-Producer:* Ginny Nugent; *Associate Producer:* Jamie Beardsley; *Production Company:* Concorde Pictures; *Cast:* Harvey Korman (Cecil Watterman/Simon Watterman), Charlie Stratton (Paul Watterman), Nadine Van Der Velde (Cindy), Jon Stafford (Dude Watterman), Alix Elias (Melvis), Charlie Phillips (Eddie), Hardy Rawls (Big Ed), Robert Picardo (Bob Marvalle), Wendy Schaal (Marge Marvalle) and Scott Sherk (Buddy Holly).

An archaeologist, who believes that aliens have visited our planet in the past, finds a strange and pretty creature in an Incan temple in Peru. The man, believing that the little creature is the living proof in support of his theory, brings it back with him to California and entrusts it to his son and girlfriend. Unfortunately, the archaeologist's despicable twin brother, a fast-food unscrupulous businessman involved in shady dealings, kidnaps the little animal and entrusts it to the custody to his son, an idiot, who does not know better than to engage a desperate fight with it, tearing it into pieces with a knife. The tender creature multiplies into many evil monsters that take a short time to create havoc in the city. *Gremlins, Ghoulies, Critters, Hobgoblins*. Could Roger Corman have assisted the invasion of so many small evil creatures and stand idly by?

## Lance Smith
### (Writer)

A funny story about *Munchies* on Maui, Hawaii. I moved here about eleven years ago and since I'm honest I was trying to get some local kids to sell me some ganja. They asked what I did and when I told them I wrote movies, they wanted to know which ones. I knew that they wouldn't know about the films I did after Roger Corman so I went with *Munchies*. They freaked out saying it was one of their favorite movies growing up and saw it over twenty times. I was dumbstruck how much they were into it. So I guess the movie got me a good hook up on Maui wowee!

Stephen Herek made *Critters* [1985] for a then small indie New Line Cinema. Roger Corman offered to do this project for $1 million. Stephen Herek went with New Line who put up about 3 millions or a little less. Well, *Critters* was released and made over 2 millions opening week. I liked it way more than *Gremlins* which was racist at times and hated how the ratings suck-ups invented a whole new "PG 13" rating cause Spielberg could never be rated "R."

I had given a pretty funny script I wrote at the American Film Institute to Roger's assistant about one year earlier. I worked in the editing room as an apprentice on *The Last Ride* which was pretty bad. So, *Critters* wowed everybody and a day later, I got a call that Roger wanted me to come in for a meeting. I had already met him during dailies but don't think he remembered me. I was hired on the spot and was way happy as hell even though it was on the day the nuclear reactor blew up in Ukraine. That's pretty much how it all started. God bless you, Steve Herek. I owe him.

Roger definitely wanted the project to be comedic without killing the horror part of the story. If I ever asked a question, he always would reply, "Do it how you think it would work best." Coming from a filmmaker as great as Roger has always been, this blew my mind. Unlike most producers Roger is never controlling in any way. He appreciates that the filmmakers he chooses make the creative choices.

Actually, there was a movie that was a huge influence on *Munchies*. It was *Used Cars* [1980, Robert Zemeckis] and it had the same sort of goofy Americana feel to it, but more importantly it had the fighting twin brothers. Roger liked this because it really is a getting two actors for the price of one. Harvey Korman [1927–2008] was a huge comedy star on *The Carol Burnett Show* which I watched as a kid. He's so damn funny and wouldn't change a line of dialogue without asking me if it was okay. I'd always say, "No, it's a great idea. You're the comedy genius, not me."

Roger is always great to work with and never looks down on the material or genres. I remember it was just me and him most of the time. The Iran-contra bullshit was the big thing in the U.S.A. then. I watched the congressional hearings with all the lies the right-wing Reagan assholes were saying while claiming they were the real patriots. I put some of this Oliver North lying crap into the script and Roger flipped. He said, "I love what you did when you gave all the best self-serving speeches to the evil twin. It's just like George Bernard Shaw's 'Arms and the Man.'" I didn't tell him all I had to do was turn on CNN.

There was the hippie or dead head character, Dude [the loony son of the evil twin]. Roger thought it would be funny if Arnold ate Dude's hash brownies. I would've never brought up ganja because I didn't think he would go for it and it was the bleak Reagan 1980s when even ganja was just as bad as heroin. Roger later changed his mind probably for this reason. So, the name stuck but the drug humor was out. Before I ever went to A.F.I., I always said, "If I ever do a creature feature, I'm gonna have the dead head die first" just cause they're such annoying assholes.

The script had a working title after a while. I think I named it "Hucas" or something like that because it was an Inca word for the palace guards. The Munchies were the guards brought to life by lightning. They weren't aliens even though everybody in the movie thought they were. It was Roger who named it "Munchies."

The Munchie was named Arnold. "Arnold Ziffel" was a Western watching, going to school pig from the only American surrealist TV show ever, *Green Acres* [1965]. He could also change channels with his snout.

Bob Short designed the Munchies. I put in the script that the Munchie was 18 inches tall. I didn't really think they'd do it exactly like I wrote it but they did. When I saw the puppet, I said very quietly to the film's producer Ginny Nugent, "It looks too short." She said, "It's a foot and a half tall," so I shut up and never mentioned it again. I'm not totally

The last "Munchie" to surrender in the final battle between the creatures and Simon Watterman (Charlie Stratton) and his girlfriend Cindy (Nadine Van Der Velde) that occurs within the factory. The Munchie is reduced to a small stone statue by way of an electric discharge (courtesy of Robert Short).

sure but I think Roger did like the puppet. However, he also knew that it wasn't going to look as good as Gremlins or Critters.

When the crew started coming together, we had a meeting in the big room. Ginny Nugent was talking to people who had already come on board. So, Roger pops his head and says hi to everybody. We thought this was all there was to it. Then, he grabs a chair to sit down at the head of the table. This meant everybody had to get and move down one seat. It was like the Marx Brothers. Roger says, "Don't let bad taste hold you back on anything." So, we all left and I went back to work on the script. Two weeks later I delivered the next draft. Roger starts reading it and gets really freaked out at some of the things he didn't want to do. He had Ginny call me to come into the office right away. So, I go into the office and he's pretty freaked out. He starts telling me the things to cut out. I said I could change it all in just a few days and I won't go overboard anymore. Roger was still a little rattled and said, "Why does everybody who works for me is so hip & cynical?" Ginny laughed and said, "I wonder why, Roger?" She was the only one who could get away with that. I've put "hip & cynical" into everything I write. It is the funniest line ever delivered by Roger...

There was a production meeting when most of the crew was already hired. We were all in a pretty small conference that had too many chairs. So, we all had to shift around so Roger could sit down. It was like a Monty Python gag or something from *Brazil* [1984, Terry Gilliam]. Roger said, "I don't think we're going to wow anybody with our effects or our budget so don't let bad taste stand in the way." I kind of took this too literally because I made some jokes in the next draft that Roger didn't really like.

Tina Hirsch and I worked on the script after she was hired after the third draft or so. We worked together well. It was only after she let the most of the crew comment and/or change the script that I got really pissed. Tina brought some actors over from *Gremlins*.

Both Wendy Schaal and Bob Picardo were great on *Munchies* [they manage the ice cream shop raided by the creatures] thanks to Tina.

The caves [at the beginning of the film, when the archaeologist and his son are about to explore the Incan temple] are up in Hollywood Hills by the Hollywood sign. They've been used since the 20s. The caves are very short so you have to shoot it from many different angles, then it looks huge. The Incan priest ceremony that was cut [which showed the origin of the Munchies] was shot at Roger's lot in Venice Beach.

Almost all the locations were in the horrible San Fernando Valley. The houses were in Sylmar and were still vacant, I believe. The desert scenes are out in Palmdale along with the ice cream shop, I think. Melvisland [the miniature golf course] is in the valley near the San Diego Freeway. Malibu Lake is where the Munchies run the bikers off the road and attack the teen girls.

When we were on the set in Palmdale for the desert locations, both of the Charlies, Charlie Stratton [the son of the archaeologist] and Charlie Phillips [Eddie, the young policeman who makes up an inseparable twosome with his father, Big Ed] and I were talking to Harvey Korman. He's a great guy all around but out of nowhere, he says, "Don't get all excited about this movie, it's gonna be horrible." We, of course, were floored. Charlie Phillips said, "What? You're kidding right?" Harvey Korman, "No, it's going to be bad because I'm in it. Anything I'm in will end up sucking." We were stunned and somebody said, "What about *Blazing Saddles*? That's a huge movie that's really great." Harvey Korman, "It was a fluke and it looked horrible when we were doing it and they somehow pulled everything together."

*Munchies* hit the redneck movie circuit meaning it played mostly in the Midwest and the South. It was, however, on a double bill with *Jaws 3* in Downtown L.A. which my agent thought meant something. I didn't. The redneck releasing strategy actually benefitted my family because *Munchies* played in my hometown of Savannah, GA. My mom took my granddad to see *Munchies* on the first showing on Friday. They were the only people in the audience so I told them it was a special screening just for them. They knew I was full of shit but it was a good joke. The Saturday shows were almost packed. My uncle and aunt took their kids and they all screamed when my name came up on the screen. My little cousin made sure that every sleep-over party had to include *Munchies* because it was her cousin's movie. My dad went to a later showing and said people were really laughing a lot. He continued that one guy was laughing hysterically throughout the whole movie. I said, "Damn, I hope you gave that guy twenty dollars for me." Of course, my shit-talking dad replied, "I wasn't going nowhere near that motherfucker, he looked insane as hell." Actual quote.

There is a review of the movie in *The Hollywood Reporter* in 1987 by Duane Byrge. It says what Roger and I both thought. Roger wanted me to write the *Munchies* sequel but I stupidly did a Julie Corman movie about corporate sex [*Corporate Affairs*, 1990, Terence H. Winkless]. I never knew the name of it because I got fired for not being corporate enough. Julie was right about that. I was kind of pissed because I had to read Donald Trump's book on business too. That was in 1988. Once Julie fired me, I didn't hear anything else till 1990 when I was already trying to get my movie *Love Shack* [1997] going in Georgia. Anna Roth, one of Roger's assistants, hooked me up with Chris Wong at Vestron Pictures. They had rights to *Ghoulies* [1984] which was written and directed by

Bernard Bercovici's grandson, Luca. I wrote a "Ghoulies Go to College" treatment but lost out since they wanted a writer on the East Coast where their office was. [Vestron's *Ghoulies Go to College*—directed by John Buechler—was eventually written by Brent Olson.] In 1990, I called Roger after I submitted the "Ghoulies" treatment to him. It was pretty stupid on my part and I should have known that "Ghoulies Go to College" would be too much for Roger's taste. Pretty funny Jim Wynorski got to do *Munchies II* [1991]. He was pretty pissed that he didn't get to do the original and never liked me, not that I gave a damn.

When the indie Hollywood scene collapsed in the late 90s, I started writing novels since scripts are not a finished product—kind of like drawing blueprints for a house that you can never build. I wrote a non-fiction book about my wife's family in Southern Thailand and the amazing brutal demons they suffered for years, "The Ghost Way" [2010]. It's a collaboration between her parents and us. It really blows the mind when you see what they endured.

## Tina Hirsch
### (Director)

I edited three films for Roger Corman in the 1970s [*Big Bad Mama/Death Race 2000/Eat My Dust*]. When I decided I'd like to try my hand at directing, I went to Roger because I'd told him, years before, that when I felt ready to direct, I'd let him know. Coincidently, he had recently asked the heads of companies that made lower-budget movies, what their most profitable projects were. All of them mentioned making money from *Gremlins* rip-offs. He was in the process of getting a creature script. I had cut *Gremlins*, so it would be a perfect fit.

I think we shot 12 days of principal photography, got into a first cut, and went on to shoot 3 days of puppets and inserts. This was always the plan and saved us a lot of time. It was obvious watching the first cut, that one of the scenes that needed puppets to complete, wasn't going to stay in the movie. So that was one less scene to shoot.

I remember day 3 of the shooting schedule. We were supposed to shoot the motorcycle gang sequence first thing in the morning, go on to the motorcycle stunt, break for lunch and then shoot a six-character dialogue scene. The first delay came about because the location was fogged in. The camera couldn't roll until 11:30 a.m. When we'd finished that scene we moved to where the stunt was to take place and found that the stunt supervisor has prepped the wrong side of the road. We broke for lunch and planned how we could shoot the extensive dialogue scene later in the schedule. This was the place that my editing experience helped me the most. I had a breakdown of the script and in two minutes figured out where to shoot that dialogue scene. The awful thing that happened was that while we were trying to figure out how to handle it, Harvey Korman arrived at another part of the location. He was late for his call (in those days none of us had cell phones) and very upset. When the producer informed him of the disastrous morning, he got very angry and quit the film. He thought we were just irresponsible. I had to call him the next day to try to convince him to come back. Thank goodness he did.

We had a scene in the film where the Munchies steal a Gremlin (a small American car

**Tina Hirsch (Director) and Scott Sherk ("Buddy Holly", the ice cream boy) (courtesy of Tina Hirsch).**

at the time) and drive around making mischief. To shoot the wide shots of the vehicle, we put Duvetyne black-out fabric on the passenger and driver side windows to hide the fact that it wasn't a Munchie driving the car. Roger called me the next day to tell me it looked phony. I said that I thought it did, but that it was the only solution we could come up with. Moving the seat back and having a driver try to lie down and drive just wouldn't work. I asked him that if he could show us how to do it, we would gladly reshoot.

Working with Harvey Korman was fun. He was a big tease. At least I hope he was teasing! He was great at improvisation. He was almost always best on the first take. Nadine Van Der Velde and Charlie Stratton were cast because they had good chemistry and I think they worked well together. As I remember it, I expanded [the] part of Melvis [the wife of the evil twin] just so that I could cast Alix Elias. I'd seen her in a couple of Paul Bartel films and thought she would make an adorable, kooky, character. She and Harvey ad-libbed their scenes and created great little moments. Jon Stafford was a huge surprise. I had imagined the character of Dude (who was kind of a dope head) as a short, small-boned guy with dark circles under his eyes. That's how I described him to the casting director, Gary Zuckerbrod. Gary brought in four of those. None of them felt right to me. The fifth actor was Jon. He was tall and blond and healthy looking, but he acted like a druggie. He was a little crazy. He and Harvey were also a perfect team. That's what a good casting director can bring to a film.

Having cut *Gremlins*, I was a little disappointed in how the Munchies worked. Of course we didn't have anything close to the budget we had on *Gremlins*. On *Gremlins*, there were 5 people operating each puppet, one or two for the face, one or two on arms and legs. The stage had deep sub floor sections so that the puppets could be operated below stage level and the camera could be placed below the floor. On *Munchies* we had one person operating two puppets. We had absolutely no special gear. I was really lucky that I'd learned a lot of tricks on *Gremlins*. Mostly I learned what you could get away with. *Munchies* is not a slick movie, particularly by today's standards, but, if you were a 12-year-old boy when you saw it, chances are, you would have liked it…

*Munchies* played for two weeks in theaters in various large cities throughout the country. I saw it on the big screen at the Egyptian Theater in Los Angeles. I was surprised at how really good it looked on that giant screen.

I edited three films for Roger and I have to say, he never gave a bad note. He was absolutely on the mark every time. When it came to editing, he was the best producer I've ever worked with.

## Robert Short
### ("Munchies" Designer/2nd Unit Director)

[Author's note—You should know that after *Munchies* Roger Corman was about to give us "Goblins." I asked Robert Short something about this unproduced project.]

I designed the Munchies after Mayan hieroglyphs. We used hand puppets, remote controlled motorized running puppets and built large close up heads for expressions (the heads were never used). We made the movements simple enough so each one could be puppeteered by a single puppeteer. There was a hero puppet for each of the different styles

**Preliminary design for "The Goblin." Despite the initial interest by Roger Corman's Concorde Pictures, "Goblins" was not produced (courtesy of Robert Short).**

of the Munchies. Because the film was done in a very camp, over the top style, we did the puppeteering and presentation of the characters in the same campy way. Unfortunately this worked against the puppets and the approach I should have taken was to go for more realism with the creatures. Unlike Gremlins or Critters which worked great because at times they had real menace, we just kept playing it for laughs except toward the end of the film. Here they become much more serious and therefore convincing. Even though I have reservations about the creatures there were still several reviews that made a point of the "simple energetic puppets" being a highlight of the film.

I enjoyed working with Tina because she always knew what she wanted and the communication was very easy. As the second unit director I shot the car chase sequence between the Munchies and the Old Lady [Ellen Albertini Dow] as well as much of the battle in the factory at the end. Working on a show like this you have to be able to solve all kinds of problems. When we were shooting the car chase the bigger car's engine stopped working and I had to have the little car push the big car down a hill to make it look they were chasing each other. It's these kinds of experiences in the field that gave me problem solving skills which I've used on my bigger projects like *Beetlejuice*.

I've enjoyed working with Roger Corman because he is such a knowledgeable filmmaker in his own right and always brings credible and imaginative input to every one of his projects. That's a very rare thing in Hollywood. I've worked on several shows for Roger including *Piranha* [1978, Joe Dante] and *Killbots* [1985, Jim Wynorski] both of which were challenging and rewarding at the same time.

When Roger approached me about doing *Munchies* I thought I'd see if he would be amenable to the idea of me directing the next monster film his studio might do. He said it was possible so I put together a script called "Goblins" [1986]. The idea was based on putting a group of teenagers trapped in a house with creatures similar to the face hugger from *Aliens*. The tone I wanted was just like the scene where Ripley is trapped in the medical bay in *Alien*. Roger liked the script and told me if we could find a way to make it work we would. While doing *Munchies* I put together designs for the creatures which were slug like creatures with tentacles and suction cups along their backs. They also had a strange side mounted mouth. As we got closer to the end of *Munchies* interest in "Goblins" began to wane and new projects began to fill up Roger's schedule and eventually "Goblins" was passed on. The only thing that came out of it was that I used the side mounted mouths of the creatures as inspiration for my studio's *Predator* [1986] designs we did for John McTiernan between Boss Films and Stan Winston's involvement.

## Jonathan West
### (Cinematographer)

*Munchies* was one of the higher budgeted films Roger Corman was doing at the time. I believe the budget was about $1.2 million. Our shooting schedule was 4 weeks, 6 days per week. Most of the crew were not making a lot of money. We worked from 12 to 15 hours a day.

We filmed an entire opening sequence which showed how the Munchies were created in an ancient Mayan cave, a thousand years ago. The scenes were cut from the movie and only the Mayan ruins scenes were used.

We had a number of locations, although everything was in the Southern California area. All of the interiors were built on a small stage in Venice, at Corman's facility (Quest). Harvey Korman's house exterior was a new house built in the hills of the northern San Fernando Valley. It was part of a development and the houses were all still for sale. The Caves were in the Hollywood Hills at the Bronson Caves, a location used in many movies and television series for decades. The miniature golf scenes were shot at a recreation area in Van Nuys, next to the 405 freeway. The factory scenes took place in Santa Clarita, north of Los Angeles. It was a factory that manufactured bathroom cleansers. We filmed on the weekend and at night. When we finished our scenes with the actors, another 2nd unit crew came in and shot more action scenes with the puppets. The lake and forest areas were in the Angeles Crest Mountains, northeast of Los Angeles. Desert scenes, ice cream shop and driving chases were near the Pearblossom Highway, Palmdale, north of Los Angeles.

## Rodman Flender
### (Director of Advertising Concorde Pictures)

I was head of advertising when *Munchies* was made and I was responsible for the campaign. I remembered the campaign for *Ghoulies* [1984, Luca Bercovici], where one of the creatures popped out of a toilet bowl, and I wanted to come up with a single image that was as memorable. I had an idea to riff on the classic Marilyn Monroe photo—the one where she stands on a subway grate and the breeze from the passing train blows her skirt up (*The Seven Year Itch*). Only in my version, one of the Munchies lurked under the grate and gazed up her skirt. I did a sketch for Roger Corman and he loved the idea. Usually we tested different marketing concepts but Roger told me to go straight ahead with this one. We finished the campaign and the final step required an approval from the MPAA, the group that gives American films their rating. Not many people know this, but the MPAA also has to approve all ads that contain their movie ratings. Without their approval, you can't include the rating—without the rating, few newspapers will run the ads or theaters show the film. I brought the campaign to the MPAA offices with little concern. I had far edgier campaigns approved by them (a woman draped on a knife for *Stripped to Kill*; a giant cockroach mounting a lingerie-clad model for *The Nest*), but for some reason, my *Munchies* campaign was rejected! "I don't like the way that creature is looking up her skirt," the MPAA rep told me. I appealed and emphasized the cartooney satirical nature of the poster, how it nodded to the classic Hollywood lore of Marilyn Monroe and after all, wasn't one of the roles of the MPAA to further the legend of Hollywood history? I gave a good song-and-dance and the rejection was overturned. Little did I know that many years later, after the advent of cell-phone-cameras, "upskirt photography" would actually become a perv-ey genre all its own. Of course nothing like that happened in the movie but that never stopped a good campaign.

# *Never Cry Devil,* a.k.a. *Night Visitor*
## (1988, U.S.A.)

*Genre:* Horror; *Director:* Rupert Hitzig; *Writer:* Randal Viscovich; *Cinematographer:* Peter Jensen; *Editor:* Glenn Erickson; *Producer:* Alain Silver; *Associate Producers:* Randal Viscovich and Richard W. Abramites;*Executive Producers:* Tom Broadbridge and Shelley E. Reid; *Production Company:* Premiere Pictures Corporation; *Cast:* Derek Rydall (Billy Colton), Allen Garfield (Zachary Willard), Elliott Gould (Ronald Deveraux), Shannon Tweed (Lisa Grace), Teresa Van der Woude (Kelly Fremont), Richard Roundtree (Capt. Crane), Michael J. Pollard (Stanley Willard), Henry Gibson (Jake) and Bruce Kimmel (Townsend)

A dissolute student is an involuntary witness of a crime while he is spying on his sexy new neighbor. The murderer in a satanic mask is his hated history professor. A retired detective is the only one who believes the boy's farfetched tale.

## Randal Viscovich
## (Writer/Associate Producer)

I was working on a film entitled "Studebaker." It was financed by Richard Corey, who also financed David A. Prior's first film *Killzone* [1984]. As a matter of fact, David A. Prior [1955–2015] helped Corey to direct the Studebaker project. Richard Corey knew about my background in film, and he knew I wanted to direct.

I'll get back to this thought in a minute.

First, a little about my background. I started my interest in film before I was 10 years old. When I was around 10 or 11, my dad bought me a Regular 8mm camera. This was before Super 8mm was even invented. And the camera had no batteries. You had to wind it up, and if you were lucky, it might run for 25 seconds. So all your takes would be short. Also, when you finished with one side of the reel, you would have to go into a dark room, open the camera, flip the reel over and rethread the other side of the film through the aperture, and then you were ready for the next 3 minutes. Each roll of film had a total running time of around 5 to 6 minutes. I had a lot of fun filming my friends as they would kill each other on film.

Then came the invention of Super 8mm, and the cameras ran on batteries!!! This allowed me to be a little more creative. Still, it was difficult telling a story with no sound, but I learned through trial and error how to make it work.

Then came the invention of Super 8mm Sound. This changed everything. Now I could use dialog, having my actor friends verbally assault each other with 4-letter words.

Then came filmmaker Howard Hawks. My life was about to change. Mr. Hawks was a neighbor at the time I was attending Palm Springs High School. A family friend, Dr. Ronald Fragen, introduced me to Howard Hawks, and I was about to learn a thing or two. First, I had no idea who he was. My idol through grade school was Sam Peckinpah. When I showed Howard what I thought were my best two films, he proceeded to tear me apart little by little. He also added that he thought Peckinpah was the worst director of all time. I brought up what a great movie *The Wild Bunch* was. Howard said to me, "I was at a private showing for that trash. I walked out after the first 20 minutes. I went to my office and called Bill Holden and demanded to know why he agreed to be in that movie." So much for that. Anyway, Howard gave me advice on story structure and character development. I learned a lot from him. He was a nice man, and I was sorry to hear when he passed away.

When I was going to USC Film School, I met two producers at Universal Studios through a friend. They were Dean Zanetos and John McPherson. Dean and John knew I wanted to direct. They saw my amateur films. Both suggested I start writing. That would be a way to get my foot into the door. So I started writing scripts with both men, while still attending Film School. I was writing episodes for *The Incredible Hulk*, *Simon & Simon*, *Voyagers!*, and a couple of others.

This takes me back to "Studebaker" and "money man" Richard Corey. He told me if I would write a script that could be made for $200,000, he would finance the project.

First, I knew I had to write something that would have only 4 or 5 shooting locations because of the budget. I had to think of the demographics of the target audience, which would be 15- to 25-year-olds. I asked a fellow USC Film School friend, Scott Hill, for some help with the budget. Scott was good with budgets, and he would be the cameraman as well as one of the producers.

I decided that I would write a horror film. They call them "grind-house" movies, filled with exploitation and made for pennies on the dollar. Richard Corey agreed. There is one thing I know, all school students have at least one teacher they can't stand. I now had my protagonist and my antagonist: the high school student and his teacher. The next step was, what kind of horrible secret can this teacher have? I wanted to avoid Vampires, Zombies and Werewolves, as they were overdone then, just like they are today.

I had a nightmare, and came up with a guy who lives two lives: school teacher by day, satanic, devil-worshiping cannibalistic serial killer by night. Ideas were coming to me faster than I could write them down on paper. Then came the actual story of the film.

I drew inspiration from the following movies: *Rear Window*, *Craze*, *Body Double*, *Race with the Devil*, *Soylent Green*, *The Evil Dead*, *Pets*, *The Sinful Dwarf* and *Bloodsucking Freaks*.

The entire story was in my head. I started writing the script, handing the scenes over to Scott who was working on the budget at the same time. Richard Corey was calling me everyday asking, "How's it coming? How far are you?" etc. I finished the script in 2 weeks. Scott finished the budget, just under $200,000. Richard read the script and loved it. The script was entitled "The Boy Who Cried Devil." Richard thought that I had a dark side to me. Some of the scenes were a little too vile for even him. I explained that you have to "push the envelope" with this genre—and I certainly did do that. It was the ultimate grindhouse screenplay.

The fall of "Studebaker" during post-production ended up bankrupting Richard Corey. Now what?!?

I had a finished screenplay with a detailed budget for under $200,000. I recall turning to television producer/friend Dean Zanetos for suggestions. He told me to try and raise the money. That idea didn't go very far. Then it was Scott Hill who brought up the idea of me giving the script and budget to Chris Black at the William Morris Agency. Chris was also another alumni of the USC Film School. Scott had been in constant contact with Chris at the time.

To make a long story short, Chris read the screenplay and told me that he thought he could do something with it. I was thrilled. After a brief passage of time, the phone rang and it was Chris Black. He told me that there was a production company from Australia called Premiere Pictures. They wanted to do the film.

Chris told me that there was a film producer, Rupert Hitzig, who was looking to direct his first film for under a million dollars. Rupert was angry with his agent. He had gone through about 100 scripts, and none of them were up to his standards. Chris heard this conversation taking place in the office next door. Chris quickly grabbed a copy of "The Boy Who Cried Devil," went into the other office and passed along my script to Rupert. It all came down to "luck." If Chris never heard the conversation in the office next door, the script would probably have remained on the shelf. I was very lucky. The people responsible for the birth of the project were Richard Corey, Scott Hill, Chris Black, and Rupert Hitzig. The rest is history.

The budget was very LOW, somewhere in the six figure neighborhood. The film was shot in 20 days. The basic locations used were in Venice, California. The final week of

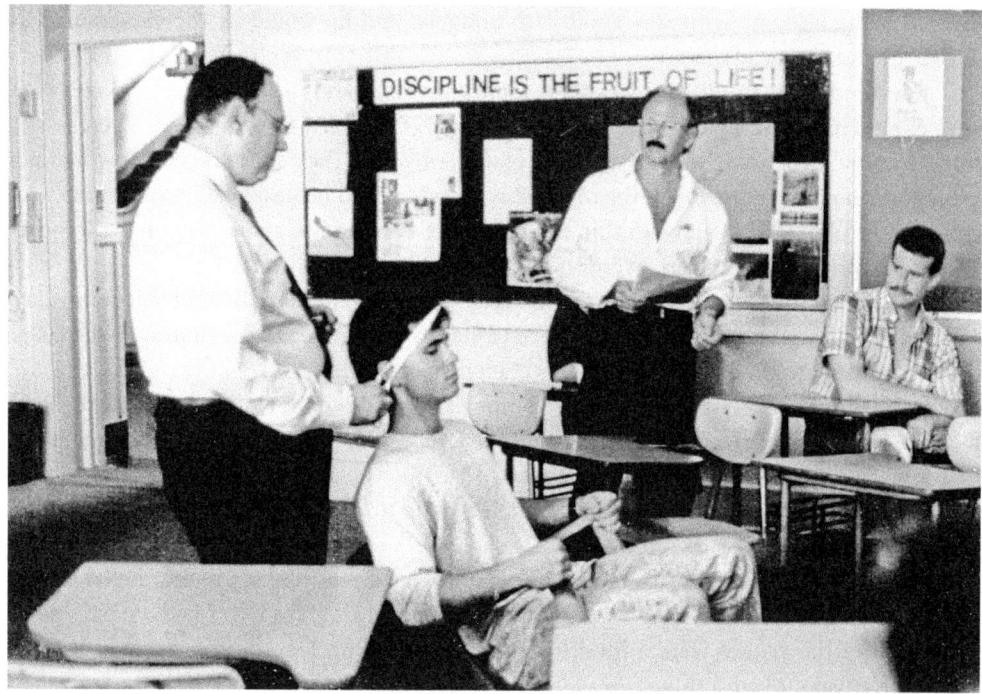

Filming *Never Cry Devil*. Location: classroom. Allen Garfield ("Zachary Willard"), Derek Rydall ("Billy Colton"), Rupert Hitzig (Director) and Randal Viscovich (Writer/Associate Producer) (photograph by Elizabeth Ward; courtesy of Randal Viscovich).

shooting was done on a sound stage at the Culver City Studios, which used to be the MGM Studios, California.

During pre-production, Rupert changed the title to "Cry Devil." Then in post-production, the editor, Glenn Erickson, suggested to Rupert and the producer that the title should be "Never Cry Devil." When the film was purchased by MGM/UA, they thought the word "Devil" sounded too exploitative, so they changed the title to "Night Visitor." The film was released in the United States and Canada under the title of *Night Visitor*. The film was released in the United Kingdom and Australia under the title of *Never Cry Devil*. I know there are different titles in different countries, but I really don't know what they are. I just recently found out that it was released in Greece under the title of *The Beast*.

A lot of things happened during the shoot. Some good, some bad, and some that were very strange. There were about half a dozen "supernatural events" that had a lot of people spooked. I remember everything like it was yesterday. I don't feel like discussing those events at this time. I would like to take a moment to address some of the people who worked behind the camera.

I had a list of actors that I wanted in the film. The executive producers only used two of my suggestions: Shannon Tweed and Richard Roundtree. All the others were selected by Rupert and the producer Alain Silver. And I must say that every actor on this film was a true professional. Allen Garfield delivered a knock-out performance. He was into that character of the teacher from day one. It was like magic, and all of the actors played perfectly off one another. The crew was awesome. Some really great professionals who worked their asses off for minimum wage.

Alain Silver, the producer, was the "axe-man" for the executive producers. I found Alain Silver to be a nice guy, at least to me. He has written a couple of books on Film Noir, and they are all good.

Alain Silver was told by the executive producers to "water down the script." So Alain and partner Bruce Kimmel went to work on my script. Everything related to cannibalism was removed. Every 4-letter word was removed. All excessive violence was removed. Anything considered crude or obscene was removed. Basically, I was baffled. The executives at Premiere Pictures bought a grind-house screenplay, but wanted to make "The Sound of Music." It just didn't make sense. A perfect example—Shannon Tweed is in a short, heavily edited sex scene, FULLY CLOTHED!!! Incredible.

Also, I did not write the scene with Henry Gibson [1935–2009] and Richard Roundtree (the scene where Henry Gibson is being interviewed by Richard Roundtree). It's a very short scene—a little more than a minute, I think—and gave Gibson a chance to do a cameo for his friend, Rupert Hitzig. To this day, I'm not sure who wrote it. I also did not write the scene where Derek Rydall throws a watermelon through the windshield of the Black Sedan. I also didn't write the ending collage of Derek Rydall and Teresa Van der Woude having "fun" before the end credits. The unused ending I wrote was very dark, and ended the movie like a *Twilight Zone* episode, as if everything was going to repeat itself as Derek meets his new neighbor, who was a witch involved with voodoo. The scene was photographed, but scrapped by the executive producers as being too dark and foreboding. It sits in a vault somewhere at MGM. Even the actress who played the part of the witch is in the ending credits, but you won't see her in the film. Too bad.

I complained vehemently to Rupert Hitzig, and he understood my anger. I argued that they were going to ruin the film. Rupert remained positive, and still allowed me to remain on the set. That tells what a great guy Rupert was, especially with all the stress and pressure he had on him during the production. Most directors would have had me thrown off the set after my first complaint. I really liked Rupert, and kept in close contact with him for a couple of years after *Night Visitor* got released. Rupert was not only full of positive energy, he really was a great human being and I'm proud to call him a friend.

The finished product came across as a comedy/thriller, but was advertised as a "hardcore horror film." There is more blood in an episode of *I Love Lucy*. This was the film's downfall.

On May 12, 1989, United Artists gave the film a very limited theatrical release under the title *Night Visitor*, and it fared below expectations. I wasn't surprised. I read a number of reviews in different newspapers and magazines, and the critics attacked the film for NOT having the creepy elements that were removed from the original screenplay. I felt fully vindicated.

MGM/UA released *Night Visitor* on video in 1990. It was in every video store throughout the United States, with a new, redesigned poster hanging in the windows. MGM/UA then released *Night Visitor* on DVD in 2005 in both full-screen and wide-screen versions, with some new flashy artwork. There are no extras, but the DVD does have the original theatrical trailer. *Night Visitor* still pops up on late night cable channels like HBO, Showtime, the Movie Channel, Cinemax, and Encore.

# *The Oracle*
(1984, U.S.A.)

*Genre:* Horror; *Director:* Roberta Findlay; *Writer:* R. Allen Leider; *Cinematographer:* Roberta Findlay; *Editor:* Roberta Findlay; *Special Effects:* Dean Mercil; *Producer:* Walter E. Sear; *Production Company:* Reeltime; *Cast:* Caroline Capers Powers (Jennifer), Roger Neil (Ray), Victoria Dryden (Dorothy Graham), James Styles (William Graham), Pam La Testa (Farkas), Chris Koronios as "Christopher Koron" (Pappas), Dan Lutsky (Tom Varney), Stacey Graves (Cindy), G. Gordon Cronce (Ben) and Ethel Mark (Dr. Ryker)

A young woman and her husband move to a new home, previously inhabited by a medium. Through a Ouija board, found in the house, the woman enters in contact with the lost spirit of a man, recently murdered. The spirit possesses the young woman and uses her as an instrument to seek revenge against those responsible of his death.

## R. Allen Leider
(Writer/"Gordon Mannering")

I met Roberta Findlay and the producer Walter Sear when they were producing adult films in the 1970s. I was interviewing adult film actors and producers/directors for domestic and international men's magazines. In 1983, Walter and Roberta were ending their careers as East Coast adult filmmakers when the advent of home video drove most of the production to the West Coast. They had been making feature length adult movies for theatrical release. I wrote many of their top-grossing films—*Liquid A$$ets* [1982] and *Glitter* [1983] were two of the best. They were R-rated scripts that I had written years earlier and later sold to Walter when they needed quality scripts. The films had both R and X rated release prints.

When the adult production in New York dried up, Walter and Roberta decided to make horror films. They owned the sound studio, the cameras and equipment and the editing tables. This meant their costs were lower than other production companies. They put out a notice in the film business trade papers for scripts and got a lot of very bad scripts. Finally, they asked me if I had anything. I was working on a novel "The Oracle" based on a true story of an event with a ouija board that my wife had experienced when she was in high school. I showed them the unfinished short story and they wanted it in script form. I abandoned the novel and wrote the script in a week. It was more atmospheric ... like *The Haunting*, but Roberta wanted blood and gore and graphic violence so we did a re-write. I got $5000 for the script and the job of unit photographer for another $1000.

The film was supposed to be a union-made film and I had some local name-talent lined up, people I had interviewed for legit publications, but Roberta and Walter decided to get cheap, cut the budget to $36,000 and went non-union. We had to re-cast the whole film and re-hire the crew. So, we worked with second-rate actors and moonlighting union crew. To save more money, the special effects were done by two high-school kids [Dean Mercil & ?] who, among other economical methods, used a life-sized puppet for the ghost instead of an actor in make-up which would have cost them $200 a day. Walter wrote the music and produced it in his studio and edited the film there as well.

The first release was in Florida at a single theater where it grossed more money in a week than a new film starring Gene Hackman. They opened it in a theater in Colorado and made little money. The film never had a New York City release because the theaters demanded $200,000 in newspaper and TV/Radio advertising and Walter did not have an advertising budget. Subsequently the film went to home video VHS release in a deal that recouped the production costs. 15 years later the film was sold in a package to a company that released the DVD version.

The short story version has not been published yet but will be in a volume of my "Hellfire Lounge" anthology series (Bold Venture Press). My new projects will include a James Bond novella "The Devil's Due" (for Canada only), a new pulp magazine series called "AWESOME Tales" and the "Wicca Girl #3" novel…

# *Parasite*
## (1981, U.S.A.)

*Genre:* Horror; *Director:* Charles Band; *Writers:* Alan J. Adler, Michael Shoob and Frank Levering; *Cinematographer:* Mac Ahlberg; *Editor:* Brad Arensman; Parasite *Effects designed and created by:* Stan Winston, James Kagel & Lance Anderson; *Special Makeup Effects:* Douglas J. White; *Producer:* Charles Band; *Executive Producer:* Irwin Yablans; *Production Company:* Charles Band Productions; *Cast:* Robert Glaudini (Dr. Paul Dean), Demi Moore (Patricia Welles), Luca Bercovici (Ricus), James Davidson (Wolf "The Merchant"), Al Fann (Collins), Tom Villard (Zeke), Scott Thomson (Chris), Cherie Currie (Dana) and Vivian Blaine (Miss Elizabeth Daley)

Due to an atomic disaster the world is reduced to poverty. A scientist has to find the cure to defeat a mortal parasite, he himself created and that lives in his stomach, as soon as possible. With the help of a local girl, the scientist has to face a gang of thugs who rob him of his samples and are infected by the parasite as well as a ruthless government agent (the Merchant) who intends to use the parasite as a formidable weapon.

## Alan J. Adler
### (Writer/Associate Producer)

I met two of my wife's old boyfriends at a party: Michael Shoob and Frank Levering. They had a title only; I said it didn't matter. The title was great and over breakfast one morning I sold the idea to Charlie Band. We wrote the script in a week taking different parts and improving the lines and action into a tape recorder. I did a polish of the script with three other writers [Albert Band and two other not-credited authors] that took about a week. Then, Irwin Yablans came on board, the budget for *Parasite* was bumped from 750K to 1 million dollars. Charlie said we were going to do the movie in 3-D. I went back into script and put INTO CAMERA into all the shots! Voilà, a 3-D script!

I was sitting outside Charlie's office and a young dark haired beauty—about 18—sits down and starts talking with me. It was Demi Moore and she was beautiful, tough, aggressive, sensual and intelligent. Demi said about three sentences and I walked into Charlie's office, said I had the girl for Patricia, brought her in, she read and got the part. The part was originally written for an actress named Patty Townsend who used to stand in front of me in yoga, but her agent wouldn't let her do it as I remember. Patty was the ex-wife of big independent director, Henry Jaglom.

*Parasite* did quite well—lots of good publicity for me and Shoob and Levering, too. I developed "Parasite 2" [1982/1983] with Larry Carroll—Band's senior line producer—a good writer and very experienced filmmaker. We were going to shoot all of it on an old aircraft carrier that was to double as a futuristic underground city where the parasite got loose. I am not sure why "Parasite 2" never clicked.... I thought for sure it would get made, and had a lot going for it.

## Michael Shoob
### (Writer)

The project started at a party at my house in Venice, California. An ex-girlfriend of mine showed up with Alan Adler. Like me, he was from the South. I'm originally from Atlanta. He's from North Carolina. He told me that he had just written a low budget horror film [*The Alchemist*, 1981] for a director [Charles Band] who wanted to do other similar projects. He said, "If you have any 'ideas' for a film, let me know." I said, "What about 'Parasite?'" I had worked on a project with that title in a horror writing class I had taken at the Sherwood Oaks Experimental College in LA. I was basically kidding around with him—I didn't expect anything to come of it.

On Monday, I got a call from Alan, "We got a deal on that idea." "What idea?" I asked. "Parasite." So, that's how it started. I never showed Alan the script we wrote in the class. We got a deal basically on the title alone. I phoned screenwriter Alan Ormsby (*My Bodyguard* and other films) who taught the horror writing class and he said that he had no problem with us taking the title.

I then asked Alan if I could include my screenwriting partner Frank Levering—Frank and I had come to Hollywood together to write more serious films like the Jack Nicholson/Bob Rafaelson film, *Five Easy Pieces*. Alan said it would be fine to include Frank. Charles Band's company would pay the three of us a small fee to write the movie.

We sat down and wrote the film together in about a week. Frank and I had a particular way of working because we had worked for many years together. Alan had a completely different way of working, and it took a little time to mesh the two approaches. My memory is that Alan had the basic idea of a small post-nuclear town and some sense of the main characters. I'm not sure honestly where all the elements of the story came from. It was a combination of all of us, I would say.

Then, after we were finished, a couple of guys were brought in to change the opening (which became much more bloody and violent), to add some dialogue and to accommodate some of the bloodier possibilities presented by 3-D. My feeling was that a lot of the dialogue we wrote was meant to be a little "tongue-in-cheek," but Charlie Band directed it dead straight. The effect, in my view, is that the film came off as kind of "campy."

In the fall of 1981, I began a stint as a Director Fellow at the American Film Institute so I missed all but a day or so of shooting. I do remember the "table read" with the actors. I had written a "dying speech" for the Ricus character [the leader of the gang who steals the scientist Paul Dean's metal pipe containing the parasite] saying something about the "nuclear ambience" of the film, something like "Look around you, Scarface, I'm the lucky one," and then Ricus dies. During the table read, Irwin Yablans said, "No, No! That's too philosophical. The line should be 'Fuck you, Scarface' and then he dies!"

# Frank Levering
(Writer)

I come from a farm family in rural Virginia, where I grew up on the family fruit orchard. We grew cherries, apples, peaches and plums. When, in the fall of 1983, I spent my honeymoon in Italy, near Perugia, in Umbria, at a house belonging to the Fitzgerald family, that overlooked an olive orchard, I felt right at home! The olives were being harvested, as I remember, and I might as well have been back at the family orchard in America! In 1984, I partnered with Benedict Fitzgerald, whose family owned this house, on an independent film project that was to star Dennis Hopper and Mary Elizabeth Mastrantonio. I wrote the screenplay, and Ben was one of the producers. Anyway, this film got to location, and much money was spent before the situation arose where money that was expected to complete the financing for production fell through. So the film was never shot. However, Benedict Fitzgerald went on to co-write, with Mel Gibson, the blockbuster film *The Passion of the Christ*.

Prior to the making of *Parasite*, I had attended Harvard Divinity School in Boston, where I got a degree but subsequently never entered the ministry. I had never been to film school or made a formal study of film. However while at Harvard I took a playwriting class with William Alfred, who won a Pulitzer Prize (the most prestigious award for an American playwright). In Alfred's class I learned many things about dramatic structure, character and dialogue that I was later able to apply to screenwriting. Then in 1979—three years before the release of *Parasite*—Michael Shoob and I moved to Los Angeles and were hired by actor and director Ralph Waite (star of the hit TV show *The Waltons*) to write a television movie script. This was my first job in Hollywood. The TV movie was never made, nor were a number of screenplays that Shoob and I, who were writing partners, wrote before 1982, several of them for hire by Hollywood film producers.

So this was my background coming into the writing of *Parasite*, with Shoob and Alan Adler. When *Parasite* was released, I had essentially been a Hollywood screen and television writer for three years, as well as a freelance journalist, writing many articles for newspapers and magazines.

*Parasite* was born at a Hollywood party—this is my recollection. At this party, which was in Venice, the beach community in West Los Angeles, Shoob and I met Alan Adler, a charming, engaging fellow who spoke in the soft drawl that characterizes natives of the American South. It turned out that Alan Adler was from North Carolina, where I had gone to high school, and together with Michael Shoob we were three young men from the American South, which is unusual in Hollywood, though Shoob's and Adler's ethnicity—Jewish—is not (I myself was a Quaker, a Christian sect known for its mystical apprehensions of divinity). Our common Southern heritage quickly united the three of us. As did our common interest in old horror films, particularly American horror films from the 1950s, and in the classic TV show *The Twilight Zone*, which had been my favorite show as a child.

I think it's safe to say that, when Shoob and I met Adler, all three of us were eager to make a real success out of ourselves, as screenwriters. It's true that Adler had achieved some measure of success already—he had, as I recall, already worked successfully as a writer with Charles Band. And while Shoob and I had been working—and were in the

Writers Guild of America (WGA) thanks to our work—none of what we'd written together had reached the silver screen. And we were very hungry for that next step.

So at this party—in the way that you do, in the effervescent atmosphere of a party—the three of us "hit it off" and agreed to work together on a screenplay that would ultimately be written for consideration by Charles Band to direct as a film. It was Adler who had the relationship with Band—and Adler who very generously (and perhaps also, shrewdly) reached out to us and embraced Shoob and me as co-conspirators in our collective attempt to elevate our level of success, as success is measured in Hollywood—by writing a hit film. At the same time, none of us, I believe, on the evening of that party, imagined or even dared to imagine the degree to which *Parasite* was to become a hit film. Primarily—speaking at least for Shoob and Levering—what we wanted, or at least more modestly hoped for, was some money coming in with this screenplay, enough to keep us going as screenwriters, and perhaps, with luck, an actual film, with modest expectations for its exposure and distribution. In other words, by partnering with Adler we hoped to advance our careers to some degree, and make a little money—and have some fun, as writers—in the process. Little did we know what was in store for us, or for the conception—essentially comical for all three of us at the party—of a monstrous parasite that would spring to life and inflict its terror on American (and world) moviegoers!

As mentioned earlier, Adler, Shoob and I were all aficionados of American horror films—Vincent Price, of course; the low-budget films of Roger Corman; in general, the atmospheric, melodramatic, you might even say "campy"—or so they seemed to "intellectuals" like Shoob and me (Adler was not so intellectual in his sensibility)—films from the 1950s and in some cases earlier (*Frankenstein*, Boris Karloff in general, Lon Chaney). Of the three of us, Adler, unquestionably, was the most knowledgeable about American horror films. They were an intense passion for him. With Shoob and I, while we loved what we'd seen of American horror films, we were primarily interested in the real classics of American drama. So, for us, embarking on writing a horror screenplay was not what we'd yearned to do from our roots in Atlanta, Georgia (Shoob), where Shoob's father was a prestigious federal judge, or from my roots, which were rural but also surprisingly intellectual (my older siblings hold Ph.D. degrees from Harvard, Princeton, and Johns Hopkins, three top universities, and a fourth did Ph.D. work at Oxford University in England). At the same time, though horror was not our absolute passion, it's true that Shoob and I undertook the writing of the screenplay for *Parasite* as an absolute challenge. While acknowledging that Adler was more knowledgeable and passionate than we were in the horror genre (and also older than we were), we were determined to hold our own with Adler—who emerged as the leader of the team—and make contributions to the screenplay that were uniquely ours to make.

Collaboration is a mysterious and hard-to-pinpoint human enterprise. I've done it many times, first as a screenwriter, later as writer of many books, plays, and a popular show for American public television. In my experience, at least, it is—different—singular—unique—every time you do it, varying in great degrees according to who you are working with and what the collaborative venture is. Entering the collaborative process of writing the screenplay for *Parasite*, Shoob and I were veterans with each other, and knew very well our tendencies as writers. We'd been a writing team for three years. We spoke a common language. Suddenly and for the first time, we were working with a third writer. Who, most significantly, had a kind of inside knowledge of Charles Band, based on their own collaborative projects, a knowledge that Adler brought to bear on our collaborative process. For neither Shoob nor I—Shoob in his youthful exuberance to push boundaries, challenge horror conventions; I, in my more studied, cautious approach to simply craft an acceptable screenplay for Band—knew very much about the man we were writing this screenplay for. We'd never really talked with him. And—taking this as gospel truth from Adler—we were not yet qualified to have a real, living and breathing conversation with the legendary Charles Band.

My memories of the writing process are dominated by several indelible images. The first is sitting outside, in the California sunshine, on the deck or porch, a deck I believe, of Alan Adler's apartment in, if memory serves, the Silver Lake neighborhood of Los Angeles. Then as now, Silver Lake was a neighborhood of diverse ethnicity and middle to lower middle class economic status. If you were affluent, chances are you did not live in Silver Lake, which was a haven for younger people aspiring to greater economic status, artists, and ethnic minorities, many of them fairly recent immigrants to America. In short, most people living there hoped to "pass through" Silver Lake and reach a more elevated destination. In writing *Parasite*, the same could be said of the three screenwriters: each of us hoping to parley this screenplay into nobler achievements—perhaps win an Oscar, down the road.

Anyway, that is the first image. The second image is quite a bit—unusual, in screenwriting, I believe—of improvisational dialogue, at times spoken out loud among the three of us. Because once we had our story—and the leader in creating a story was Adler—we created dialogue and fleshed out scenes in a very informal, spontaneous, improvisational way. Either that, or each of us wrote scenes we assigned to each other by hand. Wrote these scenes right there on Adler's deck—not taking them home to write them. With pen and ink. I still have some of the scenes that I wrote by hand. And what would happen then was, these scenes would in a manner of speaking be fed into a kind of blender, a metaphorical Veg-O-Matic (Veg-O-Matics were a popular vegetable juice blender at that time, much advertised on late night television) with Adler essentially at the blender's controls. Adler, our senior partner and more experienced in writing horror screenplays, was, essentially, the arbiter of what would "work for Charlie" (Band). This was his ultimate power—for, after all, Shoob and I had no idea whatsoever what would work for Charlie. To us, Charlie was a kind of "Wizard of Oz." So all ideas, good and bad, and all scenes, good and bad, passed ultimately through Adler, with his owlish glasses and rabbinically quizzical expression. At the same time, Adler himself was a driving creative force. Time and again he would burst into the sweet music of his drawl, often feeding off of one Shoob's or my ideas, "I have an i-dee-ah." And because of his relationship with Band, every one of Adler's "i-dee-ahs" freighted extra significance.

There was a typewriter on that deck, too. Mostly, it was Adler who typed up the results of our hand-written efforts. Because—then as now—when you "get it on the page," you've accomplished something real. And can go home happy. Three young men from what many Americans thought of then as "the Sticks"—the South. Creating in the most casual way imaginable a screenplay with modest expectations—hanging out on Adler's sunny deck and having a very good time, as if we were diners at an outdoor barbeque with hamburgers on the grill and the scent of suntan lotion on the breeze.

My own contributions to the final screenplay? Three things, I think.

—First, there were a number of occasions in the very short period (shockingly, no more than two weeks, and perhaps even less) when the first and decisive draft of *Parasite* was written, when Adler and Shoob were at odds with each other. The dynamic was essentially this: Adler, the senior partner, exercising his knowledge and ultimate authority; Shoob, the romantic, impulsive rebel, pushing and pushing Adler, and trying to push the horror genre itself (about which Adler knew much more than Shoob). To offer an analogy from poetry: Adler was the poet of metrical verse; Shoob, the free-spirited poet of free verse. And into this gulf, time and again, I was the bridge-builder—and the peacemaker. Because there were times when Shoob was visibly and audibly angry at Adler, feeling that Adler was constraining his creative latitude, and diminishing his efforts. Though Shoob had been my partner for three years, I recognized in Adler a fellow traveler: a peace-loving, just-get-it-done, practical workman from small-town North Carolina. Much as I admired Shoob's bucking bronco creativity, and its lineage of untrammeled big-city Atlanta aristocracy, I came more from Adler's world. So I think, in part, the role I played was a kind of mediator, able to speak to both sides of issues, and by my unruffled presence, calm things down and lower the temperatures of heated conflict.

—A second contribution, I think, was my background of keen social awareness. My Quaker parents—even as we were writing the screenplay—were working at the United Nations as peace and international law and Nuclear Freeze activists. Quakers, they were lifelong activists for world peace and social justice—this was my heritage, and inspiration. And into the screenplay, whenever the opportunity arose, I quietly but I think forcibly pushed for what horror films of the 1950s so often did in America—spoke in a coded language of protest and warning, much as the literature of Eastern Europe did under the Cold War yoke of Soviet oppression. So that in scenes such as the bar scene in *Parasite* [Collins' bar, where Dr. Paul Dean meets Patricia and Ricus' gang] which speaks of nuclear war apocalypse in New York City, and in the concept of the "Ray-Guns" (think: Ronald Reagan), and in the whole concept in *Parasite* of a horrific, post-nuclear war world—I think my background, and influential consciousness, were felt very strongly. As writers have always done in the best of horror films (and I think this is a major reason why *Parasite* did so well at the box office), I hoped to harness the reality of horror in the real world and translate that horror into a metaphor that anyone watching the movie would feel intuitively. Perhaps that moviegoer watching *Parasite* would not grasp the metaphorical language of the film directly. But from their knowledge and experience of the world in 1982, they would feel the metaphor viscerally, just as viewers of the original *Invasion of the Body Snatchers* felt, viscerally and incontrovertibly, the political horror in America of Senator Joe McCarthy and his chilling attempt to silence and punish American dissent to right-wing authoritarian politics. Hollywood screenwriters, time and again, have taken on the burden of daring to challenge the frightening power-grabs and outrageous lies of prominent American politicians. At his worst, Ronald Reagan was one of these politicians—and *Parasite*, inextricably, was written in the era of Reagan's prominence. So here you had a film, consciously (and metaphorically) written as an antidote to Ronald Reagan, which much to the surprise of its creators spoke powerfully to a mass audience. I believe this was because the story of *Parasite* provided powerful metaphor upon metaphor for a world in which the individual (the Demi Moore and Robert Glaudini characters) must fight to survive among gangs and Merchants and government authoritarians in a post-nuclear world—metaphorically, Reagan's world of death for the little guy.

—And the third contribution? To character nuance and specificity, I believe. These were elements, crucial to plays and screenplays, I had learned from William Alfred, at Harvard. The screenplay, I believe, for all its not-so-subtle add-ons by producer Irwin Yablans during production—retains, in the film, a number of surprisingly nuanced moments. This is what a screenwriter works hard for. In the case of *Parasite*, I think my best character contributions had to do with the development of specific character quirks and traits for the Demi Moore character. With four older sisters in my family, I grew up with a working (and intuitive) understanding of women. I tried to make Demi Moore's character as specific, and real, as possible within obvious constraints.

Generally speaking, Alan Adler was at the various filming locations much more than Michael Shoob and I. Immediately following the completion of the screenplay and its relatively few revisions, Shoob and I returned to our old partnership and pursued other work. What followed, as it turned out, was a collaboration on a screenplay with Benedict Fitzgerald, called "War in Illinois," based on a true story about a Jewish gangster in small-town Illinois in the Prohibition era of the 1920s. This screenplay was never filmed, but it did

Mac Ahlberg (Cinematographer), Alan J. Adler (Writer/Associate Producer) and Charles Band (Director/Producer) on location for the opening scene of *Parasite* (courtesy of Alan J. Adler).

launch a partnership with Fitzgerald, most notably on the project with Dennis Hopper in 1984. Prior to my working with Fitzgerald, he had written a film directed by the great director John Huston, called *Wise Blood*, which was based on a novel by the equally great American (and intensely Catholic) writer, Flannery O'Connor.

Shoob and I, however, did drive out from Los Angeles into the desert from time to time to observe the filming of *Parasite*. We witnessed Charles Band in action as a director, with his low-key, impassive approach to his low-budget art. It was clear to Shoob and me that Adler now occupied the position of chief screenwriting consultant to Band, so that they were now essentially renewing their prior relationship. In a sense, by choosing not to be on the set every day, Shoob and I were expressing our willingness to have Adler take the lead, at this point, in interpreting our screenplay with Band. So that, in fact, Adler did play the pivotal role with Band during the shooting, which it was clear, to me at least, he fiercely wanted to do. In fact, I always suspected that Adler may have felt some relied that Shoob and I receded, in a sense, from our creation on paper in the nebulous, gossamer-winged state of mind that held sway on that deck in Silver Lake. But that is mere speculation.

In our time on location, a friendship developed with James Davidson, who played the sinister Merchant (Wolf) in the film. I can remember being present for a number of the scenes featuring "Jim" Davidson, including what I think is one of the tensest, most arresting scenes in the film, in which Davidson buys gasoline from a leerie, almost paranoid local gas station attendant in this isolated, apocalyptic world. Jim Davidson brought what I think is a classic "B movie" presence to the film—both sinister and campy, which is very hard to do simultaneously. His rugged good looks belied his villainry and malevolent intent—that was very good casting, I think. And Jim knew what the moment called for, as a film actor. He didn't miss a note.

At that time, the best-known performer was Vivian Blaine, who is well known today for her role in a Judy Garland classic, *Meet Me in St. Louis*. In the credits, Blaine got what her agent wanted, I suspect: a special designation, apart from the other actors. Interaction with her was opaquely difficult. I can only guess that she was not thrilled to be—at her advanced age, and with her status as a "name" actor from the past—in what would have appeared to be, during the filming, a low-budget, lowbrow enterprise with no attached prestige. But I think she was superb in the role we'd all written for her—coquettish, lonely, vulnerable, suspicious, and above all, a faded flower, in the Tennessee Williams manner—just what we had in mind. I think Blaine's performance is one of the most distinctive and memorable aspects of the film.

The lead actor, Robert Glaudini, described in an astute, genre-savvy, and positive review of *Parasite* by David Chute in the *Los Angeles Herald-Examiner* as "the horse-faced hero," was a real trouper, as the expression goes in theater. He did yeoman work, appearing in virtually every scene and carrying the story on his back. The international success of *Parasite* owes a great deal to Glaudini's ability to bring nuance and mesmerizing alarm—and somewhat leaden hope—to a role that may perhaps have been a little underwritten. At least that is the way the role of Dr. Paul Dean now appears to me. I would love the chance to reconstruct that role a bit, make Paul Dean more specifically a real scientist, as he is meant to be, conceptually. Though Shoob and I, as part of our research, did actually interview a parasitologist at the University of California Los Angeles (UCLA), in watching the finished film I thought we'd done a better job as writers with minor characters, villains, and the Demi Moore character, than we did with Glaudini's leading role as Paul Dean.

Demi Moore, of course, is a special case. She was, I believe, all of nineteen at the time of the filming, and was not much interested in consorting with anyone as irrelevant to the reality of her sparkling bubble as mere screenwriters. She was known, at the time, to fans of soap opera television, God help them wherever they live, where she had a leading role in the hit soap show, *General Hospital*. So there was a kind of pop culture corona around Moore's pretty head, like some depictions of the Virgin Mary—but what was inside her head, on the film set, was an open question. No signs of future greatness or originality of consciousness were evident. It turns out, however, that Moore was "more" than up to the role. There was more of my writing in Moore's character than in any other role (having four older sisters has steered me to a lifelong interest in the female world view), and I liked what she did, very much, and could not have predicted it from personal encounters with her (as is so often true—I just didn't know it at the time). The role she had to portray on screen was not an Ingmar Bergman woman character; not Tennessee Williams; not Ibsen, Cechov, Tolstoj; not a Beth Henley portrait of a woman in despair who clings to hope, and dark humor, to get to a momentary safe place that you know won't last very long. It was an underwritten, story-driven, pure horror genre role. Pure and simple, As an actor, how do you make the most of a prison meal of bread and water? What Demi Moore did was anchor the female side of the film—which she had to do, in full, to make the film work. She anchored it with an exquisitely poised, unruffled, husky-voiced vision of self-confidence and hope in a shattered, menacing world. Along with her inescapable sexual allure, there was in Moore's every scene a clear, simple, immediately persuasive authenticity, and earnestness. She had, I think, an intuitive understanding of what the film needed from her, to be believable, and—dare we say it, with such a thin sketch (as written) of a young woman in horrible circumstances—she shouldered the fantasy, the sexual fantasy, that horror films have always required, each and every one, to enthrall and enchant a mass audience, both male and female. Tough, brave, compassionate—sexy. That was Demi Moore, in *Parasite*. If you were a man, or a woman, watching the film, what more could you ask for? Why else would you have paid good money to see this never-to-be-nominated-for-an-Oscar mass-market movie?

Charles Band, a handsome, mild-mannered man with strong family ties to Italy, seemed always, to me, while very much a gentleman, a somewhat distant and aloof figure. In a sense, Adler was Shoob's and my "ambassador" to Band, for their relationship was much more professionally intimate. I can say that, at least with *Parasite*, Band's energies with the actors were well placed, for I don't think there's a single bad or even lackluster performance in the film. Clearly he had finesse with his actors, at least in that one project. And, overall, I think the film is very competently directed.

The premiere of *Parasite* was a blast! More fun than P.T. Barnum and his circus showmanship could ever have dreamed of. For one thing, donning the 3-D glasses before the film appeared on the big screen created the kind of anticipation of new and transcendent experience that Hollywood has always traded on. There we were, in a Los Angeles theater, every face in the dim and holy light of an impending horror experience, decorated in the same democratic costume—the at once ludicrous and exhilarating nonsense of 3-D glasses! Everyone loved wearing those glasses. How cool! To be there, with a new, albeit fleeting disguise! In which no one could see your eyes anymore. You were fully costumed now to experience Horror. The horror! And everyone loved the film. Amazing. For me, expecting the worst, of course, what I couldn't escape, most viscerally—and this experience repeated itself, over and over, worldwide, in theaters as far-flung from this first screening as Asia and Australia and, for all I know, the dark side of the moon (maybe even Mars!)—was the horror COMING AT YOU! Everything in 3-D JUMPED OFF THE SCREEN. And "got you!"

This was the work of many real talents—but especially Mac Ahlberg, the director of photography, a real gentleman when you were talking with him, as well as a 3-D mastermind; and of course the great special effects wizard Stan Winston, who is now legendary in Hollywood as a special effects pioneer and boyish "cowboy" of the Wild West of what films can be, visually, the fantasy and horror genres especially. Writers, I learned with *Parasite*, only get the party started. The real fireworks at the party that is the making of a movie are the guests who arrive later. Ahlberg and Winston arrived later—and made magic out of the bare bones of a screenplay.

One more thing. One of my older sisters, Betsy, saw *Parasite* in New York City, in the year of its release and wild, unanticipated box office success, when only *Chariots of Fire* was pulling in more moviegoers in New York than *Parasite*. It was a theater in Manhattan, one of many there on that island of all of our dreams, where *Parasite* was playing. And what struck Betsy most was—everyone in that theater seemed to be TALKING BACK to the screen!

"Watch out! Watch out!"

"Look out!"

"Here it comes—run!"

"Get out, get out!"

"What are you doing! Get the hell out of there!"

And on and on. That's what it's all about, with horror.

"Are you crazy! Get the hell out of there! BEFORE IT'S TOO LATE!"

That was *Parasite*. For an hour and a half, in a dark movie theater, scaring the hell out of people who came there to be scared!

With the success of *Parasite*, a sequel seemed likely, if not inevitable. I can't remember the exact date, but it may have been the autumn of 1982 when Adler, Shoob and Levering reunited to begin work on the treatment for a sequel, working with producer Larry Carroll. Charles Band remained in the background, as I recall, as the three screenwriters worked on the treatment, but I understood from Adler that he intended to direct the film and act as at least one of the executive producers. The role of Yablans was unclear to me. Adler himself did not seem clear on that, though Adler's ties with Band remained strong. We did do a significant amount of speculative, unpaid work on the treatment, and publicity art and, as I recall, a promotional package for "Parasite 2" were completed, making the project seem very real. However, word arrived to the three of us that "the project is dead." Neither Shoob nor I talked to either Carroll or Band, and to this day I don't understand why "Parasite 2" died before it was ever fully alive. I do know that the sequel's demise came as a severe disappointment, as I thought our story concepts had great potential, and the public's appetite for our combination of horror and dystopia in the desert was proven and strong. But it wasn't to be.

Ironically (and we would never have guessed it at the time) *Parasite* Number One was the high water mark for the screenwriting careers of all three of us—at least to date. Adler went on, I believe, to write another low budget film or two (*The Concrete Jungle*, *Metalstorm*), but nothing anywhere close to the success of *Parasite*. He eventually became a film archivist at Twentieth Century–Fox, among other work. Shoob since 1982 has directed an independent feature film (*Driven*), and co-directed at least one documentary (*Bush's Brain*), but again, nothing to rival the success of *Parasite*. For my part, after the collapse of the independent film in 1984 that would have starred Dennis Hopper, I left screenwriting and, early in 1986, left Los Angeles for a very different sort of life. However, in the past four years events have taken another turn, which I will describe shortly.

In 1986 my then wife and I left Los Angeles, where she had been a newspaper journalist, and moved to my family's orchard in the Blue Ridge Mountains of Virginia. It's beautiful country. Several hundred miles to my north is Monticello, the home of Thomas Jefferson, also within sight of the Blue Ridge Mountains. We came to Virginia because my father, at the age of 78, had a severe heart attack, and was no longer capable of operating the orchard without family help. I was the one to do it—none of my five older siblings had time or interest—and so I made the decision to leave Los Angeles and come home, with my wife, to continue the orchard operation. My grandparents had founded the orchard in 1908, and so by coming home I hoped, among other things, to continue the family tradition there.

I also hoped to begin a career as a book writer. And this I did, initially in collaboration with my wife. From 1989 until 1996, my wife and I wrote three books together, one of which was a national bestseller, a triumph that perhaps exceeded the feat of co-writing *Parasite*, at least in my mind. That book, published in 1992 by Viking/Penguin in New York, was "Simple Living," a narrative of our new lives. A kind of sequel to that book followed, "Moving to a Small Town," published by Simon & Schuster in New York (which also did extremely well in the marketplace). My wife and I also wrote a novel together, published by Warner Books in New York. So we made a good team as writers.

In 2003, an opportunity arose for the two of us to produce a television show for PBS, the public television system in the U.S. This show was based, originally, on the success of our book *Simple Living*, and was called *Simple Living with Wanda Urbanska*, Wanda being my wife, who was also the host of the show. Again we experienced great success. Distributed by American Public Television in Boston, the show over the course of five years had 1.6 million regular viewers, and was the first regular television series in America to focus on environmental issues, including global warming. We traveled both domestically and internationally to create the show, filming in many diverse locations and often profiling leaders on environmental issues. I wrote, directed, and co-produced the show—this in addition to continuing to operate the orchard—so this was a very busy time, along with raising our son, Henry. The show ended in 2008, and can now be seen in syndication on Hulu, the popular channel emanating from Los Angeles. Meanwhile, however—and even before the show ended—my wife and I divorced, amicably, and went our separate ways.

Altogether now I have either written or co-written eight books. The latest book, called "Far Appomattox," is being published this month. It is actually a play I wrote, now in book form. Because, in addition to writing books, since 1999 I have become a playwright, drawing on skills I learned as a Hollywood screenwriter, as well as my studies in playwriting at Harvard. I have had seventeen produced and performed plays, to date, and "Far Appomattox" is the second play I've written about the American Civil War, a subject of abiding interest in this country. On April 9th of this year I travelled to Appomattox, Virginia, three hours from my orchard, to take part in the commemoration of the 150th anniversary of Robert E. Lee's surrender to Ulysses S. Grant at Appomattox on April 9, 1865. Thousands of people were there for the ceremonies.

As I mentioned, more recently things have taken a different turn, as in 2011 I met Beth Henley, a renowned American playwright, living in Los Angeles, who won the Pulitzer Prize (the top prize for a playwright) for her play "Crimes of the Heart." (The play was later adapted for the screen, and the film version starred Diane Keaton, Sissy Spacek, Jessica Lange, and Sam Shepard. Beth's screenplay was nominated for an Oscar.) In addition to her many plays, Beth has had a number of her screenplays adapted into films, with actors like Holly Hunter, Tim Robbins, Eric Roberts (brother of Julia Roberts) and many others featured in her films. Most recently, her play *The Jacksonian* was a huge hit in New York, starring Ed Harris, his real-life wife Amy Madigan, and the great film and stage actor Bill Pullman. Beth's career has been phenomenal—she is, I believe, the best known and most successful living American woman playwright.

Born within two months of each other, Beth and I have fallen in love. So that, to the extent that I can, I now spend much time in Los Angeles, where Beth lives, and for the first time since 1986. This has led to a renewed interest in screenwriting, as many of Beth's friends, and old friends of mine there as well, still work in the movie business. I now have several screenplays in the works, and hope to return to that profession, to some degree, for the first time in thirty years, while continuing other writing projects and, perhaps, again undertaking an independent film project. Who knows—maybe there will be another horror film!

## James Kagel
### (Parasite Effects)

I designed and sculpted the actual parasite itself. I believe Lance Anderson sculpted a smaller version. Stan Winston was overseeing and art directing all of us as well as the effects, makeup and so on. The actual description from the script was kind of vague. So Stan let me wing it. I designed the parasite with a tadpole, lungfish, slug sort of theme. I remember Stan wanted me to put some bigger lips on it. So it had more of a *Creature from the Black Lagoon* effect. So I did it. Then I was gone for a week. When I came back I saw a cast of the parasite. He had second thoughts so he cut the lips off after the model had been cast out of urethane. I didn't really mind. Since I didn't want to put them on in the first place. But Stan turned it around and said he didn't tell me because he didn't want me to be mad. He just didn't want me to say "I told you so." What a character he was. As I remember the parasite looked pretty good in 3-D.

I liked Charlie Band. Working with him was pretty good compared with most of the producers I have done business with. Stan and I actually presented a story synopsis to Charlie, that Stan and I had written together. He was very interested in it. It was called "Things That Go Bump." Charlie took our ideas. He made his own version of it called *Ghoulies* [1984, Luca Bercovici]. We were too naïve. Hollywood is about money not relationships. The unproduced script of "Beasties" that Stan Winston wrote with Tim Curnen was an attempt to salvage the story idea Charlie Band stole from us. The old Irish poem goes: "From ghosties and 'GHOULIES' and long-leggedy 'BEASTIES' and 'THINGS THAT GO BUMP' in the night … good Lord deliver us." I found the poem reprinted in a book by Bernie Wrightson the famous illustrator. Charlie and Stan thought it would be a good thing to borrow from too.

## Luca Bercovici
### ("Ricus")

The TV-movie *Flesh and Blood* [1979] was my first professional credit. Prior to that, I had been acting in college theater. I had discovered acting while attending College of the Redwoods in Eureka, California, and continued in the Theater Program at Santa Monica College.

The audition for the part of Ricus was at Irwin Yablans' office on Sunset Blvd. I was a young and passionate actor.… I think I actually pulled a real knife on a fellow actor as part of the scene. Happy to say, nobody got hurt and I got the job.

Demi Moore was fun, as was her husband at the time, Freddy. James Davidson was wonderful. I always wondered what happened to him. What a delightful man Tom Villard [1953–1994] was. I liked him very much. May he RIP. I loved Scott Thomson. We were instant friends and I would cast him in *Ghoulies* [Luca Bercovici's directorial debut]. I liked the DP Mac Ahlberg very much. A prince of a man, may he RIP. We would work together again on *Ghoulies*.

I liked working with Charlie Band at the time. We had a shared history, both growing up in Rome in the 1960s. Charlie was a few years older than me so our paths didn't cross, but we both attended the American Overseas School of Rome, and have people in common from those days. I'm certain that *Parasite* did quite well for Charlie, but not nearly as well as *Ghoulies* would do a couple of years later.

## Scott Thomson
### ("Chris")

I appeared in *Taxi Driver* (a silent bit part of a guy walking off with Jodie Foster as Robert De Niro looked on). I believe that the next film I was cast in was *Frightmare* [1982], a teen horror film that went through many title changes before its delayed release. I mention this because *Frightmare* is where I first met Luca Bercovici. The film was cast by Johannah Ray, a wonderful lady who cast us along with Charlie Band for *Parasite*.

The script of *Parasite* portrayed a dystopian world where among its many ills, oil was scarce and a very costly commodity. I remember discussing the character of Chris the gas station attendant with Charlie, and joked with him about Chris being the antithesis of the 50s era Texaco service guy who had a spotless uniform and provided service with a smile.… We discussed that he probably was not very bright and he compensated by trying to be tough. I liked my costume but it needed to get dirtied down. I wanted to look filthy and greasy, I think I even tore off the sleeves of my shirt.... Looking back now I have to laugh because everything about me was dirty except my hair which was perfectly coiffed in a 70s style.

It was great to be reunited with Luca Bercovici again. Luca is an affable fellow who is a very serious actor. In lighter moments on the set we would joke about the 3-D aspect recalling an *SCTV* sketch with John Candy spoofing a cheap TV show that boasted it was filmed in 3-D. It wasn't at all in 3-D, just actors leaning closer into the camera lens from time to time! Every now and then we would crack each other up by leaning into the lens leaving Charlie to wonder what we were doing.

The Wolf's car was wonderful. Since the film is set in the future they found some exotic sexy car with gull-wing doors that opened out and rose up. It might [have] been a concept car. What a wonderful sexy beast it was! When the guys weren't ogling the car they were ogling some of the girls in the cast. I was infatuated with Demi Moore and would hang around her asking her stupid questions just so I could hear her reply in the warm scratchy voice of hers. She was quite wonderful and polite putting up with my endless questions.

I've moved to New Orleans, Louisiana, where a lot a filming is being done (so much so they call it Hollywood South). I finished a film last year called *Greater* [2014, David Hunt] and I'm waiting for it to be released. Lately I've been keeping busy by writing screenplays I never finish or doing my paintings.

# *The Pink Chiquitas*
## (1985, Canada)

*Genre:* Sci-Fi/Comedy; *Director:* Anthony Currie; *Writers:* Anthony Currie (Story and Screenplay) and Nick Rotundo (Story); *Cinematographer:* Nicolas Stiliadis; *Editor:* Stephen Withrow; *Special Visual Effects:* David Stipes Productions; *Optical Effects:* Film Effects; *Special Mechanical Effects:* Brock Jolliffe; *Producers:* Nicolas Stiliadis and Syd Cappe; *Associate Producers:* George Flak and Carl Zittrer; *Production Company:* SC Entertainment; *Cast:* Frank Stallone (Tony Mareda, Jr.), Bruce Pirrie (Clip Bacardi), Elizabeth Edwards (Mary Ann Kowalski), Claudia Udy (Helen Walkman), John Hemphill (Ernie Bodine), Don Lake (Deputy Barney Drum), Laura Robinson (Trudy Jones), Cindy Valentine (Stella Dumbrowski), Diana Platts (Anita), Gerald Isaac (Dwight Wright), Robert Bredin (Dennis), Peter McBurnie (Jesse Cornfield), Sharon Dyer (Grindle), T.J. Scott (Dave) and Kevin Frankoff (Ken)

A pink-colored meteorite of alien origin falls near a small town. The influx of the meteorite transforms the women to sex-crazed amazons and gives them the power to control the male population. A private detective investigates the origins of this extraordinary phenomenon.

## Anthony Currie
## (Writer/Director)

*The Pink Chiquitas* was my first feature film as writer and director though I had made 1 professional and 49 amateur short films before that. I thought perhaps writing a feature film might provide me with the opportunity to direct. I certainly wasn't on anyone's radar as a known director.

After writing several other unproduced scripts I tried a genre that was very hot in Canada at the time, the low budget teen comedy. Canadian films such as *Meatballs*, *Hog Wild*, and *Pinball Summer* were among this genre. And in some respects that strategy worked. *The Pink Chiquitas* script immediately drew interest and was optioned by several different producers before it was eventually picked up by SC Entertainment.

The concept for *The Pink Chiquitas* arose out of some informal discussions I had with Nick Rotundo [1954–2011], someone I had also known in film school in Toronto. We were looking for something that could be done relatively cheaply. The 50s Sci-Fi genre seemed to lend itself to this. Something where the special effects didn't take itself too seriously. I believe Nick came up with the idea of alien women invading Earth or some such thing. I know that I added the idea of the meteorite falling to Earth as the catalyst. When I was a small boy I had in fact seen a meteor flash across the sky when I was at a drive-in with my parents. That was the inspiration for that and the start of the film. The subsequent search for the meteor by the various teenagers is a reference to *The Blob*. The small town where the invasion occurs is modeled after Mayberry from *The Andy Griffith Show*.

Though the film was set in the present, I wanted it to have a 50s, early 60s feel. Not just because this was the heyday of the low budget science fiction film, but also because of the portrayal of women in those days, particularly on American series television. Women in television shows such as *Leave It to Beaver*, *The Andy Griffith Show*, etc., were mainly housewives and certainly didn't compete with their men. It was a world where they may be fit to be librarians, but certainly not mayoral candidates.

At the start of *The Pink Chiquitas* there are several male characters whose jobs are already under threat from women. I thought it might be funny if these men couldn't comprehend that women could possibly challenge them in their careers and that this evolution had to be the work of some alien force. Though I'm not sure if those comedic elements were entirely successful and drawn out in the film.

The rather thick private detective [Tony Mareda, Jr.] who is as much in love with himself as are the women was a character I had created for another project and was just inserted into this story.

That's about as far as Nick and I had taken it when he got a job as a picture editor on the film *Cross Country* [1983]. It required him to relocate to Montreal for a period. As I wasn't working I then wrote the first draft. That would have been the summer of 1982. When the film was in its early stages it was very briefly known as "Black Widows." Nick Rotundo came up with "The Pink Chiquitas" which seemed to have a ring about it.

I was working primarily as a sound editor when I was trying to get *The Pink Chiquitas* produced. In 1985 I made a short educational film on commission for SC Entertainment a company run by Nick Stiliadis, another friend whom I had gone to film school with. Following that Nick optioned *The Pink Chiquitas* and we went into production in the fall of 1985. It was to be their first foray in the feature film market. I think the budget was about $ 1 million (Canadian). Most of the crew were first-timers and worked very hard indeed. It was a grueling shoot with very long hours.

We filmed the sequences for the movie seen at the drive-in, "Zombie Beach Party III" on the first day of shooting. We then had that processed and edited and then projected the cut sequence on the big screen at the drive-in and filmed the action in the foreground. I was quite amazed that our cinematographer was able to get such a good exposure of both the screen and the foreground action.

The town of Beamsville was actually a small town east of Toronto called Claremont. Most of our shooting took place in and around this area. The cave sequences were shot in Collingwood just north of Toronto. We were late in getting started due to financing, so it was an autumn shoot. We were very lucky with the weather considering many of the cast had to wear such skimpy costumes.

Casting took place in Toronto and Los Angeles. Frank Stallone was cast out of LA as well as Claudia Udy. Originally, I had hoped to cast Victor Mature as Tony Mareda, Sr., but this was deemed too costly—though he was never even approached. But I think Frank Stallone was quite good in the end in the dual role of his own father.

Many of the cast came from the comedy troupe Second City in Toronto. Bruce Pirrie who played Clip Bacardi was a friend I grew up with and had made films with since the

**Frank Stallone ("Tony Mareda, Jr.") and Anthony Currie (Writer/Director) (courtesy of Anthony Currie).**

age of 12. John Hemphill, Don Lake and Kevin Frankoff were some of the others. Peter McBurnie and Robert Bredin were friends.

Overall, I think the film was a bit too ambitious for its own good. We made it before the age of CGI and many of the special effects were just not doable on our lowly budget. The Nessie monster shoot [the scene in which Tony Mareda, Jr., fishes something enormous and, pulled by the creature who has taken the bait, ends up with him water skiing on two boards of the jetty] was an absolute disaster which we had to try to cut around to salvage. The person who constructed the "monster" was just not up to the challenge. I think the only reason it remained in the film was because the stunt skier was so good. The producers cut the comedic scene where the Mayor sets up things by telling the story of Nessie, the town's main tourist attraction.

The director's cut of the film, if you could call it that, ran 96 minutes. When the producers had difficulty selling the film to a major distributor they decided in their wisdom to cut out about 10 minutes out of the film. They thought it might sell easier if it was shorter. This they did without my involvement in the space of one day. So, I don't think a lot of care went into the deletions. Unfortunately, many of the strictly comedic scenes with the Second City cast members were lost which I don't think helped matters. Much of the film's criticism was that it just wasn't that funny. In addition to the comedic scenes that were cut, the producers also cut the only scene in which the meteor, Betty, actually speaks to Tony Mareda. So, if people are puzzled as to why Eartha Kitt is credited as the voice of the meteor, these cuts are the answer. I managed to keep a 35mm print of the 96 minute cut. Perhaps one day...

The film was finished in 1986 and was released theatrically in Canada in 1987. It had a very brief run and was received unkindly by the local critics. I know that it was sold around the world on VHS and now subsequently on DVD. A friend has a Japanese copy. I know people told me they saw it on video shelves in the Middle East, Africa, Japan, Malaysia, throughout Europe, etc. And I know it played for years on Canadian television and has had similar runs in the States on cable television. It is my understanding that *The Pink Chiquitas* is a bit more popular today with young teens.

I have spent the following years working mainly as a sound editor on feature films in Canada, England and the United States. But following *The Pink Chiquitas*, I continued to write screenplays. I am currently working on two screenplays. One is a teen comedy and the other a political thriller.

## Bruce Pirrie
### ("Clip Bacardi")

I was born in 1956 and grew up in Scarborough, a suburb of Toronto from which my Second City buddy, Mike Myers, also hails. I studied Film Production at York University, graduating with a Bachelor of Fine Arts degree. Always somewhat of a self-described comic actor, I took some classes at the famous Second City improvisation theatre (an organization that gave the entertainment world Bill Murray, John Candy, Catherine O'Hara, Tina Fey, Steve Carell and many, many others). I was asked to audition for the stage show and after one failed attempt, I was hired as an actor-writer. I left Second City after three years and shot *The Pink Chiquitas* right afterward. The film had a limited release, wasn't well-received and it didn't directly lead to any other major roles for me. Then I continued on as a journeyman actor, writer, and improviser, making a living writing for the *Red Green Show* on the CBC and a few guest roles on Canadian television shows like *The Psi Factor*, *Really Weird Tales*, *The Ron James Show*, etc.

I suppose I got involved with *The Pink Chiquitas* in 1967 when I was eleven years old and I met Tony Currie. My mother had re-married and we moved to Scarborough, a suburb of Toronto. Tony was one of my new classmates that I struck up a friendship with. Tony and I were both huge fans of movies but he was taking it to a whole other level. He formed Currie Productions when he was not yet a teenager and wrote, produced, directed, and appeared in a series of Super 8 films covering the genres of horror, war, and comedy. At the age of 13, he was even ambitious enough to adapt William Golding's "Lord of the Flies" into a one hour film. I starred in most of the productions, essaying such roles as Victor Frankenstein, Dr. Van Helsing and a variety of roles in comedies which Tony and I often co-wrote. Years later when we were in our late twenties Tony got backing to shoot *The Pink Chiquitas* and I was cast, without an audition, in the role of weatherman Clip Bacardi. By that time I had already made a name for myself as a comedic performer, having finished up a 3 year stint onstage in the world renowned Second City comedy troupe. I had also appeared in innumerable commercials, and a made-for-TV film about the Canadian inventors of the phenomenally popular board game, Trivial Pursuit. The CBC film was entitled *Breaking All the Rules*. Tony called me up to do it, and I did.

I had worked for two years onstage at Second City with Don Lake and John Hemphill where Tony saw them and cast them in the film as well. I was unacquainted with the bulk of the other actors before we met. It was of course very enjoyable spending the bulk of your days surrounded by scantily-clad beautiful women. Lolita Davidovich, one of the "Chiquitas," has gone on to do extremely well as an actress. Everyone got along very well. As I recall, Frank Stallone, labouring under the notoriety of his more famous brother had his occasional lapses into expecting "star treatment" virtually impossible given the film's low budget, but all in all he was pleasant to work with and a pretty good sport.

Although the story was set in the summer, to replicate the beach party/drive-in movies that it was parodying, it was actually shot in the late autumn, finishing up as I recall sometime in November. In some of the long shots of the countryside, you can see that the leaves have already changed colour. Naturally a Canadian fall is far colder than a Californian summer and it got uncomfortably cold performing at night in bathing suits and towels. A particularly frosty evening was my confrontation with the meteorite, Betty, where water from a nearby pond was pumped and sprayed on me as I attempted to destroy Betty with a flamethrower.

I've known Tony for over 40 years. Twenty years ago when we were working on *The Pink Chiquitas* it was just like when we were making Super 8 mm films together, twenty years before that. We had the same movie reference level, could speak in a kind of shorthand and he often solicited my input on some of the comedy quotient in the film. He was always open to suggestion. Directing *The Pink Chiquitas*, especially for a first feature, was a major achievement on just the production end. A huge cast, dozens of locations, all spread out over Central Ontario, special effects, night shoots, action sequences, car chases, huge set-pieces like the drive-in sequence, a semi-star lead and a very low budget. I believe that he did a remarkable job given the scope of the film and its budget. An added wrinkle was that one of the producers, Nick Stiliadis, the guy who watches over how the money was being spent on the movie, was also the cinematographer. So Tony had the dubious privilege of having a producer on the set all the time. On more than one occasion, Nick and Tony would get into a high-spirited debate on whether another take was needed, or even if the scene was necessary at all.

As I said, *The Pink Chiquitas* didn't lead to another major film role for me. That being said, it was a very fun experience shooting the film; I was working with a lot of my friends and nothing was taken too seriously. Would I have preferred it to have been a critically acclaimed smash hit? Well of course, but it wasn't and I still look back fondly on the experience. I own an unopened DVD of the film. The circumstances under which I'll crack it open and watch it again, are unknown to me. But I have it.

## Elizabeth Edwards
### ("Mary Ann Kowalski")

I grew up in Hong Kong as the child of missionaries and moved to Canada when I was 12 years old. When I was 14, a neighbor of mine suggested that I could get a job modeling, so I tried and was successful. As a teenager I was a model for catalogues like Sears and various publications, which led to doing TV commercials. I think I was successful because I really enjoyed people, I had fun at auditions and I was not intimidated. I started studying acting in earnest and began landing small roles.

I remember when I got the call to audition for *The Pink Chiquitas*. I first had to make sure it was not a porno flick as the name suggested! When I was told it was a comedy but I would have to be a nerdy librarian type that transforms into a sex crazed bikini clad amazon.... It sounded like a lot of fun! I especially liked the part about the nerdy librarian and went right away to purchase some glasses. I put my hair in a bun and bought some clothes at a thrift store and arrived at the audition so convincing that I sat in the reception area well past my audition time. People would walk by me, look at me and walk away! FINALLY after sitting there for an hour, someone asked why I was there. I said I was there to audition for the part of Mary Ann. They then had me read and explained that I was very good and indeed looked very much like a mousy librarian and thank you very much for coming, BUT you will have to come back again tomorrow and try and look like a sex goddess because it is hard to believe you can. Well, I had put so much work into looking bad they now thought I could not look good! The next day I came back and got the job! I was SO excited. I remember driving home from the audition not wanting to get into an accident because I had so much to live for.

Anthony Currie, was such a sweet approachable man. Really, the whole crew was great. The Second City people Bruce and John and Don gave the production credibility. I remember the hours were long and we had some night shots that were cold and wet but everyone was there to do their best. No one complained. Anthony allowed a lot of ad-libbing and gave us a long creative leash.

My 12-year-old nephew and his friends thought I was a star! The movie does have an adolescent appeal. It was fun. Looking back, *The Pink Chiquitas* was a highlight.

I was a single mother and needed a lot of help caring for my daughter during the production. I was just about to move to LA when I landed the role so as soon as the shooting finished I took off for Hollywood with my daughter. I realized quickly that I could not be the mother I wanted to be and have a full acting career. So I continued doing TV commercials at which I was very successful and still able to be there for my child. I studied art as well and developed my artistic talent and after moving to San Francisco, I now have four children a wonderful husband and a career as a painter. I now stand before bland canvases and direct and produce my own work in oils. I am happy.

# *The Rejuvenator*
## (1987, U.S.A.)

*Genre:* Horror; *Director:* Brian Thomas Jones; *Writers:* Simon Nuchtern and Brian Thomas Jones; *Cinematographer:* James McCalmont; *Editor:* Brian O'Hara; *Special Makeup Effects:* Ed French; *Producer:* Steven Mackler; *Production Company:* Bedford Entertainment; *Cast:* Vivian Lanko (Elizabeth Warren), John MacKay (Dr. Gregory Ashton), Katell Pleven (Dr. Stella Stone), James Hogue (Wilhelm) and Jessica Dublin (Ruth Warren).

A scientist tests a serum for eternal youth, obtained from the human brain, on a rich elderly actress. The serum is miraculous but has the side effect that the elderly lady has to keep increasing the serum's dosage for it to keep working. The supplies of serum come to an end and the former actress becomes a monster, obtaining the human brains she needs on her own in order to continue staying young and beautiful.

## Simon Nuchtern
### (Writer)

[Simon Nuchtern's *Silent Madness* was distributed by Almi Pictures. Almi went bankrupt shortly after the release of the film.] While Almi was still alive, they asked me to come up with another "horror" story and I wrote "Rejuvenatrix." I met Steve Mackler as he was the local distributor for *New York Nights* [1982, Simon Nuchtern]—he did very well with it. Steve had obtained a 3 picture deal [*The Rejuvenator/Escape from Safehaven/Underground*] with Sony Pictures for horror/suspense film and he offered to buy the "Rejuvenatrix" script from me. Almi was in terrible trouble and I knew that "Rejuvenatrix" would never be made by them any more so I made a deal with Steve and sold the script. I did the editing and post-production in my company, August Films, and it turned out very well. The film was directed by a young director called Brian Jones who also did some recrafting of the screenplay to alter it some to fit the new vision for the film and it turned out quite successful [the film was rechristened "The Rejuvenator"]. I was happy to share the scriptwriting credit with Brian. I was told the following year that Cinemax—the sister cable station to HBO—had a horror festival period on their channel, and *The Rejuvenator* was voted the best horror flick of the festival. Fun...

## Brian Thomas Jones
### (Writer/Director)

I came to New York in 1976 to attend NYU film school in my junior year of undergraduate university. I dropped out in the summer between junior and senior years because

I got a job with a TV commercial production company that became an opportunity I couldn't pass up. I stayed with that company for two years, then started freelancing as a production assistant on independent and studio feature films. I realized that in order to become a director I needed a show reel, so I went back to NYU in 1981 after a 4-year hiatus to make a narrative film. I also finished my Bachelor of Fine Arts degree, which made my mother extremely happy. That film, *Overexposed*, is a story in itself, but now I'll jump to the 11th Student Academy Awards of 1984.

*Overexposed* was a semi-finalist in the North Eastern U.S. region of the competition. It was a 58 minute "featurette" concerning photojournalists on assignment in El Salvador. My producer, Robert Altschuler, had done an amazing job of hustling incredible production value for very little money and the film looked like a real movie, not a student film. However, I lost to Alan Kingsberg's short film *Minors*, which went on to win the Student Academy Award in the final competition. That night of the judging I walked back to my apartment in the rain, stopped off at a hotel bar on the way and drowned my sorrows in some expensive Scotch.

A few days later I got a call from Steve Mackler. He introduced himself and told me he had been on the jury for the student awards and was really impressed with what I'd done for no money. He told me I'd only lost by 2/10ths of a point of the rating system the jury was using. Steve made a deal with Robert to take *Overexposed* around and try to raise money to shoot another 20 minutes of story so he could sell it as a feature. He was never able to accomplish that, but we became colleagues and began looking for ways to work together.

Coincidently, I had met Mark Patrick Carducci [1954–1997] on the first indie film I worked on as a production assistant in 1979. He was an office P.A. and I was on set, and we bonded over screenwriting. We more or less lost touch until 1984 when his name came up in a conversation with Steve. They were working on *Neon Maniacs* [1985] at that time. I moved to L.A. for 9 months in January 1985 and hung out on the set with Mark and Steve and director Joe Mangine while they were shooting some of the movie with L.A. standing in for San Francisco.

I moved back to New York later that year and was making a living directing corporate videos for different production companies. In the Summer of 1987 Mackler called me with a shot at "the big time." He had made a deal with Sony Video Software (SVS Films) to make 3 feature films which would get theatrical release before going to home video, which was VHS at the time, and that market was booming. Sony had just lost the Betamax versus VHS war and had begun making their own VHS video players. This was also before Sony had bought Columbia Pictures.

The idea behind SVS Films was to make low-budget genre movies, put them in theaters for a week, then use that as leverage to video store owners. "Straight to your store from the theater." They would also cross-market the movies with the video players.

The budget for each of the three films in the deal with SVS was between $200,000-$300,000. I vaguely remember *The Rejuvenator* coming in around $230K, but I could be wrong. I assume Mackler was taking his fees off the top of whatever the total number was, but who cares? Steve always was and will always be one of the nicest, most honest guys in the film business. A man of true integrity. Every deal I made with him started as a handshake and ended with the same. He always treated cast and crew with respect and is a genuine human being ... a real Mensch!

It was July of 1987 when Steve called me into his office to talk about a script called

"Skin" which he had bought from Simon Nuchtern. It was to be the first in the 3 picture deal with SVS and he wanted me to direct it based on our now solid relationship. Simon owned an editing company in the TVC Labs building and did post-production for most of the low budget producers in New York at the time. I'm pretty sure a lot of the best vintage porn of the 70s and 80s was cut in those rooms.... Back when they had stories and were shot on 35mm film.

Simon had written "Skin" specifically as a vehicle for the work of special effects make-up artist Ed French, who in fact did all the creature fabrications and appliances for *The Rejuvenator*. Steve gave me the script to read and I left his office very excited. I went to a little pocket-park in the mid-40s between 5th and 6th Avenues and sat there reading it in one sitting. It was a typical hot, humid New York City summer day, but there was a waterfall which helped cool the air and drown out the city noise. When I finished reading I said to myself, "I can't direct this script ... but I know how to make this movie. It's *Bride of Frankenstein* meets *Sunset Boulevard!*"

I pitched the idea to Steve and he turned me loose to re-write it. I think it only took 4 weeks to get a first draft. I was a night owl in those days so would usually work between 11:00 p.m. to around 6:00–7:00 a.m. I was writing about 7 pages a night.

I kept some of the structural elements and make-up special effects Simon had come up with but basically started from page one to make it my own movie. When I turned in the first draft Steve had very few notes and that was the script we basically shot. Simon also liked the script, which was cool.

I have never been a true fan of blood & guts gore horror, but I grew up on the classic Universal Studios monster movies ... *Frankenstein*, *The Wolf Man*, *Dracula*, *The Mummy*, *Creature from the Black Lagoon*, etc. I've also always been a fan of great Gothic literature and had read the source books for all of the monster movies I loved. I wanted to make this a movie with heart that was about a dramatic theme, not just gore and effects. As I was writing it the themes I tried to weave in concerned vanity, obsession, greed, addiction and loss of innocence. I think I succeeded because the reviews it got in the *N.Y. Daily News*, *Variety*, *Cinefantastique* and *Fangoria* all mentioned the depth of characterization, the performances and the story that set it apart from most low-budget genre horror films.

We tried out a number of titles along the way. The only one I remember was "Scream Queen," sort of a play on "Screen Queen," going with the faded-actress-seeking-the-fountain-of-youth motif, which never flew, thankfully. It was actually Mark Carducci who came up with the title "Rejuvenatrix." It took us all a nanosecond to love it! It had a "psychotronic" feel and the combination of "rejuvenation" with "dominatrix" really captured the essence of the film both thematically and visually. So that became the working title throughout production. When we finished the movie and screened the final cut for SVS Films, the idiot executive who knew nothing about the horror genre or fandom decided to retitle it "The Rejuvenator" ... It sounded a lot like *Re-Animator*, the brilliant Stuart Gordon film, and the marketing brain-trusts of SVS Films thought that the confusion would help to sell more videocassettes. Sadly, those same idiots are still working in the motion picture industry as I write this! When Steve Mackler and his foreign sales rep, Bernie Goldberg, starting pre-selling the film in foreign territories, the title "Juvenatrix" was used, apparently because the English language prefix "Re-" has no equivalent in Europe. I don't know if this is true, but it's what I was told.

Speaking of marketing, the original poster design for the film was completely different than the final artwork, and was far superior. The two images of Elizabeth Warren transitioning to the monster were separated by a highly stylized hypodermic needle. It was a brilliant design that really symbolized what I was trying to say socially with this movie. But this was the age of Nancy Reagan and "just say no to drugs" so the MPAA (the censor organization in the pockets of the major studios) would not approve the poster art, and this is what we have instead.

We began pre-production right after Labor Day weekend in September 1987. Steve hired Bob Zimmerman (not Bob Dylan!) as Line-Producer/Production Manager. We all called him "Zimmo." He truly loved movies, especially horror and genre films, and he had also worked with Simon Nuchtern [they had co-written *Silent Madness* in 1983]. Another "Mensch!" We took rented production offices in an office building on 5th Avenue and 42nd Street, which we shared with friends of Mackler's. Jim Dudelson and Taurus Entertainment were in one suite, and another distributor friend of Steve's had the other suite. We bounced between some vacant offices and the conference room. The offices overlooked the New York Central Library, and was a 10 block walk from my apartment. It was an inspiring space to work from.

The original schedule was for 20 days and I think we went over by two days, then had a day of pick-up shots in a studio once we had a rough cut to get some missing transition shots we needed. Still, I think the whole movie came in around $230,000 after post. We shot on re-cans and short ends of 35mm film from other productions, and used the Arri 35 BL for our A camera and an Arri 35 IIc as B camera. We had a pretty good package of both prime and zoom lenses. My Director of Photography was James McCalmont, who had shot a large part of my NYU student thesis. Jim had a great track record as a concert shooter, working for Don Lenzer and photographing everyone from John Lennon, Eric Clapton to Led Zeppelin. He also shot some of the classic vintage porn films starring Annie Sprinkle, who is now a highly respected feminist performance artist. Jim really knows how to help a director block a scene for camera "guerilla style" so that you not only get the shots you need to tell the story in an interesting visual style, but so that you can get the scene in the time allotted and make your days. Sometimes in low-budget you feel like you're not shooting a movie ... but shooting a schedule.

The first big obstacle was casting. Mackler and Zimmo had a meeting with the Screen Actors Guild and told them that we were making three feature films, each with budgets under $300K, and wanted to work with SAG actors, so let's make a deal. In those days the NY head of SAG was a really arrogant prick with a power complex. He told them, "Our union members don't work on films with budgets less than $1 million!" So we had to go with a non-union casting director and non-union actors. The irony is that actors are always desperate to ply their craft and get film for their reel. So I don't even remember how many SAG actors we worked with who changed their names so they could be in our movies! Fortunately today the situation is entirely different, and there are SAG contracts for every budget level, including experimental films.

I had a type of actor in mind for Dr. Ashton. We looked at so many leading men types and nobody worked. Then John McKay came in. I think Zimmo had actually recommended him. I would have never thought of him if I had only seen his picture. But when he read the part a nuclear bomb of clarity exploded in my head! He WAS Ashton! I completely re-imagined the part and he was one of the best things that happened to the movie.

For the lead of Elizabeth Warren/The Monster I only ever considered Vivian Lanko. She was part of an experimental theatre company I was involved with at the time, La Cucaracha, and I was familiar with her versatility, range, and willingness to take risks. She was married to Martin Donovan, a brilliant actor who was in the same company and has had a very interesting career in indie films and television. She was uncomfortable with the nudity required for the role, but was intrigued by the characterization and the transformative aspects of the part. At her audition she convinced Mackler and Zimmo she was right for the part and we cast her. She committed 1,000%, enduring hours in special effects make-up application and removal, and her chemistry with John McKay was stellar. The movie works on so many levels because of their portrayal and ownership of the characters.

The location for Elizabeth Warren's mansion we found right away. It was an incredible property in New Jersey used for a lot of filming. We shot the first 4 days there in late October and it was a magical experience. There's nothing like Fall on the East Coast. The days were warm and the nights crisp, the leaves turning golden colors. I actually crashed there a couple of nights on the set rather than going home just to get some extra sleep. There really were ghosts in that place!

The hardest location to find was Ashton's lab. Zimmo and our location manager, Phil Dolan, kept taking us to hospitals and university labs but nothing had the right look or feel. One day I was in Zimmo's office and saw these two Polaroid SX-70 photos on his desk. My heart jumped out of my chest and I said, "What's this? Where is this?!?" Zimmo said, "Oh I wasn't even going to show you those…. It's just an old abandoned tuberculosis hospital on Staten Island." Phil had scouted it but didn't think it was right so only shot the two Polaroids. Plus, it was on Staten Island, a major pain in the ass for transportation. It was the perfect mad scientist's lab! Exactly what I had in mind when writing the script. When we went to do a crew scout it was even better than imagined. Truly one of the scariest places I've ever been on this planet. It had everything we needed for props, set decoration, all just laying around … untouched from the 1940s! A few years later in 1990 Adrian Lyne shot *Jacob's Ladder* there with Tim Robbins. I can't tell how thrilled I am that I used it first!

*The Rejuvenator* was released theatrically in several all-night grindhouse theatres in Manhattan. It opened on Friday, July 15, 1988, and played at the Cine Twin on 7th Ave. in Times Square and at the Essex on the Lower East Side. It also played in the Bronx at the Cinema Center, the Dover, and the Kent Twin. I recall it also played some indie theatres in Los Angeles but don't know which ones. The tragedy of the situation is SVS Films only booked it in those theaters for a week. On Wednesday, July 20 the *N.Y. Daily News* published a very favorable review … but

*The Rejuvenator*: **The final stage of the "brain lady mutation" (courtesy of Bruce Spaulding Fuller).**

it was too late. *The Rejuvenator* was already gone from theatres. The same SVS idiot who changed the title to "The Rejuvenator" said he didn't feel the movie "had legs." That was before the reviews came out. It also got an extremely positive review in *Variety* on the same day as the *Daily News* review. It was going to be Mackler's strategy to then take the positive reviews and try to book it as a midnight movie at the 8th Street Theatre in Greenwich Village, which showed a lot of cult films. It had the potential to become a cult midnight movie, but alas, never got the opportunity because of the asshole at SVS Films. He is a prime example of how the incompetent rise to the top.

The irony is that the movie actually did quite well at the box office for what it was. For its one-week run in limited release it made *Variety*'s list of 50 Top Grossing Films for the week ending July 20. It was #36 and grossed $15,000 U.S. on 5 screens in New York. Had it run another week or two with word of mouth growing, and perhaps a run as a midnight movie, it would probably have recouped its cost and turned a small profit from theatrical alone.

When the movie was released on VHS it again got very positive reviews in the May 1989 issues of both *Cinefantastique* and *Fangoria*. I don't recall the actual number of units it sold in home video, but I do recall Mackler telling me it did quite well. Sadly, the movie has never been released on DVD. I actually bought a couple of LaserDiscs on eBay, but nobody has ever resurrected the three SVS films or contacted me to do a release with bonus features on DVD.

There are so many stories from the filming so I'll just mention a few. My favorite is the night we were shooting the scene outside the nightclub where Elizabeth has transformed into the monster and needs to use a payphone to call Dr. Ashton to come pick her up. There is a woman on the phone—one of the dancers from the club—and the monster whacks her in the head, killing her. I've always been a believer in what you don't see is more horrific than graphic gore, letting the imagination do the work. So we did the killing in cuts. What you see is blood and brains splat on the glass of the phone booth, then the dancer's bloody hand slides down through the goo as she slumps to the ground. The location for that scene was in an alley in Chinatown, right around the corner from The Mudd Club, a legendary nightspot of the Downtown Scene in 80s New York.

Another scene that was very simple but effective low-budget filmmaking was the scene where Ashton meets the fishmonger Hunter on the waterfront to order some more cadavers. The building where the dialogue takes place was just a dilapidated building on the grounds of the TB hospital where we shot most of the lab interiors. On our pick-up shot day we went to the waterfront and shot a long-lens establishing shot of a commercial boat sailing down river. Using maritime sound effects over the cut to the interior, and then throughout the scene, the illusion is created that the whole scene takes place on the waterfront. I held back showing what Hunter was fishing for. As an afterthought Ashton says "Catch anything?" Hunter then holds up a 3 foot black eel, pretty nasty looking. It was perfect for his character and a fun reveal. We got the eel from yet another Chinese restaurant. Roy McArthur who played Hunter is one of the best character actors I've ever worked with. I went on to cast him as the villain, Preacher, in *Escape from Safehaven* [1988, Brian Thomas Jones & James McCalmont], then as a low budget film director in *Posed for Murder* [1988, Brian Thomas Jones].

Shooting the climactic scene where Elizabeth/The Monster disintegrates into a pile of goop was pretty funny. That scene is on YouTube as "Gory Barfing Creature Woman," which pretty much sums it up! We had about twelve people all around the prosthetic device with tubes and plungers and bladders running all over the place. Everyone was wearing plastic garbage bags in anticipation of the impending mess. The goo was cottage cheese, oatmeal, stage blood, colored water, and who knows what else. On "action" everybody started pumping and spraying. Goop was shooting everywhere. On "cut" the whole crew broke up into hysterical laughter. It was one of the shining moments of my career. I stepped back and thought to myself, "Wow … I went to college for this?" It was too funny.

Post-production was kind of a blur. We finished shooting right before Christmas and our editor, Brian O'Hara, had a 1st assembly right after the holidays. By that point I'd already started working on the script for the next SVS film. The working title was "Bloodscape," and was eventually released as *Escape from Safehaven*. Jim McCalmont shot the day of pickups from our shot list and those shots helped make the movie seamless. One shot we needed took place in Ashton's lab and we no longer had access to the location. It was a fairly tight insert, so we drew a grid of tiles on a sheet of white Foam Core with a black Sharpie that matched the tiles in the actual location. It's a perfect match.

I'm really fortunate to have edited this and my next two films on a KEM flatbed console and upright Moviola. This is how it was done in the studio days. Now everything is computers and digital, which actually makes the editing process so much faster and easier. But I'm glad I got to do it the old-school way for the experience. I wouldn't trade that for anything.

The scoring and sound mix were a lot of fun for me. Larry Juris created a really haunting score, but not wall-to-wall music. We were really lucky to do all the sound editing and mixing at Sound One, one of the top studios in New York to this day, used by all the major studios. Hearing the movie come to life was yet another thrill on top of shooting the movie in the first place. I got to work with sound artists who work with A-list directors, and they treated this movie with as much respect and professionalism as with any studio project. What a treat!

It was extremely disappointing that *The Rejuvenator* never got the exposure and recognition I feel it deserved. It's not a brilliant movie, but for the money, genre and time period I consider it extremely successful as entertainment and it has developed an international fan base of those lucky enough to see it. I suppose I should let it go, but I will forever have a sore spot for that SVS Films idiot that didn't have the intelligence, taste, vision or creativity to understand the potential of what he had in his hands!

My directing career never reached the level I had hoped for either. After *The Rejuvenator* I co-wrote and co-directed *Escape from Safehaven* with Jim McCalmont, which was the second in the series of Mackler's three movies for SVS Films. When that movie was in post I was approached by indie producers Jack Fox and Carl Fury to direct an erotic thriller entitled "Obsessed," later released as *Posed for Murder* by Double Helix Films. It was to be a starring vehicle for Fury, who had some cachet as a WWF wrestler at the time. The original script was written by John Gallagher, who was slated to direct. For whatever reason Jack and Carl didn't want to continue the working relationship with Gallagher and approached me based on seeing *The Rejuvenator*. I took the job because I needed a job. That destroyed my friendship with Mark Carducci for many years because he was close with Gallagher and felt I shouldn't have taken the job out of solidarity. But it's show business.

These things happen all the time. Years later when I was living in Los Angeles I ran into Mark at a *Fangoria* convention. We made amends but lost touch. Then in 1997 I learned that Mark had tragically taken his own life. I heard through the grapevine that he was distraught over a deal regarding *Mars Attacks!*. He had been developing a script based on the Topps Trading Card property for years. It was his baby. Then he lost it to Warner Bros. and Tim Burton. It's only my opinion, but I think Mark let "the business" kill him. He had a young daughter too. So sad.

In 1989 Double Helix Films took *Posed for Murder* to the market at the Cannes Film Festival. I went over for the festival and it was one of the greatest experiences of my life. The South of France, movies, beautiful women, all night parties, wearing a tuxedo every night…. It was like playing James Bond. It was good for business too. In a 5 minute conversation with Mitch Galin, George Romero's partner in Laurel Entertainment, he offered me an episode of their horror anthology series *Monsters* to direct. I ended up directing two episodes ["The Mandrake Root" and "A New Woman"], then I moved to Los Angeles.

Through the casting director for *Monsters*, Leonard Finger, I met producer Bruce Cohn-Curtis, who is noted for the 80s classics *Roller Boogie*, *Fear City*, *Hell Night* and *Dreamscape*. We worked together over the 90s developing several movies that got right to the point of pre-production, then the deal would fall apart for some reason. One of these was a re-make of *Hell Night* that Bruce is STILL trying to get made! Through Bruce I met Lance Robbins at Saban Entertainment and through him I directed multiple episodes of the Saban TV series *Sweet Valley High* [1995] and *Big Bad Beetleborgs* [1997]. I finally directed a movie for Bruce, *Slammed*, which we shot in 2001 right after 9/11. It's a "bromance" sex comedy in the vein of *American Pie*, with backyard wrestling as its action hook. It wasn't my script so I was basically a hired gun. However, it's actually the best looking of any of my movies, all shot on 35mm film with Panavision cameras.

By 2002 the home video market had shifted dramatically … for the worse. All the little companies that were making straight-to-video films either went out of business or were gobbled up by larger companies, or started making movies with budgets like *The Rejuvenator*'s back in the 80s. So, for even LESS money factoring inflation! By this time I was married, and then divorced, with a 2-year-old daughter and had to make money. So I focused on my original first love, still photography, and fell into shooting architecture and interior design as a commercial photographer. All those years on sets watching D.P.s taught me how to light a room for dramatic effect. And that's what I'm doing today … eking out a living as a still photographer and teaching film and photography in community colleges.

In closing, I'll have to say I was lucky to have had the opportunities I did. I'm one of the few people from my class at NYU that ever got to direct more than one feature film. I consider *The Rejuvenator* my best movie and still enjoy watching it once in a while. I'd like to make movies again, but at this stage in life it would have to be something really fun that just falls in my lap, or a script I'm so passionate about I'd be willing to go through what you have to go through to raise the money and get it made. The advantage today is digital cinema. With a RedCam, Final Cut Pro and After Effects you can do things on a micro-budget you could never do in the days of *The Rejuvenator*. But no matter what, it always comes down to having a good script!

# Bruce Spaulding Fuller
(Special Makeup Effects)

*The Rejuvenator*, or "Brains for Beauty" as it was called during shooting, is the story of an aging Hollywood actress who is losing her career as her youth fades. She cannot bear it, so she funds illegal scientific research into youth restoration which ends up involving regular addictive injections of "brain juice" from other people. And she is willing to kill to get what she needs. Basically, it's another version of the Roger Corman classic *The Wasp Woman*. For this feature, Ed French hired Eric Schaper and myself to form a design team and handle the several stages of "Brain Monster" makeup as her condition goes horribly wrong, and a couple transformations of lab rat test subjects that presage the hideous transformations to come. Plus Gore Galore! For the kills!

The whole feature was a very special time for me as it was only my second feature film. There were a great many effects to be built and only the three of us so I got to put my hands on just about everything—even producing a drawing of a woman with a bee-hive hairdo made of brains which lead to what would become the middle, little seen stage of the creature. Ed loved the drawing and intended that stage of the transformation to be the final look; a strange, but "high fashion monster" if you will, but it proved too odd for the producers to get behind and so the huge brained, over-the-top final monster was born.

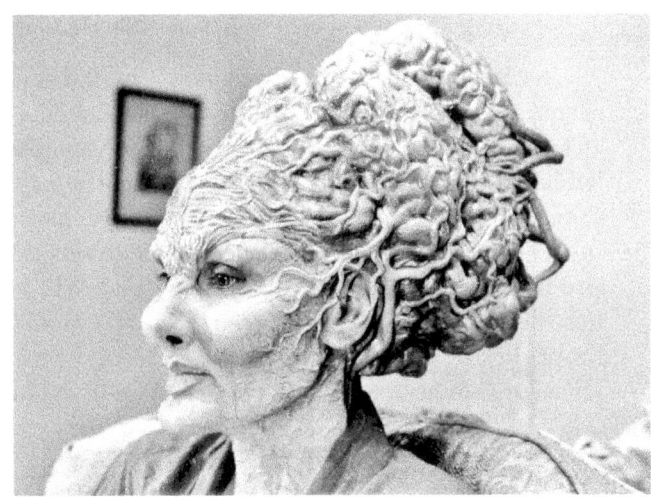

The little seen "elegant brain monster." This is what the special makeup effects team intended the final stage to be, but the producers wanted something more horrible (courtesy of Bruce Spaulding Fuller).

A funny story about this VERY low budget feature was the use of food products for gore whenever we could. There is a scene where the brain monster kills someone in a phone booth outside on the streets of New York. That night, the crew was treated to dinner at a Chinese restaurant. Many plates of food were passed around, but when I saw the plate of shrimp and lobster sauce I yelled out, "Nobody eat that!" It looked like brain curds on a plate to me, so we saved it to mix with our fake blood and blast it all over the glass of the phone booth. Another great use of food was for the final "Brain Monster" meltdown puppet. We had at least a dozen tubes running up the center of the hastily built puppet with many, many bottles of colored goo ready to be squeezed out on cue, but the crowning glory was running a giant tube up through the puppet's mouth and filling it with creamed corn that we could blast out for vomit on cue! It made for a delightful mess and looks disgusting on film!

# *School Spirit*
## (1984, U.S.A.)

*Genre:* Fantasy/Comedy; *Director:* Alan Holleb; *Writer:* Geoffrey Baere; *Cinematographer:* Robert Ebinger; *Editor:* Sonya Sones; *Visual Effects:* Motion Opticals, Inc.; *Producers:* Jeff Begun and Ken Dalton; *Executive Producers:* Roger Corman and Ashok Amritraj; *Production companies:* Chroma III Productions and Amritraj Productions; *Cast:* Tom Nolan (Billy Batson), Elizabeth Foxx (Judith Hightower), John Finnegan (Pinky Batson), Larry Linville (President Grimshaw), Roberta Collins (Helen Grimshaw), Marta Kober (Ursula Grimshaw), Frank Mugavero (Lasky), Nick Segal (Gregg), Daniele Arnaud (Madeleine), Brian Frishman (Barducci), Leslee Bremmer (Sandy) and Toni Hudson (Rita)

A playboy student is finally about to "hit the target" with his most highly anticipated conquest when he realizes he has forgotten condoms. This is not a big deal for him, but is an insurmountable problem for the girl. The student thus takes the car to go and buy them but has a serious accident and dies on the operating table. The young man is so eager to complete the job that he goes back to college as a ghost. The student only has only one day to accomplish the goal before being forced to follow his mentor (an old uncle, who was also an avid Don Juan in his day) to the beyond. While the traditional annual party is about to be held in college, the student tries to seduce his favorite girlfriend again (he can regain his physicality by simply waving his hand over his head) without neglecting the other schoolgirls (to be invisible is a net advantage in the women's shower).

## Geoffrey Baere
### (Writer)

*School Spirit* was my first screenwriting credit. I had a variety of jobs after leaving college aspiring to be a writer of some kind. I followed friends to Los Angeles in the mid-1970s and became a screenwriter. I wrote several original screenplays, a few of which were optioned and none of which was made. At some point I had an idea for a movie about a "College Ghost" who had been a legendary Casanova-like figure on a campus before his death, and who came back to the school to assist some nerd in getting laid. I pitched the story all over town and no one was interested in it. I discussed it with Alan Holleb who wanted to direct another movie and he felt it had some possibilities. We tried a few things to make it more outrageous—the school would be Harvard and the promiscuous ghost JFK—but obviously that was never going to get made. We wound up pitching it to everyone's last choice, Roger Corman, and with our expectations of becoming successful and our dreams of unlimited wealth suitably readjusted, we agreed to make the movie with them.

I think Corman released everything through his companies to make sure he got his hands on the money first. I don't know if *School Spirit* made money. It almost had to, it was made so cheaply, and I got royalties for many years so I assume it was shown or sold as a tape somewhere on Earth. We went to an opening day screening in LA and there were about 5 people in the theatre besides us. To be fair, I think some major giant Belushi or Bill Murray film opened the same day and probably drew away our other two potential customers.

Reviews weren't very good. In one review I was singled out as a philistine for writing a scene that disrespected classical music. I laughed because I specifically put the quintet in the scene to help some classical musicians make money and maybe record an original composition.

## Alan Holleb
### (Director)

I grew up in Chicago, went to college at Yale, and graduated school in film at UCLA's Film School. Roger Corman and his wife Julie had seen a short film, a musical, I had directed at UCLA, and so they contacted me about working on *Candy Stripe Nurses* [1973, Alan Holleb]. After *School Spirit*, I continued to work as a screenwriter for a number of years, and although I continue to work on screenplays, I have also been doing a number of other things, most recently dealing in fine art.

R. Michael Givens (Assistant Cameraman), Robert Ebinger (Cinematographer), Stephen Buck (Assistant Director), and Alan Holleb (Director), in the hat (courtesy of Alan Holleb).

I developed the project and worked with Geoff Baere and later with another writer on the script. In a way, the idea for *School Spirit* was inspired by a [1962] Italian film I had seen many years before (*Il sorpasso*), and though I barely remembered any details of it, the film stayed with me. Actually, when Baere and I were working on the concept for *School Spirit*, one version of the story that occurred to me (which we ultimately rejected as a bit too outré) would have set the story at Harvard University and had the Batson character be the ghost of the late president John F. Kennedy (a notorious Lothario). That might have made an interesting film.

I recall how a number of the scenes that were theoretically set at the college were actually filmed at a place called the Veterans Administration Hospital here in Los Angeles [Brentwood], a large sort of campus of collegiate-looking buildings which had been built for the army and veterans of World War II. A number of the buildings had subsequently been used for research on germ warfare (anthrax, etc.) and were so dangerous and toxic that they still hadn't cleaned them up and instead, had simply locked the doors and sealed the windows. It was those buildings that they allowed us to use the exteriors and entryways of. In the film, whenever you see people going into or out of one of those buildings, if it looks like they're worried or moving a little faster than normal, now you know why.

Roger Corman always did his own distribution back then, even if he didn't raise the money or directly produce the film. That was one of the keys to his financial success—he kept all the money!

I remember one evening when we were shooting late and I turned around and noticed a small group of Indian gentlemen standing at the back of the set, watching the filming. I was later told that part of the financing for the film came from a consortium of Indian doctors. It seemed a long way to go to invest in a low budget American film, though, of course, one of the producers was Ashok Amritraj, who has continued to be a successful producer and was also, along with his brother Vijay, part of a dynasty of great Indian tennis champions.

## Ken Solomon
### (Special Effects/Second Unit Director)

I have been in the entertainment or related field since I was 15. I started out in live theater, Broadway, then theater and television in Chicago, my home town. Then I started writing and producing industrial and business shows and films. I did that for almost twenty years. I then decided to go out to California in the 80s and work in the feature film business. Jeff Begun was a high-school friend of mine in Chicago and we did many things together as young people. We started a college humor magazine, did live radio and TV shows in Chicago, started an art-house movie theater and produced live comedy and folk music concerts. We stayed in touch throughout the years and when I decided to move permanently to Los Angeles, I went to work with Jeff and Chroma III Productions. We did low-budget T&A stuff [*Hardbodies/School Spirit*] for Roger Corman's Concorde Pictures and several other films [*Hardbodies 2/Pretty Smart*] for theatrical release, TV, video for ourselves and other production entities [Cinetel/New World Pictures]. Currently, I am still actively doing mostly animation and documentary projects. I am currently involved in the production of a very large animated series project.

*School Spirit* was a very, very low budget film and in our pre-production meetings with Roger Corman, it was made clear to the production team and producers that I had to find the "cheapest" way to do all the ghost effects. So I decided to do things the way they did in the *Topper* movies from the thirties and forties. The first one starred Cary Grant and Gilbert Roland. I did some research into those old productions and discovered that most of it was done with the "Smoke and Mirrors" technique.

In-camera double exposures, fine fishing line for moving things, directed jets of compressed air, half-surfaced mirrors in front of the camera and a whole bag of cheap tricks. But … they worked! For some of the shots I used an old Mitchell Camera because it had wonderful registration so that I could wind the film back to a selected frame and do double exposures without much frame floating (where the picture kind of wanders around). For all the in-camera ghost effects, I was actually the DP and Director due to the fact that I was the only one that knew what I was doing. I had to control lighting, camera, actors, and a very cumbersome camera setup with a 1m by 1.5m piece of plate-glass mirror on a dolly attached to the camera. It was a great challenge, but a lot of fun. The owner of Deluxe Labs, where we processed our film was so impressed with what we were doing that he called me up and took me to lunch to talk about it. He was an old-school filmmaker and just fell in love with the old-fashioned ingenuity.

The Corman involvement in any of his films required that everything be done under his banner and in his facilities and with his equipment. The unspoken deal with Roger Corman was always "You can make your film, I get the money." The "Corman School of Filmmaking" worked for a lot of now famous filmmakers. Actually, I found him to be an extremely smart, savvy and highly successful gentleman. You just did it his way. You sure did learn how to make movies! On another film that I was peripherally involved with called *Saturday the 14th* [1981] the director [Howard Cohen] in a conversation with Corman, asked to get a helicopter for a spectacular opening shot to the film. Without hesitation, Corman replied, "Forget it, get a tall ladder!" One thing Corman liked to do was show up on set the first day of shooting. He would hang around watching for a while and quietly leave. Later in the day, the production manager, producer and director would get a note to appear in his office at the end of the day. There would be a meeting where he would give everyone notes on what you did wrong and right. Everything better go right after that or you were looking for a new project. Also, Corman demanded that you start shooting on Thursday or Friday so that you had the weekend to replace any of the production crew that wasn't up to the job.

# Tom Nolan
## ("Billy Batson")

I grew up in Indiana, one of eight kids. My dad was a lawyer. I was a drummer, football player, and poet as a teen-ager. I went to Harvard College with no real plans of what I was going to do. I fell in love with the theater, and studied it both at Harvard and then at Cornell, where I received an MFA. I went to New York City to work in theater, but rapidly found it difficult to make a living. I did all kinds of blue collar jobs—moved furniture, waited tables, drove limo, laid stone, and enjoyed my early years as a gypsy actor. John Schlesinger gave me my first job in *Yankees* [1979]. After that, I came back to the U.S., did experimental theater, and then got cast in a mini-series called *Beggarman, Thief*. I fell in love and married an actress-writer-director named Peggy O'Brien, and we started a family (Peggy and I are still happily married after 32 years). I became involved with songwriting and playing music. I had a lot of down time between gigs, so music became very important to me, and is to this day. Music is probably the artistic through-line of my whole life (www.tomnolanband.com).

The audition for the part of Billy Batson was fun. I always had luck in auditions where I got to clown around, and Alan Holleb and I had immediate chemistry. He wanted me to dye my hair for the part, so I did. The whole experience was quite playful. I was basing my character on Harpo Marx, one of my heroes, so it was fun to "break the rules."

Like many American actors, I was excited to do anything starting out. *School Spirit* was a great break for me because it was the first time I got to carry a film. I love comedy, and getting to work with some really funny people was a blast. Elizabeth Foxx [Billy Batson's love interest in the film] was lovely. John Finnegan [Billy Batson's uncle, 1926–2012] was particularly kind to me, and really put me under his wing. Alan is a really bright guy, very kind, and he and I understood each other well. We were trying to make as funny a movie as possible. This was an early opportunity for him as well. I remember the shoot being very pleasant. It was fast, you had to be ready to deliver on set—kind of guerrilla movie making. It was great training.

The irony that the movie anticipated the whole safe sex movement in America, due to the AIDS epidemic, was evident a few years after the movie was released. But at the time, we were just making a sex-college romp, trying to make people laugh. It was low-budget, and unpretentious.

I went on to do several other silly movies [*Fast Times at Ridgemont High*, *Up the Creek*, *Voyage of the Rock Aliens*] and later, a kids' series called *Out of this World*, which did well. I had the good fortune to work for John Schlesinger again on *The Falcon and the Snowman* (shot in Mexico, with Sean Penn). In the mix there, I did big plays both in New York and Los Angeles, and worked on *Pretty Woman* and *Tequila Sunrise*.

I had a very good time being an actor. I loved the work, I just hated auditioning. And I was very interested in family life, and being a good and present father. So I began to look for ways to create domestic stability. In between jobs, I started teaching young kids, and I became interested in education. One thing led to another, and 29 years later, I am still teaching, helping to run a great school called Crossroads in Santa Monica, and often working with very talented young artists as a mentor. I am the assistant director of the upper school, so I still have "school spirit." As acting waned in my life, music became more and more important. I started recording and running bands, and now I have a 9 piece soul and blues band that plays all over southern California. Some of the people in the band have been with me for 22 years! We like to play dance music, and I have become a great harmonica player, an instrument I started playing as a kid. My wife teaches theater, my daughter has been an actor and teacher, my son is a gifted musician who runs a band called Caught a Ghost (another irony). So we are a family of artists and educators.

When I look back at *School Spirit*, I am happy to have been involved in something so silly. Humor and music are the best medicines, and sex is always funny, if you ask me. It was not a sophisticated movie, but it was fun to do. I grew up watching B movies, and it was fun to do a few of them. I fantasize about doing some more acting in my retirement years, so we'll see. I love to make people laugh, and I think I'm funnier than I used to be. I did some good dramatic work, but comedy is really my favorite. It is also the most difficult thing to do.

    I have been very fortunate, and I have led a surprising life for a kid from Indiana, whose family had no show business connections. I dreamed big, and some of them came true. I am grateful for the opportunities that have come my way, and I am particularly glad that I met Peggy O'Brien. I try to model creativity, joy, and humor for my students, and I am fortunate to have found a life that blends education and art. Life is sweet.

# *Shadowzone*
## (1989, U.S.A.)

*Genre:* Horror; *Director:* J.S. Cardone; *Writer:* J.S. Cardone; *Cinematographer:* Karen Grossman; *Editor:* Thomas Meshelski; *Special Makeup and Creature Effects:* Mark Shostrom; *Visual Effects:* Perpetual Motion Pictures; *Producer:* Carol Kottenbrook; *Executive Producer:* Charles Band; *Production Company:* Full Moon Pictures; *Cast:* David Beecroft (Capt. Hickock), James Hong (Dr. Van Fleet), Louise Fletcher (Dr. Erhart), Shawn Weatherly (Dr. Kidwell), Miguel A. Nunez Jr. (Wiley), Frederick Flynn (Tommy Shivers), Lu Leonard (Mrs. Cutter), Maureen Flaherty (Jenna) and Robbie Rives (James)

In a secret lab, a team of scientists study the oneiric dimension, carrying out sleep experiments. Something goes wrong and a monstrous creature, coming from a parallel dimension, passes the threshold of the dream and appears in real life. The team of experts, a NASA agent sent to investigate the death of one of the volunteer test subjects in the project, and the personnel of the lab face a living being, capable of taking the shape of the most morbid fears of each individual.

## J.S. Cardone
## (Writer/Director)

Charles Band had seen my MGM/Cannon film *Thunder Alley* [1985, J.S. Cardone] and liked it. He then looked at *The Slayer* [1982, J.S. Cardone] and decided we should meet. It was during the transition days from Empire Pictures to Full Moon Pictures [1987/1988]. We talked about different projects and then there was a period of time when we went our separate ways. I liked Charlie. And even though we have had a rocky relationship over the years I always thought he was a very smart film maker. Finally, he came to me to re-write the original *Puppet Master* [1988, David Schmoeller]. I did, and they used it as the final shooting script but I wanted to remain "uncredited." That is how we started out the relationship. He had just made the deal with Paramount for distribution. It was at that time that Stuart Gordon and myself started working on projects for Full Moon.

It was during a time when Paramount wanted a pipeline of product for its video arm and Full Moon was the supplier. Charlie would come up with a title and one sheet, with a vague concept, and then pitch it to Paramount. If they liked it they advanced financing and Stuart and I picked the projects that we liked.

*Shadowzone* was an original idea I had for a sci-fi script that was originally titled "31F." When I saw the art work for *Shadowzone* I felt "31F" would fit the story structure. It was a wholly original idea that I brought to the process. The inspiration for *Shadowzone* was more than likely fueled by my obsession with the great fantasy horror writer H.P. Lovecraft. His stories of dreamscapes and creatures who dwell in the dream world has always fascinated me. It was no single piece but a combination of things from Lovecraft that inspired me.

*Shadowzone* was completely shot on location in an old abandoned hospital that we found in the North Valley of Los Angeles. It was very creepy because there were many rooms that were left as if abandoned during a disaster. There were machines and old medical equipment everywhere. Rainwater had destroyed many walls and ceilings and there were bizarre looking things everywhere that were covered in mold and slime. It was perfect for what we wanted.

*Shadowzone* was the first film my wife and partner Carol Kottenbrook had produced for me. She'd done others on her own but this one was the beginning of a long and prosperous partnership. She was and is a great producer. It was also the first time I worked with my brother Michael as the camera operator. He went on to become my Director of Photography on three more films after that.

The budget was 1 million. Because of my reputation our deals were structured by Paramount. The only way we'd work with Full Moon was to do it on our terms. Over the years I have heard horror stories about other companies deals but ours were always structured on our terms. We had total control of the production. In fact it was because of problems with control over production concepts with *Crash and Burn* [1990, Charles Band] that we backed away from producing. We were originally set to produce and direct. Financing came from pre-sales that Paramount made. It was an ongoing pipeline deal that Full Moon had to fulfill.

On set of *Shadowzone*: J.S. Cardone (Writer/Director), Louise Fletcher ("Dr. Erhardt") and Carol Kottenbrook (Producer) (courtesy of J.S. Cardone).

It was a great pleasure working with James Hong and Louise Fletcher. I had written James' character as an Anglo character originally but when his agents submitted him I immediately jumped at the idea. I had wanted to work with him for a long time. Louise Fletcher was incredible. Again, she was someone I had wanted to work with and her agents liked the script a lot and wanted to submit it to her. We held our breath and got lucky when she agreed to do it. David Beecroft brought a hard working professional approach to everything he attempted. I had a lot of choices to cast for that role and I was very pleased with David's talent and dedication. Shawn Weatherly was very new to the business and although she wasn't a seasoned performer the freshness she brought to her work was something that complemented the older, more experienced actors in the cast. In many ways Shawn mirrored Louise and some of the scenes I like the best are between them because of the subtle differences between them. Fred Flynn is not only a great friend but one of the most underrated actors I ever worked with. He always brought an unique personality to the roles I cast him in. He was fearless in his portrayals and would never limit his approach to the psychology and physicality of the character I wrote. He was a classic character actor in every sense of the word, who could always be counted on to deliver a great, dark, complex performance. A talent, especially effective in both the horror and thriller genres.

The shoot was one of the easiest I've ever had. Mark Shostrom did an awesome job on the physical effects at the time. And even though we had a tight schedule everything went quite smoothly.

Karen Grossman was one of my favorite cinematographers to work with. She was the DP on *The Slayer*. Back then it was very hard for women in the industry to reach the position of Director of Photography and her talent and dedication proved she belonged in the position. We did three films together [*The Slayer/Thunder Alley/Shadowzone*] and all three I consider some of the finest visual work done on any of my films.

[As for the "R" rating of the film], we had originally shot full frontal nudity on both the female and male lab subjects in the pods [Jenna and James, played by Maureen Flaherty and Robbie Rives]. But to release theatrically, which Full Moon did for a short run, we had to cut the male nudity for an "R" rating. Only in America!!! God forbid we see a penis!!!

Some years later Paramount came to me to write a big theatrical release of *Puppet Master*. I really liked the script that I did for it and so did they. But once again there was a sad falling out between Charlie and me and the project never saw the light of day. Looking back on it all there were obviously the good and bad times but for the most part I really remember it to be a very productive and satisfying time for me. We don't make films like that anymore. I mean the process, and I miss that. As the years passed the business grew more complex. I love what we eventually did with other horror/thriller genre like *The Forsaken, The Covenant, Prom Night, Wicked Little Things* and *The Stepfather*. But the "old simple" days were in many ways a lot more fun.

Charlie Band was one of the geniuses of the "B" movie world. I'd put him up there with Roger Corman. Without these guys there would be far less talented directors and writers around today. They both created an atmosphere for young talent to grow in that allowed for many successful films, not only in the 80s, but that are even being made today. Many directors and writers still working owe their success and talent to B movie moguls like Charles Band.

# Mark Shostrom
## (Special Makeup and Creature Effects)

I got the job on *Shadowzone* via my friend Michael Cardone. Michael had been 1st assistant camera on a show I directed (*Monsters*, for Laurel Television), and he mentioned one day that he did video editing. A few months later, I hired Michael to help me edit my first effects reel at his home in Pasadena. He mentioned that his brother Joe was going to be directing a horror film and that I should meet him. Joe showed up one day while we were working and we got along well. A few months (or weeks) later, I started work on the *Shadowzone* effects.

My team comprised Greg Smith and Bruce Spaulding Fuller as sculptors, Eryn Kreuger (now Eryn Kreuger-Mekash) as lead mold maker; I also had on board my brother John Shostrom as co-ordinator, Dave Stinnett for mechanics and Mark Sisson doing lab tech work.

I liked Joe and I liked his script (he's a great writer), so I was glad to take on the project. And of course there were many effects to create. I was most interested to create the autopsy body of the security guard—even more so than the creature. Other effects included a rat head, a mutated monkey, and an hallucinatory circus freak, "Madam Pip" [the various transformations of the creature] and the various vein pulsing and head exploding effects for the characters of the lab subjects James and Jenna.

When I met with Joe to ask about the look of the creature [it calls itself "John Doe"], he said two words: "Bad thoughts." It was a specific answer while at the same time not specific. Then Joe looked at me and said, "I trust you, just run with it," or words to that effect.

Ironically, the creature is the one effect in the film I was never happy with. Time was fairly tight, and I tried some ideas which didn't really come together. But the clock was ticking, so I had to move forward with my first approach. I

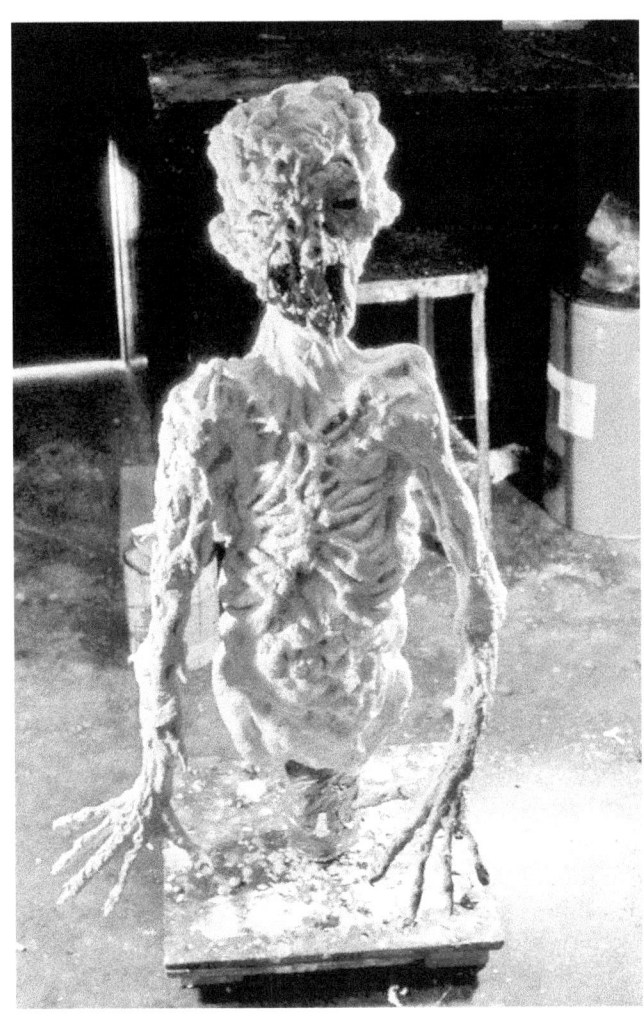

**The creature in *Shadowzone* (courtesy of Mark Shostrom).**

sculpted the head while Greg Smith sculpted the body. The body was misshapen, burned and twisted. I got the idea to make skin texture for the head similar to texture on Christopher Tucker's great *The Elephant Man* makeup, which I'd seen while visiting him in the UK. I decided to save time on the detailed sculpture work (very time demanding) and instead molded cauliflower. Into that mold, I poured melted clay and pressed the cooled clay pieces onto my head sculpture—instant cauliflower skin texture. I made the teeth by mixing clear dental acrylic and twisting the material in my fingers as it set and hardened. We made the creature puppet from the waist up. The only thing I really liked about the creature was the mechanics (animatronics) which Dave Stinnett created by himself. They were fantastic. Not only did the eyes move around, but his hands were nimble enough to almost pick up objects. One caveat Joe wanted was that the creature have human eyes. While I understood and agreed with his decision for this, in the end I don't think it worked with the totally weird looking face.

"Madam Pip" was another case where Joe gave me free reign. I decided to do an old lady combined with a real circus freak named Bob Melvin. To save time and not wait for casting, Joe and Carol agreed to hire my brother John for the brief role. I was able to make a mold of John's teeth and head at my studio and immediately begin work. It was a pretty ambitious makeup for a low budget film, but I decided to go for it. I had just finished 10 weeks of sculpting on *Dick Tracy*, so felt I could blast through any project with confidence. Madam Pip was about 12 different overlapping foam latex pieces. I sculpted an incredible amount of detail in and prepainted a lot of it. Eryn Kreuger molded the sculptures. All this took many weeks. Filming Madam Pip took perhaps half an hour and she is on-screen for a few seconds. Such is the nature of special makeup effects.

Bruce Spaulding Fuller handled most of the sculpting on the huge rat head and the monkey. Mark Sisson helped with molding everything and pouring the items in plastic and rubber.

Meanwhile, Greg Smith was doing a lot of the painstaking work on the James and Jenna heads, the lab subjects. I showed Greg how to make the veins from the inside out, using a method I'd learned from Dick Smith, which he'd used on *Scanners*. Those James/Jenna heads took a long time—and because the veins were tricky, we had to make several to get one of each that worked perfectly. Incidentally, the same Jenna vein-head ended up in another film I did, *Love Is a Gun* [1994, David Hartwell]. I needed to make a cleaved-in-half head quickly for a crime scene photo Eric Roberts sees in the beginning of that picture. We used an early version of something like Photoshop to meld the Jenna head onto a naked model's body. A little movie trivia for the fans. I was the lucky guy who got to do the photography. The tough life of a special makeup effects artist.

As I said, I was keen to make a full body replica of the security guard, played by Jack Leal. Joe said he was fine with me making just a chest appliance, but I wanted to create the entire body. This cost a bit extra in our budget, which I had to go over with Carol, and I think I ended up eating some of the cost myself since I was so dead set on creating an entire figure.

My whole staff was needed to mold Jack's entire body in sections, a process which would take all day. Since Jack could only make it on a Saturday, it cost me a little extra to bring my entire crew of people in. Saturday morning at 9:00 a.m. Jack arrived. His face was swollen huge and it was obvious he was in incredible pain. He had a major dental abscess, but said he could go through with the head and body molding. I'd had a dental abscess and I knew he could not. I phoned my dentist who worked nearby and she agreed to see Jack. Against Jack's wishes, I sent him off to see her. He came back the next week and we began the molding.

I had seen photos of the autopsy bodies Carl Fullerton made for *Gorky Park*, and Carl told me he did them in one single mold, the entire body at once, except for the heads. I decided to make life a little easier on everyone and mold Jack in sections: head, two arms, two legs, and torso. I would combine the plaster Jack sections later and re-mold that, then pour the body from the final mold.

Before molding any of Jack, I marked his body where the sections would overlap with a straight blue water color pencil line. The pencil mark would dry, but would re-activate when touched by water. I used alginate (PGC, or Prosthetic Grade Cream alginate) to mold Jack, and White Hydrocal plaster to pour the pieces. Since both materials were water-based, each of them reactivated the blue pencil mark, which transferred to the next material. The final plaster pieces were sanded smooth on the straight blue line and glued together. A little jeweler's wax was used to fill the gaps—and voilà, we had a one piece plaster body of Jack to re-mold. One awkward moment occurred when it came time to mold around Jack's genitals for the torso part. I cut a sheet of latex dental dam to fit over his private parts and got on my knees in front of him with my glue brush. The second Jack dropped the towel I had to look away. I mumbled, "Maybe you'd better do this," and gave the glue brush to Jack. Greg Smith sculpted him a brand new penis—and a brain as well. Everything else on the final Skinflex body was Jack.

The day of filming, the animal trainer came to see me as we were unloading the plastic Jack body from my truck. He would have his trained Capuchin monkey in the scene and said we needed to let the monkey "get used to it" first. He advised that we put the body in place, cover it completely with black plastic bags and then we'd bring in the monkey. We brought the monkey in, and little by little, we eased back the plastic as he crawled over the plastic Jack exploring. Then the animal trainer asked us to dress the body with the fake blood, slowly, bit by bit. He said primates know what wounds and blood are, and that the sudden sight of Jack with his guts exposed and covered in blood—would make him panic. We did this very slowly, and by then end of an hour, the Capuchin was crawling all over the bloody Jack like he was an old friend.

P.S.—I love working with Joe. We later did *Shadowhunter* [1992] together and are still friends today. He's the most easy-going, intelligent guy. I wish every director was like him.

## Richard Malzahn
### (Visual Effects)

*Shadowzone* was an ambitious film on a small budget. Joe Cardone and I talked about the effects quite a bit in order to get the most compelling visual without spending a lot of money. The two main effects in the film were in the finale when the woman doctor [Louise Fletcher] gets pulled into the other dimension. The look for this dimensional portal was very important to Joe, for good reason. Distilled down, the portal consisted of a split screen with a light effect over it along with lots of hand animated electricity that interacted with the actors. The split allowed us to make the actor disappear and the electricity could grab them and pull on them, compelling them to enter the portal. The light effect over the split gave a presence to the portal that is nearly overwhelming and becomes the center of attention which is sort of the point. The electrical animation gives the portal life and the ability to actually interact and examine the world which it has invaded. The portal actually becomes a character in the story.

Working on a small budget is always challenging, but not necessarily in a bad way. Joe is great because he understands that there is a limited amount you can do with small budgets. We have gotten used to huge visual effects budgets recently, but that was not always the case. The interesting thing here is that Joe was willing to keep it simple and in effect he strengthened the overall film by not over thinking this sequence. It would have been easy to be over ambitious and create something really bad and then blame it on bad visual effects. But keeping it simple allowed the sequence to work well and not get too silly or campy by trying to achieve more than they could afford. Often the best films come from the innovation and creativity that bubbles to the surface when money is tight. Conversely, we've seen over and over the bad films that result from unlimited budgets.

*Shadowzone* was all produced optically; in other words there were no digital effects in it. All the effects were done by hand on an animation down-shooter and on an optical printer. Working that way is very different to how things are done now. Concepts were very much thought out because the time between starting the work and seeing results was much greater. And many people had to be involved from a concept artist to an animator and finally the optical camera operator. So keeping the idea intact was a much more collaborative process than it is today. And, as always, working with Joe and Carol was/is always a pleasure. The relationships are what make the filmmaking experience so great.

# *Slave Girls from Beyond Infinity*
## (1987, U.S.A.)

*Genre:* Fantasy; *Directors:* Ken Dixon and Don Daniel (uncredited); *Writer:* Ken Dixon; *Literary source:* "The Most Dangerous Game" (Short Story) by Richard Connell, 1924; *Cinematographers:* Kenneth Wiatrak and Thomas Callaway; *Editors:* Bruce Stubblefield and James A. Stewart; *"Androids" and "Phantazoid Warrior" designed and created by:* John Carl Buechler; *"Zombie" and "Mutant" designed and created by:* Joe Reader; *Special Makeup Effects:* David Cohen; *Models:* Wizard Works; *Visual Effects:* Motion Opticals, Inc.; *Producers:* Ken Dixon and Don Daniel; *Co-Producers:* Mark Wolf and John Eng; *Executive Producer:* Charles Band; *Production Company:* Titan Productions; *Cast:* Elizabeth Kaitan (Daria), Cindy Beal (Tisa), Don Scribner (Zed), Brinke Stevens (Shala), Carl Horner (Rik), Kirk Graves (Vak), Harry Narunsky as "Randolph Roehbling" (Krel), Jeffery Blanchard (Phantazoid Warrior #1), Bud Graves (Phantazoid Warrior #2), Jacques Schardo (Zombie) and Fred Tate (Mutant)

*Slave Girls from Beyond Infinity* is an adaptation of Richard Connell's classic story "The Most Dangerous Game." Two young female convicts escape from a space prison on board a lifeboat shuttle and land on a small unknown planet. The owner of a castle in the middle of a jungle welcomes and provides shelter to the two girls with apparent generosity. Two robots are to serve humanity and defend the castle from the monstrous non-human creatures that roam nearby. The manor house already hosts another couple (brother and sister), survivors of another crash-landing. The four youngsters become involved in the sadistic pastime of the owner of the castle—a cruel game where the stakes are high, their own lives. In 1973 Ken Dixon directed the short movie *Shadow House* for the American Film Institute. This short film, with John Carradine and John Fiedler, won an award. The debut of Ken Dixon as director occurred in 1975 with *The Erotic Adventures of Robinson Crusoe*, a sexy parody of Daniel Defoe's novel, shot in Italy and produced by the legendary Dick Randall (1926–1996) and Sheldon Silverstein. The California producer Sheldon Silverstein entrusted Ken Dixon as director of *The Erotic Adventures of Robinson Crusoe* advised by Larry Woolner (1912–1985) who intended to finance the movie. At the time Ken Dixon worked in L.A. for Larry Woolner's Dimension Pictures. Unfortunately, Ken Dixon was unable to shoot the film in 16 days and was fired. The experienced Italian director Guido Zurli (1929–2009) finished the movie. Between 1980 and 1986, Ken Dixon made four trailer compilations (*The Best of Sex & Violence*, *Famous T&A*, *Filmgore* and *Zombiethon*) for Charles Band's Empire Pictures. *Slave Girls from Beyond Infinity* was Ken Dixon's second and last movie and, like *The Erotic Adventures of Robinson Crusoe*, it was finished by another director (Don Daniel).

## Mark Wolf
## (Co-Producer/2nd Unit Director/Special Effects Supervisor)

I met Ken Dixon through an associate, Paul Davids, who had attended the American Film Institute with Ken. I had a facility for prop-making and special visual effects, Wizard Works, which was based at Roger Corman's Quicksilver Studios. Ken met with me at my Sherman Oaks apartment and we hit it off; he asked me to participate in a futuristic version of "The Most Dangerous Game," which excited me as I am a huge fan of the Cooper-Schoedsack version of the story (made on the same stages *King Kong* was using). I was the answer to Ken's prayers because I could deliver stage space, props, and visual effects.

Asked what the budget was and I was a bit shocked when he told me only $120,000. I told him if we worked together we could make it look like it cost a lot more than that, which certainly appealed to him. Not long after, I introduced him to Jon Eng.

*Slave Girls from Beyond Infinity* was one more thing coming through my shop—from *The Nest* to *976-EVIL* to *Captain EO*. As co-producer, I came on board to help facilitate the stage rental, lighting/grip packages and supervise props and visual effects, all on the understanding I had a limited amount of time to commit to "Slave Girls" because of obligations to upcoming projects.

My company, Wizard Works, was a full-service boutique handling makeup effects,

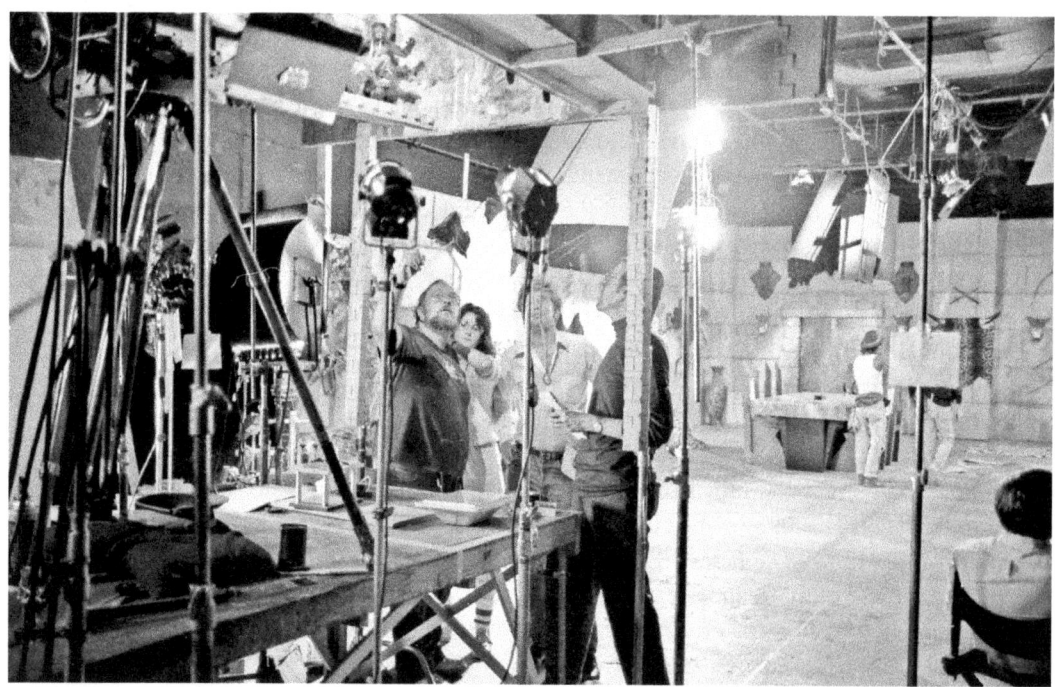

Mark Wolf (Co-Producer/2nd Unit Director/Special Effects Supervisor), a woman who maybe was helping with set-dressing, Ken Dixon (Writer/Director/Producer) and Harry Narunsky ("Krel"/Model-Building Crew). Mark Wolf is explaining the Great Hall miniature to Ken Dixon. Harry Narunsky is taking notes for an article on the making of the film (courtesy of Mark Wolf).

stop-motion, foreground miniatures, motion control, etc., for a lot of clients, from Francis Ford Coppola to William Friedkin and many others. My shop also provided special props as needed—ray guns, lightweight plastic chains for the girls in their captivity, etc. Because of Wizard Works' relationship with Quicksilver Studios, it was decided to shoot "Slave Girls" there—600 S. Main Street, Venice, CA.

Charlie Band owed Ken "X" amount of money but declined to pay him in cash; instead, typical of Band, he essentially blackmailed Ken into making the movie for him. Knowing Band's reputation fully, I recall thinking that I hoped Ken took a chunk off the top of the budget for pain and suffering.

The picture was seriously under-financed, so I invested about $30,000 to support the film with rolls of 35mm FUJI raw stock, a wealth of supplies (everything from wood screws to chicken wire & plaster), as well as making available props and existing miniature elements that I normally rented to other productions. At that time I regarded "Slave Girls" as an investment in my career.

I called Charlie Band's office repeatedly the first week to explain that the production was already in trouble. John Buechler showed up on Charlie's behalf and I told him that while I personally liked Ken, even with "The Most Dangerous Game" as a literal blueprint, Ken was struggling to hit his stride and we were falling behind schedule.

**Elizabeth Kaitan ("Daria") entering the great hall of the castle. This is the visual effect shot by Mark Wolf that the *Variety* reviewer thought was a real set (courtesy of Mark Wolf).**

In those pre–CGI days, doing visual effects in-camera on original camera negative was the best way to ensure the highest quality possible. Therefore, I made the decision early on to use an old technique referred to as hanging miniatures or foreground miniatures. For instance, the Great Hall miniature [the entrance hall of the castle of Zed where he keeps his hunting trophies exposed] was arranged near the camera in such a way as to blend with a set further away from the camera, where the actors were performing; the end result was that the miniatures and live action looked like a single location. The *Variety* review of "Slave Girls" praises the vast interior set—testimony to how successful the in-camera effects shot was.

The escape lifeboat [used by Daria and Tisa to escape from the prison in space] was a miniature built by Carl Horner and his associate, Terry M. Huud; Carl appears in the film. I filmed it in flight as a Lydecker shot—named after the two brothers, Howard and Theodore, who did marvelous high-speed miniatures for Republic Studios (on films like *The Flying Tigers*). The escape ship taking off at the end [used by the two girls to escape from the castle of Zed and from his planet] was another Lydecker shot staged as a full miniature, sliding the ship down wires into Zed's castle and running that in reverse.

Don Daniel came on board after I had to leave due to prior commitments, and he shepherded a week or ten days of pick-ups, I believe. As I recall, the log bridge [the tree bridge in the middle of the jungle we see in the scene where Zed, armed with a crossbow, is busy hunting his "prey"] was among the last things we shot, so it would make sense that Don did jungle shooting to take advantage of what resources were on hand. I recall being awakened in the wee hours one morning by a panicked call wondering if I had a prop they needed…

Charles Band never visited the set, to my knowledge. He did a brilliant thing with the double-bill release: it gave the films U.S. theatrical "legitimacy" which he then used as marketing leverage to sell the films overseas at MIFED. Others tried to duplicate his success and failed miserably.

"Slave Girls" was a smash success; I've been told it financed the bulk of the films that followed. The film has been released on VHS, Laserdisc and DVD, and has played cable releases here in the U.S.; it's the little movie that keeps on earning. For years afterwards, I met dozens of companies, producers and distributors who wanted me to re-make a version of "Slave Girls" for them—but they wanted to do it cheap, which was no inducement for me to get involved.

# John Eng
## (Co-Producer/Visual Effects Supervisor)

I grew up in New York and had watched a lot of TV at an early age. Science fiction and fantasy movies were my favorite. But as a young boy it wasn't until a high school friend showed me an 8 MM movie camera that I actually thought we could make movies. Practically the next day, we were on the rooftops of New York making Kung-Fu movies made popular at the time by our hero Bruce Lee. I went to the School of Visual Arts where I majored in Illustration (I drew since I was 10 years old) and minor in Film. While still in school, I was hired to produce storyboards for a commercial production company called Image Factory. They liked me so much that I was hired full time and we produced many TV commercials, network ID,

TV show openings, etc. This would later be called Motion Graphics. It was a combination of graphic design, animation, special effects, opticals and filmmaking. The opportunity for longer form, narrative filmmaking was limited in New York so I relocated to Los Angeles in 1981 where I opened my own animation company called Icon R&D Inc. We produced many TV commercials and worked in 35 MM as well as 65 MM Showscan and IMAX.

After 3 years I sold my half interest in the company and heard that Ken Dixon was looking for a special effects company (or supervisor) to produce the effects for his low budget feature called *Slave Girls from Beyond Infinity*, an updated space version of "The Most Dangerous Game." I met him, we talked for a whole day where we discovered that we had a lot in common. We grew up loving the same movies and knew that we could make a quality feature film on a limited budget. Ken had convinced Charlie Band that he was able to both direct and produce this film. However, in reality his experience as a producer was limited and he knew he needed help. I had produced many projects through my company and knew how to handle complex budgets and schedules. In addition, I knew many people who would work for little or no money as favor to me. I convinced Ken that not only would I be an asset as a producer, but I could art direct and produce the special effects as well.

The money for the movie came from Empire Pictures. But aside from approving the script, Charlie Band had very little involvement during production. At least for the first 3 weeks of principal photography. I didn't have any interaction with him aside from meeting him once in a hallway.

The original schedule was: 3 weeks of principal photography and 1 week of pick ups. This was unrealistic mainly because the director of photography, Ken Wiatrak (who was extremely likeable and full of enthusiasm), turned out to be difficult on the set and unable to produce more than 4 set ups a day. We needed 30–40 set ups a day. It was like Murphy's Law, once we started to shoot, everything went wrong. It took Wiatrak 4 hours to place ONE light for our first set up (the "slave cell" where Liz Kaitan was trying to break free), then Dixon refused to show up because he was too busy in the dressing room "studying" the costumes of the actresses.

Then while waiting for Dixon to show up, the ceiling of the stage caught fire. Lucky for us, the stage manager was able to put it out within minutes. This was a former lumber yard turned low budget movie studio owned by Roger Corman. 95% of the film was shot on stage. This shooting stage was about 45 × 100 ft. We also shot in a warehouse in North Hollywood. The other 5% of the film was shot on locations like Leo Carrillo State Beach by a second unit [Daria on the beach following the crash-landing; Tisa who takes a swim under the surveillance of Zed's two robots]. The cameras and film stock were supplied by people that was connected to the porn industry and we even had porn stars auditioning for what they saw as legit roles. For the time, it was the best and worse experience of my life.

During the shoot, I was heading the art department where I was building the next set while they were shooting the prior set. We had to stop work and freeze in place when we heard "action" then started again after we heard "cut." I also supervised the various foreground miniature shots (the main hall with the animal trophies) and glass painting shots (where Zed and the girls go over the log bridge).

The exterior spaceship shots were done later after principal photography. Mark Wolf is a stop motion animator with a huge collection of puppets and props. In contributing his collection and his expertise (he talks a lot), he was made co-producer.

Elizabeth Kaitan was a serious actress and extremely nice throughout. She was Hungarian and asked if it would be okay for some family/friends to attend the shoot. It was approved but the sight of our three main girls in skimpy slave girls attire running around while a group of elderly men and women in their 70s and 80s watched, was an odd juxtaposition.

Four weeks of slow torture and disasters somehow evaporated and shooting finally stopped. They edited what they could while I oversaw the special visual effects unit, shooting outer space shots on a motion control animation system that I helped build for my former company Icon. A few weeks later, we discovered that only about ⅓ of the film was in the can but that the entire budget was now gone. Charlie Band was not happy but he agreed to put a little more money into the production in order to finish. There was one big change however, he put Don Daniel in charge since he no longer trusted Ken. Who would blame him, Ken had fucked up royally. Ken was still the director on the set but the budget and schedule was out of his hands.

In the so-called 1 week of "pick ups," we shot in a smaller warehouse in North Hollywood. The new director of photography was Tom Callaway, different than Ken Wiatrak in almost every way. He was cooperative, easy to work with and most importantly, FAST. He shot an average of 35 set ups a day. Don made sure things got done and we had usable footage every day. During the shot, I was art directing and because the budget was so low, we actually RENTED plants in pots to create the jungle we didn't get around to shooting the first time around. We got the most mileage from a pick-up truck full of ivy we had "borrowed" from the side of a liquor store one night when we went out for some midnight gardening (the shoot was during the night in order to keep a low profile). Over ½ of the film was shot in this one week period.

"Slave Girls" was released theatrically for one week and played in limited theaters (so it could get better video dollars later). It double billed with *Creepozoids* [1987, David DeCoteau] which was also shot by Tom Callaway, a film made for even less money than "Slave Girls."

I've moved on to other things. Mainly animation and most recently I directed episodes of *Dragon Riders of Berk* [2012], the TV series based on the DreamWorks movie *How to Train Your Dragon*. It has 10 nominations for Annie Awards (Astroluxe.org).

## Don Daniel
### (Producer/Director)

I came to *Slave Girls from Beyond Infinity* rather late in the game. The film had been in production for three weeks and was almost that much behind schedule when production had been halted. I had been brought in to take over a number of troubled productions in the past and was asked to take over "Slave Girls." As the film was already in profit from presales, Charlie Band wanted the film finished as quickly as possible. I worked with the editor, Bruce Stubblefield and we determined what was needed to finish the story.

Charlie has a small warehouse in the San Fernando Valley that I took and turned into a jungle with rented plants. There were a number of real problems with this location: it was not air conditioned and it was in the flight pattern of Van Nuys airport. Fortunately, both of these obstacles were overcome with the same solution: we shot at night after the airport closed and it had cooled off a bit.

Mark Wolf (Co-Producer/2nd Unit Director/Special Effects Supervisor) directing 2nd unit with one of the "Phantazoid Warriors" (played by Jeffery Blanchard and Bud Graves) (courtesy of Mark Wolf).

I replaced most of the crew and brought in folks that I knew could do the job. Tom Callaway had done work for Charlie [*Creepozoids*] and he was my choice for Director of Photography. He and his team were instrumental in getting the job done.

I hate to say it but Ken Dixon was the weak link in the chain and I ended up directing most of the rest of the production. I think it is safe to say that for the most part, I directed the jungle sequences in the film. Ken had a vision as to what he wanted but it consumed him to the detriment of the process. As best as I can tell, that is what slowed down the original part of the production.

I am thankful that I was able to work with the actors. Under trying conditions, they were able to give very believable performances. The experience was very challenging and invigorating. I got very little sleep due to our shooting schedule. I regret not working more with Charlie to direct more films for Empire Pictures.

## Thomas Callaway
### (Cinematographer #2)

The director Ken Dixon was an interesting director. One of the lead actresses complained that Ken was trimming the chamois outfits each night making them smaller and smaller. Ken was fun to work with but seemed to be more interested in female leads than actually finishing the film. I remember working incredibly long days (several 17+ hours). Ken just wanted to keep shooting and shooting. If it were up to him we would still be shooting.

## Bruce Stubblefield
### (Editor #1)

*Slave Girls from Beyond Infinity* was an amazingly bad film, and therefore very painful to work on. Of all the bad movies I worked on in the 1980s "Slave Girls" has probably been the most enduring. Certainly the most notorious, mostly I'm sure because of the title.

I remember Ken Dixon as a nice and sincere fellow. He was very passionate about the film, but wasn't experienced and turned in a lot of footage that was quite talky, and frankly silly. There were long scenes of exposition around some table in the mansion where the girls found themselves, etc. It was quite painful to just watch the dailies long enough to cut the scenes. After cutting out the footage that was just too awful or too boring to use, the film was quite short, probably around an hour. The producers decided that they needed to shoot more scenes, so Don Daniel was brought in to produce the new material. He literally "saved" that film.

I don't remember why I left the film, I might have been fired for having a bad attitude, or I might have been laid off due to the hiatus between the original and the second production periods. Jim Stewart came on after I left the film, to finish it. I remember talking with him at some point and hearing from him that the producers finally let him cut out all the rest of the boring exposition that he inherited from me.

## James A. Stewart
### (Editor #2)

I was brought in near the end of editing for a week. I tried to make the action a little more exciting. I remember mostly picking up the pace here and there because there had been a little too much lingering on the girls.

## Joe Reader
### ("Zombie" and "Mutant" Designer)

I was a child of the 50s and 60s, grew up in Los Angeles, and like everyone else loved the old Universal monster movies and pretty much liked anything that had a devil, demon zombie, etc., in it. I loved the old *Famous Monsters of Filmland* magazine and devoured every issue I could get my hands on. My brother and cousins and I did the 8MM movie thing and made our own monsterfests. Lots of fun, but never thought of doing anything professionally with it.

Then in 1977, *Star Wars* came out and I was fascinated by all the cool aliens. I started to pick up magazines of the time and found out that people my age were making these things. So, I thought, "Hey, I'd like to try my hand at this." So I called up Don Post Studios in Glendale, CA, a company that manufactured Halloween masks, and asked if someone there could show me how to make masks. Academy Award winner Bob Short was a department head there at the time, and he said sure, come on down. So I immediately went there and met Bob. He gave me the "$.05/nickel tour" for about 15 minutes, and I came away with an "I can do this" feeling. So I went out, bought supplies, and started making my first masks. By the late 1970s I had my own little company and was selling my creations to local merchants and, through ads in *Starlog* and *Fangoria* magazines, collectors. It was on a return trip to Don Post that I ran into an old friend from high school, who it turns out was working there. He introduced me to now make-up artist Rick Stratton, who was just branching out into movies and TV. I eventually worked with him and Steve Neill on some films and TV series: low budget (*Saturday the 14th*, *The Stuff*) and better budget (*The New Twilight Zone*, *Fright Night*). That was how I entered show business. But all along I still had my mask company, House of Horror Studios, paying the bills.

I don't recall how my credit on *Zombiethon* [1986, Ken Dixon] came about. I think it may have been that I knew some of the people that were zombie extras for the film. They were mask collectors that I had become friends with. I know that they let Ken Dixon use some their pieces and I think some of my stuff was in the mix. I think Ken thought it would be a nice gesture to give me a credit. I was never on set for Ken's stuff—I actually met him later when he was starting *Slave Girls from Beyond Infinity*. Ken called me at my shop, introduced himself to me, and asked if he could come over and see what I might have available for the movie. I remember him being a very nice, quiet man who was trying hard to make a mark as a director. Charlie Band had finally tossed him a bone and "Slave Girls" was it. There was of course no budget, and Ken was trying to make every penny count. I showed him some things I had and told him I could paint them any way he wanted. He purchased a few pieces and used them in the movie. I didn't hear from him again until he called inviting my wife and myself to a cast and crew screening of the finished film. It was held at the home of a friend of his who had transformed the living room of his old house into a movie theater. In fact, it's the same movie theater used in some shots/photos for Zombiethon. I don't think I ever heard from Ken after that.

I'm still in the film business. It's changed quite a bit and I'm now working with companies that do more specialty costumes than make-up effects. In recent years I've worked on several features (*Watchmen*, *The Last Airbender*, *Tron: Legacy*, etc.) and TV series (*True Blood*, *Daredevil*, *Supergirl*, etc.)

## Cindy Beal
### ("Tisa")

I was born in Minnesota and came out to California when I was three years old. My parents were farmers and wanted to start a new life. I grew up in the San Fernando Valley in Southern California. I started modeling at a late age (24 years old). I was doing a favor for a friend of mine (who was going to Art Center College of Design in Pasadena) and posing for one of his photography assignments. All the other students wanted to use me as a model when they saw the photos and that is how I started. I shot with many now famous photographers back then and got an awesome portfolio for free. One of the first things I did was to go to Florence, Italy, after being recruited by an Italian modeling agent that came to Los Angeles. I modeled for six years, mainly in Los Angeles, with trips to Florence, Milan, Paris and Munich. I quit modeling (and acting) when I was thirty years old—the same year I got the role as Tisa in *Slave Girls from Beyond Infinity*. I always wanted to act but I have to be honest and say I have absolutely no acting talent. I am not a natural. I would have to take classes and study to be good.

I was a waitress at Rive Gauche Café in Sherman Oaks, California. I waited on Ken Dixon, director of "Slave Girls," many times. He thought I was beautiful and was a little infatuated with me. I started taking acting classes at his Whitefire Theatre in Sherman Oaks. I remember he filmed me doing a monologue that he wrote solely for me. I really wish I could see that. While he was directing "Slave Girls," they lost one of the lead girls and Ken asked me if I wanted to do the role of Tisa. I don't remember doing an audition. I believe I got the role of Tisa solely due to my looks; I had the right type body (although I think they would have preferred larger breasts), was available right away and willing to do it. Also, maybe Ken Dixon wanted to see me in a bikini. I also had no problem wearing 3 outfits during the entire movie, a bikini made from chamois, bra and underwear and a black evening gown (I was told it was the same dress that Yvonne De Carlo wore in her role as Mrs. Herman Munster … although I never checked that fact out to see if it was true). I think there may have been a lot of people involved in the film that would have wanted a more talented actress for Tisa, but I believe Ken had the final word at that time, otherwise I may not have gotten the role.

I filmed every day and loved it and had a little wad of cash at the end as I was too busy during filming to spend one cent. I really liked the experience of acting, especially being one of the leads. I loved studying my lines and had a good memory. I felt my best scene was at the dinner table when I said, "What if you were the hunted instead of the hunter?" I also liked being in the spaceship and working all the imaginary knobs—that was a blast. I am so glad I was given the opportunity to be in the film. It was a great experience.

Liz Kaitan and I became fast, close friends on the set. We were both vegetarians and she has a wicked sense of humor. We laughed so much. I remember one day, we both put Styrofoam cups in our chamois bikini tops and did a shimmy dance across an open office door where Ken Dixon was having a meeting. Only he could see us; his face was so red as he tried not to laugh and ignore us.… It was hilarious. (I am laughing as I write about it.) I lost touch with Liz after "Slave Girls" but in 2002, I was able to run into her again. When I met my present husband, I found out he did two films with Liz and he was still friends with her. We set up a dinner to meet Liz and her husband and when she saw me, she screamed in typical Liz fashion. She is a real fireball and a wonderful human being. I still see her once in a while. I was also close with Don Scribner. He seemed an experienced actor to me and I looked up to him. He gave me some acting tips. I still am in touch with Don. I always hoped he would become successful as an actor as I felt he really deserved it. He is very talented.

All the crew and actors on the set were so great. It was a fun shoot. I don't remember any bad feelings or bad experiences at all. When Ken Dixon is on the set, you are guaranteed to have a good time. I wish I could have lived up to his expectation of me becoming a great actress but it was not in the cards. I always thought when I retire I will take acting lessons so there may be another role for me in the future.

I had a long term relationship with a photographer (Rudi Weislein) during my modeling days and developed a passion for photography. Rudi gave me my first camera and taught me a lot. I started shooting bands and headshots/portfolios for models and actors while I was modeling in Europe and continued to shoot after I stopped modeling. After spending some time doing a lot of work and not making much money, I decided to go back to school to get my accounting degree. I had always taken part time or temporary accounting jobs while I was modeling as I was good with numbers. My first job at 16 was typing envelopes for a garage door company to mail out their brochures and when I left that company 4 years later, I was running the office and doing all the accounting … by hand … this was before computers! I got my accounting degree from Cal State Northridge in 2002, passed the CPA exam and started a master's program in tax—which I decided not to complete. I have been doing accounting and management work for companies. I still do photography but it is strictly for pleasure and I find that much more enjoyable. I do have a longing to go to Art Center College in Pasadena and become a professional photographer which I will do … just not sure when I am going to take that step as I kind of like having a nice steady paycheck. I remember the days when I had no money and lived paycheck to paycheck. Some of my shots can be seen at: www.CindyBealPhotography.com.

## Don Scribner
### ("Zed")

I came from Wisconsin and from a background in education. I was the youngest principal in the state at one time. And, I was given so much in that field … free master's program … offered the principal's position. I did not apply. I always knew I would be doing what I am today. I realized I would be an actor in the 8th grade, the first time in front of an audience telling an improv story. That thrill never left me and even while in education I knew I would be in Los Angeles or New York … as an actor. One of my songs "Big Fish," from my album "I Know the Devil" [2006], tells that story: "…to leave security for obscurity. But, it's a stepping up…." While in education I did a ton of theatre in the Wisconsin, Minnesota area and had my own dinner theatre company, Two Is Company … also did commercial and radio work whenever I could … always pursued that knowing I would not stay in education.

After 13 years my wife and son and I left for Los Angeles and struggled to pay bills, etc. *Outlaw Force* [1987, David Heavener] was my first movie. *Moon in Scorpio* [1987, Gary Graver] was my first union film. *Slave Girls from Beyond Infinity* was my first lead role. I was at home reading a two-week-old actor's paper called *Dramalogue*. It gave the breakdown for "Slave Girls." The lead male character Zed sounded like me and the ad had a phone number … rare to ever have one listed. I called to see if it had been cast. It hadn't. I asked if I could mail a headshot and resume. They gave me the address. I got in my car and drove the 45 miles to the studio and handed it to the secretary.

The director walked by, looked at me and called me in his office to read right then. I did and during that time he made a phone call. I told him that I found that rude and stopped reading. He said that was all right and that I was his Zed! I started shooting the next day I believe. I got lucky … right place … right time. They needed someone and I fit the bill.

We shot for approximately a month and the production was over-budget and halted. We didn't expect to have it go farther. However, they put together a rough-cut and decided the movie had possibilities and shot two more weeks. Ken Dixon was replaced as director and Don Daniel directed two weeks until we wrapped. They asked the cast to work for free to just be able to finish the movie and came to me saying the entire cast agreed to do that. I said, "NO! I cannot work for free. I have a wife and son to support." They said they didn't believe I would agree to that and paid me…. (Actually, they gave me a bonus.) I loved every second of shooting this movie.

I was this guy from small town Wisconsin and was introduced to much of the LA life through "Slave Girls" primarily by the beautiful Cindy Beal. She bought me my first sushi and had to show me how to eat it. She chuckled at my unawareness and said, "Oh Don you are so naive." She was a truly wonderful person … her one and only film. She also had a successful modeling career. She told me I belonged there and she would introduce me to whomever to do film. Part of me thinks that may have been a wise choice, but I didn't go. Cindy was my closest friend among the cast.

Ken never gave me a note about my character and how I was believable as Zed. I took that as he trusted my approach and it must be what he wants. Thank you, Ken Dixon.

My mother was visiting California and we went to the theatre to see "Slave Girls." It was fun to watch as a simple audience member and surprising to hear the audience repeat lines such as "It's a cold cosmos." My mother commented, "They're repeating what you said."

## Carl Horner
### ("Rik")

*Slave Girls from Beyond Infinity* was a lot of fun, and a lot of hard work. Working on the film was like a big home movie, the kind I used to shoot back in Pennsylvania as a young man on super 8 film—except for the slightly larger budget.

My background is in production, actually, and I had done some acting previously, in local, regional, and national commercials back East, but my primary role during the past three decades has been as a visual effects artist, and as an art director and production designer to a lesser extent. I won a THEA Award for production design, which is the themed entertainment industries Academy Award, for my role as a Senior Production Designer at Walt Disney Imagineering for five years on the Tokyo Disney Sea theme park, and I was nominated for my first VES [Visual Effects Society] Award while working for the amazing New Deal Studios and its co-founder Ian Hunter in 2012. Unfortunately, we lost to Martin Scorsese and his team on *Boardwalk Empire*! Just being nominated was an extreme honor.

It's an interesting story how I got involved with "Slave Girls." My roommate was working for a producer, Mark Wolf, on an industrial video for a toy trade show for the toy company Mattel. My roommate told me that Mark Wolf was also producing a low-budget film, and that he, my roommate, would also be helping with some design work and building

Carl Horner ("Rik") shows Mark Wolf (Co-Producer/2nd Unit Director/Special Effects Supervisor) the miniature lifeboat he built (courtesy of Mark Wolf).

miniatures for it. He happened to have a copy of the script laying around, which I read. While reading it, I realized that I would, in my own humble opinion, be perfect for the role of the intergalactic space playboy, Rik! My roommate introduced me to Mark Wolf, who was incredibly nice, very funny, and after reviewing my portfolio, hired me to work on the video for Mattel. After getting to know me a bit, Mark asked me if I had done any acting, because there might be a part for me in a film that he was producing. Conveniently, I had done some acting, and he introduced me to Devorah Hardberger [the production manager]. In the way that things can only work out at Hollywood sometimes, she thought that I would be ideal to play Rick as well, and arranged for a reading with the film's producer, writer and director, Ken Dixon!

Meeting with Ken went well, as well as could be expected. Ken was an interesting person—in that you never really quite knew where he was coming from. He had an interesting way of giving you a compliment, but it was also part insult, too. If I had breasts and a small leather bikini, I would've fared much better!

Apparently, a number of other young men read for the part as well, but I heard from Mark Wolf that I was the lead contender, and Ken had pretty much decided that I had gotten the part, but I needed to hear it from Ken directly. So, I called Ken to see if I had gotten one of the leads, or not.... So Ken, in his inimitable way, says to me, "Yeah, we had a number of other guys read for the part, but no one else read better than you did, so I guess you got the part." Thus began our glorious working relationship on *Slave Girls from Beyond Infinity*...

From what I thought I heard, Ken Dixon and Charles Band had made a bet. Apparently, Charles Band had the rights to a bunch of Italian, and I believe Spanish poor films, in particular a bunch of zombie movies that had not been released in America. The clause was that Ken had access to the Empire film library and the bet stipulated that if Ken managed to make a film with the ridiculous budget of $20,000, Charles Band would have given him the chance to write and direct another film, this time without using archival/stock footage [the movie was *Zombiethon* and apparently Ken Dixon won the bet]. While we were filming the beach sequences in "Slave Girls" at Leo Carrillo Beach in Southern California, some of the crew talked about filming some of the bridging sequences in *Zombiethon* at one of the nearby beaches. I've not actually seen *Zombiethon*, but I could swear that Brinke Stevens [Rik's sister, Shala, in "Slave Girls"] played in the bridging sequences that Ken shot to stitch the Italian and Spanish films together!

Cindy Beal was a fun counterpoint to Liz Kaitan. Liz was not the original female lead, Daria, in "Slave Girls." They had originally cast a former porn star. She is literally only one of two or three people I have ever met in my life that the temperature would drop 10 or 15 degrees when they entered the room. Seriously ... I literally cried the night that I found out that she had been cast as the Daria character. They filmed with her for two or three days, and she was so horrible that they let her go, and bumped Liz from the second lead up to the first lead, Daria.

The director wanted Daria and Rik's love scene to be far more salacious, bordering on pornographic. Liz, myself, and the DP Ken Wiatrak put our collective foot down and absolutely refused to film anything of that nature. I was very proud of us, as we were actually on-set, with him giving us direction, and we said no. You always hear the big A-list actors talking about what hard work it is to film a love scene, and how difficult it actually is. They ain't lying!

The first scene that we filmed with me was after making love to Daria. I am walking out of the bedroom to walk down the corridor. Ken wanted me to be like, "Yeah, I just got lucky!," where my take on it was we just had this poignant, serious love scene, and he (Rik) shouldn't be like some sophomore who just scored in the backseat of the car after the prom. Ken won out, and I walked down the hallway with a smirk on my face.... Immediately thereafter, Ken lost almost all interest in directing me, because I didn't have a tiny leather bikini that he could continually adjust, which he did with the girls. It wasn't until literally halfway through filming that I realized, "I'm actually directing myself..." I wish I had realized that sooner, because my performance could've even been better. Ken and I didn't really get along, but I don't even think that he even realized that.

In between set ups, I was also helping build sets, and work on the visual effects under the tutelage of Mark Wolf. It was a lot of fun, and I met a lot of really super cool, super hard-working people toiling to break out of the low-budget underbelly of Hollywood. There were a lot of very talented people just entering the film industry, anywhere from aspiring models, to interior decorators, to [an] electronic warfare specialist from the Navy! There were so many truly nice people that in many ways I believe working on the film was a once-in-a-lifetime experience. It was kind of like going to camp every day, and you really didn't want to go home.... "Slave Girls" was very much so like a whole movie, or a high school play, where everybody pretty much chipped in and did whatever they could to help make the film be a success because of, or in spite of, the director!

During the introduction of all the main characters in Zed's gigantic trophy hall—including me and my sister [Brinke Stevens]—Ken the writer had visions of Zed playing some cosmic pipe organ, like something out of "The Phantom of the Opera...." Before lunch one day, I happened to hear Ken discuss with one of his cronies about filming the grandiose pipe organ after lunch—or the next day or something like that. As I was helping build sets, in addition to helping out with miniatures on the film, I was pretty aware of what all the art department has been working on, and a grandiose pipe organ was most certainly not in the works. Not at all. When I brought this to the director's attention, he just laughed at me and gave me a hard time for being one of the assistant directors. I shot back, "You should be thanking God I am playing at being one of your assistant directors!" When I brought this to the producer's attention who was supervising the art department, he was stymied that this grandiose, non-existent organ had to go before the cameras after lunch! Necessity sometimes being the mother of invention, especially on a low budget film, our intrepid producer, who shall remain nameless, grabbed a mug rack, spray-painted it silver, found a piece of acrylic rod, and Zed's miraculous amazing grandiose pipe organ of the future was born!

At a certain point, the production ran out of shooting days, and money. We all went on hiatus, not sure of what was going to happen to not only our jobs, but of course the film itself. Several weeks later, I believe, we reconvened, and there was a new producer on board, Don Daniel, brought on it to make sure that things actually got finished. The original cinematographer, Ken Wiatrak, was also replaced by a new cinematographer, Tom Callaway. I respected and liked both men very much, and each of them had their different strengths. After we came back from hiatus, Ken was given some latitude to direct, but as we slipped behind once again, Don Daniel became more assertive, sometimes taking over scenes in the middle of filming. It was certainly interesting receiving direction from two different directors at the same time.

I was invited to a screening of "Slave Girls" at the Academy of Science Fiction Fantasy and Horror Films in Los Angeles. All of us who had either worked on it or been in it got a shout out from Dr. Reed, the founder, and I stood up to get my moment in the sun. Ken hadn't realized I was there, and was anxious to talk to me after the screening.... Again, in his inimitable way, Ken was dumbfounded as he screened the film around the country that people actually enjoyed watching me, and actually even liked me in the film. Even more so than the girls, which he didn't understand! Shaking my head at him once again, I thanked him. Ken excitedly mentioned that he was working on his next film, and asked me if I wanted the lead in it, the starring role. My immediate response was to say no, but then I realized that it was another lead in another movie, and my perfect opportunity to get paid to torment him! How could I say no? I told Ken to keep me posted—let's do it, but unfortunately the financing never really came together. And that's the last I ever heard of Ken Dixon…

I saw "Slave Girls" during its limited theatrical release in Southern California. A bunch of my friends and I all went to the theater, and I think we took over about two rows. There was some drunk guy sitting directly in front of me, with his two kids, and I guess our loud laughter kept prompting him to turn around and look at us. At one point he looks at me in the row behind him and then looks at me on the silver screen in front of him, and he turns back and looks at me and says, "Hey buddy that's you!" It was one of those moments that you'll just never forget…

Interestingly enough, I heard through the grapevine that the vice president in charge of production at Empire Pictures, Frank Hildebrand, said that I actually had a chance to really making it, which I thought was a high compliment and very nice. I did take a break from my visual effects career to pursue acting for about six months, but the hand-to-mouth existence of an actor really didn't appeal to me, nor did waiting tables. I have been offered the lead in two other films, but the material really didn't agree with me (the part for the first film was actually quite nasty, portraying the nice guy next door who is actually a serial rapist and murderer—the other film never got made). After working the graveyard shift as a security guard for six months, and tired of dealing with the nonsense that is known as Hollywood, I went back to my day job being a visual effects artist!

Much to my surprise, "Slave Girls" came out on home video, it was actually talked about and featured on one of the largest late night talk shows in America (*Late Night with David Letterman*) and was also featured in *Playboy* magazine, amongst a number of others. Years later, I found out that "Slave Girls" had actually done quite well overseas, making a few million on basically a $300,000 investment. I also found out that I was very popular in Turkey! I heard that directly from Empire later incarnation, Full Moon Pictures…

Tired of all the nonsense in Hollywood, I moved back home to Pennsylvania in 1989 for the next four years. In 1991, I was teaching in the Industrial Design Technology department at the Art Institute of Pittsburgh, and one of the games that the other members of the faculty and I would play would be, how long would it take someone, one of the students, to recognize me from "Slave Girls," as it had been on heavy rotation on several of the cable TV networks! Each new term we would place bets to see how long, how many days it would take for one of the students to recognize me! It was actually a lot of fun, and actually helped to create a bond with me and my students.

It's been a hell (heaven?) of a ride these past few decades, and I am very excited to see what the future holds; as I have recently gotten married to the most amazing woman, and I am growing into the role of a lifetime, being the stepfather to two teenagers and a daughter who also recently [got] married herself! I am learning on the job, each and every day! Also, I have put all of my own personal film projects in development, namely "Enigma" and "Trajectory," on hold as I am taking some time out to write a book about my involvement with the occult that I have struggled with whether or not to write for decades now. Apparently, it is the season in my life to write the most difficult thing I have ever written. It's literally the grace of God that I live and breathe, and it's time to roll up my sleeves and get serious about it…

## Harry Narunsky
### ("Krel"/Model-Building Crew)

When I went to Los Angeles in 1975 Ken Dixon was making trailers for low budget exploitation films for such producers as the Woolner brothers and Charles Band. Ken then did several compilations for Charles Band, including *The Best of Sex and Violence* [1981], with John Carradine as the host introducing film clips, and *Filmgore* [1982], with Elvira, Mistress of the Dark.

After that Ken wanted to do something a bit different. For *Zombiethon*, another compilation, instead of an on-screen celebrity introducing the clips, he filmed various pretty girls pursued by zombies. The girls flee to a zombie theatre where, in the midst of an all-zombie audience they watch an all-zombie program of films. Ken shot the footage with his 16mm silent film camera. His crew consisted of an assistant. Wearing rubber masks and an old suit Ken frayed, I played several of the zombies. Locations include the outside of the Pan Pacific Auditorium (also seen in the M-G-M two-reel Technicolor short *Cinema Circus* and the King Brothers' *Suspense*), an alley off Gardner Street between Sunset and Hollywood

Boulevard in West Hollywood, and the beach at Malibu. While were shooting there, a house owner came down to see what was going on below his home; it was Buddy Hackett. The zombie theatre was the El Ray, a movie house on Wilshire Boulevard in West Hollywood (which was also used in *The Happy Hooker Goes Hollywood*). The theatre interior was in a bungalow in East Hollywood, near Melrose Avenue, just east of the Hollywood Freeway. A film fan had turned the house's dining room into a screening room furnished with rows of seats salvaged from a demolished theatre, an "Exit" light, and a 35mm projector installed in a small projection booth.

After *Zombiethon* Ken persuaded Charles Band to have him do a feature film. They settled on *Slave Girls from Beyond Infinity*, which was basically "The Most Dangerous Game" set in outer space, also including dialogue from such sources as *Charlie Chan in Egypt*. As I was told by Ken, on the strength of the title and the artwork for the poster, Charles Band sold the foreign rights to the film, and that essentially provided the budget, which was approximately $200,000.

There wasn't a great deal of money, and I devised a modular system for the hunting lodge walls, with the idea that hanging miniatures would augment the stone walls built with styrofoam blocks. The budget was so low that, even though I can't draw, I was almost made the production designer. John Eng was hired to be the production designer, and essentially elaborated on my idea for constructing the sets. With Mark Wolf in charge of effects, I worked on the model-building crew. I could fit into an android suit John Buechler's company had built, so I got the part of Krel.

**Fred Tate ("Mutant"/Production Assistant/Electrician), Kirk Graves ("Vak") who is wearing the robot costume and Ken Dixon (Writer/Director/Producer) on the stairs (courtesy of Mark Wolf).**

The film started production at Roger Corman's studio, a converted lumber yard in Venice, California, across the street from a bus terminal. Hunting lodge interiors were done there, as was the log bridge, an imitation of the log bridge in *King Kong*, and the space prison ship and escape ship. Mark Wolf supervised special effects, including the hanging miniatures, an old technique that has fallen out of favor. The hunting lodge made use of a hanging miniature. In the long shot of the main room the balcony is a miniature closer to the camera than the full-scale set of the first floor. The entrance to the hunting lodge was filmed outside the sound stage. The stage door was repainted to be the entrance to the lodge, and a model stone wall was another hanging miniature, suspended nearer the camera. The path is the asphalt paving outside the stage, and the jungle foliage on either side of the path is also a miniature.

## Kirk Graves
### ("Vak"/Set Carpenter)

I am an actor and theater technician living and working in Los Angeles. I still act occasionally but I work mostly in props and set dressing. It was January 1987. I was 22 years old and 6 months out of college. I had been working at small theaters, acting and doing technical work when my friend and neighbor Escott Norton [Art Director] asked me if I wanted to work on a film that he was art directing. I came on as a set carpenter and we started building the scenery. We built and shot at one of Roger Corman's warehouse/soundstages in Venice, CA.

After about a week of set construction I found out that the film had not completed casting. I mentioned to the production staff that I was an actor and that, if possible, I would like to see the script and audition. I read the script and I thought it was a pretty basic "B" movie adventure story based on "The Most Dangerous Game"—made sci-fi with a bit of *The Jetsons*' style futuristic dialogue thrown in. In reading the script I thought that the part that suited me best was one of the robots. This was partly because if the movie was awful and if I never showed my face then I would have the ability to deny that I was the "Kirk Graves" listed in the credits. I had spent the previous summer with a student group touring Europe as a street performer and I had some basic pantomime skills. I auditioned with some basic robotic movements and a voice reminiscent of C-3PO (*Star Wars*). The decision had been made that Vak would be more of an indoor butler robot and Krel would be the outdoor patrol robot. I went back to building scenery and a couple of days later I was cast as Vak (I heard a rumor that more than anything it was because I was already there and I was the right size to fit in the robot costume that had already been built). I did most of the work in the movie where the robot is doing something with its hands. They used me in most of the scenes where there was detailed movement as they liked my version of robotic movements better than the actor playing Krel.

There are two scenes in the movie where I was not on set and one of the other set carpenters was put into the robot suit. The first was a scene in the grand hall and shooting that day was running long and I had to leave because I was acting in a production of *Man of La Mancha* on my nights and weekends. The second scene was in the jungle that we shot during the week of pick up shooting. I had to leave at the scheduled time on the last day and the shooting went longer so the same set carpenter was put into the suit again.

Early on, while we were building the scenery but before we started shooting, there were concerns among the cast and crew that the film would not be properly funded. So, as a group, it was decided that we would rather be paid in cash rather than to wait and hope the check came the next week and that the check wouldn't bounce. This was a non-union production and to give some idea of the economics at the time I was paid $150.00 per week as a set carpenter. I can't remember if they were 10 or 12 hour days at that time. When I was cast as Vak I went up to $300.00 per week when we were filming and I no longer had to do the set construction. However I didn't want to abandon my friends on the set crew so I came every day and worked on the sets when I wasn't filming as Vak.

Much of the set we built were the Styrofoam covered walls and pillars that make up most of the scenery in Zed's compound. They were designed to be utilitarian and we reconfigured them as needed for the various rooms. I think we had one sliding door unit which was reused for each new application. There was no second level built for the sequences in the grand hall. There is a sequence where they're having dinner and you can see all the trophies on the second level with an entry door at the top of the stair. The second level was a model that was mounted just above the camera so that you could see all of the miniatures in the same scale with the rest of the room. The staircase was reused from an earlier production and was not tall enough to reach the second level so the top four stairs are decorative only. We built them out of very thin wood and painted them to look like the rest of the set. In any scene where people are going up or coming down that staircase you will notice no one ever steps on the top four steps because they're not structural. You'd fall through. Often a scene would start with the actors on the highest usable step and then walking down or walking up but the camera would cut away before they reached the top 4 steps.

All of the jungle scenes were filmed indoors at the warehouse. We brought in a lot of real and fake plants and we painted a mural of the jungle on the wall of the warehouse. Many of the plants were still in pots and we disguised these by covering them in camouflage netting, extra foliage and moss. Our originally scheduled number of shooting days ran out and we had not finished all of the scripted and scheduled scenes. Principal filming, if I remember correctly, went from late January to early March 1987. At the point when we ran out of our scheduled days we had only completed a few of the many jungle scenes and we did not know when the other scenes would be completed.

If I remember correctly it was May 1987 when we got the call for a week of re-shoots. This was in another warehouse in Burbank or North Hollywood. At that warehouse we could only shoot over night as we weren't supposed to be there. We had to park down the block and keep hidden in the warehouse so as not to arouse suspicion. And we also had a problem with the Burbank Airport as we were directly in the flight path of landing planes. The flights at that time did not come into Burbank from around 10 p.m. to 6 a.m. So for the remainder of the shoot in the other warehouse we were coming in and filming from 7 p.m. to 7 a.m. both to avoid detection and to avoid the interruptions from the sound of landing planes.

The only sequences that we filmed outside of the warehouses were the beach scenes. These were filmed at Will Rogers State Beach. We ran into a problem with those scenes as it was an open public beach and the park ranger assigned to our shoot wouldn't let us shoot any of the topless sequences. We shot what we could that day and a small crew went back

Filming *The Erotic Adventures of Robinson Crusoe*, 1975, Beach of Sabaudia (Italy). Ken Dixon—writer/director of the film—is on the tower next to the camera. Roberto Girometti—cinematographer on the film—is next to Ken Dixon, with his leg on the cube. The actor who plays Robinson Crusoe, Lawrence P. Casey, is the one with arms folded on the seashore (courtesy of Roberto Girometti).

at a later date to quickly get the topless shots. This is why on the continuity of that scene Tisa's top keeps going on and off depending on the day of filming.

The robot suit was made out of laminated pieces of flexible foam and it was in a number of pieces. There were separate pieces for the feet, lower leg, upper leg, waist with codpiece, chest, gauntlets, forearm, bicep into shoulder and a helmet. Underneath it all was a black leotard with wires attached and some painted detail—mostly at the waist and knee and elbow joints. This was to cover my body and make it look robotic at the various seams between the foam pieces. When we first started filming we were so concerned about the robots being damaged that we couldn't do very much movement. The suit was fairly constricting. When I was wearing the outfit I couldn't sit down and it would take 20 to 30 minutes to get me in and out of the various pieces. I never had a dressing room on the shoot. I would just go into the bathroom at the warehouse and change from my street clothes into the leotard and come into the set where someone would help me get into the rest of the suit. I learned to relax while in the suit by leaning up against the wall while standing. As the shoot went on I was able to get a little more flexibility out of the robot suit. I was never able to sit down in it but I got a little more movement out of it, to the point where I was able to run in the suit during the week of pick up shooting.

The helmet was made of cast resin rather than from foam. It was a little heavier and the eyes were filled with reflective sunglass lenses. This made it difficult on the darker sequences because I could not see out of the helmet in low light. For certain scenes I would have to memorize my steps to make sure that I could get where I needed to go without bumping into anything. There is one section in the torture chamber where I'm standing in front of Zed and then I turned move around the table go up the staircase and operate a door handle on the wall. I wasn't able to see any of that when we did it so I did that by counting out the steps on the floor and I did it blind. We had a similar section with the jungle sequences. I learned how to navigate and actually run through the jungle in that robot suit.

There was one scene in the hallway where I knock out Rik as he is coming down the hall. We were told that we would only be seen from the chest up and they didn't have me put on the bottom half of the suit. In the finished footage you see well below the chest piece and you can see the leotard and the wires without the waist piece on the suit.

I never spent a lot of time hanging with the other actors as I started originally on the set crew and I tended to hang out with them. I mainly focused in the work on the scenes with the other actors and oftentimes I was working building the set when I didn't have scenes until later in the day. I would be out of the robot suit but still wearing the leotard with a pair of sweats over it painting scenery or operating the automatic door. As I recall everyone was pleasant and professional on set.

Rumor had it that Ken Dixon was one of the guys who edited the trailers for Charlie Band's Empire Pictures and he had been doing it for so long that Charlie owed him a big favor. I heard that the way this movie got made was that, if they (Ken and the other producers) could put together a concept and sell the rights for distribution in Europe then Charlie would let Ken film the movie with the budget being a portion of the money raised from selling the foreign rights. This is all hearsay but that's what the rumor was on set. They took a synopsis and a poster and went to European distributors and sold the idea and then they had to make the movie for less than that amount. I believe the original shooting budget was $90,000. And if I heard correctly later the total shooting budget including the re-shoots finished somewhere around $125,000.

In July of 1987 I got a call from Ken asking if I wanted to record the dialogue for the finished product. We were in a recording studio with video playback and I recorded all of the dialogue for Vak matching the timing of the final edited footage. The dialogue for Krel was recorded in the studio by Ken Dixon. I don't know whether or not the other actor was available or whether Ken wanted to do it himself but Ken did record the actual dialogue that was used in the film. When I was on set I was doing the dialogue inside the helmet I was also making a little whirring noises to mimic the servos and motors running inside the robot whenever I moved. I wasn't mic'ed at the time but you can hear them a bit in the background. Some of those noises can actually be heard on the audio track for the finished film.

*Slave Girls from Beyond Infinity* opened in only 5 theaters in Los Angeles in October of 1987. That was the week of the Whittier earthquake and 2 of the 5 theaters were closed from damage due to the earthquake. I saw the film in its opening week with friends at an old movie palace, I believe it was the State Theater, in downtown LA. It was weird seeing a low budget sci-fi movie in an opulent movie palace filled with the excesses of design left over from the early part of the century. One note is that this film has a place in the record books as one of the last films released on a double-bill. This practice had ended as a rule years before in the States but it was revived when "Slave Girls" was released.

I ran into Ken several times over the years. I have been selling comic books at a local convention since 1993 and I would occasionally run into him at the convention. He was often selling items that he had collected over the years from movie sets, some props and posters. He also, as I recall, was a collector of animation cels and he was often selling those. I haven't seen him since around 1997.

# Sorority Babes in the Slimeball Bowl-O-Rama

(1987, U.S.A.)

*Genre:* Horror/Comedy; *Director:* David DeCoteau; *Writer:* Sergei Hasenecz; *Cinematographers:* Scott Ressler and Stephen Ashley Blake; *Editors:* Thomas Meshelski and Barry Zetlin; *Special Makeup and Creature Effects:* Craig Caton; *Producers:* John Schouweiler and David DeCoteau; *Associate Producer:* Thomas A. Keith; *Executive Producer:* Charles Band; *Production Company:* Cinema H.V. Productions ;*Cast:* Andras Jones (Calvin), Linnea Quigley (Spider), Robin Stille as "Robin Rochelle" (Babs), Hal Havins (Jimmie), John Stuart Wildman (Keith), Brinke Stevens (Taffy), Michelle Bauer as "Michelle McClellen" (Lisa), Carla Baron (Frankie), Kathi O'Brecht (Rhonda) and George "Buck" Flower as "C.D. LaFleur" (Janitor)

In order to be able to join a sorority, two girls have to spend the night in a bowling alley and are asked to steal a trophy, escorted in the initiation by three boys. The girls are unaware that the head of the sorority, as well as two of her friends, are also hidden in the bowling alley, aiming to pull a prank on the small group. Unfortunately, the trophy to be stolen is a cup inhabited by an evil genie, who promises to satisfy the youngsters and a female thief, who is also present in the building, with one wish each. The wishes act like a boomerang, turning against those who expressed them, so that the pleasant evening quickly becomes a nightmare for everybody.

## Sergei Hasenecz
### (Writer)

[Author's note—"Thane" was intended to be Nick Marino's third film as a producer, after *Death House* and *Terror Night*, both shot in 1987. Unfortunately, "Thane" never saw the light. No need to repeat that I love the stories behind unproduced screenplays. In addition, Nick Marino's *Terror Night* and *Death House* are both included in this book. So, on my request, Sergei Hasenecz agreed to make an interesting digression at the end of his story, sharing his memories of working with Nick Marino on "Thane."]

I worked on *Android* [1981] as part of the set construction crew, and I had previously done the same for *Forbidden World* [1981]. Both were at Roger Corman's New World studio. *Android* was written by James Reigle and Don Opper. I knew Don a little bit, but knew Jim much better since Jim had been head of the set construction crew for *Forbidden World*. Jim was an intelligent man, full of ideas, and it's a pity he didn't write more than he did. The script he and Don did for *Android* was a little gem. *Android* also gave me the chance to work on a movie starring Klaus Kinski.

The "Sorority Babes" project began with David DeCoteau and John Schouweiler, the producers. They were turning out direct-to-video movies. I had known David previously, and he asked me if I wanted to try my hand at a screenplay for him. At the time I had just finished working on a movie as an apprentice sound editor. I'd written performance pieces for local stages and nightclubs. I'd also written a few other things under a pen name or two. David told me up front that it wouldn't pay very much, and that the schedule would be very tight. I agreed to do it. I was hoping to get further along as a writer and this was a paying job, at least.

When I met with David and John, they had a one sentence idea about an imp, a little demon, trapped in a bowling trophy. That was the working title, "The Imp." It escapes and begins raising hell. David loved the movie *Revenge of the Nerds*, so he wanted college fraternity boys and sorority girls involved. During the meeting, David and John would think out loud of things they might want to see in the movie, and I joined in. Brainstorming. I don't remember who came up with the idea of having some of the girls become possessed. And, of course, I was reminded that the movie needed a certain amount of nudity and gore. Not that I needed to be reminded. The only other idea I took away from that meeting was David's. He wanted someone to be hung upside down in the bowling alley and have a bowling ball hit their head as if a strike was being scored.

I was told to take a couple days and come back with a plot synopsis. All of the rest was left up to me. If I remember correctly, they were hoping to have both Linnea Quigley

Filming *Sorority Babes in the Slimeball Bowl-O-Rama*. Location: Bowling alley. Hal Havins ("Jimmie") and Stephen Ashley Blake (Cinematographer #2) during a break in filming (courtesy of Stephen Ashley Blake).

and Michelle Bauer in the movie, but at that point I don't think it was definite. I told them I didn't know who either of the actresses were. John showed me a very sexy photo of Michelle Bauer that would have made a bishop jump the fence. Then I remembered I had seen her in a movie before but didn't know her name.

A couple days later I had a story ready and presented it to David and John. David said he wanted more comedy with the college students before they got to the bowling alley, but other than a few minor changes they approved what I'd come up with. Then they told me I had ten days to write a finished script, ready to shoot. The reason for the short time schedule, again if I remember correctly, was that they had found a bowling alley where they could shoot at night, after it had closed, and they had already booked those nights.

And I did it. I wrote the entire script in ten days. I wish I would have had more time and could perhaps have written something better, but within the limitations imposed on me, I guess it didn't turn out too badly. The only thing in the script that was changed was David asking me again to add more *Revenge of the Nerds*–type comedy in the beginning. The problem was that I hadn't seen that movie. At first David didn't like that part of the script as I rewrote it, but later he said that it would work. He told me he changed his mind because initially he hadn't visualized it as he read it.

Since Michelle Bauer or Linnea Quigley were possibly going to be cast, I knew I had to have a good part for a woman, however I didn't want her to be part of the sorority. I wanted an outsider. I also didn't want a victim, the way women so often were in the slasher movies, so I simply went in the opposite direction. I had been around the LA punk scene for some time, and knew a few local musicians and bands. The look of those punkers, and some of their attitudes, was part of the inspiration for Spider [the thief], the character Linnea Quigley would eventually play. I made Spider a woman who was tough and could take care of herself, and take care of someone else if she had to. The name came from a woman I knew at the time who was nicknamed Spike, although Spike was nothing at all like Spider. I just used the name as a starting point. Spider grew from there. I really enjoyed writing her.

Once I had Spider, the other characters began to fall into place: a male ingénue to play opposite her, then the possessed women. I tried to make the sorority girls more than simply victims as well, make them the aggressors. Just trying to turn the clichés around a little bit.

However, I tried not to make the movie too self-conscious of itself, even though characters were recognizing the clichés they were involved in. "The Imp" was probably the most aware of the conventions of the genre, but then why shouldn't he be? I had fun writing Uncle Impy, too.

In the end, what it came down to was this: try to write something that wasn't too constricted by the limitations imposed by budget, genre, or meeting the producers' expectations. I was also taking myself a little too seriously as a writer, at times, and had to not let that get in the way. Both David and John wanted to have fun with the movie. And I wanted to have fun writing it, but without turning it into something witless.

I wasn't on the set during filming (I was already working on another project), but I know David allowed Buck Flower to ad lib some lines. "The Imp" wasn't changed to *Sorority Babes in the Slimeball Bowl-O-Rama* until after filming had finished, I believe. I don't know who came up with it. I didn't care much for either title, although "Sorority Babes in the Slimeball Bowl-O-Rama" certainly stands out. Once you've heard it, you don't forget it. For a while I was a bit embarrassed to say I wrote the movie because of that title, but as I said I sometimes took myself a little too seriously as a writer then.

I saw the movie for the first time during its brief theatrical run, if you can call it that. While "Sorority Babes" was intended as a direct-to-video feature (at least in America, I wouldn't know about elsewhere in the world), it was given very limited distribution to movie houses. Or movie house. It played exactly one theater in Los Angeles, and it wouldn't surprise me if that was the only theater it ever played.

"Sorority Babes" ran for maybe a week at the Cameo, a decaying grindhouse in downtown LA catering to a Spanish-speaking crowd. I went with a friend on an overcast Saturday afternoon. Upon entering the lobby, the atmosphere was immediately foreboding. It smelled as if a toilet had overflowed. Fortunately the odor did not permeate the theater itself, although the foreboding did continue. It was difficult for my friend and I to find two seats together that were not broken or did not have springs coming through the seat. The sound system was a single speaker hanging precariously from a nail above the screen. The audience consisted of maybe a dozen people scattered about (probably because of the bad seats), most of them carrying on conversations in Spanish.

The coming attractions began, showing scratched and faded trailers for older Mexican movies. I remember one was for a Cantinflas movie, *Por mis Pistolas*, from 1968. The audience talked through the trailers, and when *Sorority Babes* began, they talked through that, too. Other than my friend and I, no one seemed to have come to actually watch a movie. I got the impression they were all just killing time.

And that's how the screening went, "Sorority Babes" accompanied by a continuous murmur of Spanish-language conversation, until the scene where Michelle Bauer pulls off her top—and there was SILENCE. Every eye was fixed on her. Not a person moved. Then, perhaps in awe, someone whispered (it's a cliché, but I'm not making this up), "Ay, chihuahua!" A little while later the scene finished, everyone's attention drifted, and the talking resumed.

When the movie ended we left, although everyone else kept their seats. My friend and I walked a few blocks to a nicer section of downtown, where we found a quiet bar and she bought me a couple glasses of scotch. It had not been a red carpet premiere.

Over the years since then, I would occasionally meet people who saw the movie and recognized my name, which I always found rather surprising. But I tended to be dismissive of "Sorority Babes" because I wasn't satisfied with it. I thought it could have been better, that I could have written it better, and I always wished I'd had more time to work on the script.

"Sorority Babes" got a lot of showings on cable TV through the 1990s, and what I didn't realize was that a lot of people saw the movie that way and became fans of it. A few have tracked me down just to say how much they enjoyed the movie, which I found baffling at first. You want to talk to the writer? The movie has Michelle Bauer, Linnea Quigley and Brinke Stevens in it, and you want to talk to the writer? It did change my attitude toward the movie, though. I still wish I had had more time to write a better script, yet a lot of people enjoyed the movie. A lot had fun watching it. So that's worth something. One of the people who contacted me said "Sorority Babes" is one of his favorite movies, and he's now an independent filmmaker in part because of it. His name is Theo Lemasters, and this June he will be shooting his own horror feature entitled "Demonic Aborted Sewer Fecal

Fetuses Revenge." If a script I wrote inspired someone to be creative, yes, that's worth something.

I met Nick Marino through David DeCoteau, because David knew Nick was looking for writers, so he introduced us. This was before my work on "Sorority Babes." Nick had already begun actively soliciting scripts, and before the start of filming for *Terror Night* [1987, Nick Marino, Fred J. Lincoln & André De Toth], he had the script for *Death House* [1987, John Saxon] and several other potential projects (one script was titled "I Remember When Coke Was Still Cola," though I no longer recall the writer's name). It wasn't long after "Sorority Babes" had finished when Nick asked me to read *Death House* to give an opinion and make suggestions. I did, but by then he decided to take the *Death House* script in a different direction, which ended my involvement with it.

I wasn't involved with *Terror Night*, although I was frequently at Nick's offices on Sunset Blvd. and would hear about the movie's progress. André De Toth [1912–2002] was only helping Nick out by directing a few scenes, so did not want to be credited as the director. There was an incident on *Terror Night* where a stunt was supposed to be filmed in slow-motion. Unfortunately, André didn't cue the slow-motion camera. Nick was upset because of the added expense of renting the special camera yet losing the shot. I don't believe the stunt was re-shot. My understanding was that Nick directed a few scenes himself as well.

Nick kept trying to change the movie as it went along. At first it was supposed to be yet another slasher movie, but when Nick began to feel there were now too many of those movies, he tried to change the emphasis, adding or taking out scenes. He was very happy to get John Ireland, but he hated Aldo Ray who apparently was drunk much of the time.

I saw the movie with Nick before it was shown in a theater. He had a VHS copy made and we watched it on his television. He was still somewhat enthusiastic about the movie at that point. When it later had a public screening, he introduced the movie. I wasn't there, but was told that Nick was apologetic and almost embarrassed by how *Terror Night* had turned out.

One night Nick gave me a call and said he had a great idea for a science fiction movie: it would be "Macbeth," set in outer space. I still remember him pitching it to me by exclaiming, "Instead of swords, they use lasers!" He was very excited with his idea. Shakespeare has been adapted to various genres before, including "The Tempest" becoming *Forbidden Planet*, so it was an intriguing idea. And I needed a job.

Nick asked me to write a treatment of a dozen or so pages. He wanted me to keep the plot, but didn't want to use Shakespeare's dialogue. He also wanted all of the characters' names changed. I no longer remember what I called the treatment I first turned in to Nick, but it was Nick who chose "Thane" [1987/1989] as the title. I had used the word in the treatment. (A thane is a Scottish feudal lord. In Shakespeare's play, when Macbeth meets the three witches, they greet him each in turn: "Macbeth! hail to thee, Thane of Glamis! / All hail, Macbeth, hail to thee, Thane of Cawdor / All hail, Macbeth, thou shalt be king hereafter!" which predicts Macbeth's rise to power.) I always thought it was a good choice.

Although I was familiar with the play, I began by re-reading it several times through, making my notes, and then started on my adaptation. My approach was to write a futuristic story with a medieval atmosphere. Yes, the characters would be traveling through the galaxy in space vessels and, as Nick wanted, they would use laser guns. But I wanted to create a society that had fallen from its former glories and was decaying. Advanced technology was still in use, but the people were losing the knowledge of how it worked. They had lost the ability to manufacture the technology they used. Space vessels were cobbled together from various junked ships, computer parts were cannibalized from other computers. Everything was being jerry-rigged. At the same time, culture and morality were in decline and brutality on the rise. To the characters' minds, there would be little difference between science and the supernatural. For example, the three witches of the play in my adaptation became a sybil manifesting on dead computer monitors.

When I finished the treatment, I gave it to Nick. Then waited to hear back from him. After a couple weeks with no response, I gave him a call and asked him what he thought of it. He was a bit vague with his opinion, but told me to go ahead and write a first draft. If I remember correctly, I wrote the first draft in about a month, because despite Nick's vagueness, he was anxious to have a script in his hands.

I gave him the first draft and that night received an angry phone call from him. Nick said he didn't like this, he didn't like that, why was I putting these things in the script? This wasn't what he wanted. I got angry back at him. I said, "What are you talking about? Everything you're complaining about is in the treatment. If you didn't like it, why didn't you tell me before I wrote the script? You gave me the go-ahead!" There was an embarrassed silence from Nick, then he reluctantly admitted that he had never read the treatment. I told him that I'd make any changes he wanted, but he'd have to pay me more. And that's where things rested for a while.

Nick gave the script to someone else to rewrite. I don't know how André De Toth met Nick Marino, but at some point André became involved in "Thane" with the intention that he would direct. André later told me that Nick gave him the rewrite to read, and André told him it was terrible. André then read my first draft, liked it, and told Nick to throw out the rewrite and get me back for a second draft. Nick told me where to meet André to begin a second draft.

I first met André in the hospital. He had broken his neck in an accident. (He owned a Doberman Pinscher, and while walking the dog one day it had suddenly bolted and yanked André off his feet. Not the first time André had broken his neck. He had done it previously in a skiing mishap.) Walking into the hospital room I saw André in bed, in a reclined sitting position. He wore a black patch over his bad eye, and with his good one was watching the Winter Olympics on television. His hair was white, close-cropped very short. Encircling his head was a metal halo which was screwed directly into his skull to hold his head steady. The halo was attached to a cervical brace, which in turn kept his neck from moving. I introduced myself, he reached across his immobilized body to shake my hand, and without hesitation he said, "Let's begin!"

The man was unstoppable. I sat next to the bed and would read a scene. We'd discuss it, decide what changes we wanted to make and how to improve it, then go on to the next scene. I'd take notes the entire time. When we finished for the day, I would go home and write out what we had agreed upon, as well as add things as inspiration struck me. Every two or three days, I would again visit André in the hospital. I'd read aloud the rewritten scenes, and we would polish them until we were satisfied, then go on to the next scenes.

It was an odd method for an odd situation, yet it worked very well, and I very much enjoyed writing with André. He never dictated or demanded, instead it was a good give-and-take. He always liked to try something new and different, as well as to experiment with an idea to see where it would go, no matter if it was his idea or mine. He had no ego that way. His only concern was that we create as good a script as possible. I learned a lot from him.

When writing anything of length, it isn't unusual to occasionally hit a snag, where something isn't going right. It may be a plot point or a character or a scene, but you find yourself stuck. André had an excellent method for working out those problems. We once became stuck and couldn't come up with a solution. André closed his good eye and was quiet for a little while, then opened his eye, looked at me and said, "What if the main character was a woman?" My reaction was, of course, "What? It's Macbeth. It can't be a woman." André waved my objection away, saying, "No, no. Just go home and think about it. We'll talk tomorrow." So I thought about it half the night, and when I went back the next day, I had all of my arguments ready as to why the character shouldn't be a woman. And I had also found the solution to our problem, which had been André's intention all along. He had gotten me to view the character from a new angle, and that fresh perspective gave us our answer. Our galactic Macbeth remained male.

I think we finished that second draft by the time André got out of the hospital. Nick read it and began to shop it around to the major studios. It was clearly too expensive for him to finance alone. But Nick wanted some changes, too. I didn't think that any were necessary, and felt that all the script needed was a polishing. One thing in particular Nick wanted to add was an alien race. I resisted that, until André and I came up with the idea that the aliens were a conquered race, now living as servants to the humans. The aliens were secretly manipulating the overthrow of their human masters. It was a touch of Othello in Macbeth, as if Macbeth had not one Iago but many. That seemed to be working out fairly well, when Nick decided he wanted a second alien race as well. The more changes and additions Nick wanted pushed the story farther away from the central "Macbeth" story. Finally André and I argued Nick back to the original concept of the script.

Part of the problem seems to have been that Nick was very sensitive to criticism. When someone read the script and made a negative comment to him, he would want us to rewrite whatever had caused that criticism. This was without regard to how the change would affect the rest of the story. This happened more and more as Nick was unable to get a studio to commit to making the movie. By the end there were six drafts that I worked on, all but the first with André. Nick believed in the script—or, at least, in his idea—yet he kept tampering with it, and that definitely hurt "Thane."

Twentieth Century–Fox showed some interest in "Thane" for a while, however in the end they backed away from it. I don't know why. Perhaps they thought it would be too expensive. Perhaps because Nick wouldn't sell the script outright, since he wanted to be the producer. Perhaps the script was too dark. This certainly wasn't a swashbuckler like *Star Wars*. All of which is speculation on my part. I wasn't privy to the meetings Nick had with the studio people.

"Thane" never went into pre-production. No major studio ever committed to doing our script. Nick kept trying for years to interest a studio, and he never did. Nor was he able to raise the money independently. After a long while he even offered "Thane" as a basis for a video game. Again, no takers. He had gone on to other projects, some realized and some not, but he always kept trying with "Thane." In the theater, "Macbeth" is traditionally regarded as a "bad luck" play. Perhaps the "Macbeth" curse affected "Thane" as well.

The most important thing to know about Nick Marino is that he loves movies. He grew up at a time when television was constantly showing movies from the 1930s, '40s and '50s, Hollywood's golden era. He told me that he watched movies every day, even while eating dinner. He never outgrew that. When I was writing for him I would sometimes stop by his home for a meeting, and he would always have a movie on. By that time VHS tapes were available, and Nick must have had hundreds. I'm sure he now has hundreds of DVDs and Blu-rays.

That love of movies brought him to Hollywood, of course. He was enamored of the first two *Godfather* movies, and he came to Hollywood wanting to write the third. Nick worked with another writer (whose name I've forgotten) [Thomas Wright] on a script for *Godfather III*. Paramount desperately wanted a third movie, and there were several writers working on scripts for the sequel then. The *Los Angeles Times* did an article about all of the scripts, illustrated with caricatures of the various writers standing side by side with their arms over each others' shoulders. Nick was included, along with Puzo, Coppola, and others. Nick later got the original artwork from the *LA Times*, framed it and hung it proudly in his home. He's quoted in the article as well.

But his script was turned down, like so many others. When *Godfather III* was finally filmed and released, only Puzo and Coppola got a writing credit. Nick complained to the Writers Guild that many of his ideas were used. His complaint went into arbitration (or however the Writers Guild resolves such things). In the end, the Guild sided with Puzo and Coppola. I read Nick's script [1985/1987] after seeing the movie. There were ideas which would have grown logically out of anyone's seeing the first two movies. However, I did think he had a few ideas that might have been unique to him and his writing partner, and that their case may have been stronger than the Writers Guild wanted to admit. The thing is, Nick wasn't chasing the money. I'm sure he would have been happy with a writer's credit, or even an acknowledgment.

I'd say that Nick was probably the idea man while his co-scripter did the actual writing. To be honest, Nick wasn't a very good writer. He could come up with an idea and hand it to a writer, yet even that could be a problem, because Nick didn't always trust his writers. He tended to second-guess and third-guess things, and not always for the better. I've told about my experiences writing "Thane" for him. I know that both *Terror Night* and *Death House* went through their share of changes, too.

It wasn't always easy working for Nick. What did help, though, was seeing his genuine passion for movies. I want to emphasize that. If in the end he didn't make great movies, Nick was pursuing his passion. I respect that.

## Thomas A. Keith
### (Associate Producer/1st Assistant Director)

I came to Los Angeles in 1982 and was able to get a job as a production assistant working on TV commercials through a contact I had made in college. Then I got together with two friends so we could show Hollywood what great filmmakers we were by producing a short film called *Heaven Help Us*. We used our own money and called in as many favors from the crew members I had met working on the commercials. We interviewed several people to work with us as production assistants but we gave the job to one particular guy because he owned a pickup truck. That was David DeCoteau.

The first theatrical film I worked on, as an assistant director, was *Cold Steel* [1987]. David had directed several movies by this time so I called him up and asked him if he would let me be his 1st assistant director. Our first movie together was *Sorority Babes in the Slimeball Bowl-O-Rama*. The crew met at the bowling alley at 7:00 p.m. and bowled until 9:00 p.m. when we could take control and begin filming. We could shoot until 6:00 a.m., but had to stop because that was when the alley opened again in the morning. We had a lot of dialogue, stunts, and special effects to shoot each day but we were able to finish our work in six hours. I believe we were only in the bowling alley for five days of filming.

## Scott Ressler
### (Cinematographer #1)

[Author's note—*Sorority Babes in the Slimeball Bowl-O-Rama* was shot by two directors of photography. Although Scott Ressler left the film after a few days, I managed to obtain from him two very interesting pieces of information. The first concerning the final title of the film; the second concerning "Star Pupil"—a sort of sequel of *Dr. Alien* (do you remember the sexy alien schoolmistress Judy Landers focused on conducting experiments on the student Billy Jacoby to find a cure against the decline of virility plaguing her species?)—that would have been his second produced screenplay, following *Warlords*.]

I was contacted by David DeCoteau shortly after shooting *Hollywood Chainsaw Hookers* [1987, Fred Olen Ray] for Fred Olen Ray. My principal profession was, and is, camerawork. David essentially hired me over the telephone to shoot "The Imp." Charlie Band had run a contest for his employees, to come up with the best name for the film. I believe the winner, the man who named "Bitchin' Sorority Babes in the Slimeball Bowl-O-Rama," was Eric Gruendemann, who I coincidentally knew through school friends. Eric went on to be a film and television producer for Sam Raimi, amongst others. The "Bitchin'" in the title was later dropped due to restrictions with newspaper advertising. I didn't complete that shoot but left on decent terms with David. After a screening of *Warlords* [1988, Fred Olen Ray], I was again contacted by David about writing "Star Pupil." [1988/1989] David had the general idea already worked out, essentially an exchange student from another world. He was looking for a similar feel to his earlier film, *Dr. Alien* [1988, David DeCoteau]—in this case a teen sexploitation comedy with science fiction elements. Broad comedy is definitely not my strong suit and it was a struggle to write. My final draft had more of a retro feel, I think, with elements of '70s black comedy. I gave the main character a sort of binary name, OXO, which a crowd would chant once he became a cult hero at the school. David showed the script around but there were no takers, so he asked Ken Hall, the screenwriter of *Dr. Alien*, to do a rewrite. To be honest I was grateful for this, as I was never happy with my script. Unfortunately his later version never sold, either.

## Stephen Ashley Blake
### (Cinematographer #2)

David DeCoteau knew my work from a picture I had shot for AIP [David Winters, David A. Prior and Peter Yuval's company] called *Deadly Prey* [1986], and called me to shoot "The Imp," which was already in production. The first DP, Scott Ressler, had left the shoot after just a few days of work, so with no notice and absolutely zero prep, I came onboard. That's why there are two very different looks to the movie: the opening scenes in the sorority house and a few scenes in the bowling alley were Scott's work—his look was quite dim and smoky. After completing principal photography, we spent another half day in a tight little office space in Hollywood shooting the close-ups of the imp on the video game.

## Craig Caton
### (Special Makeup and Creature Effects)

I've been friends with David DeCoteau for years and had always wanted to work with him. We always laughed at the notion of that, we were always so busy on different projects and thought that it would never happen. Then one day, David calls me out of the blue with "The Imp" and not only was I not busy at the time, but the whole idea sounded really fun because of the dark comedy aspect, so I jumped on it.

I was in charge of designing and creating the Imp puppet and also puppeteering him. There were a number of other effects that I helped out on, mostly a burn make up appliance and a fake head that was used for a bowling ball. Both David and I were very impressed the design of Audrey II [designed and created by Lyle Conway], the plant monster from *Little Shop of Horrors* [1986, Frank Oz], especially how well it's lips articulated when it spoke and sang. So I incorporated a little of that into the imp's mouth design. My other main inspiration came from a drawing done by the great Bernie Wrightson. It was a illustration of several goblins taunting a man beneath a bridge done in 1974. It was a piece Bernie had done for a coloring book and I'm not sure if it has a name. Creating the Imp puppet was done on an incredibly short schedule of two weeks

**"The Imp" and Craig Caton (Special Makeup and Creature Effects) (courtesy of Craig Caton).**

before David needed him for shooting in San Marcos, near San Diego. The imp was a hand puppet with a fully articulated head. His right hand was mechanized, the left had poseable fingers.

A lot of "The Imp" was filmed inside a real bowling alley and there was one scene where I had to crawl inside the bowling pin setter mechanism. I was a little nervous because if the machine had activated I would have been folded into a pretzel, but of course that didn't happen. There was another scene where I had to puppeteer the imp from the inside of a video arcade machine. I climbed inside with the puppet thinking this would be easy! Then they put in a 5K light to illuminate the video screen and things got very hot and cramped. You find yourself in some pretty ridiculous places when you are performing, and this was no exception.

Most of the filming was done at night on a extremely short schedule. David DeCoteau had made so many movies by this time, so we couldn't be in better hands. Hal Havins kept everyone in stitches in between takes and did a great mock on set interview with the Imp puppet.

## Andras Jones
### ("Calvin")

I remember when I auditioned I was very impressed because Jeffrey Combs was in the waiting room. I was a big fan from his role in *Re-Animator*. We ended up working together on *The Attic Expeditions* [2001, Jeremy Kasten] about ten years later but that day in the waiting room I was still new in Hollywood and it felt very cool to meet a movie star like Jeff.

I had a huge crush on Robin Stille [1961–1996], like the kind that's so strong it hurts. She was absolutely gorgeous and clearly out of my league, dating a very big shot performer from Las Vegas. I still get a hungry young feeling when I think of her. Probably will 'till I die. Can't tell if that makes me shallow or her special. Probably a healthy dose of both.

Hal Havins was funny. Talented. Great guy. I'm surprised he didn't have more of a career but then, who am I to talk? Hal is probably the person from the shoot I'd be most interested in speaking with, other than Robin. I bet he's had a really interesting life.

It felt like I had a rock and roll connection with Linnea Quigley. I spent most of the time when we weren't shooting writing songs on my guitar and, since Linnea was a musician too, that's mostly what we talked about. Least that's how I remember it. This will make no sense to most people but, as an actor, her way with a line kind of reminds me of Jerry Stiller. She plays off rhythm and I think this is going to make her an interesting actress well into her elder years.

Brinke Stevens and I didn't hang out much on the set but we've become better friends over the years at conventions, and through mutual friends like Rhonda Baughman (who's one of the biggest *Sorority Babes* fans I've met). Brinke is a deep and profound woman. "Taffy … pull…" has become a line people in my family like to shout out from time to time. It always gets a laugh.

I once had the good luck to attend a recording session with Pete Townshend and George Martin. I'm a huge Who fan and a huge Beatles fan, but Townshend got all my attention, although under almost any other circumstances I would have shadowed George Martin looking for any opportunity to connect and learn something, anything from the man who produced the Beatles. Similarly, if I could have torn my eyes away from Robin Stille, I probably would have been smitten with Michelle Bauer (equally out of my league). What a treat to be young and surrounded by such professional beauty.

"Sorority Babes" was one of Dave DeCoteau's first films and what's he made? Like three hundred pictures since then? Clearly, he's one of the gutter greats, and I speak from the vantage point of the gutter, so that's a kindred compliment. Beck had "two turntables and a microphone." U2 had "three chords and the truth." Dave DeCoteau has "no budget and a sense of humor." What an honor to be his first leading man.

We were in a post production recording session in a kind of low-rent area in Hollywood. Me and Hal Havins and John Wildman and the girls, recording dialogue that had been missed or insufficiently recorded, when we were informed by the film's producer that it would not be released as "The Imp" but as "Sorority Babes in the Slimeball Bowl-A-Rama." I remember one of the women (I think it was Carla Baron) saying, "But now no one's going to take this film seriously." That is still one of the funniest things I've ever heard.

## John Stuart Wildman
### ("Keith")

I had just finished *Deadly Weapon* [1987, Michael Miner] and was sent to David DeCoteau by Anthony Barnao who was the casting director at Empire Films. Anthony had become a big supporter during the audition process for *Deadly Weapon* as I wasn't an obvious casting choice for the leader of a high school gang and he was impressed (I guess) that I could pull it off. Ironically, I wasn't an obvious choice for the leader of a group of college nerds either, but fortunately I had a great meeting/audition with David and was signed on almost immediately afterward.

The budget was so low that we were speeding through and shooting 18 hour days to get the film made. There wasn't any room for subtleties and as one can see the film is shot for the most part using master shots with very few close ups, etc. Not a lot of nuance there or detailed work on performances. David was working hard just to complete the film with the money he had to make it, but that was also kind of his specialty already by that point.

The three guys (myself, Andras and Hal) were about as different from each other as we could possibly be, but we worked well together, they were fun to team up with and Andras struck me as being particularly smart too. Michelle Bauer could not have been nicer or more kind in how she dealt with everyone, especially me. She may have been the most mature behaving person there, kind of like the "set mom" and I remember in particular me being full of myself with actor's ego and her bringing me back down to earth (or at least trying to) and being nicer than she needed to as she did that. I also connected with Brinke Stevens on that shoot and we get in touch every few years or so.

"Sorority Babes" was a huge lesson to me as a young actor getting his footing in the business and learning what it was like to act for film and be on a set, etc. I find it hilarious that the film has such a cult popularity now—another big lesson in that you never know what is going to connect with people and gain fans or notoriety.

# *Terror Night*
## (1987, U.S.A.)

*Genre:* Horror; *Directors:* Nicholas M. DeMartino as "Nick Marino," Frederick J. Piantadosi as "Fred J. Lincoln" (uncredited) and André De Toth (uncredited); *Writers:* Nick Marino (Story), Murray Levy (Screenplay) & David Rigg (Screenplay) and Kenneth J. Hall (Screenplay); *Cinematographers:* R. Michael Stringer and Howard Wexler; *Cinematographer 2nd Unit:* John V. Fante; *Editor:* Art Luciani; *Special Visual Effects:* Mark Wolf; *Special Makeup Effects:* Cleve Hall and John Goodwin & Ron Wilson; *Special Effects:* Kevin McCarthy; *Producer:* Nicholas M. DeMartino as "Nick Marino"; *Co-Producer:* Nancy Paloian; *Executive Producer:* Barry Gottheimer; *Production Company:* Nick Marino Presents; *Cast:* Staci Greason (Kathy), William Butler (Chip), Ken Abraham (Greg), Carla Baron (Lorraine), John Stuart Wildman (Todd), Jimi Elwell (Angel), Michelle Bauer (Jo), Denise Stafford (Sherry), John Ireland (Lance Hayward), Cameron Mitchell (Detective Sanders), Alan Hale, Jr. (Jake Nelson), Aldo Ray (Capt. Ned) and Dan Haggerty (Ted Michaels)

A group of teens and a biker couple decide to spend the night in the abandoned mansion of a long-missing Hollywood actor (Lance Hayward). The villa of the silent movie star (presumed dead) is soon to be demolished. The young people are being slaughtered one by one. While the posters and pictures of the actor's old hits flow on the screen, the fake murders as represented in his films become true in the villa, with the same exact modalities.

## Murray Levy
### (Writer)

I'm a retired professor of Business at Glendale College in California where I taught Economics, Marketing and Finance for 25 years. I've written a play called "Dead Calm" that was produced (workshop for new playwrights) by the Academy of Arts and Science. Currently I have 15 short stories (horror, ghost, dark fiction, etc.) on a UK short fiction site [www.short-fiction.co.uk].

My background in film consists of running a film festival of classic films in New York in 1979. I left NYC in 1981 for a position in distribution with 20th Century¬–Fox. It was there I met some contacts including Nick Marino.

Before I taught I was a traffic reporter and Dave Rigg was a client. We went to lunch talking about writing ideas for films if we had the opportunity. We got the chance. Nick Marino gave us a story idea about an old film star [Lance Hayward] killing people in costumes from his old films. We wrote the original script, and Ken Hall re-wrote and polished.

They filmed the beginning of the movie on the remains of the old Errol Flynn mansion.

I met André De Toth at the beginning of production. He was a dapper old man with an foreign accent and an eye patch. I saw the first few scenes he directed, I thought we had a hit on our hands, with a real pro director, and five stars. Things went south as André De Toth had to leave because of health issues. They tried a new director, but he had women, and drug issues. Nick took over with no experience. I witnessed one scene with Aldo Ray [1926-1991], he was in a very bad way and needed any paycheck he could get. He was an alcoholic, and he lost his pants just before he was due on camera.

We had a major screening for distributors at Century City theater in L.A. in 1987. No one could pick up the film, they didn't get clearance for using the old film scenes [the old film footage accompanying the murders]. So we had legal problems. Nick just disappeared. The film was lost until a copy surfaced in Germany in the early 2000s. Then it went to DVD.

## Kenneth J. Hall
### (Writer)

*Terror Night* was a script brought to me by Nick Marino (a porn producer who was introduced to me by Dave DeCoteau) to rewrite and direct. I rewrote it as best I could, and cast the film. The original script was absurd. The killer was supposed to be a matinee idol similar to Errol Flynn who was popular in the 1930s. Only it was 50 years later so the guy would be in his 80s, if not older. He would not be running around killing people. In fact, he wouldn't be running at all. I recalled a fun B movie called *Castle of Evil* [1966, Francis D. Lyon] where a mad scientist had made a cyborg of himself to terrorize guests on his island. I came up with the idea that he [Lance Hayward] had invented some kind of bio-mechanical suit that enabled him to look and act young. This made the whole thing even sillier but I felt a crazy explanation was better than none at all. As I recall, they kept some element of that in the final film.

I clashed too much with Nick and resigned the film before shooting began. I was replaced with Fred Lincoln [1937-2013], an adult film director who had also acted in *The Last House on the Left*. Fred directed the majority of the picture but also had differences with Nick Marino. Some time later, André De Toth was brought in. He shot that ridiculous Shakespearean ending [Lance Hayward/Othello strangles Kathy/Desdemona] with John Ireland [1914-1922],which was not in my script or any of the previous drafts. Again, there were problems and André De Toth did not want his name used on the film. That's when Nick took the credit. To my knowledge, he never directed a single scene.

Nick had very unrealistic expectations for a film shot on such a short schedule and I did not want to be blamed for his inevitable disappointment. Apparently, he had similar problems with Fred Lincoln and André De Toth. Nick had only produced porn up to this point and this was to be his first "legitimate" feature, which explains his lack of perspective on low-budget filmmaking. I assume he had worked with Fred previously on his earlier adult stuff.

*Terror Night* went directly to home video but was screened at least once here in LA. The movie has been released recently on DVD as *Bloody Movie*, another pathetically generic title.

This project was not a pleasant experience for me or anyone else that worked on it. It remains the only film I ever worked on that I truly detest. However, some of the people involved are still friends after all these years. I originally cast Linnea Quigley in the film

Howard Wexler (Cinematographer #2), André De Toth (Director), John Ireland ("Lance Hayward") and Staci Greason ("Kathy"). In this scene, John Ireland plays scene 2 of act 5 of Shakespeare's "Othello" where Othello chokes Desdemona—Staci Greason wears a blonde wig. "It is the cause, it is the cause. My soul..." This scene was not included in the original script and was probably De Toth's idea. He was, at the time of *Terror Night*, trying to make "Thane" with Nick Marino and Sergei Hasenecz. "Thane" was a science fiction version of another Shakespeare play, "Macbeth." Perhaps the Shakespearian ending in *Terror Night* was a sort of "test" for "Thane," to be used as a teaser to raise money to make the film, which was never produced (photograph by Abe Perlstein; courtesy of Nick Marino).

but she quit when I did. Richard Gabai was an unknown at the time and was runner-up for William Butler's part. Billy was a good friend at the time (and still is) so I told Richard he wouldn't get this part but would keep him in mind for future projects. Shortly thereafter, I recommended him to Dave DeCoteau, who cast him as the male lead in *Nightmare Sisters* [1987, David DeCoteau]. This launched Richard's career as not only an actor but as an independent filmmaker in his own right. Staci Greason had done very little prior to being in this film. Later on, she had a long run on the popular soap opera *Days of Our Lives*. She has since retired from acting but is now a screenwriter and a novelist.

## R. Michael Stringer
(Cinematographer #1)

As a cinematographer for low budget and television projects I had the ability to shoot quality images quickly. What that means is, I could block and light the scene quickly. This is an attribute prized in low budget filmmaking. I was the original cinematographer on *Terror Night*. I worked with Nick Marino on this low budget film. I shot everything in the original script. When we were finished shooting the editors created a rough cut of the film and it was decided that some additional photography was required.

Fred Lincoln was the original director on *Terror Night*. Fred had an adult film history, and this film was a way for him to be taken seriously in the mainstream industry. Fred directed the movie and I seem to remember that he and Nick had creative differences. I'm not sure, but perhaps he lost his job the last few days of filming. During the primary shooting schedule André De Toth was an overseer or the man who kept us on track and gave us "Horror Movie" advice. At least that's how André was presented to me.

At the time one of the low budget tricks was to dig up out of work actors with a name in the industry and pay them for a day or two of work, which added production value to the film. Aldo Ray worked very hard the few days he was there and did a fine job. Alan Hale, Jr. [1921–1990], likewise came in on time, knew his lines and hit his marks. Dan Haggerty also did a great job because he has always been a good actor and consistently worked well with the cast.

Nick Marino was a businessman who understood the low budget filmmaking. There is an artistry in the process of producing low budget films, which differs from the artistry required to direct them.

In the 90s I returned to my roots as a lighting person. The last fifteen years of my career I worked as a key grip, which I found very rewarding. I think grip work is the best kept secret in the business. Becoming a Local 80 grip was the smartest move I made during my 44 years in the business. It was the first time in my career that I had medical insurance, and as I discovered later I had built up a modest pension. I retired from the business in 2012 and relocated to South Florida.

## Mark Wolf
### (Special Visual Effects)

My company, Wizard Works, was hired to produce a long shot of a key setting of the film. We shot one afternoon near the abandoned Errol Flynn estate, and added the hanging miniature to the actual location. The model was made by using carefully selected photo blow-ups of a girl's school where the production had been shooting; there was no money to fabricate a full three-dimensional miniature. To that basic configuration I added some dimensional elements such as miniature trees and then my art director, Kurt Zendler, applied a light airbrushed misting of white to simulate aerial perspective. The model was suspended into frame on a support rod disguised as a tree branch, to blend it into the scene. Some hand-held branches with leaves on them were placed near camera to increase the sense of perspective. This was by far the most economically-done effect I was ever involved with.

## John V. Fante
### (Cinematographer 2nd Unit)

*Terror Night* and *Death House* [1987, John Saxon] were Nick Marino's first feature films. I worked on *Terror Night* with André De Toth as the director on 2nd unit. Most of the film was shot on an abandoned, and ruined house in the Hollywood Hills.

Mark Wolf (Special Visual Effects) on location near the Errol Flynn estate, preparing to shoot a foreground miniature (courtesy of Mark Wolf).

The most memorable part for me was working with the old master, André De Toth. He wore an eye patch over one eye, but is remembered for one of the best 3D movies of the 1950s, *House of Wax*. He was a true gentleman in the European tradition. Soft spoken, impeccable manners and funny.

The night I worked with him he had an accident on the set. We were working in the Hollywood Hills in darkness and André stumbled and fell down, hitting his head on the large generator we were using for power. The impact cut his forehead and tore off his eye patch. He was nearly knocked out and in a very dazed state stumbled up to me bleeding profusely from his head wound. We tried to convince him to go to the hospital, but he refused and insisted that he continue working, which he did through the entire night. I believe it was the following day that André went to the hospital and the doctors discovered that he had fractured his neck. He recovered, but had to wear a halo brace around his neck as part of his rehabilitation for a number of weeks. He was in his 80s and behaved like a much younger man.

Nick Marino was skilled at finding actors in Hollywood who were, let us say, beyond their prime. I assume he took a director credit on the film because he felt that he had done that job, but I would guess also that André De Toth asked not to have his name on the film.

## Malcolm Marmorstein
### (André De Toth's Assistant Director)

[Author's note—Do you remember *Dead Men Don't Die*? Elliott Gould played the role of a TV journalist brought back to life with a voodoo ritual after he was killed by a gang of drug traffickers he was investigating. The idea for *Dead Men Don't Die* was born while

André De Toth was shooting *Terror Night*. I asked Malcolm Marmorstein about the story behind his 1989 zombie comedy, which was to be produced by Nick Marino.]

André De Toth was a very respected director who should not have worked on this project, but loved to pull rabbits out of hats. He asked me to assist him in the reshoot of this film, due to injuries he had suffered.

It is little known that André made one of the most important shots in motion picture history. David Lean asked André to direct the second unit of *Lawrence of Arabia*. André did it under a different name. David Lean wanted a shot of Omar Sharif coming across the desert. André and the cameraman went out on the desert with a camera and a 500mm lens. They shot what appears to be Omar Sharif astride a camel coming toward the lens. The heat of the desert made the images waver like a flame. It was a sensational shot and was copied by every director.

[Another story about André De Toth.] André, while on location in Hollywood, directing *House of Wax*, cast an actor named Charles Bukowski. Charles was not thrilled with his surname which did not sound very commercial and asked André for his opinion. André looked up at the street sign where they were shooting and christened the young actor in his strong Hungarian accent, "Your name is now Charles Bronson."

I had been writing with André De Toth on assignments in London, in the early 1970s, most notably for Albert "Cubby" Broccoli, though not on the Bond films. These were a Mafia and a caper script. Cubby was too busy with Bond and never made them. André and I remained friends. He lived in Switzerland.

On his return to Los Angeles in the eighties, André agreed to do someone a favor and

Cameron Mitchell ("Detective Sanders"), Andrè De Toth (Director) and Nick Marino (Writer/Director/Producer). André De Toth wears a halo brace for the neck fracture that occurred in an accident on set (photograph by Abe Perlstein; courtesy of Nick Marino).

took over the shooting of *Terror Night*. During the shooting, he fell and his activities were limited. He asked me to assist him on the set for the rest of the shoot to ease the pressure. Cameron Mitchell [1918–1994] was brought in by André. Cameron worked two nights. He did it because he owed money to bookies to cover some gambling debts. André convinced John Ireland to appear in the film by telling him he was shooting a version of "Othello." Ireland jumped at the opportunity, not knowing there were only a few scenes from Shakespeare.

It was during this time that André encouraged me to direct. He suggested I write a horror film in ten days, and Nick Marino, the producer of *Terror Night*, would produce it, with André backing me up. Fond of zombie films, I plunged in.

My background is a little different from most writers. My father was a theatrical electrician. As a child I was sort of raised backstage, seeing many shows. I acquired a union card. When I was twenty, I became an assistant electrician on the Broadway production of *A Streetcar Named Desire* with Marlon Brando and Karl Malden (Anthony Quinn later replaced Marlon). I worked on more than a dozen Broadway shows. I was also a stage manager on *A Thurber Carnival*, where I got to know James Thurber, who encouraged me to write.

I'd always been a fast writer, having written 82 episodes of the original *Dark Shadows* [1966–1971] and created the character of the vampire Barnabas Collins, recently played in the film version—awful film!—with Johnny Depp. I did not receive any credit whatsoever for my original creation of Barnabas Collins; nor did I receive a single penny for the use of the character—the producers refused to meet with me. [Speaking of vampires], I saw Bela Lugosi "in person" on stage in 1948 where he was performing in a cheesy summer stock production of *Dracula*. He was terrible … didn't seem to know his lines. Also, I live in the Hollywood Hills below the Hollywood sign. In the 40s/50s, Bela Lugosi lived in this area about a mile up Beachwood Canyon.

I wrote the script of *Dead Men Don't Die* in ten days. We began to pull the production together. I brought some financing in, but Nick failed to come up with his share of the money … or any money at all. Nick Marino was out, so one of my sons, Wayne Marmorstein, stepped in and pulled it together. Elliott Gould was cast. Elliott had appeared in two of my films, *S*P*Y*S* [1974, Irvin Kerschner] and *Whiffs* [1975, Ted Post]. However, I had known Elliott from Broadway. When I was a stage manager, I first met Elliott when he was a chorus boy auditioning for *Irma la Douce*. His rise to theatrical stardom was fast. We met occasionally during that period. Our friendship increased when we met on *Whiffs*. *S*P*Y*S* was shot in Europe and I was not there. Elliott is brilliant and was aware of every aspect of the production as we shot. He was also very supportive of his fellow actors. We are still in touch.

I have written a new zombie screenplay and will put it on the market shortly. Also … Disney is remaking *Pete's Dragon* [1977, Don Chaffey], the lovable monster musical I wrote for them. Robert Redford is starring. No one from the company has talked to me as yet. I shall have to wait to see what my credit will be.

## Howard Wexler
### (Cinematographer #2)

Nick Marino was a difficult person to get along with, but under the surface he was a pussycat. He looked the part of a New Jersey mafia person, and could have been, with a white Rolls Royce, pretty blond and plenty of cash. He did not know much about filmmaking, but was a quick learner.

I came to meet him in his cheap, moldy office on Sunset Blvd. near Wilcox, in the heart of Hollywood, and I was thrilled to meet John Saxon in the same office. Apparently Nick needed to finish some scenes for both *Terror Night* and *Death House*, and I was an up and coming DP and probably got the job because of my young naiveté, easy manner, and reputation for being fast. In his office, Nick was very proud of the posters of *Terror Night* and *Death House*, and he showed me the first copies of each, carefully unrolling them on a table in his cluttered office.

We shot *Terror Night* in an empty warehouse space, and it was a thrill to work with both André De Toth, John Ireland and Cameron Mitchell. These were some of the greats of the film world, and I was honored to work with them. André with his eye patch was an imposing figure, and he knew the film craft like no one else—f-stops, focus, depth of field, lens millimeters, and lighting. He respected me and what I brought to the set, even being the youngest person in the room. I think André was wearing a neck brace for the duration of the shot, having broken it in a recent fall. He could walk with aid, and sat in his chair ramrod straight. The shooting schedule was always changing, depending on the money, mood and health of André.

Another person on the set sometimes was Malcolm Marmonstein, who was helping André get back into the business. Mal was a successful writer of several Disney movies, and I eventually continued with Mal to work on his feature film.

One night we had to shoot Cameron Mitchell in a small house in West Los Angeles.

**André De Toth (Director) and John Ireland ("Lance Hayward") (photograph by Abe Perlstein; courtesy of Nick Marino).**

The crew was basically me and a camera assistant, but the NBA playoff finals were on the radio that evening. I loved the LA Lakers and especially the radio play by play announcer Chick Hearn, who brought the game alive on radio. I elected to arrive at set late, first time ever, and parked outside and listened to the play by play for as long as I could, and then was reprimanded by Mal when I finally rang the doorbell and arrived on the set. But that playoff game was so exciting I just could not pull away from the radio.

John Ireland had a long dramatic soliloquy that he worked hard at, and tension was on the set during that day. Ireland was a professional, although aging at the time. I remember we were shooting in a drafty open warehouse, and it was a challenge for all departments, and Ireland blew up a few times at the miscues and false starts, and the fog machine overdoing it. John Ireland was awesome to watch, and later on I shot a feature film for his son, John Ireland, Jr., called *Johnny Moran*. He was great to work with, and remembered talking with his dad about the *Terror Night* days.

Nick Marino gave himself co-director credit because he helped stage a few scenes, he was the producer and had final say over the credits, and always had a fascination with Hollywood. He did not have the patience with actors or the whole filmmaking process, and he could be a handful, but in spite of the fancy car, the gold necklaces and big rings, he was a nice man at heart. Many years later, he opened a Greek restaurant near Venice Blvd. and La Cienega, and I met him there on occasion, and his white Rolls was always parked prominently outside.

## Cleve Hall
### (Special Makeup Effects #1)

Fred Lincoln directed the entire movie except for the "Othello" scene, which was André De Toth. Fred was a great guy. I was brought on to do effects for a "family-rate" because my brother Ken Hall was directing. When he left, Nick Marino went to Fred Olen Ray and asked who he should get to do the effects. I guess he thought I would leave because Ken did. Fred asked who was originally doing them and Nick said I was. Fred told him, "You already have the best!"

Since we shot the film in a nunnery which did have nuns in it (we gave them a fake script), I recall having to be on our guard at times. When shooting the sex scene with Michelle Bauer [and Jimi Elwell] we had people stationed at each end of the hall to stall any nuns from coming by.

Nick was always ranting about one thing or other, once chewing out a PA for not getting white bread for sandwiches at 2nd meal. My favorite story is when Nick Marino and Fred Lincoln were in the production trailer at the Errol Flynn estate location—the night which everything that could go bad … did. You could hear yelling from inside. Eventually Fred stepped out and walked over to my trailer with the saddest look on his face. I asked him what's wrong. He said, "I just got a lesson in economy from Nick…"

The night of the Errol Flynn location shoot … I think I had four killings scheduled that night. Production manager Nancy Paloian told us we had to park our cars at the top of the hill for some stupid reason. They had no security up there. It turns out a group of transients come up that side of the hill and sleep up there at night. They pretty much broke into our cars and took everything not nailed down, which included a compound bow and arrows I bought for the shoot. We were not happy thinking a guy up there had a weapon and might shoot us any minute. When we found my assistant Johnnie Saiko's vehicle had been ransacked I told him and the rest of my crew to just go home. I felt bad they'd been robbed. The late Mark Williams stayed with me however and we got through the planned killings.

[In the original screenplay] there never was an actor intended to play Lance Hayward [the original ending was changed and replaced with the "Othello" scene]. In the original climax Lance Hayward, in his bio-suit, is unmasked and is revealed to be shriveled and deformed looking. This we did with a puppet head. Ken sculpted the Lance Hayward puppet head (I guess he felt he kind of owed me for leaving me to the sharks with little budget). I believe Bill Butler and Staci Greason lived in the original ending. Knowing Ken, he wouldn't kill Billy…. We LOVE him! All I remember about the [original] climax is that they [William Butler and Staci Greason] had a confrontation with Lance Hayward and I believe pulled some hose that caused his precious bodily fluids to leak out, and he died … I think. [In the original ending] it was a dummy and he [Lance Hayward] was dressed kind of like a knight, if I recall. The only part of the bio-suit we made was the hand they [William Butler and Staci Greason] find on the table. I think the hand was supposed to be a working prototype they found. That was actually a glove left over from *Masters of the Universe* [1986, Gary Goddard] that I added some tubes to and operated from under the table. Quick and dirty man! I believe they [William Butler and Staci Greason] find the hand searching the place near the end. Bill touches it and it grabs his wrist very tight. When they were doing the new footage [the scene with Cameron Mitchell and the "Othello" scene] Nancy Paloian called me and asked what I'd charge for the effects. I told her $10,000 for one night. That's the last I heard from her.

## John Goodwin
### (Special Makeup Effects #2)

Ron Wilson and I worked only two days on *Terror Night*. At the climax someone was supposed to pull off part of John Ireland's face to reveal he is an android underneath. What was designed to be a larger effect on John Ireland turned into what we were able to get on him: a false cheek appliance that when pulled off revealed an aluminum surface underneath. But John Ireland didn't want to shave off his beard, and really didn't want to do the makeup gag at all—and the director André De Toth was one of these guys that just let the actors have their way and let the DP do all of the decisions on what to shoot and cover. So they spent all their time letting John Ireland do Shakespeare and strangle the girl [Staci Greason]. It's hard to tell but I think John Ireland has the cheek piece in that scene…. The picket fence impalement in *Terror Night* [William Butler is thrown out the window by Lance Hayward and ends up impaled on a fence] was also shot that day (and maybe a few other things I can't remember). I remember Ron had to do the picket fence impalement while I was making up John Ireland and came back to me laughing that the so called deadly picket fence was only a foot high!!!

# Ken Abraham
## ("Greg")

Nick Marino was a hot head and had a temper, though I don't recall him ever yelling at me. He had a huge white Rolls Royce that like his temper tended to intimidate people. I remember two things during my audition with Nick Marino. One was that I recall a young woman (perhaps his assistant, I don't know) going through a pile of actors' headshots. She held one up and said the actor looked handsome. Marino took the picture and said, "You like this guy?" His assistant said yes and then Nick tore it up, "Then he's never going to fucking work in this town!!!" It struck me as very funny. Another incident was during an audition I had with him. I think he was reading me for the film *Death House*. I'm not too sure. I just remember auditioning and Nick was reading the script opposite me. When it got to the part in the script where his character yells, Nick Marino screamed like a lunatic and with one clean swipe of the arm cleared all the contents of his desk onto the floor. It was nuts.

A lot of the film was shot up in the Hollywood Hills in what used to be the Errol Flynn estate. One night while filming a ton of effects stuff was stolen from the special effects crew's vehicle. It's my understanding that they were supposed to have a bunch of cool effects stuff for my death scene (and other scenes, for that matter), but in the end it all boiled down to them simply saying, "Here hold this arrow against yourself and pretend to die."

Another memory I have from the film was my bathtub scene with Denise Stafford. This girl could not have been cuter nor appeared more innocent. I was smitten. Beyond smitten. In fact, I felt the poor girl was being exploited when they had her naked in the bathtub. That's why I seem so reserved in the scene; I was worried about her. It wasn't until well after production had ended that I found out she was a famous porn star named Jamie Summers aka "The Brat." I was so naive. During the time of filming *Terror Night* I had a girlfriend that was tiny and blond like Denise, and one evening when Denise wasn't available for shooting my girlfriend stepped in as a replacement for the long-distance wide shots of us walking to the mansion.

Alan Hale, Jr., played the Skipper on a TV show I grew up with called *Gilligan's Island*. I mean I grew up watching this guy. It was thrilling to be on the same set as him, and when I approached him and told him so he turned and said to me in this big, gentle, kind fatherly-voice, "Well young man, that's the KINDEST thing anyone could say to me." I just melted in an "aw shucks" kind of way. I wanted to ask, "Can you call me 'little buddy'?" like he always referred to Gilligan on the show but I was too shy. What a nice man. And tall. He towered over me.

I also hung out in Aldo Ray's trailer. He was extremely talkative and personable. It seemed as if he had been drinking, but who knows. He had the distinction at the time of being the only SAG member thrown out of the guild for appearing in non-union movies. A scary thing. When I asked him about it he went off on a tangent and called Patty Duke a cunt. It was a little shocking to hear that freely flying out of his mouth, but quite funny. He also stated that "Chuck got me back in." Patty Duke was the then SAG president that had thrown him out and it didn't occur to me until years later that he was referring to Charlton Heston when he said "Chuck got me back in." Charlton Heston had become a later SAG president after Patty Duke. What a hoot.

## John Stuart Wildman
### ("Todd")

Of the four films I did that year, two were really from "cold" auditions [*Deadly Weapon* and *Lethal Pursuit*] and the other two [*Sorority Babes in the Slimeball Bowl-O-Rama* and *Terror Night*] were really off of recommendations based on my work in previous films.

Kenneth Hall was supposed to direct *Terror Night* and then Fred Lincoln came on to replace him and then after we completed filming, André De Toth was resurrected from the dead to do some rewriting/reshoots which basically re-imagined the entire film. So, Nick Marino never actually directed the film, I'm sure it was just easier for Nick to take credit for it all. They could have easily credited "Alan Smithee" as the director.

I think, for the most part, the film was shot in a house in the Mid/Central Los Angeles (the Melrose/Pico area), the old ruins of the Errol Flynn estate in the Hollywood Hills and a convent (I kid you not) closer to the downtown LA area.

Meeting Aldo Ray and Alan Hale, Jr., was the biggest kick and the best part of doing that movie. Of course, I only actually did a scene with Aldo Ray and then met Alan Hale, Jr., in makeup. Dan Haggerty wasn't shooting while I was around and John Ireland and Cameron Mitchell were added on with the André De Toth silliness (long after I was gone).

Fred was great to work with. The funny thing was that I had no idea of his background while we were working with him and I actually recommended him for another film I auditioned for (*Teen Witch*) while we were filming *Terror Night*. Hilarious to look back on that now, but I'm sure that contributed to me not getting that part...

*Terror Night* was almost cliché in how wrongheaded, ridiculous and silly making a film can be and how inept and "wrong" people making films can be—on almost every level. You could call the final result entertainingly bad, but you would probably be either very generous or just related to someone in the cast or production if you made that assessment.

## Jimi Elwell
### ("Angel")

I moved to LA in 1985 after finishing school at University of Wisconsin, intent on being a director. I joined a theatre company to study acting to help my directing. I enjoyed the acting and started auditioning for film roles. AIP [David Winters, David A. Prior and Peter Yuval's company] hired me for a couple of small roles [*Deadly Prey/Death Chase*]. In the meantime I was auditioning like crazy. One of my mates from the theatre, Whitefire Theatre in Sherman Oaks, was Luke Perry. We were doing a play at Powerhouse Theatre, in Santa Monica, when we both went to a "Cattle Call" for a new soap opera starting named *Loving*. We both made it to the final four actors and after the choice was made, Luke got the role. The casting director offered me the part if I would join him on the "couch." I turned him down. I never asked Luke what he did, but he got the part, hmmmm. He obviously went on to *Beverly Hills 90210*. I always wondered how much mouthwash it would cost for fame.

Freddy Lincoln directed most of *Terror Night*. We shot most of the film in a nunnery in the Hollywood Hills. The cast I worked with were great. We had a good time together.

I ended up becoming friends with Bill Butler and Ken Abraham, after the shoot. I played a biker with Michelle Bauer as my girlfriend. I remembered her as a Penthouse Playmate of the Year in the early 80s. She also went by the name of "Pia Snow" and starred in one of the greatest sex/cult film, *Cafe Flesh* [1982, Stephen Sayadian]. We had a nude sex scene shot at the nunnery as the nuns were hanging out in the hallway wondering what was going on inside the room. I remember she was sitting on my face and then sliding down to my crotch. After the second or third take, I looked down at my chest and seeing a trail of female juice, I said to her, "Nice Snail Trail, you're having fun!" She said, "It's just animal, baby!" Ha ha! It was quite surreal!

After we finished our sex scene Freddy offered me work in the porn biz. Compliment, I guess. Several years later I ended up working in the porn biz, behind the camera, to pay bills (1990–2000). I ran into Freddy, in 1991 at a porn awards show, and we ended up working together for several years. I was his video tech and editor. We became good friends. That guy sure had some awesome stories!

*Terror Night* was a great experience and I'm proud of it. I started hanging with a rough crowd (Guns n' Roses) and dropped out for a few years. Started back up in 1996 and started getting lead roles in independent films, and voice-over. Voice-over became my money maker. I met a great chick from Australia and moved here in 2000. I'm doing theatre and doing music videos in Sydney now. Also, playing a shit load of ice hockey!

# *Time Walker*
## (1982, U.S.A.)

*Genre:* Horror; *Directors:* Tom Kennedy and Skip Schoolnik (uncredited); *Writers:* Jason Williams (Story), Tom Friedman (Story and Screenplay) and Karen Levitt (Screenplay); *Cinematographer:* Robbie Greenberg; *Editors:* Tom Kennedy (uncredited) and Skip Schoolnik (uncredited); *Special Makeup Effects:* Robert Short; *Visual Effects (Transformation Sequence):* New World FX; *Producers:* Jason Williams and Dimitri Villard; *Executive Producers:* Roger Corman and Robert A. Shaheen; *Production Company:* Byzantine Productions; *Cast:* Ben Murphy (Prof. Douglas McCadden), Nina Axelrod (Susie Fuller), Kevin Brophy (Peter Sharpe), James Karen (Dr. Wendell Rossmore), Robert Random (Jack Parker), Sam Chew, Jr. (Dr. Bruce Serrano), Melissa Prophet (Jennie), Austin Stoker (Dr. Ken Melrose), Gerard Prendergast (Greg Hauser), Shari Belafonte (Linda Flores) and Jack Olson (Ankh Venharis).

A mummy (Ankh Venharis), recovered by a Californian University professor during the exploration of Tutankhamen's tomb, is transported to the university's lab. The mummy turns out to be an alien who comes back to life and starts looking for some crystals that were stolen from him by a student. The mummy needs the crystals to activate an interplanetary transportation device by which he will finally return to his planet. The mummy spreads terror inside the campus trying to find all the crystals, which are each in the hands of a different student.

## Dimitri Villard
### (Producer)

Roger Corman, who co-financed the film and distributed it in the United States, told me, "You will learn 99% of everything you will ever know about filmmaking on your first film"—and that was certainly true. Everything that could go wrong happened, from harassment by the Teamsters Union—because we couldn't afford to hire them—to problems with the director who had never directed anything before. I learned a lot.

*Time Walker* is very similar in story to *Super 8* [2011, J.J. Abrams]. The alien in both movies is collecting jewels/tiles which need to be all together in order to beam him home. In both cases the alien ends up terrorizing kids to collect these things. Coincidence? I prefer to think of it as an "homage"...

## Tom Friedman
### (Writer)

My specialty was in the creation of audio-visual marketing materials for movies: trailers, featurettes, behind-the-scenes documentaries, TV and radio ads for movies. I travelled from Hollywood to New York to do a "featurette," a short promotional documentary on the making of *The Sunshine Boys* and on the lead actors, George Burns and Walter Matthau [*The Sunshine Boys*, 1975]. I interviewed them both on camera, along with Richard Benjamin, and, probably, Herb Ross [director], Ray Stark [producer] and several other cast members. Back in Hollywood I oversaw the editing and finishing of the featurette under the direction of my boss, Andy Kuehn [1937–2004] of Kaleidoscope Films (where I worked from 1970 to 1977 as head writer-producer). I worked on many other ad campaigns and featurettes, the high point of which was probably spending a month in England with Stanley Kubrick during the making of *Barry Lyndon* (1976, I believe).

I wrote *Flush* [1976], and was an associate producer. The film was directed by Andy Kuehn of Kaleidoscope, where the film was edited, and where the trailer was created. I wrote at least one more screenplay for Kaleidoscope, a version of "The Wonderful Wizard of Oz," that was not produced. Shortly after that, in 1977, I left Kaleidoscope and began my independent career in trailer and film production, through my company, Euphoria Productions.

While I was still at Kaleidoscope we took as clients Bill Osco and Jason Williams. Osco and Williams were successful porn producers who had made a cross-over to legitimate films with *Flesh Gordon* [1972, Howard Ziehm and Michael Benveniste], starring Jason Williams as Flesh, and produced by Williams and Osco. Williams was the line producer, while Osco handled financing and distribution. *Flesh Gordon* was made as a hard-core porno, but was released as a soft-core adult film; it did very well. After *Flesh Gordon* came *Alice in Wonderland* [1976], a film produced by Osco and Williams through Kaleidoscope. I became involved in the marketing of *Alice*, another film that was shot as a hard-core but released as soft-core. *Alice* also did quite well, and starred Kristine DeBell, a sweet and lovely young Alice who later was featured in a *Playboy* spread shot by Helmut Newton. While working for Kaleidoscope I wrote a feature for Osco, "The Training of Tricia." I named the lead character after one of President Richard Nixon's daughters because I despised Nixon, whose presidency I felt was truly pornographic. The movie was never made. After I left Kaleidoscope I wrote another script for Osco and Williams, "Flesh Gordon on the Pyramid Planet." Reflecting the times, the Pyramid Planet was actually a planet-sized crystal of cocaine. The movie was never made.

At some point Bill Osco and Jason Williams parted company, and Jason and I worked together on several films that actually were produced, first *Time Walker*, and then *Danger Zone* [1986, Henry Vernon], *Vampire at Midnight* [1987, Gregory McClatchy] and *Danger Zone 2* [1989, Geoffrey G. Bowers]. Jason went on without me to make *Danger Zone 3* and *Danger Zone 4*, both of which had some original footage but made extensive re-use of footage from *DZ 1* and *DZ 2*. Jason was not a great artist, but he was a very clever and resourceful producer, bursting with marketable ideas.

Jason came to me with an idea for a movie he called something like "The Mummy from King Tut's Tomb." I came up with the title "Time Walker." I sometimes got jobs renaming feature films; for example, I changed the name "Die Hard: Simon Says" to "Die Hard: With a Vengeance" for Fox. I think "Time Walker" was one of my best titles.

Jason and I wrote the story together, and then I wrote the screenplay. As we headed toward production through New World Pictures (a deal arranged by Jason and Dimitri Villard), I got very busy with my independent trailer business. Two weeks before the start of production Roger Corman wanted changes to the script. Because I didn't have time, I hired one of my copywriters, Karen Levitt, to do a polish on the script. Levitt and I were girlfriend and boyfriend at the time and were living together—or perhaps we had already broken up (I can't remember). Levitt spent two weeks on the project polish along with me, for which she wanted equal credit. Though I later felt that was an unreasonable request, at the time I felt pressured and agreed. I can say her input was useful but minimal, but she is credited as co-writer of *Time Walker*.

One thing I remember about my creation of the script for *Time Walker* that I thought was a clever in-joke at the time but now think is childish, is that I decided to name as many characters as possible after streets in Hollywood where I lived: McCadden, Fuller, Rossmore, Serrano, Hauser, Hayworth, Plummer, Willoughby, Melrose.

I think the budget was about $500,000. I assume New World was involved in securing financing. We went to New World with a completed script and an original teaser trailer Jason and I created. (I believe New World committed because of the teaser trailer as well as the script.) They agreed to distribute the film before it was made, but had very little to do with script or production. The teaser, which I think was Jason's idea, was very simple but effective. We found a place in Hollywood's Griffith Park, where a park bench was placed with a concrete walking path behind it. We got one of Jason's childhood friends, Jack [Jack Olson], a very tall, big school teacher, to play a mummy with an alien face. We bought a $15 mask on Hollywood Blvd., and we bought several rolls of Ace Bandages, stretch material for protecting sprained wrists and ankles. We wrapped Jack in ace bandages. We hired an actress to sit on the park bench. We put Jack on a skateboard off-camera, and pushed him across the scene behind the girl on the bench. Because we couldn't see the board or the bottom of the mummy, it looked like this creature was floating across the scene. He floated past her and off-camera to the right. Then, a beat later, he floated half-way back, until he was behind the girl. He stopped and reached toward her ... and we cut to title: "*Time Walker* ... Nothing can stop him, not even time." That got us into Roger Corman and got the movie made.

The movie was shot entirely in Los Angeles. The university at which the story was set was UCLA, LA's great research institution, but the film was actually shot at California State University Los Angeles (Cal State LA), just to the east of downtown LA. We shot at night and on weekends. I don't remember where the other locations were, but all were in LA, and probably Hollywood.

Shari Belafonte, who I think was then Shari Belafonte-Harper, was the daughter of the great calypso singer Harry Belafonte, and was married to Bob Harper, then head of advertising at Fox and one of my clients. Don LaFontaine, who played a reporter, was one of my first mentors in Hollywood, along with Andy Kuehn. Don became the most famous and successful narrator of trailers in Hollywood, credited with creating the line leading into half the trailers produced, "In a world where..." Ben Murphy had a TV career (*Alias Smith & Jones*).

I was told *Time Walker* was one of the most successful independent feature films of its time, grossing either 2.3 million dollars or 3.2 million (I forget which). Of course, independent films have since done far better, but at the time I believe it was a minor hit. Though I don't recall making any money from it, maybe $5,000, I assume its success gave us credibility when we started raising money (which we did ourselves) for *The Danger Zone* movies and *Vampire at Midnight*. Perhaps *Time Walker* got us in the door at Skouras Pictures, the distributor of those three movies. Tom Skouras was also my client for trailers (I produced several trailers for his film pickups from overseas).

I personally was not happy with the "To Be Continued?" title at the end [of *Time Walker*]. I thought it was presumptuous and was asking for trouble; and I believe I recall that when the title came on during a screening before a paid audience the response was cries of "Nooo!" along with hisses and boos. That's probably why we did not proceed with a sequel. I felt the ambiguous ending [once the intergalactic transportation device is reactivated, Prof. Douglas McCadden disappears, dematerializing with the alien] was perfect, as it would propel the imaginations of the audience (and the writer, for sure) beyond that room where the final events unfolded and out across space and time. I already had a title in mind for the sequel: "McCadden on Mars," though I was not necessarily expecting to set the action on Mars—I think our Time Walker came from farther away than that. As to why we did not make another *Time Walker*, I also recall that I received just half of my contracted writer's fee. Perhaps Jason Williams was similarly short-changed, which might have also discouraged us from proceeding.

I remember that *E.T.* was released the same year as *Time Walker*, and I was dismayed because I thought people would think our story was ripped off from *E.T. The Extra-Terrestrial* (the two films had some similarities—alien lost on earth, trying to get back home). This was not true. *Time Walker* was written before *E.T.* was released and before I knew anything about *E.T.* It was an original story.

I remember thinking the movie was not very well-executed. I thought the script was pretty good (of course—I wrote it!) but the production was not as good as the script. This was Tom Kennedy's [1948-2011] first feature, maybe his first directing job. I don't know if he ever directed another feature, though he remained a well-respected trailer editor. I think he rose up to head one of the trailer departments at one of the studios, maybe MGM. Jason Williams, as I said above, has many good ideas and is far better able to line-produce a movie far I can, but his taste is not very refined, and he isn't a writer. Any time I would want to make a change or put in something he didn't like he would exclaim, "You're stupid! We're not doing that!" I very rarely see or speak to Jason any longer; I haven't had much to do with him since I moved 70 miles out of Hollywood about 17 years ago (1996). I wouldn't be surprised if he's produced many more movies. I did appear in two of his little direct-to-video soft-core exploitation films, *Malibu Bikini Weekend* [1995] and *Nude Bowling* [1995]. I got the acting jobs because I own a tuxedo. In Malibu I played a butler and had such lines as "Is madame aware that she is naked?"

I have always been much more attracted to character, nudity and sensuality in movies than to action, violence or paranoid plot-turns. I'm bored by hard-core sex scenes, which I find about as exciting as watching the pistons of an engine move in and out. However, I've always liked women-in-jeopardy scenes, especially if they feature generous amounts of naked flesh and don't get too explicit in the violence. The two *Danger Zone* films and *Vampire at Midnight* were designed and written to provide just that kind of cheap adolescent titillation. Unfortunately (by my standards), Jason went through a religious conversion (I would call it being "born again"—I don't know how he characterizes it) during the production of *Danger Zone*. Suddenly, the plot was stripped of its explicit erotic content, and the girls, who were supposed to be stripped, ending up keeping on all their clothes. The resulting $300,000 film was pointless, thrill-less, lame and ludicrous—and it did quite well

(I know, I was one of the investors, a limited partner as well as a general partner). The limited partners from *Danger Zone* decided to roll their earnings back into a second movie, *Vampire at Midnight*. The movie was more expensive (about $500,000) and better, and did worse than *Danger Zone*. We found ourselves in the not-uncommon position in Hollywood where we had to deliver a third movie to Skouras in order to get what was owed from the second movie. We did a third movie, D*anger Zone 2—Reaper's Revenge*. The movie was yet more expensive (about $700,000), was of the best quality yet, and did the worst. By that time I had lost all my money and my desire to play this game. As I said, Jason continued doing feature films. I wrote and produced a documentary on Martin Luther King, a documentary on jazz of the 1940s and a documentary on storytelling.

One of the reason for the downward trajectory of our films in the mid–1980s was the change in the home video business. In its early days there was a market for almost anything that could be produced. That was true during the days of *Time Walker* and of *Danger Zone*. By the late 80s, the time of *Danger Zone 2*, if your movies were not star-driven, and therefore much more expensive, they had very little chance of succeeding. Also, with regard to the financial outcome of *Time Walker* for me, in the very early 80s home video was still quite a new business. I believe we had nothing about home video in our contracts, and I'm not sure *Time Walker* was even released on video until some time later. I certainly never saw income from video, and have never received anything like a residual check for any of my movies. That's one thing about Hollywood accounting: they can always demonstrate that a movie has lost money and nothing is owed.

It's been a few years since I've seen *Time Walker*. I saw it once in the version created for *Mystery Science Theater 3000* [MST3K]. The result was horrifying. The specific purpose of that version was to make fun of the movie and belittle it. A couple of years later I showed the original version to my high school video class. The students liked it and I didn't find it as terrible as I thought I would.

## Skip Schoolnik
### (Director/Editor)

Mark Allan, the production manager on *Time Walker*, was a friend. He called to ask if I could help them out, and I agreed. The picture was in trouble. If memory serves, the picture wasn't at all scary, nor particularly creepy, and didn't make a whole lot of sense.

I recut and directed new scenes. My involvement was late in the process, and, I think, helped to clarify and give it a sense of heightened suspense. In the end, I don't know how successful I was, but the producers seemed to think I made a difference. I worked on a number of Dimitri Villard's pics after *Time Walker* [*Hide and Go Shriek*, 1988, for one].

## Robert Short
### (Special Makeup Effects)

I designed and built the Mummy and Alien make-up for *Time Walker*. My assignment was to create an alien head that would fit under a mummy mask that could be removed.

The alien design was based on a Constantin Brancusi sculpture that the director liked, which had a teardrop-shaped head and very large eyes. Without knowing it at the time, this was the first film iteration of an alien design that would eventually become popularly known as standard "Greys" which allegedly abduct people. Looking back on the assignment, perhaps the Brancusi sculpture itself was somehow connected to tales of alien abduction—in any case it is an interesting coincidence. I sculpted the alien head in a couple of days along with the base shape of the mummy head which was then wrapped in bandages. The sequence went smoothly and was shot in one night at a college just on the outskirts of downtown Los Angeles.

## Julia Gibson
### (Visual Effects—New World FX)

New World FX, a subsidiary of Roger Corman's New World Pictures, was put together in 1978 or 1979 by Corman and his production team in order to produce visual effects for *Battle Beyond the Stars*, an outer space epic modeled after *Star Wars*. The studio was in a warehouse in Venice, California, a couple of blocks from the ocean. We who worked there rarely got to see the ocean, as we put in long hours in the black rooms that were the motion control stages and animation departments. Though Corman's intention for New World FX was to provide visual effects services for films produced by his company, other jobs came through the effects studio as well.

My first job with New World was in the Brentwood office as legal assistant to the executive vice president, Barbara Boyle. I loved working for Barbara, who is an extraordinary woman, but I had an animation background and longed to work with cameras and models, so when I was offered an opportunity to learn to operate the Elicon motion control system that Corman had purchased for miniature photography on *Battle Beyond the Stars*, I took it. My first job at New World FX was on *Escape from New York*, which wasn't a Corman movie. For that movie I was an assistant motion control operator working with the estimable Ken Jones. I ended up working at New World FX on and off for several years. I did rotoscoping art and camera, worked on special lighting effects, did some stop-motion animation, and then moved into production management, coordinating the various visual effects departments: roto, animation, models, miniature photography, opticals, etc.

I worked on a number of projects with many other talented and skilled effects artists. The famed Skotak brothers (Robert and Dennis) worked there, and so did James Cameron, who later became a successful feature director. I met Aaron Lipstadt there, who is now my life partner. He directed his debut feature *Android* [1981] at the New World studio and went on to a career producing and directing television. The atmosphere at New World was, for the most part, convivial and cooperative. Some of us were new to the industry when we started there and others, like the Skotaks and Cameron, had experience with filmmaking and were visual effects scholars and adepts. The more experienced crew people were incredibly patient and generous with those, like myself, who were green.

*Time Walker* was a relatively straightforward job. The client wanted a transformation effect [for the movie's final scene where the mummy/alien activates the intergalactic transport system and returns to his planet]. There was very little money or time, so it had to be done simply and quickly with minimum R&D or design time built in. The sequence was rotoscoped on an animation stand and artwork was created on cells for the glow. The animation cells were shot on 35mm black and white film. Color tests were shot to determine the color treatment for the effect. The compositing was done on an optical printer. The studio didn't have an optical department, so opticals were farmed out. Most likely various tests were shown to the client before the final compositing was attempted.

Roger is a highly creative individual who is both bold and thrifty. He is legendary for offering people opportunities to work on movies in capacities that could have taken them decades to achieve in the major studio system (or at a traditional effects house). I had many opportunities to discuss various aspects of production with Roger and found him logical, decisive, and willing to consider unconventional approaches. He usually prioritized budget over other considerations. "Quick and dirty" was the catchphrase that many of us used who worked with Roger. The time I spent at New World FX was extraordinary. I learned a lot about filmmaking and art and design and various visual effects techniques (some of them archaic even then), about creative discipline, about working as a team. I met incredible people that I worked with many times over the years on much bigger movies than Roger liked to make. I feel privileged and fortunate to have been given the opportunity to learn about effects work in such a stimulating milieu.

## Steven B. Caldwell
### (Visual Effects—New World FX)

Julia Gibson and I at this time ran New World FX. January Nordman designed the effect for the mummy transformation. Julia and I basically oversaw and helped with the shooting of live-action plates and were hands on through the whole project from beginning to end. The effect was very old school with cell animation, and if I recall correctly the effect was created on the animation stand—the animation stand is where we shoot extra footage of the live-action and hold some latent which means we only develop enough of the film to do line up on the animation stand for creating the animation cells for creating the effect. For the wide shots you will notice the camera doesn't move during the mummy/alien transformation: that is what we call a lock-off where we had a special camera, actually one of the cameras they used for filming the first atomic blasts—they were great cameras that were pin registered, which means that every frame of film is pushed into pins in the camera gate and locked in place so every frame of film is exactly the same, so we can do our animation and it won't move against the original live-action back ground plate. Then, after animation is complete we get the un-developed latent film and re-expose it with the animation and create a wedge where we adjust exposure one frame at a time and develop that. We then look at our wedge and pick exposures for all the elements used in the effect. Once picked we shoot the complete animation one frame at a time until end of shot and send that to the lab for developing. The next day we get to look at the dailies and keep our fingers crossed that it looks good and if not we make adjustments and shoot it again until we get correct.

## January Nordman
(Visual Effects—New World FX)

We worked on whatever Roger Corman had in the pipeline, often multiple productions at the same time. The effects in many of Roger Corman's pickup movies were afterthoughts, done in a frenzy in a short post-production schedule. The main inspiration [for the alien's dematerialization at the end of the film] was the robot transformation in *Metropolis* (still one of my favorite movies), without the time or budget to realize it—that makes for stress in the best of times.

# *Transformations*
## (1987, U.S.A.)

*Genre:* Horror; *Director:* Jay Kamen; *Writer:* Mitch Brian; *Cinematographer:* Sergio Salvati; *Editor:* Victoria Martin; *Special Makeup and Creature Effects:* Mechanical and Makeup Imageries, Inc.; *Producer:* Bob Wynn; *Executive Producer:* Charles Band; *Production Company:* Empire Pictures; *Cast:* Rex Smith (Wolfgang Shadduck), Lisa Langlois (Miranda), Patrick Macnee (Father Christopher), Christopher Neame (Calihan), Michael Hennessy (Stephens), Cec Verrell (Antonia), Benito Stefanelli (Vapes), Donald Hodson (Kane) and Pamela Prati (Woman Succubus)

While traveling in space, an astronaut has a sexual intercourse with a monstrous creature that suddenly appears in the form of a beautiful woman. The disappearance of the woman, immediately after the act, convinces the astronaut that it was only a dream. Forced by a mechanical problem to land on a space penal colony, the man is involved in the escape of a group of convicts, but the monster now is inside him.

## Mitch Brian
## (Writer)

[Author's note—I asked Mitch Brian to continue his story after *Transformations* right up to the unproduced screenplay "The Bloodsight" that could have been his debut as director.]

The job came to me through my agent at the time. It was very straightforward. I think they were paying 7,500 dollars for a script in those days. I was given a title, poster and copy of the blueprints of the sets for *Robot Jox* [1986, Stuart Gordon] which had to be used for the film! Then I was given 2 weeks to write the first draft! I saw the poster, which had the title line something like "The Nightmares inside Carl Rattner are coming out." It was this illustration with a guy sitting in a chair with different parts of his body looking like animal parts. I think my first question was "Does he have to be named Carl Rattner?" I was given the blueprints from *Robot Jox* and started working with those sets in mind. I may have seen a few photographs as well.

I didn't get to go to Italy, where the film was shot. I would have loved to go but the budget was so small that only the director would go. There was a Los Angeles casting director and the key make up and effects designers were from LA but all the labor was Italian.

I worked with a director named Jay Kamen who said I should call him "Uncle Jay." He was an editor and had worked on a lot of films. I don't know if he saw this as a break or just a job. I was naïve. *Transformations* was my first Hollywood job [Mitch Brian had previously co-written *Night Screams*, an indie slasher film shot in Kansas in 1986]. It was all very fast and I was inexperienced and so I don't know how good it really was. That said, I was committed to being a screenwriter and had already written four or five scripts that hadn't sold, so, for me I was hoping this might lead to bigger things.

AIDS was in the news and I was interested in trying to drill that age-old fear of sex leading to disease but do it in a science fiction horror way. I ran with the concept of the succubus in space. I was interested in the idea of a prison planet and somebody getting stranded there. I'm sure I was influenced by *Alien* and *Escape from New York*. And the idea that ancient evil exists off world was there too. So it was pulp horror and sci-fi. No doubt it was all too ambitious and few ideas, a smaller scale, fewer characters would have helped. That said, I'm not sure I got all that much help with the script development. I remember being told my dialogue was too conciliatory and the notes were usually very much along those lines—not be structure notes. They wanted it fast not good.

I know much of the film was rewritten in Italy and, as I said, I probably had these grand ideas and didn't really understand what my restrictions were in terms of budget, character, etc. I would have loved to have been there—would have loved to meet Patrick Macnee [1922–2015] who I admire very much. But I was only the writer.

Of course, just after the script was delivered and the director went off to shoot it (it may even have been while he was shooting) Empire Pictures went bankrupt. I remember hearing stories about how officials were going into the office and locking everyone out, taking artwork, seizing assets to pay the debts. I also heard another version where company people were going in the night before bankruptcy and getting valuables out before the bankruptcy happened. Not sure which is true. This is why it took years for the movie to ever be seen. I never saw a frame of footage for years. When all the bankruptcy was sorted out I guess they tried to release whatever they had to video. There were some other movies caught in this same limbo. I know they bought all the outer space and spaceship footage from another company (or maybe reused stuff from another film). They didn't do it for *Transformations* because the company went bankrupt before that stuff could be filmed. I think the score may also have been lifted from another movie. The film went straight to video here in the USA. I don't think it was even much of a video release.

I recently watched the film again with some friends who are aficionados of bad movies and we all came away with the same feeling. It was boring. Just plain dull.

I think the director was way in over his head. Had he wanted to play the film as "camp" that would have been totally understandable. But I don't think he had a knack for that. I have written three camp plays ("Maul of the Dead," "Sorority House of the Dead" and "The Tempermental Artist: or A Bucket of Blood," all published by Dramatic Publishing) and I understand the allure and power and fun of camp. But the movie neither steers into its limitations and embraces the campiness nor works as a "serious" genre piece.

Is most of the dreadful dialogue mine? Absolutely. That said, the action scenes that should have played out between the bad dialogue scenes are compromised if not simply missing. The director should have had the good sense to ditch the dialogue in favor of more visual storytelling, because the plot was sound enough (though admittedly tropey).

Sadly, the default in bad low budget movie making is often filming the dialogue and cutting back on the action. But movies are really about action. About visuals. We spent a lot of time rewriting dialogue in the two days of rewrite meetings we had before the project went off to shoot in Italy. I don't remember any rewriting of action scenes or visual storytelling. The result is a film that just lays there. Inert and dead. Being boring is the greatest crime any film can commit.

After *Transformations* a spec script I had written called "The Bloodsight" [1988] came to the attention of Andrew Lane and Wayne Crawford [Gibraltar Entertainment] and they optioned it in the hopes of generating foreign sales to finance the film. I had shot a promo reel to sell the concept. Since I had directed that and had also storyboarded several key sequences they were prepared to hire me as director. Wings Hauser was going to play the lead, an LAPD patrolman who gets involved in a homicide investigation involving homeless people that leads to the discovery of a vampire preying on the street people who won't be missed. This killer is ruthless and efficient, covering his tracks, disposing of the bodies. It was a very unromantic take on the vampire, even less elegant than the killer in the 70s Dan Curtis film *The Night Stalker*. In fact I think that Eddie "the Mangler" Quist from *The Howling* was a sort of model. Robert Picardo even showed up on the set of the promo video, which was a thrill. It was a mix of police procedural, chase film and horror. Other films of the time like *Wolfen* and *The Hidden* were doing similar genre mash-ups at the time. "The Bloodsight" was written for LA and budgeted around a million dollars but ultimately never came to pass. The money just never materialized.

Not long after that, in 1989, I sold a spec script to Universal, a police thriller called "Cold Sweat" that was never made, but it got me into the Writers Guild and moved me away from the horror film into other genres and bigger budget projects. Within that same year I became involved with co-creating and writing scripts for *Batman: The Animated Series*. There were a couple other horror spec scripts I wrote that didn't sell after that but I didn't really return to the horror film in any significant way until adapting David Morrell's novel *The Totem* in 2005. I also contributed some essays to *The Book of Lists: Horror* in 2008.

## Jay Kamen
### (Director)

Charlie and Albert Band had a talent for selling posters. They would have a movie poster designed and then try and sell it as if it were a finished film. Once the poster was sold, they would have a script written in about 2 weeks by some film student and then go and make the film. The big problem was—let's say he would raise $700,000 to make the movie. He would pay himself $200,000 for producing the film. But the movie would cost him $700,000 to make, so he would be $200,000 short and have to sell another poster to finish the first movie, but then have to make a 2nd movie for even less money. Then he would have to sell a 3rd poster to finish the 2nd movie. When I got the call from the Bands, they were on movie 20 … but I am getting ahead of myself. The only reason I took this job was my desire to direct was so great.

I graduated New York University Film School in 1975. As soon as I graduated, I moved to Los Angeles. My first job in the film industry was being a staff film editor for American International Pictures. American International Pictures was the studio Roger Corman discovered a number of directors at and I thought that's where I needed to be to move my career into directing. While I was at AIP, I not only recut movies they sold to television, but I ended up Samuel Z. Arkoff's (the head of the company) projectionist, which is a job I loved very much.

While I was there, I also wrote a script from the book "The Amityville Horror." They were interested in the script and I wanted to direct it more than anything in the world. Since they just hired a new exec Jere Henshaw, an executive who was let go from both 20th Century-Fox and Universal, he was not about to let a new writer have that screenplay assignment (I was very disappointed since the script they actually used for the movie was not as good as mine). I wrote another screenplay while I was there entitled "Cheapskates," a musical about roller skating in Venice Beach, California. Once again, one of the execs loved it but Jere Henshaw (who worked out of fear) would not let them have me direct it. Finally, one of the execs who liked the script asked, "Why don't we see if he can direct before we say no." So they let me direct a short film I wrote entitled *Interview*.

Just as we were about to shoot *Interview*, I got a shot to cut my first feature at Paramount called *North Dallas Forty*, so I left AIP to cut my first major movie (I was only 24 years old, so this was a big deal for me). When the short film was finished, there were not the number of festivals there are today (though it did win the Miami Film Festival and the Festival of Festivals in Houston, TX). Oddly enough, *Interview* sat around for a number of years. I began directing other things (some fell apart before the money was finalized—some, I walked off of because I didn't think the material would help my career or anyone else associated with the film). I went to the American Film Institute to get a masters in film directing thinking it would help me get some attention. Unfortunately, it depleted my funds to the point I had to go into sound editing to survive.

It was while I was at Warner Bros. on the movie *Club Paradise* when I got a call from Debbie Dion, Charlie Band's wife. I didn't know who they were—or what Empire Pictures was—but they had a copy of my film and loved it (I thought that was odd). I met with them over a two-year period. They wanted me to direct a film for them, but they always found a newer, younger director who they got excited by and then pushed me off. Finally, I got a call from Bob Wynn [1932–2013], saying he was Albert Band's friend and that he was producing a movie for them and they wanted me to direct the film. I asked if I could see a script but was told it wasn't written yet (I thought that was odd).

I drove to Burbank to meet Bob Wynn. This was an older gentleman who produced the old Judy Garland series on television in the 60s and the Bob Hope Christmas specials. I talked to him about the Judy Garland show being my favorite show as a kid and went through every episode. He was impressed that I knew so much about the show. My first job at AIP was also cutting a fund raising movie. Sam Arkoff was very involved in the Variety Club which got money for kids to get artificial arms and legs when they were born without one, and Bob Wynn knew them all and was vice president to the charity. So he hired me to direct *Transformations*.

20 minutes later, a kid from USC (University of Southern California Film School) came to the office and read the first 20 pages of the script. I sat there amazed. The story made no sense and I thought I was making a big mistake by not leaving. After the reading of the 20 pages, I was driven into the San Fernando Valley to look at this "chicken head." The chicken head moved up and down, back and forth. I was asked what I thought. I asked if there was a chicken head in the movie. Then Bob Wynn screamed out, "The director loves the chicken head!"

I went home depressed and called my old writing partner. He asked, "If you don't go to Rome and direct *Transformations*, what will you be doing?" I said, "Cutting sound on *Beverly Hills Cop 2*." Bob told me, "Look, if you turn down *Beverly Hills Cop 2* and go to Rome, Paramount will still call you to cut sound on *Beverly Hills Cop 3*." So go to Rome.

A number of complete re-writes were done to make the story more coherent and a lot simpler to shoot. The original writer made the story as complex as *Alien* only Ridley Scott had 20 million dollars and I had $300,000. The original writer also kept saying all you need to do is hold a hand-held camera and walk through the sets. I explained that this was a union shoot and if Rome is anything like Los Angeles, I would not be allowed to hold a camera on set and run around aimlessly.

So off I went to Rome. Empire put me up at the Locarno, which is a hotel I like very much. They dropped me off with 2000 lire (which isn't very much and I was off on my own). The next morning I got a call at 5:30 a.m. that the driver was here to take me to the studio. No one had told me. So I took a quick shower and came down. Getting to Dino De Laurentiis' studio in the morning took about two hours in the traffic, but eight o'clock I arrived. They showed me to my office when two minutes later the door swung open and a very angry Italian barged in screaming, "You're not one of those directors who knows every cut in every movie…" I smiled and said, as a matter of fact, I am. "You think you're Bertolucci? You think you're Fellini? You're just this rich porn director and you make these porn movies for Charlie Band." And he left. That was the introduction to my first AD.

At 9 a.m. the special effects crew came to my office to go over the script with me and I was hoping storyboards to give me an idea how they were going to achieve certain things in the script. We started at page one and I brought up the first effect. I asked, "What are you going to do about this…" and they said, "We have nothing." I thought that was strange. We turned to the next set of effects. I asked them, "What about this?" They said, "Nothing." I finally said, "Well, instead of wasting my time, what have you got for me?" They took me to a shed at the back of the studio. The shed was filled with all kinds of junk. They pulled down a rubber blob and said, "This is it." I asked, "What is it?" And they said anything I want it to be. They could cut it open and shove an actor through it—they could paint it. I asked what happened to the monies that were allotted to the movie for me. And they said the last two directors spent that and all I had left was the blob.

I was shocked. I went back to my office to reconsider staying at all. After sitting in my office for a few hours, I decided to make a go of the picture but I didn't expect anyone at the studio to help me. I went back to the special effect guys and said I wanted to go through that tool shed again. This time we talked through and I took anything I thought I could use (like 1000 pounds of KY Jelly that I had colored black).

Watching the sets go up was a nightmare as well. I thought we were going to use the *Robot Jox* set but they were building new sets of transparent thin white material. It was so thin, you could see through the walls. I told the set designer that this was supposed to be a prison not a hospital. Everything was too white. I had them spray paint everything black. There was a scene in the original script where the priest [played by Patrick Macnee] was sleeping and an earthquake wakes him. A tiny cross on the wall falls onto the floor. And the priest sits up and says, "The evil is here." They built a giant cathedral with an 8 foot cross. I was shocked. There was also no door to get the cameras through. I asked them what happened to the small bedroom and their answer was they thought this would look better. The problem I was having is I was supposed to shoot 9 pages a day and having an 8 foot high cross that was supposed to fall on cue without killing the actor was going to take longer than an hour to shoot. In fact it took 5 hours to shoot until the crew made the cross fall. They were jumping on. Wiggling it. I was afraid it was going to fall on the actor and kill him.

The actors finally arrived in Rome, a day before shooting. We had a reading of the script where I was told by Rex Smith, the lead actor, that he would not walk from the bed to the closet naked and put on a pair of pants (let alone the sex scene, which was in the script from the beginning when he approved it). He didn't think he was getting enough money for doing a nude scene. You should never tell a director who used to be an editor I won't do something. Being an editor, I pride myself on being able to cut around anything. The first day, the PM [Pino Butti], scheduled the sex scene which was not a very nice thing to do. It's hard enough getting into a shoot where no one knows anyone, but to start with people taking off their clothes—and worse, Dino De Laurentiis, who was angry he lost his studio to Charlie Band, took all the heat and air conditioning. So it was freezing on the set, even with the lights. Rex, of course, would not shoot without his boxer shorts on, so I had naked women on top of him and the camera at a low angle so you couldn't see his boxers and the scene looks more pornographic than sexy.

Rex, also, would not come to dailies or take direction. Since we were only shooting 9 days, I had to get that under control. I had a feeling Rex was having an affair with some model in the hotel he was staying at (which was different than mine) and I asked my assistant to follow him all night and take pictures of him if he was doing something that didn't seem right. Within a day I had pictures of him with the model outside by one of the fountains (not quite dressed). At lunchtime of the third day of shooting, I went to visit Rex in his dressing room with the pictures and gave them to him. I told him if he came to dailies and took direction, I would give him the negatives as a gift from me, but if he didn't I would give them to his pregnant wife who was coming to visit at the end of the shoot. He did follow direction but he hasn't talked to me since even though I did give him the negatives as I had promised him.

The crew was less easy to control. I asked for certain things through my assistant director (since I didn't speak Italian) but never got what I asked for. Finally at the end of the first week my script supervisor and assistant camera woman told me that the assistant director did not tell the camera man or crew what I had asked for; they both told me he constantly told them different things. So during the second week, Paula [Paola Barbaglia], the assistant camera woman and my script supervisor would tell me when things were translated incorrectly and intervened. Unfortunately, by the time I found out everything, there were only three days left of shooting. Not enough time to save the movie. I constantly asked the DP for smoke on the set to defuse the light. He didn't do that until the last day of shooting to show me he could do it but wouldn't for me.

Albert Band was never around but Bob Wynn, the producer and Albert's friend, would only drop by the set to tell me how many pages I had shot and how many more I needed to shoot that day and how much time I had to shoot it. It really wasn't a help.

[The studio was almost burned down on the last day of shooting.] We saved the fire scene [Rex Smith, now reduced to a monstrous mutant creature, is confronted by Lisa Langlois with a flame-thrower] for the end. When we were shooting—with two cameras—the fire kept growing but when it got incredibly large, I kept saying it wasn't going to match anything else we shot. What I didn't know is the fire department didn't turn on the water to put out the fire and everyone was running around or off the stage except me and the camera operators.

Post-production was odd as well. Just a side note, the crew was very slow until Good Friday when everyone "hauled ass" to finish, on two stages, so they could go home early. I spent a week in Rome after shooting was completed (on Good Friday of that year) thinking this would give my editor, Victoria Martin (a close friend who was an excellent sound editor I met at Paramount Studios), her first picture editing job.

When I returned to Los Angeles, I found Victoria (I called her Miss Vicki) sitting at a film bench, in a hallway of Empire Pictures, breaking down film into smaller rolls and making shot tags. I was shocked to see that no film was cut. She wasn't even given a roll of splicing tape or a Movieola, the machine we used to cut film on. She then informed me that a third of the film was still in customs and Empire had no money to get it out. I flipped out—mainly because it was such a bad experience, I wanted to finish the film as quickly as possible and move on with my life, but they weren't even giving me the basics. It took about two weeks for them to give me a closet in a small building across the street that was made into a cutting room. We finally got the film, and two Movieolas. I asked Victoria if she wouldn't mind us splitting up the film and me cutting half just so we could get done. When I couldn't get splicing tape, I called all my pals at Paramount, Universal and Warner Brothers to donate splicing tape and grease pencils to the project so we could cut the film.

I can't remember if it was four or five weeks to assemble the footage, but when we were through, we wheeled the 9 reels of film across the street to Empire's screening room to see what the film looked like. This first cut was short—maybe 80 minutes—since I disliked a lot of the footage and I cut it out. I'm ruthless with my own work. So we are sitting and watching the movie, taking notes, when in the middle the door opened, the lights went on, and a man stood there with a badge. "This is the I.R.S. Please take your personal belongings and leave the building. Please leave anything that does not belong to you here." So me and Victoria left the building. And that was the last time I saw the film (I never saw the film projected in its entirely).

Some years later, I had heard that Moshe Diamant, who ran Trans World Pictures, had bought the Empire Film Library. I called him and explained to him that I had directed one of the unfinished films—*Transformations*—and that I had an idea how to turn it into a comedy. I told him my idea of looping the entire film in Italian, with a different story altogether: Rex Smith is looking for a Big Mac in outer space and gets into all kinds of trouble and what the McDonald's food is doing to people … and then putting English subtitles over the film. Moshe loved the idea and was up for it until he found out that Charlie Band sold the film to two or more distributors in many countries so he would be liable to both if the film was finished. Therefore Moshe could not complete the film.

Years after that, James Honore, the head of post production at Columbia/Tri Star and Sony Pictures, called me that there was a possible directing job open and he wanted to submit me for it. He also said the execs wanted to see the film I shot in Rome. I told him to forget that. But the next day he called me into his office and the movie was running on his monitor. I asked him where he got it from. He laughed and handed me the tape. Me and some friends watched the film—me for the first time. We got drunk and laughed a lot, and

I relived the experience (I was laughing and crying at the same time). How did that come out of me? It was totally recut! They added shots of tits that didn't even match the women in the film and random space ships. Just horrible.

Months after that, I got a call from another editor friend of mine who told me he was up late at night and couldn't sleep, so he turned on HBO to see my credit on this space [film]. It was on television. I was very embarrassed. Then I got a call from an old friend from NYU Film School to tell me that he saw a copy of the tape at K-Mart. I immediately found one, which was hard to do, since it was selling so well.

And a final chapter. I was seeing Barbra Streisand opening the MGM Grand in Las Vegas. It was New Year's Eve and I wore a top hat with my tux. Some man stopped me the next day and said, "You were the guy wearing the hat. And I bet you saw Barbra and are going to see her again tonight." I confessed I had front row tickets through a friend. He said he wishes he could take his wife. I asked him what he did for a living and he told me that he was a small video distributor out of New Jersey and that I probably never heard of him. I told him I know many people. He mentioned he ran Star Maker Films which is the company. That was the company that was distributing *Transformations*. I offered him the two front row tickets to Barbra Streisand and $100,000 in cash for all the negatives and video masters so I could destroy them. He turned me down.

And on a film note, trying to forget this. I recently finished a musical short film which I wrote and directed entitled *Not Your Time* [2010]. It stars Jason Alexander, Val Pettiford, Kathy Najimy and Sally Kirkland. It just played 100 theatres last week in the U.S. and is now on iTunes worldwide. Currently, *Not Your Time* is being developed into a Broadway musical, something I've dreamed about my entire life. I am very excited about this.

## Michael Deak
### (Special Makeup and Creature Effects— Mechanical and Makeup Imageries, Inc.)

As far as I remember, *Transformations* was an extremely low budget movie. All the production could afford was $7,000.00 U.S. dollars for John Buechler to create a monster head for the movie and it was shipped to us. John had just finished *Cellar Dweller* [1987, John Buechler] and was back in the United States, so he was not on set during the filming. The M.M.I. crew (Bill Butler, Greg Johnson, Andrew Kenworthy and Chet Zar) and myself had to build the rest of the monster costume and all the make-up effects from things left over from other movies. The monster costume was probably left over from *Spellcaster* [1986, Rafal Zielinski] as well as a lot of the foam latex appliances. We tried to hide the seams of the different pieces with torn up clothing, slime and latex flesh. We had no feet for the monster so we tried to tear up a pair of boots to make it appear that the feet grew out of them, but the boots had steel toes and we couldn't cut through them. We ended up gluing the toes on the outside of the boots and tried to hide them with bits of leather.

We tried to make Jay Kamen, the director, happy, but he realized that there was very little we could do with what we had. When we shot the monster, he tried to keep it darkly lit and we were constantly covering it with slime.

Our make-up team all knew this was not good work. Normally, I would have worn the monster costume, having played many of the monsters for Empire movies. It was actually too small for me, but I wanted to try because whoever was wearing the costume on set would not be seen by the rest of the crew and spared being embarrassed. Well it turned out we all were thinking the same thing and after some discussion it turned into a (good natured) fistfight as to who was to wear the costume. In the end Andrew Kenworthy wore the suit on set.

That costume was so hated by everyone involved, that on the last day when it got burned by flame thrower, everyone on the crew and a lot of people from the production office crowded into the small set to watch it burn. As it burned the set got filled with thick toxic smoke and there was no way for the crowd watching to leave without walking in front of the camera, so we all coughed and choked until they yelled "cut." I think most people felt it was worth the choking to watch it burn away.

All the make-ups were handled by the other members of my crew. To repeat, they had to use foam latex appliances from other Empire movies. If memory serves me, the Rex Smith transformation make-up was a left-over piece from *Spellcaster* (I'm pretty sure it was the same make-up we used on Adam Ant). Our crew added air bladders under the make-up to make it look like it was moving.

I handled most or all of the blood effects. Since we had very little variety of make-up effects to offer, I was constantly trying to come up with as many blood spurting effects as I could. There was one scene where a prisoner gets stabbed in the stomach and slit across his belly. For a close-up, I had a pre-cut dummy and loaded it with blood filled condoms. The actor was to stick the knife in, break the condom and the blood would gush out. I even glued a razor blade on the end of the knife and (I am not exaggerating) we did over twenty tries and the damn condom never broke! We eventually gave up on that shot.

Rex Smith was a very funny guy and a pleasure to work with. Bill Butler and I were constantly joking with him on set. During one of the sex scenes, when Rex was facing away from camera he would quote lines from the Woody Allen movie *What's Up, Tiger Lily?* to Bill and I while he was "having sex" with the girl. It was difficult not to laugh during filming. This constant joking made it a lot easier when we had to put Rex through some very uncomfortable scenes, like crawling out of the burnt monster, covered in slime at the end of the movie. I think the monster skin he crawled out of was a left-over of a *From Beyond* [1986, Stuart Gordon] piece which had been sitting around the studio for close to three years. It was not pleasant for Rex, but he was very professional and made the best of it.

The rest of the cast was a pretty good collection of actors and we all got along very well. I was thrilled to be working with and a big fan of Patrick Macnee. I thought Christopher Neame was a great bad guy and when I saw him in the James Bond film *Licence to Kill* a year later I said, "That's the guy that shot me in *Transformations*!" I was also pretty thrilled when I realized that Benito Stefanelli was a stunt man/actor in all the spaghetti westerns I grew up with.

For many Empire films shot in Italy, I would end up playing small parts that required an English speaking person. In *Transformations* I played one of the prisoners that got shot. For some reason I could not get my one line of dialogue right, so I asked the pyrotechnic man to fire the explosive squib on my chest as soon as I began to talk, thankfully he did.

My crew did the succubus make-up on Pamela Prati [a famous Italian showgirl]. We also did a matching more horrific make-up on a much, much older actress, which was used briefly in the same scene. When Pamela was done filming I went back to the make-up room to remove her make-up while my crew attended to the older version of the succubus on set. Pamela had nothing on but a robe as I, trying to be as professional as possible, tried to remove the make-up around it. After awhile she got tired of holding the robe around her and, to my surprise, let it drop to the floor and stood there totally naked as I removed the make-up. I let my crew take the make-up off the much older version. Sometimes it's good to be the boss.

## Andrew Kenworthy
### (Special Makeup and Creature Effects— Mechanical and Makeup Imageries, Inc.)

I had experience in doing this sort of work from doing MTV Rock videos as well as just creating things on my own and was willing to sell myself to the lowest bidder! Honestly, I was a kid who needed work and I remember talking to some of the other employees in the MMI shop when I went for my interview. They were saying that he (John Buechler) would be more than happy to "take advantage of my abilities." Also, on my job application I wrote some ridiculous stuff about having to feed a family of twelve and having a dying mother on life support in the hospital or some such over the top nonsense. Yep, I was MMI material!

MMI was contracted to make the monster costume as well as some other effects for the film. These were done mostly in the shop in California and shipped to Italy although some of the work was done at the very last minute by the MMI crew on location. The filming of *Transformations* was done at the same time as another film called *Pulse Pounders* [1987, Charles Band]. *Pulse Pounders* was a trilogy of horror stories. I have never seen it and don't know if it was ever released.

The American MMI crew were a group of young stupid crazy kids. On the set the Italian crew would often need to talk with the effects supervisor Michael Deak. In their broken English they would call out, "Where is Mie Dick?" Which to us sounded like "Where is my dick?" We did have fun … we had some great times together back in the day.

MMI had a number of very talented artists working there at the time. John Buechler had talents of his own which include building a business which could employ and pay me, although somewhat randomly … intermittently … usually…. John had his talents and I thank him for that but, sculpting and creating creature costumes was NOT one of them.

John Buechler can take the credit/blame for the creation of what was to be dubbed: "The Chicken Monster." I vividly remember walking into the shop one early morning to see for the first time the sculpture of a creature which must have been hacked out of clay the night before. It was (sorry John) just awful…. It truly was a Chicken Monster from the films of the 1950s at best. We workers kept it to ourselves but we all thought it was just horrible.

The head of the "The Chicken Monster" was completed in California and shipped to Italy but the rest of the costume had to be done on site as I recall. One of the most ridiculous moments of my life, one that I laugh at to this every day was when I took a pair of boots, cut holes in them and glued monster toes to them as if they were poking out of the boots. I'm laughing now as I write this! That's all I had to work with!

Almost everything about MMI was low budget. Occasionally it would be announced that our paychecks would be delayed and we would all walk off work and go to the bar. Good times…

Although the idea of playing the "Monster" has been something I have enjoyed since I was a kid, the fact is that I didn't want to be seen next to this stupid Chicken suit. I remember telling my coworkers just that, I would rather be in it than seen next to it. Yes, I had fun but I was also the laughing stock of the set. I remember sticking my thumbs under my armpits flapping my elbows and making chicken noises. It was hilarious!

One thing that I'll never forget is that when the monster gets torched at the end of the film I was standing to the right of the camera and slightly behind it in a small corner pocket of the set. Once they lit it up the flames were way more intense than I think anyone thought they would be. I was stuck there on set burning up and the only way out for me was to cross in front of the camera which would spoil the shot. I didn't dare do that. Damn that hurt.

## Chet Zar
## (Special Makeup and Creature Effects—
## Mechanical and Makeup Imageries, Inc.)

I went to Italy to work on *Cellar Dweller*. I don't think I knew anything about the other two films we also worked on when we got there (*Transformations* and *Pulse Pounders*). I was only 18 years old at the time. Not only was it my first time on set working on a film but it was also my first time out of the country—my first time on an airplane, too!

I think I was hired on as a mold maker in the shop. Three weeks later they asked me to go to Italy to work on set doing makeup application. This was all for *Cellar Dweller*. I think we did all the *Cellar Dweller* stuff, wrapped, and then did a short stint on *Pulse Pounders*. *Transformations* seemed like a last minute addition. I remember doing the pus/boils on the succubus chick's back. I remember she [Pamela Prati] didn't speak much English but she kept trying to get me to give her my Mickey Mouse watch! Other than that, I did whatever makeups or special effects gags they asked me to on set.

Like I said, I was just a young flunky getting my foot in the door so I pretty much did anything they asked me to. I didn't get to design anything that I can remember, other than an early stage of those back boils I mentioned above. (I think the final stage was a sculpted foam latex prosthetic, which I may have applied.) For the first stage of the boils, I remember I figured out stippling latex and forming little bubbles by pulling spots out from the dried latex with tweezers, then filling them with methocel "pus" using a syringe. I'm not sure if it made it in the final cut or not but I thought it looked pretty cool on set. I think I applied her prosthetic foam succubus face as well.

The creature head was already built and sent to us from the states but it wasn't painted very well and it looked so bad that we covered it with nurnies (latex guts made from painting thin latex onto a smooth, flat surface and then rolling it up until it looks like a bunch of beef jerky). The head looked kind of like a chicken so we all called it "The Chicken Monster." It looked so bad, it was almost funny. So we covered it in nurnies and slime. I think on the last day or production, we took that chicken head out into the studio parking lot, covered it with spray glue and set it on fire, kind of an effigy to lameness.

I remember that for the final sequence where Rex crawled out from the burnt husk of the creature (something that was sprung on us at the last minute, if I remember correctly), we had to "repurpose" a really cool creature that was left over from *From Beyond*. It was a really cool sculpture that had a really nice paint job and I was super bummed that we had to paint it with flat black spray paint to make it looked charred. Then we covered it with nurnies and slime. Ultimately, it looked like a big pile of shit but we had to do what we had to do.

I remember during the sex scene that Rex Smith kept getting too into it and groping the actress who was on top of him and she kept slapping his hands away. I thought he was kind of arrogant and he pissed me off in the makeup chair when he insulted me for having a tattoo. I called him a cunt and the other guys from our crew (older than me and old enough to know better than to call an actor a cunt) just gave me this look like I had killed somebody. I was just a dumb kid. He was probably cool enough. I guess I had a bit of an attitude.

# Index

Numbers in ***bold italics*** refer to pages with photographs.

A-Team (TV series) 15
Abraham, Ken 76–78, 79, 261, 263
Abrams, J.J. 264
*The Abyss* (film) 107
*Act of Piracy* (film) 155
Adams, Bill 56
Adams, Lynne 43–44, 48–49
*The Addams Family* (TV series) 7
Adler, Alan J. 122, 175–176, 177–185, ***181***
Adler, Stella 78, 129
Aerosmith 67
*The African Queen* (film) 108
*Agatha* (film) 129
Ahlberg, Mac 115, 116, ***181***, 184, 187
Akin, Phil 32
Akkad, Moustapha 136
Albertini Dow, Ellen 166
Albon, T. Dow 35, 36–38
*The Alchemist* (film) 122, 176
Alexander, Jason 279
Alfred, William 177, 181
*Alias Smith and Jones* (TV series) 266
*Alice in Wonderland* (1976 film) 265
*Alien* (film) 22, 26–27, 29, 33, 73, 166, 273, 276
*Alien from L.A.* (film) 158
*Aliens* (film) 21, 30, 166
*All My Children* (TV series) 87, 88
Allan, Mark 268
*Aloha Summer* (film) 135–136, 140
*Altered States* (film) 111
Altschuler, Robert 196
*America* (film) 140
*American Cinematographer* (magazine) 76
*American Pie* (film) 202
*American Success Company* (film) 129
*Americathon* (film) 129
Amigo, Hank 138
*Amityville Horror* (film) 112
*The Amityville Horror* (book) 275
Amritraj, Ashok 206
Amritraj, Vijay 206
Anderson, Lance 186
*Android* (film) 239, 269
*The Andy Griffith Show* (TV series) 190
*Angel* (film) 30
*Angel Heart* (film) 108
*Animal House* (film) 58
Annaud, Jean-Jacques 52
*Another World* (TV series) 87
Anspach, Susan 29, 38

Ant, Adam 280
Aranda, Michael 78–79
Aravena, Arthur 59, 62
Arkoff, Louis 112
Arkoff, Sam 25, 112, 275
*Arms and the Man* (play) 160
Asquith, Anthony 98
Atlas, Bunny 40
*Attack of the 50 Foot Cheerleader* (film) 84
*Attack of the 50 Foot Woman* (film) 25
*The Attic Expeditions* (film) 249
*The Aurora Encounter* (film) 136
*Avalanche Express* (film) 129
*The Avengers* (film) 20
"AWE-SOME Tales" (magazine) 174
Azzopardi, Mario 26

*Back to the Future* (film) 78
Baer brothers (John and Robbie) 133
Baere, Geoffrey 204–205, 206
Band, Albert 123–126, 175, 274, 275, 277
Band, Charles (also Charlie) 25, 74, 110, 112–113, 115, 117, 122, 124–127, 175–179, ***181***, 182–184, 186–188, 210–212, 217, 219–223, 225, 229, 232–233, 237, 247, 274–278, 281
Bankston, Scott 143
Barbaglia, Paola 277
Barber, Glynis 100, 102–103, 105
Barnao, Anthony 250
Barnum, P.T. 183
Baron, Carla 250
*Barracuda* (film) 107–108
*Barry Lyndon* (film) 265
Bartalos, Gabe 141–143, ***142***
Bartel, Paul 164
Bassoff, Lawrence 128–133, ***132***
Bauer, Michelle 241–242, 250, 259, 263
Baughman, Rhonda 249
Baughn, David 51, 54–55
Beaird, David 130
Beal, Cindy 225–227, 228, 230
"Beasties" (screenplay) 123, 187
Beatles 249, 250
Beck 250
Becker, Martin 141
*Bedazzled* (film) 130

Bee Gees 71
Beecroft, David 212
*Beetlejuice* (film) 166
*Beggarman, Thief* (TV series) 208
Begun, Jeff 206
*Behind the Mask* (film) 140
Belushi, John 205
*Ben-Hur* (film) 128
Belafonte, Harry 266
Belafonte, Shari 266
*Beneath the Planet of the Apes* (film) 93
Benjamin, Richard 265
*Benny Hill Down Under* (TV movie) 114
*The Benny Hill Show* (TV series) 114
Benveniste, Michael 265
Bercovici, Bernard 163
Bercovici, Luca 126, 163, 167, 186, 187–188
Bercovici, Mieko 126
Berenson, Berry 150
Bergman, Ingmar 183
Bertolucci, Bernardo 276
*The Best of Sex & Violence* (film) 217, 232
*Beverly Hills Cop* (film) 133
*Beverly Hills Cop 2* (film) 276
*Beverly Hills 90210* (TV series) 262
*Big Bad Beetleborgs* (TV series) 202
*Big Bad Mama* (film) 163
"Big Fish" (song) 227
*The Big Fix* (film) 129
*The Big Lebowski* (film) 82
*Big Trouble in Little China* (film) 34
Biggs, Chris 141
*Bill and Ted's Excellent Adventure* (film) 107
Birkinshaw, Alan 146, ***149***, ***151***, 152, 153–154, 157
Black, Chris 170
"Black Cat Run" (screenplay)
Blaine, Vivian 182
Blair, Linda 59–62, 63–69, 70–71
Blake, Stephen Ashley ***240***, 247–248
Blanchard, Jeffery ***223***
Blanchard, Rick 64, 68
*Blazing Saddles* (film) 162
*Bleeding Kansas* (book) 74
*The Blob* (film) 82, 91, 190
*Blood Feast* (film) 6
*Blood Frenzy* (film) 3–19, ***9***, ***11***, ***13***

285

*Blood Nasty* (film) 72
"The Bloodsight" (screenplay) 272, 274
*Bloodstone* (film) 112
*Bloodsucking Freaks* (film) 169
*Bloody Movie* (film) 252; see also *Terror Night*
*Blue Monkey* (film) 20–39, **22**, **35**
*Boardwalk Empire* (TV series) 41, 228
Bock, Barbara Anne **135**, **137**, 141
*Body Double* (film) 131, 169
Bogart, Humphrey 108
*The Bold and the Beautiful* (TV series) 51
Bonaduce, Danny 84, 87–88
*Boogie Nights* (film) 7, 25, 81, 94
*The Book of Lists: Horror* (book) 274
"Bots, Come!" (stories) 73
Bottoms, Timothy 91
*Boulevard Nights* (film) 129
Bowers, Geoffrey G. 265
Boyle, Barbara 269
*The Boys Next Door* (film) 21
Bradbury, Ray 93
Brancato, John 5
Brancusi, Constantin 269
Brando, Marlon 118, 119, 257
Bravman, Jack 40–43, 47
*Brazil* (film) 161
*Breaking All the Rules* (TV movie) 193
Bredin, Robert 191
Brian, Mitch 272–274
*Bride of Frankenstein* (film) 197
Broccoli, Albert "Cubby" 256
Bronson, Charles 256
Brosnan, Pierce 118
Buck, Stephen **205**
Buckley, William F. 62
*Buddy Holly* (film) 136
Buechler, John 74, 117, 163, 219, 233, 279, 281
Bunyan, Paul 45
*Buried Alive* (1988 film) 96–101, 146
"Burmese Days" (unproduced play) 158
Burns, George 265
Burstyn, Ellen 68
Burton, Bennah 125
Burton, Richard 118
Burton, Tim 202
Bush, Rebeccah 132
*Bush's Brain* (documentary) 185
Butler, Jerry 7
Butler, William (also Bill and Billy) 253, 260, 263, 279–280
*Butterfly Dream* (TV series) 156
Butti, Pino 277
Byrge, Duane 162

*Cafe Flesh* (film) 263
Cage, Nicholas 73
Caldwell, Steven B. 270
Calhoun, Rory 130
*California Suite* (film) 129
Callaway Thomas 74, 75, 77, 222–224, 231

Cameron, James 21, 81, 107, 269
Campanelli, Steve 41
Candy, John 119, 188, 192
*Candy Stripe Nurses* (film) 205
*Capricorn One* (film) 129
*Captain Blood* (film) 128
*Captain EO* (film) 218
*Car 54, Where Are You?* (TV series) 17
Cardone, J.S. 210–212, **211**
Cardone, Michael 211, 213
Carducci, Mark Patrick 196–197, 201–202
Carell, Steve 192
Carlisle, Belinda 107
*The Carol Burnett Show* (TV show) 160
*The Carpenter* (film) 40–50
Carpenter, John 41, 108, 111, 125, 135, 138
Carradine, John 97, 100, 217, 232
Carren, David 126, 127
*Carrie* (film) 27, 147
Carroll, J. Larry 124, 125–127, 175, 184
Carsillo, Peter **75**
Casey, Lawrence P. **236**
Cassano, Claire 6, 8, **9**, 10, 11–14, **11**
Cassavetes, John 82
*Castle of Evil* (film) 252
Castro, David 53
*Catacombs* (film) 110
Cathcart, Tavia 66
Caton, Craig 248–249, **248**
Caught a Ghost 208
*Caught from Behind* (film) 3
*Caught from Behind 2* (film) 3, 4
Caulfield, Maxwell 21
*Cavegirl* (film) 51–57, **52**, 130
Ceausescu, Nicolae 155
Cechov, Anton 183
*Cellar Dweller* (film) 279, 282
Chaffey, Don 257
*The Champ* (film) 129
Chaney, Lon 8, 178
Chaney, Warren 134–140, 143, 144
*Chariots of Fire* (film) 184
*Charlie Chan in Egypt* (film) 233
Chayette, Jeff 56
"Cheapskates" (screenplay) 275
Cheech and Chong 8
Cheek, Molly 87
*Children of the Corn* (film) 24–28
"Children of the Corn" (short story) 24
*The Chilling* (film) 58–71
Christie, Agatha 14
*Christine* (film) 111
*The Chronicles of Narnia* (film) 36
Chute, David 182
*El Cid* (film) 128
*CineAction* (magazine) 42
*Cinefantastique* (magazine) 197, 200
*Cinema Canada* (magazine) 43
*Cinema Circus* (short film) 232
Clapton, Eric 198
Clark, Greydon 150
Clark, John 7, 9, 12, 17

Climan, Sandy 86
*Close Encounters of the Third Kind* (book) 82
Clouse, Robert 23, 24
*Club Paradise* (film) 275
Coco, James 131, 132
Coffing, Barry 144
Cohen, Howard 207
Cohen, J'Aime **9**
Cohn, Harry 83
Cohn Curtis, Bruce 83, 202
*Cold Steel* (film) 247
"Cold Sweat" (screenplay) 274
Cole, Ben 104–106
Cole, Dennis 90, 94
Columbus, Chris 66
Combs, Jeffrey 249
Compton, Jill 34
*The Concrete Jungle* (film) 185
Connell, Richard 217
Connors, Chuck 125
*Contra Costa Times* (newspaper) 63, 69
Conway, Blake 116
Conway, Lyle 248
Cook, Bruce R. 87
Cooper, Merian C. 218
Coppola, Francis Ford 219, 246
"Copycat" (unproduced film) 114
Corey, Richard 168, 169, 170
Corman, Julie 162, 205
Corman, Roger 25, 34, 72, 83, 107, 146, 159–167, 178, 203, 204–207, 212, 218, 221, 234, 239, 264–266, 269, 271, 274
*Cornell Daily Sun* (newspaper) 129
*Corporate Affairs* (film) 162
Cosmatos, George P. 107
Coulter, Scott 117
Cousteau, Jacques 108
*The Covenant* (film) 212
*Craig en Cardo* (TV series) 156
*Crash and Burn* (film) 211
Crawford, Wayne 107, 108, 274
*Craze* (film) 169
*Creature from the Black Lagoon* (film) 186, 197
*Creepozoids* (film) 72–80, **75**, 222, **223**
*Cries in the Night* (film) 21
*Crime Scenes—Movie Poster Art of the Film Noir* (book) 133
*Crimes of the Heart* (play) 186
Criswell, John 116
*Critters* (film) 113, 159–160
Cronenberg, David 41
*Cross Country* (film) 190
*Crossed Swords* (film) 129
Crupi, Tony 84, 87
Crusher, Beverly 118
*CSI* (TV series) 7
Cunningham, Sean S. 107
Curnen, Tim 123–125, 126–127, 187
Currie, Anthony (also Tony) 189–192, **191**, 193, 194
*The Curse* (film) 63
Curtain, Jane 118
Cushing, Peter 135

# Index

Cutler-Rubenstein, Devorah 90–91, 92–94, **93**; *see also* Wittcomb, Kate

*Daily Variety* (newspaper) 124, 197
Daley, Tom 136, 138–140, 144
*Dallas* (TV series) 131
*Damn Yankees* (film) 130
*Dance Macabre* (film) 150
"Dance of Death" (screenplay) 150
*Danger Zone* (film) 265, 266, 267–268
*Danger Zone 2* (film) 265, 266, 267–268
*Danger Zone 3* (film) 265
*Danger Zone 4* (film) 265
Daniel, Don 217, 220, 222–223, 224, 228, 231
Darabont, Frank 86
*Daredevil* (TV series) 225
*Dark Shadows* (TV series) 257
*Dark Tower* (film) 21, 26
Davenport, Harry Bromley 75
Davidovich, Lolita 193
Davids, Paul 218
Davidson, Foziah **149**, 156–157
Davidson, James 182, 187
Davis, B.J. 108
Davis, Desmond 151
Dawber, Pam 118
Day, Gerry 111
*The Day After Tomorrow* (film) 50
*Days of Our Lives* (TV series) 253
*Dead Calm* (play) 251
*Dead End City* (film) 76
*Dead Men Don't Die* (film) 255, 257
*The Dead Pit* (film) 58, 59
*Deadlock* (film) 59
*Deadly Intruder* (film) 81–88, **86**
*Deadly Prey* (film) 247
*Deadly Reactor* (film) 76
*Deadly Sunday* (film) 20
*Deadly Weapon* (film) 250, 262
Deak, Michael 116–117, 279–281
*Death Chase* (film) 262
*Death House* (film) 89–95, **90**, **93**, **95**, 239, 243, 246, 254, 258, 261; *see also Zombie Death House*
*Death Race 2000* (film) 163
DeBell, Kristine 265
De Carlo, Yvonne 226
"Decathlon" (short story) 5
Deckert, Blue 136
DeCoteau, David (also Dave) 72–79, 222, 240–241, 243, 246–250, 252–253
*The Deep* (film) 108
*Deep Space* (film) 37
*Deep Star Six* (film) 107
Deeth, Jim 56
Defoe, Daniel 217
Defont, Tony **35**
De Laurentiis, Dino 277
"Demonic Aborted Sewer Fecal Fetuses Revenge" (screenplay) 242
De Niro, Robert 77, 187
De Palma, Brian 41, 131, 147
Depp, Johnny 118, 154, 257

De Rieux, Jack 62, 64–66, 68
de Ropp, Valerie 67
De Toth, André 243–245, 252–260, **253**, **256**, **258**, 262
de Villiers, Dirk 156
"The Devil's Due" (novela) 174
Dewhurst, Coleen 129
Diamant, Moshe 278
*Diamonds Are Forever* (film) 117
*Dick Tracy* (film) 214
Dion, Debra (also Debbie) 112, 125, 126, 275
*Dirty Business* (film) 86
*Dirty Harry* (film) 93
*Discopath* (film) 44
Dixon, Ken 217, 218–226, **218**, 228–233, **233**, **236**, 237–238
*Dr. Alien* (film) 247
*The Doctors* (TV series) 118, 119
Dodd, Wilfrid 100
Dolan, Phil 199
Donahue, Troy 60–62, 63–65, 68–69, 71
Donovan, Martin 199
"Don't Make Me Over" (screenplay) 133
"Dorian" (screenplay) 97
D'Orthez, Christobel 155–156
Douglas, Gordon 38
Douglas, Kirk 128
*Dracula* (film) 136, 197
*Dracula* (stage show) 257
*Dracula's Dog* (film) 125
*Dragon Riders of Berk* (animated TV series) 222
*Dragonard* (film) 100
*Dramalogue* (newspaper) 80, 227
*Dreamer* (film) 129
*Dreamscape* (film) 202
*Driven* (film) 185
Dudelson, Jim 198
Duke, Patty 261
Duke, Robin 32
*The Dukes of Hazzard* (TV series) 111
Dullea, Keir 45
Duncan, Peggy 62,
Duvall, Shelley **13**
Dylan, Bob 24, 198

*Earthquake Survival* (documentary) **13**
Eastwood, Clint 41, 82
*Easy Rider* (film) 45
*Eat My Dust* (film) 163
Ebinger, Robert **205**
Ecclesine, Steve 23–24
*The Edge of Night* (TV series) 87
*Edge of Sanity* (film) 96–106, **99**, **101**
Edwards, Elizabeth 193–194
Eisenstark, David 73–74
*The Elephant Man* (film) 214
Elias, Alix 164
Ellison, Harlan 27–28
Elvira, Mistress of the Dark (Cassandra Peterson) 232
Elwell, Jimi 259, 262–263
*Elysium* (film) 36

Emmerich, Roland 50
*An Enemy of the People* (film) 129
Eng, John 218, 220–222
England, Bryan 131
Englund, Robert 150
"Enigma" (screenplay) 232
*Enter the Dragon* (film) 23–24
Erickson, Glenn 171
Erland, Cynthia 157
*The Erotic Adventures of Robinson Crusoe* (film) 217, **236**
*Errol Flynn—The Movie Posters* (book) 133
*Escape from New York* (film) 269, 273
*Escape from Safehaven* (film) 195, 200–201
"Escort to Danger" (*The Amazing Spider-Man* episode) 111
Esposito, Vesna 156
*E.T. The Extra-Terrestrial* (film) 22, 28, 267
*The Evil Below* (film) 107–109
*The Evil Dead* (film) 169
*Executive Suite* (film) 129

*The Falcon and the Snowman* (film) 208
*Fame* (film) 129
*Famous Monsters of Filmland* (magazine) 90, 224
*Fangoria* (magazine) 197, 200, 202, 225
*Fanny by Gaslight* (film) 98
Fante, John V. 94–95, 254–255
"Far Appomattox" (play) 185
"The Far Arena" (novel) 126
Fasano, John 40
*Fast Times at Ridgemont High* (film) 208
*Fatal Attraction* (film) 146
*Father of the Bride* (film) 155
*Fear City* (film) 202
Felix, Jerry 96, 97–100
Fellini, Federico 276
Fenton, Reed 53, 54, 56
Fey, Tina 192
Fiedler, John 217
Field, Sally 66
Fields, Freddie 86
Fields, W.C. 15
*Filmgore* (film) 217, 232
*Final Destination* (film) 20
Findlay, Roberta 173–174
Finger, Leonard 202
Finnegan, John 208
Fischa, Michael 130
Fitzgerald, Benedict 177, 181–182
Fitzgerald, Wayne 51, 53
*Five Easy Pieces* (film) 29, 176
Flaherty, Joe 32
Flaherty, Maureen 212
Flanagan, John 62, 66, 70–71
Fleetwood, Mick 83
Flender, Rodman 167
*Flesh and Blood* (TV movie) 187
*Flesh Gordon* (film) 265
"Flesh Gordon on the Pyramid Planet" (screenplay) 265

Fletcher, Louise **211**, 212, 215
Floores, Brian 138
Floutz, Thomas 74–76, **75**
Flower, Buck 241
*Flush* (film) 265
*The Flying Tigers* (film) 220
Flynn, Errol 133, 252
Flynn, Fred 212
Foch, Nina 129
*The Fog* (1980 film) 108
Foley, James 129
Fonda, Peter 45
*Footloose* (film) 51
*Forbidden Planet* (film) 243
"Forbidden Television" (screenplay) 133
*Forbidden World* (film) 123, 239
*Force: Five* (film) 23
*The Forsaken* (film) 212
Foster, Jodie 187
Fox, Jack 201
Fox, Tom 21
Foxx, Elizabeth 208
Fragen, Ronald 169
Franciosa, Anthony 91, 94
Franciosa, Chris 94
Francis, Freddie 21
Franco, David 41, 44
Frank, Billy 76
*Frank and I* (film) 100
*Frankenstein* (film) 178, 197
Frankoff, Kevin 191
Frazer, Devin 89–90, 91–94
Freed, Herb 53
Freeman, Hal 3–19, **9**, **11**, **13**
French, Ed 197, 203
*French Postcards* (film) 129
*Frenzy* (film) 6
*Frequency* (film) 90
*Friday the 13th* (film) 6, 135
Friedkin, William 218
Friedman, Tom 264–268
Friend, Lonn 4
*Fright Night* (film) 78, 135, 225
*Frightmare* (film) 187
*From Beyond* (film) 280, 283
"Frozen Shogun" (screenplay) 122
Fruet, William (also Bill) 21, 29, 31, 32, 36
Fujioka, Hiroshi 124–126
Fujioka, John 156
Fuller, Fleming 155
Fullerton, Carl 215
Fury, Carl 201

Gabai, Richard 253
Galin, Mitch 202
Gallagher, John 201
Garfield, Allen **170**, 171
Garland, Judy 182, 275
Garrett, Hank 15, 17–18
*The Gauntlet* (film) 129
*General Hospital* (TV series) 15, 183
George, Christopher 84–85
Gertner, Risa 21, 32
*Ghost Town* (film) 110–121, **115**
*Ghost Warrior* (film) 122–127
*The Ghost Way* (book) 163

*Ghoulies* (film) 126, 159, 162, 167, 186–187
*Ghoulies Go to College* (film) 163
*Ghoulies 2* (film) 75
Gibb, Andy 71
Gibson, Henry 171
Gibson, Julia 269–270
Gibson, Mel 177
Gielgud, John 105
Gill, Jim 141, 143
Gilliam, Terry 161
*Gilligan's Island* (TV series) 6, 261
*Girlfriends* (film) 129
Girometti, Roberto **236**
Givens, R. Michael **205**
Glaudini, Robert 181–183
*Glengarry Glen Ross* (film) 129
*Glitter* (film) 173
Globus, Yoram 100
Glover, Bruce 117, 120
Gluck, Steve 66
Go-Go's 107
*Go Tell the Spartans* (film) 93
"Goblins" (screenplay) **165**, 166
Goddard, Gary 260
*The Godfather* (film) 91, 95, 246
*The Godfather III* (film) 246
*Goin' Coconuts* (film) 129
Golan, Menahem 100, 153
Goldberg, Bernie 197
*Golden Girl* (film) 129
Golding, Gerry 82
Golding, William 192
Goldsmith, George 21, 23–30, 31–32
Goldstein, Allan A. 97
*Gone with the Wind* (film) 94
*The Good, the Bad and the Ugly* (film) 114
*The Goodbye Girl* (film) 129
Goodin, Courtney 125
Goodman, John 118
Goodwin, John 6–10, 14–15, 16, **90**, 260
*Gor* (film) 155
Gordon, Stuart 197, 210, 272, 280
Gordy, Berry, Jr. 24
*Gorky Park* (film) 215
Gould, Elliott 255, 257
Governor, Richard 113, 114–115, **115**, 120; *see also* McCarthy, Richard
*The Graduate* (film) 94
Grant, Cary 207
Grant, Ulysses S. 186
Graver, Gary 59, 227
Graves, Bud **223**
Graves, Kirk **233**, 234–238
Greason, Staci **253**, 260
*Greater* (film) 188
*Green Acres* (TV series) 160
Greene, Ellen 118
*Gremlins* (film) 113, 159, 161, 163–165
*Grey's Anatomy* (TV series) 76
Griffin, Kathy 129
Grisè, Pierre 40, 41, 42
Grossman, Karen 213
Groves, Phil 51–52

Gruendemann, Eric 247
*Gunga Din* (film) 128
Guns n' Roses 67, 263
Guy, Riccardo 156

Hackett, Buddy 233
Hackman, Gene 174
Haggerty, Dan 60–61, 63–65, 68–69, 71, 254, 262
Hale, Alan, Jr. 254, 261, 262
Hall, Cleve 259–260
Hall, Kenneth J. (also Ken) 247, 251, 252–253, 260, 262
*Halloween* (film) 83, 98, 135, 136
*Halloween 4* (film) 112
Hamilton, Linda 24–25
*Hamlet* (stage show) 105
Hanks, Tom 29
Hannah, Daryl 7
*The Happy Hooker Goes Hollywood* (film) 233
Hardberger, Devorah 229
*Hardbodies* (film) 206
*Hardbodies 2* (film) 206
*Hardcastle* (TV series) 15
Hardwicke, Catherine 131
Harkham brothers (Efrem and Uri) 126–127
Harper, Bob 266
Harris, Ed 119, 186
Harris, Richard 150
Hartwell, David 214
Hasenecz, Sergei 239–246, **253**
Hasselhoff, David 118
Hathaway, Beth **35**, 36
*The Haunting* (film) 173
Hauser, Wings 41–42, 45–46, 48–49, 274
Hauss, Harry 56
Havins, Hal **240**, 249–250
Hawkins, John 111
Hawkins, Richard 78, 79, 80–81
Hawks, Howard 169
Hayward, Susan 73
*Headhunters* (play) 91
Hearn, Chick 259
Hearst, Patti 23–24
Hearst, Vicki 23–24
"The Heat Is On" (song) 133
*Heaven and Earth* (film) 59
*Heaven Help Us* (short film) 246
Heavener, David 227
*Heavy Metal* (magazine) 90
*The Heidi Chronicles* (stage show) 63
*Helga & the Little People* (screenplay) 5
*Hell Night* (film) 202
*Hellboy 2* (film) 76
*Hellfire Lounge* (book) 174
"The Hellgramite Method" (1985 *Twilight Zone* episode) 91
Hemphill, John 191, 193, 194
Henley, Beth 183, 186
Henshaw, Jere 275
*Herald Examiner* (newspaper) 33
*Hercules Unchained* (film) 128
*Here Comes the Bride* (TV show) 16

# Index

Herek, Stephen 159–160
Herman, Pee Wee 129
Hershey, Barbara 118
Heston, Charlton 140, 261
Hewitt, David L. 137
Hickland, Catherine 119
Hickox, Douglas 108
*The Hidden* (film) 274
*Hide and Go Shriek* (film) 268
*Hide in Plain Sight* (film) 129
Hildebrand, Frank 231
Hill, Benny 37, 114
Hill, Scott 169–170
*Hill Street Blues* (TV series) 31
Hirsch, Tina 161–162, 163–165, **164**, 166
Hitchcock, Alfred 6, 13
Hitzig, Rupert **170**, 171–172
*Hobgoblins* (film) 76, 159
Hoblit, Gregory 90
Hoey McBride, Michelle 152–155
*Hog Wild* (film) 189
Holden, Bill 169
Holder, Chris 84, 87–88
Holleb, Alan 204–206, **205**, 208
*Hollywood Chainsaw Hookers* (film) 247
"Hollywood Heroes" (screenplay) 133
*Hollywood Reporter* (magazine) 162
*Honeysuckle Rose* (film) 129
Hong, James 212
Honore, James 278
*Hooper* (film) 129
Hooper, Tobe 41
Hoover, Michael F. 33, **35**
Hope, Bob 275
Hope and Crosby 76
Hopper, Dennis 177, 182, 185
Horner, Carl 220, 228–232, **229**
*The Horse Whisperer* (film) 36
Horton, Peter 24–25
*The House of Usher* (1989 film) 96, 146–148, 150, 151–152
*House of Wax* (film) 255, 256
*How to Train Your Dragon* (animated film) 222
Howard, Sandy 20–23, 25–26, 28–33
*The Howling* (film) 274
Hudson, Kate 23
*Hunk* (film) 128–133, **132**
Hunt, David 188
Hunter, Holly 186
Hunter, Ian 228
Huston, James 144
Huston, John 182
Huud, Terry M. 220

*I Know the Devil* (music album) 227
*I Love Lucy* (TV series) 172
"I Remember When Coke Was Still Cola" (screenplay) 243
*I Want to Live* (film) 73
Ibsen, Henrik 183
*The Importance of Being Earnest* (stage show) 104

*The Incredible Hulk* (TV series) 169
*The Incredibly Strange Creatures Who Stopped Living and Became Mixed-Up Zombies* (film) 6
*The Innocents* (film) 115
*Interview* (short film) 275
*Invasion of the Body Snatchers* (film) 180
*Invasion of the Mind Benders* (film) 40, 42–43
Ireland, John 243, 252, **253**, 257, **258**, 259, 260, 262
Ireland, John, Jr. 259
*Irma la Douce* (stage show) 257
Isgro, Jack 53, 54
"La Isla Bonita" (song) 109
*It's Alive!* (film) 129

Jacobs, Michael 66
*Jacob's Ladder* (film) 199
Jacoby, Billy 247
Jaffe, Stanley 146
Jaglom, Henry 175
*Jake Speed* (film) 108
*Jantjie Kom Huis Toe* (TV movie) 156
*Jaws* (film) 109, 135
*Jaws 3* (film) 162
Jefferson, Thomas 185
Jeremy, Ron 7, 74
*The Jetsons* (animated TV series) 234
Johnson, Greg 117, 279
Jones, Andras 249–250
Jones, Barbara 43, 44
Jones, Brian Thomas 195–202
Jones, Donald M. 20
Jones, Ken 269
Joseph, Genie 42, 43
"Judgment Night" (screenplay) 3, 10, 13
Julian, Janet 126–127
*Jurassic Park* (film) 36
Juris, Larry 201
Jutras, Richard 44

Kaczender, George 22
Kafka, Franz 82
Kagel, James 186–187
Kaitan, Elizabeth **219**, 221–222, 226, 230
Kalember, Patricia 118
Kamen, Jay 272, 274–279
Karloff, Boris 178
Kasten, Jeremy 249
*Kate and Allie* (TV series) 118
*Kay O'Brien* (TV series) 118
Keaton, Diane 186
Keith, Thomas A. 246–247
Kennedy, John F. 204, 206
Kennedy, Tom 267
Kenworthy, Andrew 279, 280, 281–282
Kenwright, Bill 156
Kerschner, Irvin 257
Kerwin, Harry 107
*KGB: The Secret War* (film) 21
Kida, Makio **35**

Kiersch, Fritz 25
Kiger, Robby 24
Kikoine, Gerard 97, **99**, 100–101, **101**
Kikoine, Kat **101**
*Killbots* a.k.a. *Chopping Mall* (film) 166
"Killer Bees" (screenplay) 82
*Killer Party* (film) 21
*Killer Shark* (film) 135
*Killzone* (film) 168
Kimmel, Bruce 171
King, Martin Luther 268
King, Stephen 24, 27, 86
*King Kong* (film) 128, 218, 234
Kingsberg, Alan 196
Kinski, Klaus 239
Kirkconnell, Clare 92
Kirkland, Sally 279
Kitt, Eartha 192
Klasky, Earl 53
*Knight Rider* (TV series) 51
Konig, Peter 68
Korman, Harvey 160, 162, 163–164, 167
Koseluk, Chris 29, 30–33
Kottenbrook, Carol **211**, 214, 216
Kreuger, Eryn 213–214
Kubrick, Stanley 265
Kuehn, Andy 265–266
Kuehnert, Fred 136
Kurtz, David 133
Kutcher, Steven 31–32
"The Laboratory of Hallucinations" (play) 91

*Lady Avenger* (film) 72–73
LaFontaine, Don 266
Lake, Don 32, 36, 38, 39, 191, 193, 194
*The Lamp* (film) 134–145, **135**, **137**, **142**
Landau, Martin 78
Landers, Judy 247
Lane, Andrew 107, 108, 274
Lange, Jessica 186
Langlois, Lisa 277
Lanko, Vivian 199
Lansing, Sherry 146–147
*The Last Airbender* (film) 225
*The Last House on the Left* (film) 252
*The Last of Sheila* (film) 150
*The Last Ride* (film) 160
*The Last Samurai* (film) 156
*Late Night with David Letterman* (TV show) 232
Laurel and Hardy 8
Laurence Pfeil, Valentina 51, 53–54
*Lawrence of Arabia* (film) 256
Leal, Jack 214–215
Lean, David 256
Leary, Craig 53
*Leave Bad Enough Alone* (film) 79
*Leave It to Beaver* (TV series) 190
Led Zeppelin 198
Lee, Bruce 27, 220
Lee, Christopher 135

Lee, Robert E. 186
"Legacy" (The Lamp 2) (unproduced film) 139
Leider, R. Allen 173–174
Lemasters, Theo 242
Lennon, John 198
Lenoir, Pierre 42, 43, 44–50
Lenzer, Don 198
Leonard, Brett 58
Leone, Sergio 114
*Lethal Pursuit* (film) 262
*Let's Do It Again* (film) 129
Levering, Frank 175–176, 177–186
Levine, Joel 108
Levitt, Karen 266
Levitt, Steve 131–132
Levy, Murray 251
Lewis, Herschel Gordon 6
Lewis, Robert 129
*Licence to Kill* (film) 280
*The Life and Times of Grizzly Adams* (TV series) 71
Lincoln, Fred J. 243, 252, 254, 259, 262, 263
Lipstadt, Aaron 269
*Liquid A$$ets* (film) 173
Little, Dwight H. 21, 112
*A Little Romance* (film) 129
*Little Shop of Horrors* (film) 83, 248
*Little Shop of Horrors* (stage show) 118
Lom, Herbert 152, 154, 156–158
Lommel, Ulli 59
*The Lone Ranger* (TV series) 130
*Look Who's Talking* (film) 36
*Lord of the Flies* (book) 192
*Lords of the Deep* (film) 107
Loring, Lisa 6, 7, 8, 12, 15, 17
*Los Angeles Free Press* (newspaper) 129
*Los Angeles Times* (newspaper) 129, 246
*Love Is a Gun* (film) 214
*Love Shack* (film) 162
Lovecraft, H.P. 211
*Loving* (TV series) 262
Lovitz, Jon 129
Lubo, Gerard 106
Lugosi, Bela 257
Lunde, Christine 156, 157
Luz, Frank 118–121
Lydecker brothers (Howard and Theodore) 220
Lyne, Adrian 199
Lyon, Francis D. 252

*Macbeth* (play) 243, 245, **253**
MacDonald, Wendy 6, 12, 15, 17
Mackler, Steve 195–200
Macnee, Patrick 273, 276, 280
Madigan, Amy 186
Madonna 109, 119
*Madonna: A Case of Blood Ambition* (film) 40
Magnoli, Albert 129
Mahaffey, Valerie 119
*The Main Event* (film) 129
Malden, Karl 257

*Malibu Bikini Weekend* (film) 267
Malzahn, Richard 215–216
*A Man Called Horse* (film) 30
*Man of La Mancha* (stage show) 234
"The Mandrake Root" (*Monsters* episode) 202
Mann, Michael 111
Manson, Charles 66
Mantee, Paul 129, 131
Marineau, Barbara 118, 119
Marino, Nick 89–95, **95**, 239, 243–246, 251–259, **256**, 261, 262
Marmorstein, Malcolm 255–257, 258–259
Marmorstein, Wayne 257
*Mars Attacks!* (film) 202
Martin, George 249
Martin, Steve 155
Martin, Victoria 278
Marx, Harpo 208
Marx, Rick 98
Marx Brothers 161
Masciarelli, Michael 20–23
Maslin, Janet 29
*The Masque of the Red Death* (1989 film) 96, 146–158, **149**, **151**
*Master of Dragonard Hill* (film) 100
Masters, Todd 33, 34–36, **35**, 37–39
*Masters of the Martial Arts* (video series) 23
*Masters of the Universe* (film) 260
Mastrantonio, Mary Elizabeth 177
Matthau, Walter 265
Mature, Victor 190
"Maul of the Dead" (play) 273
Maur Thorp, Sarah 101–104, 105, 106
*Mayhem* (film) 12
McArthur, Roy 200
McBurnie, Peter 191
"McCadden on Mars" (*Time Walker 2*) (unproduced film) 267
McCalmont, James 198, 200–201
McCarthy, Joe 180
McCarthy, Melissa 129
McCarthy, Richard 114–116, **115**; *see also* Governor, Richard
McCauley, John 81–87, **86**, 88
McClatchy, Gregory 265
McClure, Tane 92
McDowell, Malcolm 97
McEvoy, Anne Marie 24
McKamy, Kim 79
McKay, John 198–199
McPherson, John 169
McQueen, Steve 120
McTiernan, John 166
*Meatballs* (film) 189
*Meet Me in St. Louis* (film) 182
Melvin, Bob 214
Mennier, Louise-Marie 43, 47
Mercil, Dean 174
Merhi, Joseph 12
Merrill, Damon 143–144
Messenger, Guy 58–59, 60, 69–70

*Metalstorm* (film) 122, 185
*Meteor* (film) 31
*Metropolis* (film) 271
Meyer, Russ 54
*Mighty Movies—Movie Poster Art from Hollywood's Greatest Adventure Epics and Spectaculars* (book) 133
Miner, Michael 250
*Minors* (short film) 196
*Mississippi Burning* (film) 153
Mitchell, Cameron **256**, 257, 258, 260, 262
Mitchell, Charlie 53, 54, 56
*Moneyball* (film ) 20
Monroe, Marilyn 106, 167
*Monsters* (TV series) 202, 213
"Monté: King of Atom-Age Monster Decals" (book) 91
Montero, Tony 15–16, 17
Monty Python 52, 161
*Moon in Scorpio* (film) 227
*Moonlighting* (TV series) 14
Moore, Clayton 130
Moore, Demi 175, 181, 183, 187–188
Moore, J. Paul **35**
Moore, Saba 56
*Morbid Curiosity Cures the Blues* (book) 91
Morgan, Glen 20–21
*Morgan the Pirate* (film) 128
"The Most Dangerous Game" (short story) 217, 218–219, 221, 233, 234
*Moving to a Small Town* (book) 185
Mozart, Wolfgang Amadeus 139
*Mrs. Doubtfire* (film) 66
*The Mummy* (film) 197
*Munchies* (film) 159–167, **161**, **164**
*Munchies II a.k.a. Munchie* (film) 163
Murcott, Joel 111
Murphy, Ben 266
Murray, Bill 192, 205
Murray, Michael J. 146–151
"Mutant Spawn 2000" (screenplay) 72–73
*My Bodyguard* (film) 176
"My Chauffeur" (screenplay) 130
"My Mom's a Werewolf" (screenplay) 130
*My Sister Sam* (TV series) 118
*Mystery Science Theater 2000* (TV show) 268

Najimy, Kathy 279
*The Naked Monster* (film) 7
Napoli, Jackie 72
Narunsky, Harry **218**, 232–234
Neame, Christopher 280
Neame, Ronald 31
Neill, Gilly 34–36, **35**
Neill, Steve 22, 32, 34, **35**, 37, 125, 225
Nelson, John Allen 131–132, **132**
*Neon Maniacs* (film) 196
*The Nest* (film) 118, 167, 218
*Never Cry Devil* (film) 168–172, **170**

# Index

*Never the Same: The Prisoner of War Experience* (film) 94
"A New Woman" (*Monsters* episode) 202
*New York Daily News* (newspaper) 197, 199
*New York Nights* (film) 195
*New York Times* (newspaper) 29
Newman, Paul 119
Newsom, Ted 4–11, 12, 13, 14, 15
Newton, Helmut 265
Nicholson, Jack 61, 118, 176
Nicolaou, Ted 111, 125, 155
Nielsen, Leslie 44
*The Night at the Museum* (book) 140
*Night at the Museum* (film) 140
*Night of the Dribbler* (film) 40
*Night of the Comet* (film) 107
*Night of the Creeps* (film) 34
*Night Screams* (film) 273
*The Night Stalker* (TV movie) 274
*Night Visitor* (film) see *Never Cry Devil*
"Nightcrawler" (screenplay) 111–112
*A Nightmare on Elm Street* (film) 41, 98, 150
*Nightmare Sisters* (film) 253
*Nightstick* (film) 21
*Nijinsky* (film) 129
*976-EVIL* (film) 218
Nixon, Richard 265
Nolan, Tom 207–209
Nordman, January 269, 270
North, Oliver 160
*North Dallas Forty* (film) 275
Norton, Escott 234
*Not Your Type* (short film) 279
*Nowhere to Hide* (film) 26
"Le nozze di Figaro" (opera) 139
Nuchtern, Simon 195, 197–198
*Nude Bowling* (film) 267
Nugent, Ginny 160–161
Nuse, Deland 59–63, 65, 66, 69, 71

Obata, Toshishiro 126
O'Brien, Peggy 208–209
O'Connor, Flannery 182
*The Octagon* (film) 129
O'Hara, Brian 201
O'Hara, Catherine 192
Olivier, Laurence 17, 103, 105
Olson, Jack 266
"The One I Love" (song) 67
*One Life to Live* (TV series) 118
"One Woman Death Machine" (screenplay) 72–73
O'Neill, Eugene 129
O'Neill, Neil 62, 70
Opper, Don 239
*The Oracle* (film) 173–174
*Ordeal by Innocence* (film) 151
"Orestes" (play) 71
Ormsby, Alan 176
Orwell, George 158
Osco, Bill 265
*Othello* (play) **253**
O'Toole, Peter 29

*Oui* (magazine) 4
*Our Winning Season* (film) 129
*Out of This World* (TV series) 208
*The Outing* (film) see *The Lamp*
*Outlaw Force* (film) 227
*Outlaw of Gor* (film) 155
*Overexposed* (film) 196
Oz, Frank 248

Paloian, Nancy 259–260
*The Paper Chase* (TV series) 92
*Parasite* (film) 125, 175–188, **181**
"Parasite 2" (screenplay) 175–176, 184
*The Passion of Christ* (film) 177
Pataki, Michael 94
Patino, Steve 34
Patrick, Andrea 131
Payne, Arthur 107–109
Pearl, Daniel 125
Peck, Gregory 82, 105
Peckinpah, Sam 169
Penn, Sean 208
Pepin, Rick 5, 10, 12
Perkins, Anthony 96–103, **99**, **101**, 105, 150
Perlstein, Abe **95**, **253**, **256**
Permut, David 89
Perry, Luke 262
*Pete's Dragon* (film) 257
*Pets* (film) 169
Pettiford, Val 279
Petty, Tom 125
Pfeil, David Oliver 51–53, **52**, 130
*The Phantom of the Opera* (film) 112
Phillips, Charlie 162
Picardo, Robert 162, 274
"The Picture of Dorian Gray" (novel) 97
*Pinball Summer* (film) 189
*The Pink Chiquitas* (film) 189–194, **191**
*Piranha* (film) 166
Pirrie, Bruce 190, 192–193, 194
Pirro, Mark 130
Pisanello, Gianna 157
*Playboy* (magazine) 4, 232, 265
Pleasence, Donald 100, 151, 156
Poe, Edgar Allan 96, 97, 99, 146, 148, 150
Poindexter, Cheryl 130
Poland, Simon 157–158
*Police Academy* (film) 130
Polley, Sarah 32
*Poltergeist II* (film) 34
*Por mis Pistolas* (film) 242
*Posed for Murder* (film) 200–202
Post, Ted 93, 257
Prati, Pamela 280, 281, 282
*Predator* (film) 34, 166
Pressman, Ed 123
*Pretty Smart* (film) 206
*Pretty Woman* (film) 208
*Prettykill* (film) 22
*Prey of the Chameleon* (film) 155
Price, Vincent 178
"Primal Urge" (screenplay) 51
Prior, David A. 168, 247, 262

"The Prison Women of Theta Planet" (screenplay) 83
*Prom Night* (film) 212
*Promises in the Dark* (film) 129
*The Psi Factor* (TV series) 192
*Psycho* (film) 99, 150
Pullman, Bill 186
*Pulse Pounders* (film) 281, 282
*Pumpkinhead* (film) 123
*Puppet Master* (film) 210, 212
*Purple Rain* (film) 129
Puzo, Mario 246
Pyun, Albert 158

Quaid, Randy 130
*Quest for Fire* (film) 52
Quigley, Linnea 10, 77, 78–79, 240, 241, 242, 249, 252
Quinn, Anthony 257
Quintero, Jose 129

*Race with the Devil* (film) 169
Rafaelson, Bob 176
*Raiders of the Lost Ark* (film) 45
Railsback, Steve 21, 29, 32, 36, 38
Raimi, Sam 247
Raley, Ron 96–97, 98–100
Rambaldi, Carlo 22
Randall, Dick 217
*Rat Patrol* (TV series) 84
*Rattlers* (film) 81–82
Ray, Aldo 243, 252, 254, 261, 262
Ray, Fred Olen 37, 92, 247, 259
Ray, Johannah 187
Reader, Joe 224–225
Reagan, Nancy 198
Reagan, Ronald 160, 180–181
"Real Man" (song) 133
*Really Weird Tales* (TV movie) 192
*Re-Animator* (film) 197, 249
*Rear Window* (film) 169
Reardon, Lindsay 157
*The Red Green Show* (TV series) 192
*Red Riding Hood* (film) 131
Redford, Robert 257
Redgrave, Lynn 7, 12, 17, 156
Redgrave, Vanessa 156
Reed, Donald A. 231
Reed, Oliver 100, 147–148, 151
Reedus, Norman 79
Reeves, Keanu 107
Reeves, Steve 128, 130
Reigle, James 239
Reiner, Ira 4
*The Rejuvenator* (film) 195–203, **199**, **203**
REM 67
Renzetti, Nicholas 27
Ressler, Scott 247, 248
*The Return of the Living Dead* (film) 21
*Revenge of the Nerds* (film) 240–241
Reynolds, Burt 25
Reynolds, Kevin 129
Rhae, Chuck 8, 19
Rhae, Danica 8
Richichi, Sal 95
*Ricochet River* (film) 23

*The Rift* (film) 107
Rigg, David 251
*Riptide* (TV series) 15
*Rites of Passage* (film) 72
*River of Death* (film) 103, 156, 157
Rives, Robbie 212
*The Robber Bridegroom* (stage show) 118
Robbins, Lance 202
Robbins, Tim 186, 199
Roberts, Eric 186, 214
Roberts, Julia 186
*Robinson Crusoe on Mars* (film) 129
*Robot Jox* (film) 272, 276
Roebuck, Dan *52*, 53, 55–56
Roland, Gilbert 207
*Roller Boogie* (film) 202
Romero, George 202
*The Ron James Show* (TV show) 192
Ross, Herb 265
Roth, Anna 162
Roth, Ivan E. 33, 34–36, 38–39
Rotundo, Nick 189–190
Roundtree, Richard 171
Ryan, Meg 118
Rydall, Derek *170*, 171
Ryshpan, Arden 44

Saiko, Johnnie 260
St. Clair, Barrie 108
*St. Elmo's Fire* (film) 78
St. Ivanyi, Andra 138, 143–145
Sandefur, B.W. 111
Sandefur, Duke 111–113
Sandefur, Jane 111
Sanousi, Mohammed 136
Santana 59
Sapir, Richard 126
Sarafian, Richard 22
*Saturday the 14th* (film) 207, 225
Savage, Lisa 6, 12, 15, 17, 18
Savini, Tom 22
Saxon, John 23, 91–95, *95*, 156, 243, 254, 258
"Say It Again" (music video) 59
Sayadian, Stephen 263
Sayles, John 72
Scanlan, Joseph L. 21
*Scanners* (film) 214
*Scarecrow and Mrs. King* (TV series) 15
*Scarface* (film) 94
Schaal, Wendy 162
Schaefer, Laura 117
Schaper, Eric 203
Schlesinger, John 207–208
Schmidt, Wayne 125
Schmitz, Will 72–73
Schmoeller, David 110, 112, 125, 210
Schoedsack, Ernest B. 218
Schoen, Judy 118
*School Spirit* (film) 204–209, *205*
Schoolnik, Skip 268
Schouweiler, John 240–241
Schreiber, Avery 131
Schwartz, Ricky *35*

Schwarzenegger, Arnold 141
Scorsese, Martin 228
Scott, Derek *13*
Scott, George C. 129
Scott, Ridley 27, 114, 276
Scribner, Don 226, 227–228
Sear, Walter 173–174
*Secret Admirer* (film) 78
Segal, George 118
Segal, Steven 126
Selby, William (also Bill) 89, 90–92, 93–94
"Sgt. Fury, The Sub-Mariner" (screenplay) 5
Sestito, Fulvio 63
*The Seven Year Itch* (film) 167
*The Seventh Voyage of Sinbad* (film) 128
Sevier, Coy 136
Shadow, Monty 156
*Shadow House* (short film) 217
*Shadowhunter* (TV movie) 215
*Shadowzone* (film) 210–216, *211*, *213*
Shakespeare, William 129, 243, *253*, 257, 260
Shapiro, Marty 125
Sharif, Omar 256
Shaw, George Bernard 160
*The Shawshank Redemption* (film) 86
Sheen, Charlie 21
Shelley, Barbara 8
Shelton, Deborah 131–132, *132*
Shepard, Hilary 131
Shepard, Sam 186
Sherk, Scott *164*
*Shogun* (film) 126
Shoob, Michael 175, 176, 177–185
Short, Robert 7, 160, *161*, *165*, 166, 225, 268–269
Shostrom, John 213–214
Shostrom, Mark 212, 213–215, *213*
Siegel, Mark *35*
*Silent Madness* (film) 195, 198
Silver, Alain 171
Silvera Nadon, Monica 6, 16–19
Silverstein, Elliot 30
Silverstein, Sheldon 217
Simon, Juan Piquer 107
*Simon & Simon* (TV series) 169
"Simple Living" (book) 185
*Simple Living with Wanda Urbanska* (TV show) 185
*The Sinful Dwarf* (film) 169
Sisson, Mark 213, 214
Skaggs, Jimmy 116, 120
Skotak brothers (Dennis and Robert) 269
Skouras, Tom 267
*Slammed* (film) 202
Slater, Cher 53
*Slave Girls from Beyond Infinity* (film) 217–238, *218*, *219*, *223*, *229*, *233*, *236*
*The Slayer* (film) 210, 212
Smith, Dick 214
Smith, Greg 213–215
Smith, Lance 159–163

Smith, Rex 277–278, 280, 283
Solomon, Ken 206–207
*Somebody Killed Her Husband* (film) 129
*Someone Is Killing the Great Chefs of Europe* (film) 129
Sondheim, Stephen 150
*Sorority Babes in the Slimeball Bowl-O-Rama* (film) 74, 239–50, *240*, *248*, 262
"Sorority House of the Dead" (play) 273
*Il sorpasso* (film) 206
*Soul Man* (film) 78
Sowards, Jack 111
*Soylent Green* (film) 169
"Space Sluts in the Slammer" (unproduced film) 72–73
Spacek, Sissy 186
*Spasms* (film) 21
Spaulding Fuller, Bruce 203, 213–214
*Spellcaster* (film) 279–280
Spencer, Brenton 33
Spheeris, Penelope 21, 30
"Spider-Man" (screenplay) 5
Spielberg, Steven 83, 84, 159
*Splash* (film) 7
Spratling, Tony 106
Sprinkle, Annie 198
*S\*P\*Y\*S* (film) 257
Stafford, Denise 261
Stafford, Jon 164
Stallone, Frank 156–158, 190, *191*, 193
Stallone, Sylvester 130
"Star Pupil" (screenplay) 247
*Star Trek* (2009 film ) 20
*Star Trek: The Next Generation* (TV series) 118
*Star Wars* (film) 136, 224, 234, 245, 269
*Stargate* (TV series) 36
Stark, Ray 265
*Starlog* (magazine) 225
Steckler, Ray Dennis 6, 12
Steinheimer, Alan 62
*The Stepfather* (film) 212
Stevens, Brinke 7, 10, 13, 230, 242, 249, 250
Stevenson, Robert Louis 96, 98
Stewart, James A. 224
Stiliadis, Nick 190, 193
Stille, Robin 249–250
Stiller, Ben 140
Stinnett, Dave 213, 214
"The Strange Case of Dr. Jekyll and Mr. Hyde" (novel) 96, 98
Strasberg, Lee 129
Stratton, Charlie 162, 164
Stratton, Rick 225
Strauss, Robert 72
Streep, Meryl 129
*A Streetcar Named Desire* (stage show) 257
*Street Justice* (film) 21, 23
Streisand, Barbra 279
Stringer, R. Michael 253–254
*Stripped to Kill* (film) 167

Stubblefield, Bruce 222, 224
"Studebaker" (unproduced film) 168–169
*The Stuff* (film) 225
*The Stunt Man* (film) 29, 36
*Subspecies* (film) 111, 155
"Subterraneans" (screenplay) 111, 113
Sullberg, Jon 60
Summers, Jamie *see* Stafford, Denise
Sunseri, Jack A. 58, 59–62, 63–70
*Sunset Blvd* (film) 197
*The Sunshine Boys* (film) 265
*The Sunshine Boys* (short documentary) 265
*Super 8* (film) 264
*Supergirl* (TV series) 225
*Superior Court* (TV series) 76
*Suspense* (film) 232
Sutherland, Donald 151
*Swank* (magazine) 7
*Sweet Valley High* (TV series) 202
*Swept Away* (film) 129
Swift, Chris 141
Szigeti, Cynthia 131

Tate, Fred **233**
*Taxi Driver* (film) 187
Taylor, Doug 40, 41–43
"Teen Tour" (screenplay) 130
*Teen Witch* (film) 262
*Teen Wolf* (film) 78
"The Tempermental Artist: or A Bucket of Blood" (play) 273
*The Tempest* (play) 243
*10* (film) 129
*Ten Little Indians* (1988 film) 103, 151
*Ten Little Indians* a.k.a. *And Then There Were None* (book) 6, 14
Tennant, Tim 213–214
Tenser, Marilyn J. 128
Tenser, Mark 51–53, 128, 130
*Tequila Sunrise* (film) 208
*Terror Night* (film) 239, 243, 246, 251–263, **253, 255, 256, 258**; *see also Bloody Movie*
*The Texas Chainsaw Massacre* (film) 135
*The Texas Chainsaw Massacre II* (film) 41
"Thane" (screenplay) 239, 243–246
*Them!* (film) 38
*Thief* (film) 111
*The Thief of Baghdad* (film) 128
"Things That Go Bump" (screenplay) 186–187
*13* (film) 131
Thompson, Cindy 53, 56
Thomson, Scott 187–188
*Thor* (film ) 20
Thrasher, Jim 62, 66
Three Stooges 14
*Thunder Alley* (film) 210, 212
Thurber, James 257
*A Thurber Carnival* (stage show) 257

*Time* (magazine) 73
*Time After Time* (film) 129
*Time Walker* (film) 264–271
*Today, I Am a Man…I Think* (short film) 129
Tolstoj, Lev 183
*Tom Horn* (film) 129
*Tomboy* (film) 53
*Topper* (film) 207
*The Totem* (screenplay) 274
*Tourist Trap* (film) 125
Towers, Harry Alan 96–103, 106, 146–148, 150–151, 152
Townsend, Patty 175
Townshend, Pete 249
"Trajectory" (screenplay) 232
*Transformations* (film) 272–283
*Trapped* (film) 21
"Treasure Island" (unproduced film) 100
*Tron: Legacy* (film) 225
*True Blood* (TV series) 36, 225
Trump, Donald 162
Tucker, Christopher 214
Turner, Peter 124
Tweed, Shannon 171
*The Twilight Zone* (1959 TV series) 171, 177
*The Twilight Zone* a.k.a. *The New Twilight Zone* (1985 TV series) 34, 91–92, 225
*2001: A Space Odyssey* (film) 45
*2001: A Space Travesty* (film) 44

U2 250
Udy, Claudia 190
*Underground* (film) 195
*Unsolved Mysteries* (TV series) 1
*Up the Creek* (film) 208
*Uplink/Downlink* (book) 27
Urbanska, Wanda 185
*Used Cars* (film) 160

Vaccaro, Brenda 154, 156, 157, 158
*Valley Girl* (film) 73
*Vampire at Midnight* (film) 265, 266, 267, 268
*Vampire Knights* (film) 76
Van Der Velde, Nadine 164
Van der Woude, Teresa 171
*Variety* (magazine) 33, 115, 200, 220
Vaughn, Robert 100, 156
Vernon, Henry 265
Vernon, John 32
*Vice Squad* (film) 30
*The Video Killer* (book) 74
*The Vikings* (film) 128
Villard, Dimitri 264, 265, 268
Villard, Tom 187
Vincent, Chuck 98
Vincent, Jan Michael 85
Vincent, Ron 62, 63–70
Viscovich, Randal 168–172, **170**
*Voices* (film) 118
*Voodoo Dolls* (film) 40
*Vortex* a.k.a. *The Day Time Ended* (film) 125
*Voyage of the Rock Aliens* (film) 208
*Voyagers!* (TV series) 169

Waggoner, Lyle 16
Waite, Ralph 177
*The Walking Dead* (TV series) 79
*Walking Tall* (film) 117
Wallace, Tommy Lee 135
Walsh, Gwynyth 21, 38
Walters, Martin 21
*The Waltons* (TV series) 177
"War in Illinois" (screenplay) 181
Ward, Elizabeth **170**
*Warlords* (film) 247
*Warrior Queen* (film) 98
*The Wasp Woman* (film) 203
Wasserman, Wendy 63
*Watchmen* (film) 225
*Waterworld* (film) 129
Watkins, Michelle 138
Wayne, John 133
Weatherly, Shawn 212
*Weekend Pass* (film) 128, 130–131
Weill, Claudia 130
Weintraub, Fred 24
Weislein, Rudi 227
Welles, Orson 59
Wellington, David 40–41, 42, 44–49
Wells, Ray 5
West, Jonathan 166–167
Weston, Doug 23
Wexler, Howard **253**, 257–259
*What's Up, Tiger Lily?* (film) 280
*When Harry Met Sally* (film) 118
*When Time Ran Out* (film) 129
*Whiffs* (film) 257
*Whirlpool* (TV series) 156
Whitcher, Patricia 20
*White Ghost* (film) 108
Whitman, Stuart 84–85, 87
*Who'll Stop the Rain* (film) 26
*Whoopie!* (stage show) 118
Wiatrak, Ken 221–222, 230–231
"Wicca Girl 3" (novel) 174
*Wicked Little Things* (film) 212
Wiederhorn, Ken 21
*The Wild Bunch* (film) 116, 169
Wildman, John Stuart 250, 262
Wilkof, Lee 118
Williams, Jason 265–268
Williams, Mark 32–37, **35**, 260
Williams, Robin 66
Williams, Tennessee 182, 183
Wilson, Ron 6–9, 14–15, 16, 18–19, 260
Wilson, Roy Alan 136, 139–140
Winkless, Terence H. 118, 162
Winston, Stan 123–124, 166, 184, 186–187
*Winter Kills* (film) 129
Winters, David 247, 262
Winters, Deborah 136, 138–140, 143–144
*Wise Blood* (film) 182
Wittcomb, Kate 90; *see also* Cutler-Rubenstein, Devorah
Witter, Karen 99
Wolf, Mark 218–220, **218**, 221, **223**, 228–230, **229**, 233–234, 254, **255**
*The Wolf Man* (film) 197
*Wolfen* (film) 274

*The Wonderful Wizard of Oz* (book) 265
Wong, Chris 162
Wong, Jim 20–21
Wood, Ed 78
Wood, Jim 56
Woodford, David 133
Woolf, Alain D. 156
Woolner, Larry 217
Woolner brothers 232
Wright, Thomas 246
Wrightson, Bernie 123, 187, 248
Wynn, Bob 275, 276, 277
Wynorski, Jim 163, 166

*X-Factor* (film) 5, 6
*X-Files* (TV series) 20
*Xtro* (film) 75

Yablans, Irwin 175–176, 181, 184, 187
*The Yakuza* (film) 26
*Yankees* (film) 208
Yates, Peter 108
*You and Me Kid* (TV show) 20
"You Got Lucky" (music video) 125
Young, Darren 53, 54, 55–57
*The Young and the Restless* (TV series) 15, 87, 88
*You're Famous* (film) 156
Yuval, Peter 247, 262

Zanetos, Dean 169–170
Zar, Chet 279, 282–283
Zemeckis, Robert 160
Zendler, Kurt 254
Ziehm, Howard 265
Zielinski, Rafal 279
Zimmerman, Bob (also Zimmo) 198–199
*Zombie Death House* (film) 92; see also *Death House*
*Zombie Nightmare* (film) 40, 41, 42
*Zombiethon* (film) 217, 225, 229, 232–233
Zuckerbrod, Gary 164
*Zulu Dawn* (film) 108, 129
Zurli, Guido 217

www.ingramcontent.com/pod-product-compliance
Ingram Content Group UK Ltd.
Pitfield, Milton Keynes, MK11 3LW, UK
UKHW050541150426
5217IPUK00026B/2021